Annual Competitiveness Analysis and Impact Estimation of Exchange Rates on Trade in Value-Added of ASEAN Economies

In 2019, ACI was ranked 12th globally, 2nd in Asia, and 1st in Singapore amongst 94 think tanks worldwide under the "Best University Affiliated Think Tank" category by the Think Tanks and Civil Societies Program at the University of Pennsylvania, USA.

About ACI

The Asia Competitiveness Institute (ACI) was established in August 2006 as a Research Centre at the Lee Kuan Yew School of Public Policy (LKYSPP), National University of Singapore (NUS). It aims to build the intellectual leadership and network for understanding and developing competitiveness in the Asia region. ACI seeks to contribute to the enhancement of inclusive growth, living standards, and institutional governance through competitiveness research on sub-national economies in Asia. It identifies mitigating issues and challenges for potential public policy interventions through close collaboration with regional governments, business corporations, policy think-tanks, and academics. ACI's three key research pillars include (I) Sub-national economies level competitiveness analysis and city-level liveability analysis; (II) Firm-level competitiveness analysis in 16 Asia economies; and (III) Singapore's long-term growth strategies and public policy analysis.

ACI's value propositions may be encapsulated in its acronym:
Analytical inputs to initiate policies for policy-makers and business leaders in Asia
Capacity building to enable others through improvement in productivity and efficiency
Intellectual leadership to create pragmatic models of competitiveness and inclusive growth

The institute's core research competencies can also be encapsulated in this acronym describing our evidence-based assessments conducted on public policies for **A**SEAN in the context of the rise of **C**hina and **I**ndia.

Vision and Mission

- ACI's over-arching vision is to build up its research credibility with policy impact, contributing as a professional, world-class think-tank.
- ACI's mission is to establish our niche as a leading policy think-tank by identifying competitiveness trends, opportunities, and challenges, as well as promoting competition and synergizing complementarities amongst Asian economies and business corporations.
- ACI endeavours to articulate sound recommendations, entice discourse, and shape agenda in the arena of public policy amongst Asian governments.
- ACI undertakes evidence-based analysis of public policy issues and decisions, in order to provide assessment of their effectiveness as well as economic and societal impact.

Research Initiatives and Collaborations

I. Identify trends of competitiveness and policy analysis on trade and investment of ASEAN, within the regional context of competition and complementarities with China and India.
II. Identify competitive strengths and conduct policy analysis on Singapore within the context of regional economies with international benchmarking.
III. We are regularly releasing three indices on liveability ranking including 64 Global Cities, 100 Greater China Cities, and 17 Shandong Cities.
IV. We have established an Ease of Doing Business (EDB) Index on Attractiveness to Investors, Business Friendliness, and Competitive Policies for 21 sub-national economies of India and 33 sub-national economies of Indonesia.
V. We have signed Memoranda of Understanding (MoU) with The World Bank (2015), Enterprise Singapore formally known as SPRING Singapore (2014) and European Central Bank (2014). The MoU between The World Bank and National University of Singapore, coordinated through ACI, was signed in 2016.
VI. We have signed MoUs with various institutions in Greater China economies, including Institute of Economics at Shanghai Academy of Social Sciences (2019), Institute of World Economics at Shanghai Academy of Social Sciences (2016), Shandong Academy of Social Sciences (2015), Chongqing Municipal

People's Government (2015), China Institute for Reform and Development, Haikou (2015), Counsellors' Office of the People's Government of Guangdong Province (LOI, 2014), and Chung-Hua Institution for Economic Research, Taiwan (2015).

VII. We have signed MoUs with seven Chief Ministers' Offices in Uttarakhand (2019), Andhra Pradesh (2018, 2017 & 2015), Bihar (2015), Chhattisgarh (2015), Madhya Pradesh (2015), Odisha (2015), and Punjab (2015).

VIII. We have signed a MoU with Committee for Acceleration of Priority Infrastructure Delivery at Coordinating Ministry for Economic Affairs, Indonesia (2016), Indonesia Investment Coordinating Board (2014), Indonesian Agency for Agricultural Research and Development at Ministry of Agriculture (2014), Indonesian President's Delivery Unit for Developing Monitoring and Oversight (2013), and Employer's Association of Indonesia (2013).

IX. We have signed MoUs with Asian think-tanks and institutions, including Institute of Economic Growth, India (2018), Vietnam Chamber of Commerce and Industry, Vietnam (2016), Centre for Strategic and International Studies, Indonesia (2015), Institute of Strategic & International Studies, Malaysia (2015), Philippine Institute for Development Studies, the Philippines (2015), Thailand Development Research Institute, Thailand (2015), and Central Institute for Economic Management, Vietnam (2015).

About ACI's Research Pillars

ACI has consciously engaged in economic research that has significant relevance to Singapore and the Asian region. Over the years, ACI has focused on our expertise in quantitative competitiveness analysis and simulation, spinning off volumes of research output in the applications of our methodology and regional insight. At this stage, ACI has identified three core research pillars that will guide and define its research efforts moving forward. The three research pillars are as follows:

Pillar I. Sub-national Economies Competitiveness Analysis

ACI engages in systematic and methodical competitiveness analyses of the sub-national economies by using an evidence-based, empirical approach involving a comprehensive list of relevant indicators, which are categorised under multiple layers called the 'environments'. A number of our projects, including competitiveness analyses of Greater China, ASEAN-10, India, and Indonesia, as well as other thematic research projects, were conducted by adopting this common methodology, with potential variations in the specific environments and indicators. ACI's competitiveness analysis of Asian economies goes beyond the usual ranking to offer constructive policy recommendations on how individual member states can improve their rankings vis-à-vis their sub-national or regional peers through the application of the 'what-if' simulation, which provides the projected improvements of each state's ranking whereby the bottom one-fifth of its indicators are enhanced.

Pillar II. Micro-based Firm Level Competitiveness Analysis

Micro-based firm level competitiveness analysis is ACI's second research pillar that has been developed in view of the intrinsic importance of firm-level competitiveness in terms of productivity, efficiency, and governance. In the context of globalisation, mobility of economic activities, and blurring of borders, an understanding of the determinants and dynamics of firm-level competitiveness is paramount, in order for policy makers to adjust and prepare their industries for an increasingly competitive economic landscape. To this end, ACI has partnered with the European Central Bank to carry out research in this area, possessing a solid foundation in firm-level productivity research in the form of European Competitiveness Network database and methodology. ACI envisaged the expansion of Competitiveness Research Network (CompNet) into Asia, thereby pioneering the Asia's CompNet in encompassing 16 economies in Asia.

Pillar III. Singapore's Long-term Economic Growth Strategies and Public Policies Analysis

The third and imminent research pillar focuses on Singapore's long-term economic growth strategies in the context of changing circumstances, future trends, and emerging opportunities for Singapore in the decades ahead. In particular, ACI will take on the task of critically examining Singapore's public policy strengths and areas of improvement by assessing policy successes of the past, identifying new issues to address and the current policy gaps, through a systematic and evidence-based research inquiry using quantitative methodology and empirical data, leveraging on our network of policy experts.

Founding Patron and International Advisory Panel

Founding Patron

Mr George Yeo
Visiting Scholar, Lee Kuan Yew School of Public Policy, National University of Singapore & Former Minister of Foreign Affairs, Singapore

International Advisory Panel

Co-Chairs:

Professor Michael Porter (2006–2010)
Bishop William Lawrence University Professor

Ms Marjorie Yang (2006–2012)
Chairman, Esquel Group

Members:

Professor Kishore Mahbubani
Former Dean, Lee Kuan Yew School of Public Policy, National University of Singapore

Dr Kuntoro Mangkusubroto
Former Head, President's Delivery Unit for Developing Monitoring and Oversight (UKP4), Indonesia

Mr Narayana Murthy
Former Chairman, Infosys Technologies Limited

Mr Philip Yeo
Former Chairman, Enterprise Singapore

Mr Loh Khum Yean
Permanent Secretary, Ministry of Trade and Industry

Ms Yong Ying-I
Permanent Secretary, Public Service Division

Professor Chan Kam Leung Alan
Former Dean, College of Humanities, Arts and Social Sciences, Nanyang Technological University

Asia Competitiveness Institute

Co-Directors:

Associate Professor Tan Khee Giap (2011 till now)
Professor Tan Kong Yam (2011 till now)

Asia Competitiveness Institute - World Scientific Series

(ISSN: 2424-9912)

Series Editor: Tan Khee Giap (*Lee Kuan Yew School of Public Policy, NUS, Singapore*)

In the tradition of the Asia Competitiveness Institute (ACI) at the Lee Kuan Yew School of Public Policy, National University of Singapore (NUS), our research publications make a distinctive contribution to the understanding of economic development in Asia. These books, first published in 2013, in the Asia Competitiveness Institute - World Scientific Series evaluate and track competitiveness for the sub-national economies of China, India, Indonesia and ASEAN annually through combining leading-edge methodologies with an extensive dataset. The study covers four environments of competitiveness: (1) Macroeconomic Stability, (2) Government and Institutional Setting, (3) Financial, Businesses and Manpower Conditions, and (4) Quality of Life and Infrastructure Development. It also conducts "what-if" policy simulations to propose policy suggestions.

2018

Annual Competitiveness Analysis and Impact Estimation of Exchange Rates on Trade in Value-Added of ASEAN Economies
by Tan Khee Giap, Tan Kway Guan, Melissa Poh Wei Le & Doris Liew Wan Yin (Lee Kuan Yew School of Public Policy, NUS, Singapore)

Impact Estimation of Exchange Rates on Exports and Annual Update of Competitiveness Analysis for 34 Greater China Economies
by Tan Khee Giap, Zhang Xuyao & Mao Ke (Lee Kuan Yew School of Public Policy, NUS, Singapore)

Annual Competitiveness Analysis and Impact Estimation of Exchange Rates on Exports from Sub-National Economies of India
by Tan Khee Giap, Sasidaran Gopalan & Jigyasa Sharma (Lee Kuan Yew School of Public Policy, NUS, Singapore)

Annual Competitiveness Analysis and Impact Estimation of Exchange Rates on Exports from Sub-National Economies of Indonesia
by Tan Khee Giap, Nursyahida Ahmad, S Shalini Sivakrishnan & Doris Liew Wan Yin (Lee Kuan Yew School of Public Policy, NUS, Singapore)

2017

2017 Annual Competitiveness Analysis and Impact of Exchange Rates on Foreign Direct Investment Inflows to ASEAN Economies
by Tan Khee Giap, Luu Nguyen Trieu Duong, Chuah Hui Yin & Nguyen Duy (Lee Kuan Yew School of Public Policy, NUS, Singapore)

Balanced, Sustainable and Competitiveness Enhancement Study for Vietnam: A Critical Evaluation with Development Potentials
by Vu Tien Loc (Vietnam Chamber of Commerce and Industry, Vietnam), Tan Khee Giap, Luu Nguyen Trieu Duong & Nguyen Duy (Lee Kuan Yew School of Public Policy, NUS, Singapore)

*More information on this series can also be found at http://www.worldscientific.com/series/aciwss

(Continued at end of book)

Asia Competitiveness Institute - World Scientific Series

Annual Competitiveness Analysis and Impact Estimation of Exchange Rates on Trade in Value-Added of ASEAN Economies

Tan Khee Giap

Co-Director, Asia Competitiveness Institute
Lee Kuan Yew School of Public Policy, National University of Singapore

Tan Kway Guan

Research Assistant, Asia Competitiveness Institute
Lee Kuan Yew School of Public Policy, National University of Singapore

Melissa Poh Wei Le

Research Assistant, Asia Competitiveness Institute
Lee Kuan Yew School of Public Policy, National University of Singapore

Doris Liew Wan Yin

Research Assistant, Asia Competitiveness Institute
Lee Kuan Yew School of Public Policy, National University of Singapore

Special Remarks

Lawrence Wong
Minister for National Development and Second Minister for Finance, Singapore

Bilahari Kausikan
Chairman of the Middle East Institute at the National University of Singapore, Singapore and former Permanent Secretary at the Ministry of Foreign Affairs of Singapore, Singapore

Reviewers

Tan Sri Rastam Mohd Isa
Chairman and Chief Executive, Institute of Strategic and International Studies (ISIS), Malaysia

Dr. Lee Jae Young
Group Head and Lead Economist, ASEAN+3 Macroeconomic Research Office (AMRO) Management

Dr. Hezri Adnan
Senior Director of Research, Institute of Strategic and International Studies (ISIS), Malaysia

Dr. Frederico Gil Sander
Lead Country Economist, Macroeconomics & Fiscal Management, The World Bank Group

Lee Kuan Yew School of Public Policy
Asia Competitiveness Institute
NUS National University of Singapore
World Scientific

Published by

World Scientific Publishing Co. Pte. Ltd.
5 Toh Tuck Link, Singapore 596224
USA office: 27 Warren Street, Suite 401-402, Hackensack, NJ 07601
UK office: 57 Shelton Street, Covent Garden, London WC2H 9HE

British Library Cataloguing-in-Publication Data
A catalogue record for this book is available from the British Library.

Asia Competitiveness Institute – World Scientific Series
ANNUAL COMPETITIVENESS ANALYSIS AND IMPACT ESTIMATION OF EXCHANGE RATES ON TRADE IN VALUE-ADDED OF ASEAN ECONOMIES

ISBN 978-981-120-793-8

Desk Editor: Jiang Yulin

Typeset by Stallion Press
Email: enquiries@stallionpress.com

Printed in Singapore

Contents

Foreword

The year 2018 has marked a tumultuous year for the ASEAN-10. Domestically, the bloc has been badly hit by natural disasters and struck by the rising issue of terrorism. Globally, the many developments across the world have led to much uncertainty and worry. It is hence apt that tellingly, the theme of Singapore's chairmanship for this year was "Resilient and Innovative".

But it has not been all bad news — the solidarity and cohesion of the region has worked to ensure its ability to withstand the various events that have occurred since the founding of the bloc in 1967. Moving forward, the commitment to regional integration will be crucial to the ASEAN-10's capability to ensure equal growth and success for all.

This book *Annual Competitiveness Analysis and Impact Estimation of Exchange Rates on Trade in Value-Added of ASEAN Economies* by the Asia Competitiveness Institute (ACI) at the Lee Kuan Yew School of Public Policy (LKYSPP), National University of Singapore (NUS) has thus proved fitting and ideal.

Methodology-wise, the framework that has been developed by ACI stands out for three key points. First, the addition of the Shapley values methodology — predicated on game theory — has served to act as a robustness check, hence ensuring concise and accurate data. Second, the identification of the 20% top and bottom-most indicators allows for an individualised look into the strengths and weaknesses of each and every country in the ASEAN region. Third, the simulation studies that are carried out further strengthen these results by offering an insight into the possibility of what the future for the ASEAN bloc might look like, thus enabling constructive policy recommendations to be made.

Similarly, the chapters and content in this book reflect ACI's commitment to moving beyond listing rankings. Other than providing an extensive backdrop to the ASEAN region, the thematic chapters on the significance of exchange rates, as well as trade disruptions, offer a contextualised look at the bloc in the grander scheme of things. This is also in addition to a collection of hand-picked speeches and articles by key academics and policy-makers, hence supplementing the ongoing dialogue surrounding the ASEAN region. The concluding chapter, in particular, discusses grounded pathways for the ASEAN-10 to undertake in the goal of achieving holistic and sustainable growth.

All in all, I am confident that ACI's work has and will continue to value-add to policy discourse in the ASEAN region, and look forward to the many more book editions that are to come.

Mr. Jusuf Wanandi
President Director, The Jakarta Post Daily &
Senior Fellow and Co-founder, Centre for Strategic and International Studies
Indonesia

Preface

The year 2018 marks the 51st year since the founding of the ASEAN bloc, a testament to the strong cooperation of the region despite internal differences and external macroeconomic changes. Over the past 51 years, the ASEAN region has weathered multiple difficult periods such as the Asian financial crisis of 1997–1998, the Dot-com bubble in the early 2000s and the Global Financial Crisis of 2007. As ASEAN continues on its vibrant growth path, its members have launched important policy initiatives such as the recent ASEAN Smart Cities Network as a means of solidifying the region's potential of becoming the fourth largest economy by 2030.

Nonetheless, the challenges that ASEAN faces remain substantial. Within the ASEAN region itself, concerns such as infrastructure bottlenecks and the widening development divide will have to be duly confronted. On the world stage, issues related to the rise of technologies, global warming, changing trade and political conditions, and more, are all causes for concern. The ASEAN bloc will therefore need to continue to cooperate to ensure unity and equal development for all nation states.

This book published by the Asia Competitiveness Institute (ACI) at the Lee Kuan Yew School of Public Policy (LKYSPP), National University of Singapore (NUS) serves as a timely and comprehensive guide to navigating the uncertain waters faced by the ASEAN region. It presents the latest findings on the relative competitiveness of the ASEAN-10 economies and is supplemented by a *What-if* simulation that enables constructive policy recommendations. With the inclusion of an objective weightage method predicated on Shapley values, ACI has added another layer of robustness to its study. Further, the book provides an empirical study on the relationship between exchange rates and trade in ASEAN economies, proving itself a useful companion for all ASEAN policy-makers.

I am confident that this study will play a central role in ongoing policy dialogue, and steer the ASEAN region towards fulfilling its full and immense potential.

Ramkishen S. Rajan
Vice Dean (Research) and Professor
Lee Kuan Yew School of Public Policy
National University of Singapore

Acknowledgements

We from the Asia Competitiveness Institute (ACI) at the Lee Kuan Yew School of Public Policy (LKYSPP), National University of Singapore (NUS), have combined leading-edge research methodologies with extensive data collection efforts to evaluate and track economic competitiveness since 2000 at both national and sub-national levels for over 100 Asian economies including Greater China, India, Indonesia and the 10 members of the Association of Southeast Asian Nations (ASEAN).

In this book on *Annual Competitiveness Analysis and Impact Estimation of Exchange Rates on Trade in Value-Added of ASEAN Economies*, we present an update of the annual competitiveness analysis for the ASEAN-10. We also continue with last year's innovation introduction of the Shapley Values Weightage methodology as a robustness check in order to ensure objective data.

In addition, the book recounts ASEAN's development experience over the past year and provides an in-depth assessment of its future outlook. In terms of moving past internal bottlenecks, the book benefits from the astute insights of Mr. Lawrence Wong, Minister for National Development and Second Minister for Finance, on how to develop quality infrastructure in order to solidify the region's success. Moreover, recognising the significance of exports as an engine of growth for the region in this fast-globalising world, we conduct an empirical study on the impact that exchange rates have on the ASEAN-10's trade.

This is also furthered by an analysis of the influence that trade disruptions will have on the region. To this end, we gain greatly from the knowledge imparted by Mr. Bilahari Kausikan, Chairman of the Middle East Institute at the National University of Singapore, and former Permanent Secretary at the Ministry of Foreign Affairs of Singapore, on the ASEAN-related impacts of the Trade War.

Finally, we wrap up the book with a discussion on the policy implications and possible routes to take in gearing the ASEAN region to reach the greatest heights possible.

We would like to place on record our sincere appreciation towards Mr. Lawrence Wong and Mr. Bilahari Kausikan for their contributions to Chapters 1 and 4 of this book. Moreover, the publication of the book would not have been possible without the tremendous support from various country experts who attended the ACI–World Bank Asia Economic Forum jointly organised by ACI and the World Bank at LKYSPP. We wish to thank the following reviewers who gave their constructive comments and offered instructive insights on the respective chapters as incorporated in this book:

Mr. Tan Sri Rastam Mohd Isa
Chairman and Chief Executive, Institute of Strategic and International Studies (ISIS), Malaysia

Dr. Hezri Adnan
Senior Director of Research, Institute of Strategic and International Studies (ISIS), Malaysia

Dr. Lee Jae Young
Group Head and Lead Economist, ASEAN+3 Macroeconomic Research Office (AMRO) Management

Dr. Frederico Gil Sander
Lead Country Economist, Macroeconomics & Fiscal Management, The World Bank Group

We would also like to place on record our appreciation for the support and encouragement from Dean Danny Quah, Vice Dean of Research Professor Ramkishen, Mr. Thomas Chan Hean Boon (Associate Director, Research Support Unit) and all other colleagues at LKYSPP. Finally, this book would not have been possible without the dedicated effort of all research and administrative staff at ACI. Thus, we note with tremendous appreciation the high team spirit of all ACI staff including Luu Nguyen Trieu Duong, Nguyen Duy, Constance Siew Hui Hui, Nguyen Phan Dai Trang, Aishwarya Narayanan, Yap Xin Yi, Tracy Cai Jiao, Nurliyana Binte Yusoff and Dewi Jelina Ayu Bte Johari.

Tan Khee Giap
Tan Kway Guan
Melissa Poh Wei Le
Doris Liew Wan Yin

Asia Competitiveness Institute
Lee Kuan Yew School of Public Policy
National University of Singapore

About the Authors

Tan Khee Giap is a Co-Director of the Asia Competitiveness Institute (ACI) and Associate Professor at the Lee Kuan Yew School of Public Policy, National University of Singapore. He is also the Chairman of the Singapore National Committee for Pacific Economic Cooperation. Upon graduating with a PhD from University of East Anglia, England, in 1987 under the Overseas Research Scheme awarded by the Committee of Vice-Chancellors and Principals of the Universities of the United Kingdom, he joined the banking sector as a treasury manager and served as secretary to the Assets and Liabilities Committee for three years, thereafter he taught at the Department of Economics and Statistics, National University of Singapore, 1990–1993. Dr Tan joined Nanyang Technological University in 1993 and was Associate Dean, Graduate Studies Office, 2007–2009.

Dr Tan has consulted extensively with the various government ministries, statutory boards and government-linked companies of Singapore government including Ministry of Finance, Ministry of Trade & Industry, Ministry of Manpower, Housing & Development Board, Civil Aviation Authority of Singapore, Singapore Tourism Board, Trade Development Board, Maritime Port Authority, Ministry of Information, Culture & Arts, Economic Development Board, Ministry of National Development, Media Development Authority, Ministry of Environment and Water Resources, Singapore Design Council, Ministry of Community Development, Youth & Sports, Singapore Press Holdings, Yayasan Mendaki, StarHub, CapitaLand and Great Eastern Life. He has also served as a consultant to international agencies such as the Asian Development Bank, Asian Development Bank Institute, United Nations Industrial Development Group, World Bank Group, World Gold Council, ASEAN Secretariat, Central Policy Unit of Hong Kong, Kerzner International, Las Vegas Sands and Marina Bay Sands.

Dr Tan is the lead author for more than 20 books, serving as journals editor and published widely in international refereed journals. He is the associate editor of the journal *Review of Pacific Basin Financial Markets and Policies* (US) and is on the editorial advisory board of the journal *Competitiveness Review* (UK). His current research interests include Cost of Living and Purchasing Power Index for World's 105 Cities, Global Liveable Cities Index, Ease of Doing Business Index and competitiveness analysis on sub-national economies of China, India, Indonesia and Association of South East Asian Nations.

Dr Tan was Deputy President of the Singapore Economic Society, 2004. He served in the 2002 Economic Review Committee (ERC), served as Chairman of the Task Force on Portable Medical Benefits (PMB), served as the Deputy Chairman of the IPS Forum for Economic Restructuring (IFER) in 2003 and served as a member of the Resource Panel of the Government Parliamentary Committee for Transport and Government Parliamentary Committee for Finance and Trade & Industry and Government Parliamentary Committee for Defence and Foreign Affairs since 2007. Dr Tan is currently an Independent Director of the publicly listed BreadTalk Group, Boustead

Singapore, TEE Land and Chengdu Rural Commercial Bank, and Senior Business Advisor to United Overseas Bank Limited, Singapore.

Tan Kway Guan is a Research Assistant at the Asia Competitiveness Institute, Lee Kuan Yew School of Public Policy, National University of Singapore. Kway Guan graduated from the University of Western Australia with a Master of Economics and a Bachelor of Commerce, double major in Economics. Kway Guan is currently the project coordinator for the Annual Competitiveness Analysis and Development Strategies for ASEAN-10 Economies as well as assisting in the Annual Indices for Purchasing Power, Cost of Living and Wages for Expatriates and Average Residents for 105 Cities and the Welfare Spending and Budget Sustainability analysis for ASEAN economies. Kway Guan's research interests include development economics and energy economics.

Melissa Poh Wei Le is a Research Assistant at the Asia Competitiveness Institute, Lee Kuan Yew School of Public Policy, National University of Singapore. Melissa graduated from the National University of Singapore with a Bachelor's of Arts and Social Sciences (Hons), majoring in Sociology. She is currently involved in the Competitiveness Rankings and Simulation Studies for ASEAN-10 Economies, the Welfare Spending and Budget Sustainability project for ASEAN, the Competitiveness Rankings and Simulation Studies for India, and the World Toilet Organization (WTO) Index. Melissa's research interests include inequality and public policy.

Doris Liew Wan Yin is a Research Assistant at the Asia Competitiveness Institute (ACI), Lee Kuan Yew School of Public Policy, National University of Singapore. Doris graduated from Nanyang Technological University with a Bachelor of Arts (Honours) in Economics with Distinction and a minor in Public Policy and Global Affairs. She is currently involved in the Annual Competitiveness Analysis and Development for ASEAN-10 Economies, Competitiveness Rankings and Simulation Studies for Indonesia, as well as the Global Liveable and Smart Cities Index. Her research interests include ASEAN economics, environmental economics, international trade and development economics.

List of Abbreviations

AANZFTA	ASEAN–Australia–New Zealand Free Trade Area
ACCSQ	ASEAN Consultative Committee for Standards and Quality
ACFTA	ASEAN–China Free Trade Area
ACI	Asia Competitiveness Institute
ACIA	ASEAN Comprehensive Investment Agreement
ACN	ASEAN Corporate Social Responsibility Network
ADB	Asian Development Bank
ADBI	Asian Development Bank Institute
AEC	ASEAN Economic Community
AFAFIST	ASEAN Agreement on the Facilitation of Inter-State Transport
AFAS	ASEAN Framework Agreement on Services
AFC	Asian Financial Crisis
AFIN	ASEAN Financial Innovation Network
AFTA	ASEAN Free Trade Area
AHN	ASEAN Highway Network
AIF	Asian Infrastructure Fund
AIFTA	ASEAN–India Free Trade Area
AIIB	Asian Infrastructure Investment Bank
AJCEP	ASEAN–Japan Comprehensive Economic Partnership
AKFTA	ASEAN–Korea Free Trade Agreement
APEC	Asia-Pacific Economic Cooperation
APN	Asian Payment Network
APSC	ASEAN Political-Security Community
APTA	ASEAN Preferential Trading Agreement
ASCC	ASEAN Socio-Cultural Community
ASCN	ASEAN Smart Cities Network
ASEAN	Association of Southeast Asian Nations
ASEAN CBTP	ASEAN Framework Agreement on Cross-Border Transport of Passengers
ASEAN-SAM	ASEAN Single Aviation Market
ASPEN	ASEAN Strategic Plan on Environment
ASW	ASEAN Single Window

ATIGA	ASEAN Trade in Goods Agreement
ATISA	ASEAN Trade in Services Agreement
ATSP	ASEAN Tourism Strategic Plan
AWSC	ASEAN-wide Self-Certification
BIS	Bank for International Settlements
BPO	Business Process Outsourcing
BRI	Belt and Road Initiative
CBD	Central Business District
CCP	Chinese Communist Party
CEPT	Common Effective Preferential Tariff
CGIO	Centre for Governance, Institutions and Organisations
CLMV	Cambodia, Laos, Myanmar and Vietnam
COT	Competitiveness Over Time
CPI	Consumer Price Index
CPTPP	Comprehensive and Progressive Trans-Pacific Partnership
DOLS	Dynamic Ordinary Least Squares
DVA	Domestic Value-Added
EADM	East Asian Development Model
EIU	Economist Intelligence Unit
EPA	Economic Partnership Agreement
ERIA	Economic Research Institute for ASEAN and East Asia
ESCAP	Economic and Social Commission for Asia and the Pacific
EU	European Union
EUSFTA	EU–Singapore Free Trade Agreement
EUSIPA	EU–Singapore Investment Protection Agreement
FBMC	Financial, Businesses and Manpower Conditions
FDI	Foreign Direct Investment
FMCG	Fast-Moving Consumer Goods
FORGDP	Foreign Real GDP
FRAND	Fair Reasonable and Non-Discriminatory
FTAs	Free Trade Agreements
FVA	Foreign Value-Added
GCI	World Economic Forum Global Competitiveness Index
GCR	World Economic Forum's Global Competitiveness Report
GDP	Gross Domestic Product

GFC	Global Financial Crisis
GIS	Government and Institutional Setting
GMID	Global Market Information Database
GNI	Gross National Income
GRP	Good Regulatory Practices
GTAP	Global Trade Analysis Project
GVCs	Global Value Chains
HDI	Human Development Index
HPAEs	High Performing Asian Economies
HSSWG	Healthcare Services Sectoral Working Group
ICIO	Inter-Country Input–Output
ICT	Information and Communications Technology
IDE	Institute of Developing Economies
IHiS	Integrated Health Information Systems
ILO	International Labour Organization
IMD	International Institute for Management Development
IMF	International Monetary Fund
I–O	Input–Output
IP	Intellectual Property
ISIS	Institute of Strategic and International Studies
IT	Information Technology
ITMX	National ITMX Co. Ltd
JETRO	Japan External Trade Organization
KL	Kuala Lumpur
LKYSPP	Lee Kuan Yew School of Public Policy
M&A	Mergers and Acquisitions
MACC	Malaysian Anti-Corruption Commission
MDGs	Millennium Development Goals
MNCs	Multinational Corporations
MPAC	Master Plan for ASEAN Connectivity
MRIO	Multi-Region Input–Output
MS	Macroeconomic Stability
MSMEs	Micro, Small and Medium Enterprises
NAFTA	North American Free Trade Agreement
NAPAS	National Payment Corporation of Vietnam

NETS	Network for Electronic Transfers (Singapore) Pte Ltd
NGOs	Non-Governmental Organisations
NIEs	Newly Industrialised Economies
NSWs	National Single Windows
NTBs	Non-Tariff Barriers
NTMs	Non-Tariff Measures
NUS	National University of Singapore
OBOR	One Belt One Road
OECD	Organisation for Economic Co-operation and Development
OJK	Financial Services Authority
OLS	Ordinary Least Square
PayNet	Payments Network Malaysia Sdn Bhd
PPP	Purchasing Power Parity
PROT	Pro-Trade-Oriented
PWC	PricewaterhouseCoopers
P&G	Procter & Gamble
QLID	Quality of Life and Infrastructure Development
RCEP	Regional Comprehensive Economic Partnership
REER	Real Effective Exchange Rates
RER	Real Exchange Rate
Rintis	PT Rintis Sejahtera
RSVI	Ranked Standardised Value of Indicator
SDGs	UN Sustainable Development Goals
SEA	Southeast Asia
SMEs	Small and Medium Enterprises
SVI	Standardised Value of Indicator
TiVA	Trade in Value-Added
TPP	Trans-Pacific Partnership
TVET	Technical and Vocational Education and Training
UK	United Kingdom
UN	United Nations
UNCAC	United Nations Convention against Corruption
UNCTAD	United Nations Conference on Trade and Development
UNDP	United Nations Development Programme
UNESCO	United Nations Educational, Scientific and Cultural Organization

US	United States
USD	United States Dollars
USMCA	United States–Mexico–Canada Agreement
USTR	United States Trade Representative
VAREER	Value-Added Real Effective Exchange Rate
WCY	World Competitiveness Yearbook
WEF	World Economic Forum
WEO	World Economic Outlook
WGI	World Bank Worldwide Governance Indicators
WHO	World Health Organization
WIOD	World Input–Output Database
WJP	World Justice Project
WTO	World Trade Organization

List of Figures, Tables and Boxes

Chapter 1

Chapter 2

Chapter 3

Chapter 4

Chapter 1
Regional Developments and Economic Outlook of ASEAN

1.1 Introduction

The Association of Southeast Asian Nations (ASEAN) is a regional bloc that was founded in 1967 by five founding members, namely Indonesia, Malaysia, Philippines, Singapore and Thailand. Brunei Darussalam joined the association in 1984. During mid to late 1990s, ASEAN has expanded when Vietnam, Lao PDR, Myanmar and Cambodia joined ASEAN. Today, these countries make up the 10 Member States of ASEAN. The objectives of ASEAN are to foster regional cooperation in economic, social, cultural and other fields, and to promote peace and stability through mutual respect and conforming to the principles laid out in the United Nations Charter.[1]

Since its establishment, the ASEAN community has put in place several trade initiatives to foster economic growth in the region. As early as 1977, the regional bloc introduced ASEAN Preferential Trade Agreement that granted preferential rates of custom duties on agricultural produce, minerals, textiles, manufacturing products and machineries. Other trade agreements that have been introduced since then include the 1992 ASEAN Free Trade Area (AFTA), 1995 ASEAN Framework Agreement on Services, 2010 ASEAN Trade in Goods Agreement, and the 2012 ASEAN Comprehensive Investment Agreement. These trade agreements reduce tariff on a wide array of goods and services to boost trade volume between the ASEAN members.

The ASEAN Economic Community (AEC) that was established more recently in 2015 is a major milestone for ASEAN. Through AEC, ASEAN aspires to create a single market and production base and highly competitive economic region. AEC helps to facilitate the free flow of goods and services, attracts investment, increases labour mobility, and enhance physical as well as person-to-person connectivity that can reduce the cost of doing business, narrowing the development gap between ASEAN states and promoting regional integration with FTAs. The 2015 ASEAN Economic Community Scorecard that tracks the progress of AEC Blueprint shows that ASEAN had successfully implemented 469 out of 506 measures that they had committed to achieve. This demonstrates ASEAN's commitment and success in achieving economic development and integration into the global economy. Other than intra-ASEAN Free Trade Agreements, the regional bloc also opens up itself to create economic ties with other major economies in the world that includes ASEAN plus one, ASEAN+3 and recently ASEAN+6.[2]

[1] See the establishment of ASEAN and its aims at https://asean.org/asean/about-asean/.

[2] ASEAN plus trade agreements include the 2014 ASEAN–China FTA (ACFTA), 2007 ASEAN–Korea FTA (AKFTA), 2008 ASEAN–Japan FTA (AJFTA), 2010 ASEAN–Australia–New Zealand FTA (AANZFTA), and 2010 ASEAN–India FTA (AIFTA). ASEAN+3 is the cooperation between ASEAN and China, Japan and South Korea. ASEAN+6 is the cooperation between ASEAN and six other nations which are China, Japan, South Korea, India, Australia and New Zealand). See also Taguchi and Lee (2016) and ASEAN Secretariat (2017).

In our annual publication, the Asia Competitiveness Institute (ACI) contributes to the ongoing literature of ASEAN by assessing the economic development and competitiveness of the regional bloc.

1.1.1 ASEAN in Numbers

Decades of regional integration and economic cooperation through multilateral Free Trade Agreements and the ASEAN Economic Community have benefited ASEAN in an unprecedented way. Since 2000, the GDP of ASEAN-10 countries more than doubled in value. ASEAN as a region was the sixth largest economy in the world in 2016, with a total GDP standing at US$2.55 trillion. ASEAN in 2017 contributes close to 3.4% of the world's GDP, up from 1.6% in 1998. Table 1.1 provides the key indicators for ASEAN in 2017.

Figure 1.1 compares the economic growth of ASEAN countries to that of major global economies. Since 2000, the average real GDP growth of ASEAN-10 exceeded the world's economic growth except for two years in 2001 and 2014. The region continues to outperform major economies such as the United States, European Union and Japan. However, due to the heterogeneity of the region in areas such as economic openness, political stability and ease of doing business, the region as a whole is still growing slower than China and India in the past two decades.

Economic cooperation and open door policies have also made ASEAN an attractive investment hub. ASEAN attracts a significant proportion of FDI relative to its Gross Domestic Product (GDP). FDI inflow to ASEAN in 2017 stands at 4.9% of its GDP, higher than the world average

Table 1.1: ASEAN Key Indicators 2017

Country	Land Area (thousand square kilometres)	Population (million)	Human Development Index	GDP (constant 2010 billion US$)	GDP Per Capita (constant 2010 US$)	Trade (% of GDP)	FDI Net Inflows	
							Million US$	(% of GDP)
Brunei	5.27	0.428697	0.853	13.47820098	31,431.00	64.27	460.15	3.77
Cambodia	176.52	16.005373	0.582	18.20170072	1,079.10	114.42	2,732.15	12.23
Indonesia	1,811.57	263.991379	0.694	1,090.459494	3,974.70	32.13	23,063.62	2.27
Laos	230.8	6.85816	0.601	11.86739308	1,642.70	49.07	1,695.38	9.92
Malaysia	328.55	31.624264	0.802	364.5739033	11,031.80	130.01	9,447.21	2.98
Myanmar	653.08	53.370609	0.578	79.49583153	1,408.10	50.50	4,002.43	6.10
Philippines	298.17	104.91809	0.699	303.3558523	2,752.10	56.11	10,057.39	3.20
Singapore	0.71	5.612253	0.932	309.9956729	53,353.80	216.37	62,016.70	19.14
Thailand	510.89	69.037513	0.755	422.9406675	5,910.50	100.82	8,045.51	1.77
Vietnam	310.07	95.5408	0.694	175.2840811	1,735.30	189.67	14,099.98	6.30
ASEAN	4,325.629	647.387138	N/A	2,789.652798	4,309.10	93.08	135,620.52	4.90

Source: World Bank, World Development Indicators, ASEANstats and Human Development Report.

Figure 1.1: Growth of Real GDP in Selected Economies (%), 2000–2017

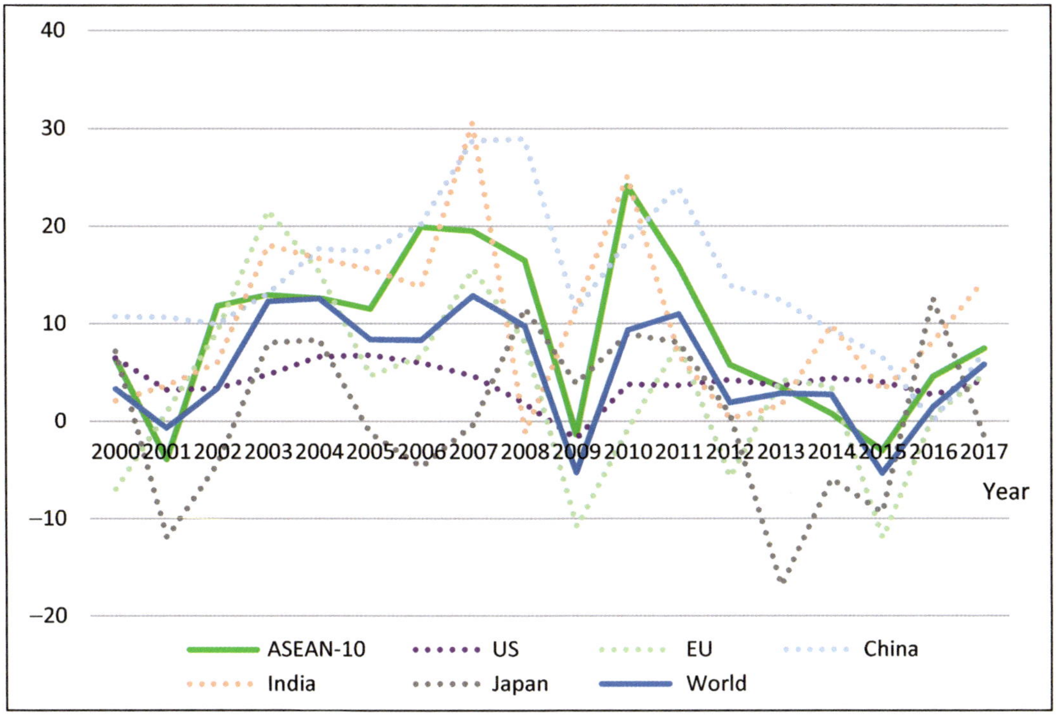

Source: Asia Competitiveness Institute based on data from World Bank, World Development Indicators.

at 2.3%.[3] In 2017, ASEAN as a whole received US$135 million in FDI, the bulk of which goes to Singapore (45.7% or US$62 billion) and Indonesia (17.0% or US$23 billion). Other countries in ASEAN get a lesser share of the FDI inflow, in which the inflow is less than 10% each for Philippines, Malaysia, Myanmar and Lao PDR.

Most of the FDI inflow to ASEAN countries comes from other ASEAN countries. Looking at Figure 1.2, intra-ASEAN FDI inflow stands at over US$26 million, or about 19.9% of the total FDI inflow into ASEAN. The major external sources of FDI comes from the European Union (18.3%), followed by Japan (9.9%). The major economies — United States and China — are less invested in the economy of ASEAN as the share of FDI from these two countries stands at only 3.2% and 8.4%, respectively, much lesser than their European Union counterpart. The composition of intra-ASEAN FDI is further illustrated in Figure 1.3. Here it is observed that Singapore and Indonesia are sources of FDI into other ASEAN economics constituting 60% of total intra-ASEAN FDI. The growing FDI inflows illustrated here are important drivers of growth for ASEAN member states. Foreign investment steers economic growth with technology spillovers, and this effect is positive in most of ASEAN through intra-ASEAN, China and the rest of the world FDI inflow.[4]

[3] The FDI/GDP of ASEAN is also higher of that of European Union (3.51%), United States (1.82%), India (1.53%), China (1.4%) and Japan (0.38%).

[4] See Ahmad *et al.* (2018); Rammal and Zurbruegg (2006) and Tu and Tan (2012).

Figure 1.2: FDI Inflow to ASEAN by Source Country (in million US$), 2010–2017

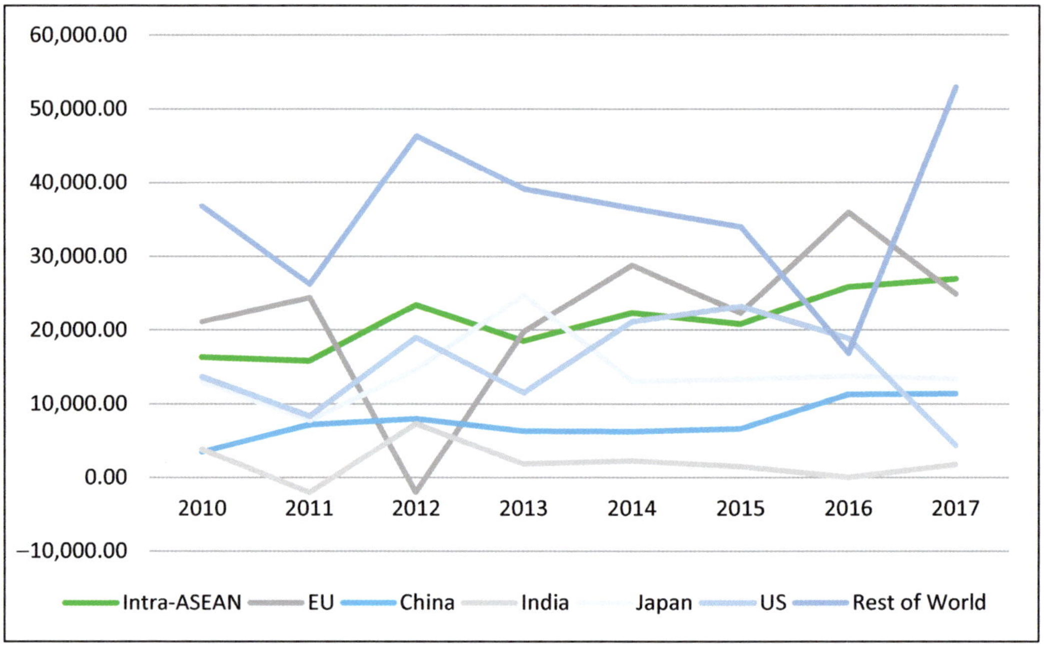

Source: Asia Competitiveness Institute based on ASEAN Secretariat.

Figure 1.3: Percentage of FDI Inflow to ASEAN by Host Country, 2010–2017

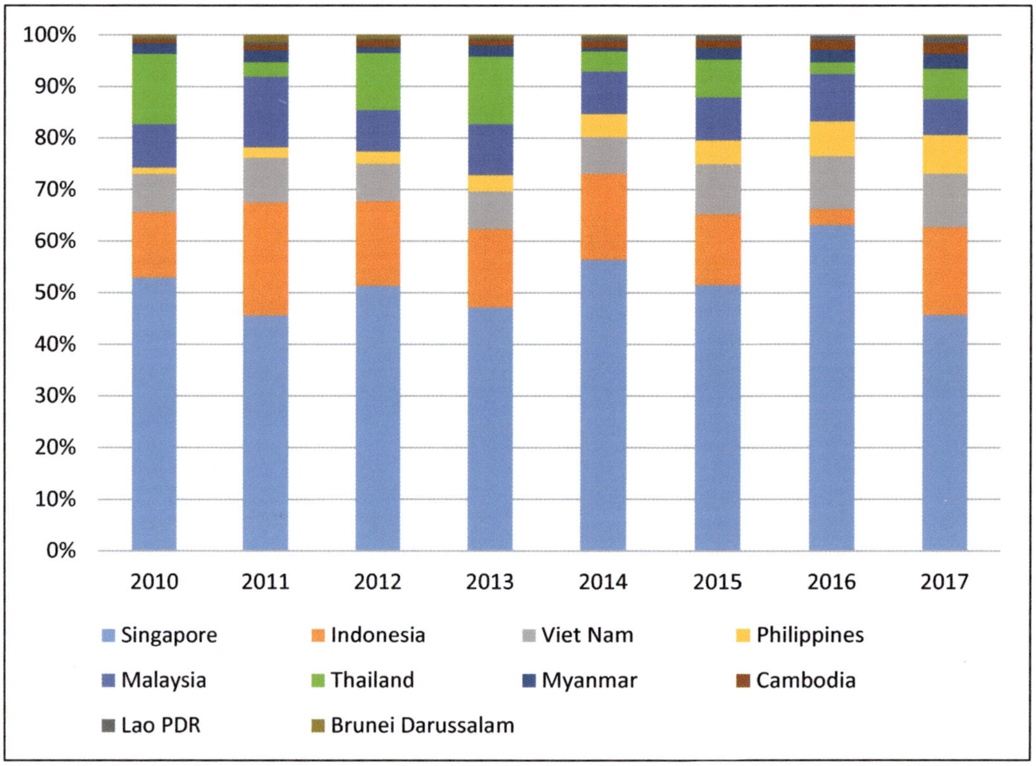

Source: Asia Competitiveness Institute based on ASEAN Secretariat.

Figure 1.4: Export of Goods and Services by Country (in million US$), 2000–2017

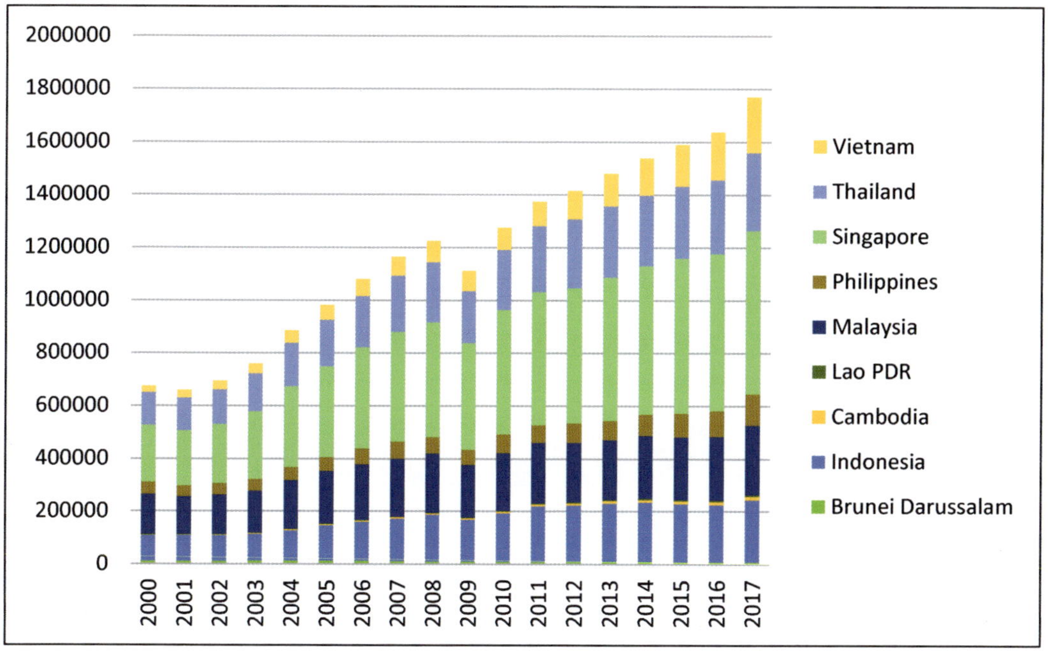

Source: Asia Competitiveness Institute based on data from World Bank, World Development Indicators.

The numbers in Figure 1.4 suggest that exports of goods and services have been increasing since 2000. In 2017, Vietnam, Thailand, Singapore and Malaysia generated the majority of the exports from ASEAN. Exports from the 10 ASEAN states have been growing more than 10% year-on-year since 2000 and export in services as a share of total export has been increasing at the same time. From 2000 to 2017, export growth had been vibrant and positive for every year except in 2009 during the global financial crisis. The export figure rebounded in the following year and continued to grow above 10%.

Trade volume makes up a significant proportion of GDP in ASEAN economies. Singapore as a regional port with no natural resources relies heavily on imports and exports to steer economic growth. Other ASEAN economies, such as Vietnam and Thailand, are also adopting open trade policies to export raw materials and manufacturing goods. As shown in Figure 1.5, trade in five out of 10 ASEAN countries surpasses 100% of their respective GDP.

In recent years, there has also been a global shift towards a provision of services other than raw materials and manufactured goods. The portion of trade in services to GDP in the world has more than doubled since 1975. Services such as back-end office support and computer programming can be provided without a physical presence. For instance, a computer programmer in one country can code and write programmes and subsequently export this piece of work over to its client at another country with close to no transportation cost.

Figure 1.5 shows that Singapore is relatively buoyant at trade in services. This is attributed to Singapore's continued emphasis on technological advancement and nurturing of high-skilled labour.[5]

[5]According to Baller *et al.* (2016), Singapore is the most technological advance country in ASEAN, ranking second in the 2016 Global Information Technology Report.

Figure 1.5: Trade as a Percentage of GDP (top) and Trade in Services as a Percentage of GDP (bottom), 2017

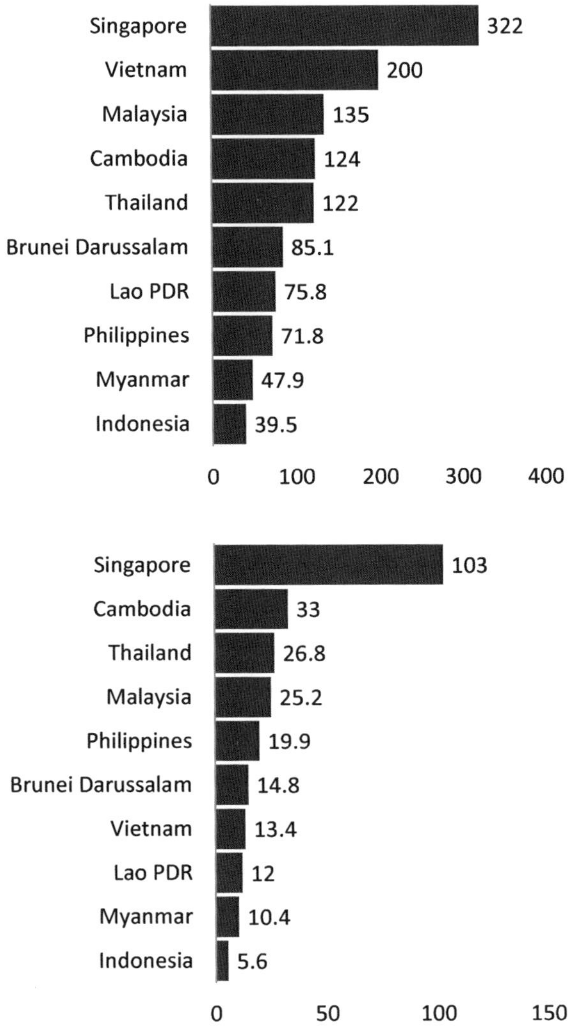

Source: Asia Competitiveness Institute based on data from World Bank, World Development Indicators.

The rest of ASEAN captures relatively lesser trade in services to GDP compared to overall trade, as majority of their trade volume consists of trade in goods. ASEAN countries need to develop their technology and human capital to capture the growing services market.

1.2 Prospects for Economic Growth

Endowed with rich natural resources, a generally young population and a growing middle class undergoing urbanisation, ASEAN is poised to become the fourth largest economic entity in the world. This section will thus provide and review possible growth paths that ASEAN can explore in regard to leveraging on today's ever-changing climate, especially with the changing geopolitical winds and the rise of digitalisation as the world stands at the dawn of the Fourth Industrial Revolution.

1.2.1 ASEAN Trade and Investment Pathways — Manufacturing

The growth of Singapore, Malaysia, Indonesia and Thailand in the 1970s has been ascribed to their industrialisation strategy focusing on export-led growth, a model which the rest of the transitional economies in Southeast Asia, namely Cambodia, Laos, Myanmar and Vietnam (CLMV) have followed.[6] As a result, exports are a crucial part of economic growth in the ASEAN region since they play a significant role in member states' Gross Domestic Product (GDP) (see Figure 3.1 in Chapter 3). In the period 2004–2017, ASEAN has shown an overall marked increment in total merchandise trade and continues to maintain its positive trade balance, despite increasing global protectionist sentiments (Figure 1.6).

ASEAN's efforts aimed at the promotion of trade liberalisation and their integration into the global trade network can be seen through their sustained initiatives at deepening economic cooperation with the rest of the world. One such pertinent example is the ongoing discussion surrounding the Regional Comprehensive Economic Partnership (RCEP) built on existing Free Trade Agreements (FTAs) that ASEAN currently has with the People's Republic of China (ACFTA), Republic of Korea (AKFTA), Japan (AJCEP), India (AIFTA), as well as Australia and New Zealand (AANZFTA). Aiming to achieve greater mutually beneficial opportunities through

Figure 1.6: ASEAN's Trade in Goods, 2004–2017 (billion US$)

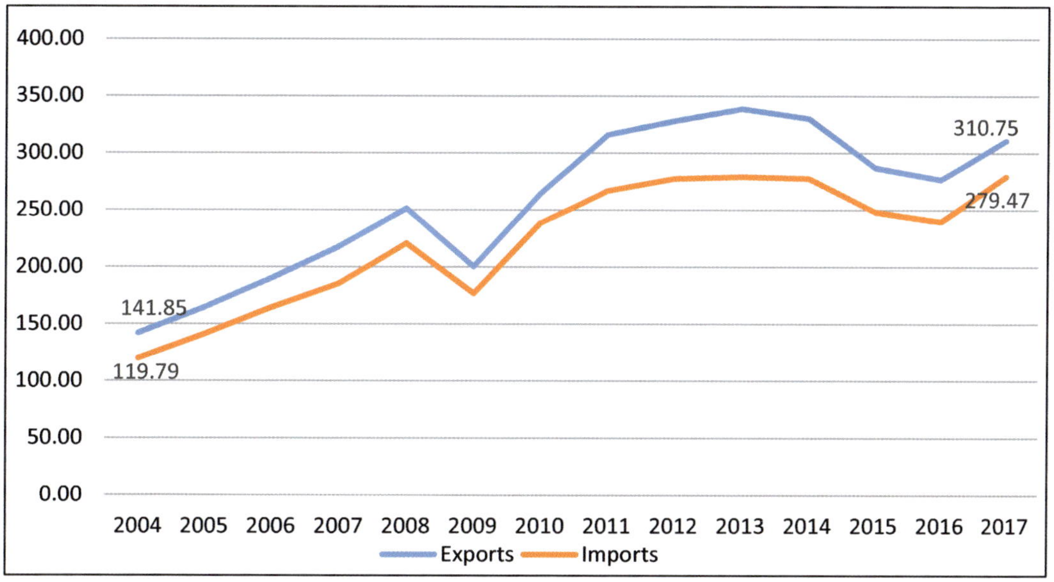

Source: Asia Competitiveness Institute based on ASEANstats.

[6] See Tan *et al.* (2017) and Chow and Kellman (1993, p. 1994).

reduced trade barriers and a more secure market access, there is vast potential behind RCEP: all 16 of the member countries in total contribute 31.6% of global output, 28.5% of global trade, one-fifth of 2016's worldwide foreign direct investment inflows, and also make up almost half of the entire global population.[7]

Other significant agreements also include the Comprehensive and Progressive Trans-Pacific Partnership (CPTPP) and the One Belt, One Road (OBOR) or Belt and Road Initiative (BRI).[8] Ratified by Mexico, Japan, Singapore, New Zealand, Canada, Australia and Vietnam, the CPTPP entered into force on 30 December 2018 and links eleven economies[9] — four of which are ASEAN member countries — in the Asia-Pacific region, making up 14% of the world economy.[10] The BRI acts as a "21st Century Maritime Silk Road",[11] where its goal is to produce multiregional cooperation in areas of infrastructure, trade and investment between some 65 countries spanning three different continents of Africa, Asia and Europe. In total, they make up for more than 30% of the world's GDP, 62% of the world's population, and 75% of energy reserves.[12]

At the same time, trade facilitation within ASEAN must not be ignored. As Figure 1.7 shows, intra-ASEAN trade has consistently made up the most significant part of ASEAN total trade, even among the other important global trading partners. Moreover, despite the changing nature of trade with other countries, intra-ASEAN trade has more than doubled in size from US$261.63 billion in 2004 to US$591.51 billion in 2017.

To this end, ASEAN's commitments such as the ASEAN Economic Community (AEC) aspire to integrate ASEAN into a "single market and production base".[13] Already, much headway has been made in this area: The ASEAN Free Trade Area (AFTA) has already been virtually established, and over 99% of the goods listed in the Common Effective Preferential Tariff (CEPT) Inclusion List of the ASEAN-6[14] have been brought down to the 0–5% range[15]. As such, measures under the AEC will work to reduce non-trade barriers, subsequently contributing to reduced trade costs as well as new production and export diversification possibilities, hence boosting each member country's competitive advantage in the global value chain.[16] Key policy initiatives include the recently "live"[17] ASEAN Single Window (ASW) digital platform that makes customs clearance easier, as well as the ASEAN-Wide Self-Certification (AWSC) Regime that enables authorised exporters to self-certify that their goods meet ASEAN preferential treatment conditions.

---

[7] See ASEAN Secretariat (2017).

[8] See Chapter 5 of Tan *et al.* (2017) for a more comprehensive coverage of the BRI.

[9] The 11 economies are Australia, Brunei Darussalam, Canada, Chile, Japan, Malaysia, Mexico, New Zealand, Peru, Singapore and Vietnam.

[10] See Ministry of Trade and Industry Singapore (2018).

[11] See Ploberger (2017); and Tan *et al.* (2018).

[12] See Huang (2016) and World Bank Group (2019).

[13] See Chapter 1 of Tan *et al.* (2016) for a more detailed discussion on the ASEAN Economic Community.

[14] The CEPT Inclusion List for the ASEAN-6 comprises Brunei, Indonesia, Malaysia, Philippines, Singapore and Thailand.

[15] See https://asean.org/asean-economic-community/asean-free-trade-area-afta-council/

[16] See Chapter 3 for more discussion on global value chains in the ASEAN context.

[17] The ASW platform went "live" on 1 January 2018 for five ASEAN states, namely Indonesia, Malaysia, Singapore, Thailand and Vietnam.

Figure 1.7: ASEAN Trade in Goods by Selected Partners/Countries in 2004 and 2017 (billion US$)

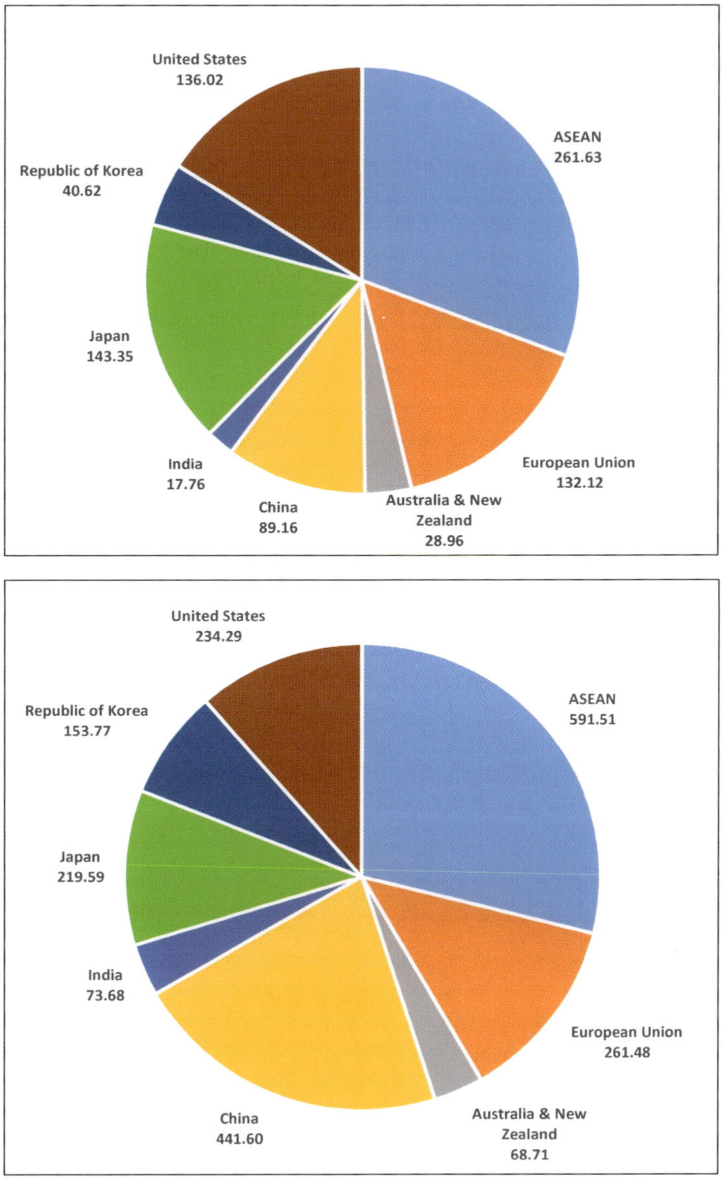

Source: Asia Competitiveness Institute based on ASEANstats.

An integrated ASEAN with a seamless intra-ASEAN trade network would also attract multinational corporations (MNCs) to set up production bases in the region. Further, ASEAN's endowments such as its possession of the third largest labour force in the world, its growing consumer base, and its proximity to large markets such as China, India and Japan gives it immense potential in becoming a highly integrated manufacturing hub — These natural factors translate into abundant human capital, increased market demand and easy access to other large markets that businesses can take advantage of. Coupled with the ASEAN region's overall macroeconomic stability, the bloc provides many incentives that can be leveraged upon in order to bring in more MNCs and FDI. Given the currently ongoing US–China trade war and the potential of production dislocation from China,[18] it is even more important for ASEAN to use these qualities to their benefit and boost growth to greater heights. Moreover, a greater consumer base in tandem with a greater amount of new companies in ASEAN potentially translates to GDP growth that is not as reliant on trade, thereby reassuring the macroeconomic stability of the region and investor potential.

It is also particularly significant to note the non-tangible benefits that trade,[19] and the relocation of MNCs and FDI bring into host countries, such as knowledge, skills and technology transfers,[20] investments in infrastructure, and the creation of job opportunities that contribute to an overall development in standard of living.[21]

1.2.2 ASEAN Trade and Investment Pathways — Services

Despite ASEAN's potential as an integrated manufacturing hub, it is also key to note the booming services sector that has increasingly become a key driver of growth in ASEAN. In 2017, ASEAN trade in services surpassed the US$700 billion mark, and FDI inflows into the sector stood at US$90,120.7 million. In the ASEAN bloc itself, total intra-ASEAN trade in services stood at US$116,008.5 million.[22] Moreover, a study by Gani and Clemes (2002) found that growth in the manufacturing sector is likely to contribute to a spill-over effect on the services sector, underscoring how the ASEAN region can make use of its strong manufacturing base to transition into a service-based economy. Furthermore, the study found a robustly positive link that exists between the impact of growth in the services sector and per capita growth, underlining the importance of measures like the ASEAN Framework Agreement on Services (AFAS), the ASEAN Trade in Services Agreement (ATISA) and the ASEAN Comprehensive Investment Agreement (ACIA) in facilitating growth in the services sector to ensure a more productive economy.

In the ASEAN region, travel is the most significant contributor to trade within the services sector. It makes up the largest proportion of trade both globally and in the ASEAN bloc itself, as seen in Figures 1.8 and 1.9, respectively. In 2017, travel made up 36.2% of total ASEAN exports and 21.1% of total ASEAN imports globally, and 58.9% of total exports and 41.46% of total imports within the region. At the same time, international air passenger traffic has been on the rise, increasing from 187.4 million in 2013 to 269.8 million in 2017.[23] The tourism sector hence remains a vital part of economic growth that the ASEAN region can tap into. This is made even more significant considering the ASEAN bloc's diversity, which makes for unique travelling experiences, and underlines the importance of measures such as the ASEAN Tourism Strategic Plan, the ASEAN Declaration on Cruise Tourism and ASEAN Single Aviation Market (ASEAN-SAM).

---

[18] For a more detailed discussion on this topic, see Chapter 4.

[19] For more on trade, see Chapters 3 and 4.

[20] See Branstetter (2006), Bwalya (2006), Lee and Tan (2006) and Tu and Tan (2012).

[21] See Haskel *et al.* (2007) and Sirgy *et al.* (2004).

[22] See ASEAN Secretariat (2018b).

[23] *Ibid.*

Figure 1.8: ASEAN's Trade in Services in 2017, by Major Service Category (in million US$)

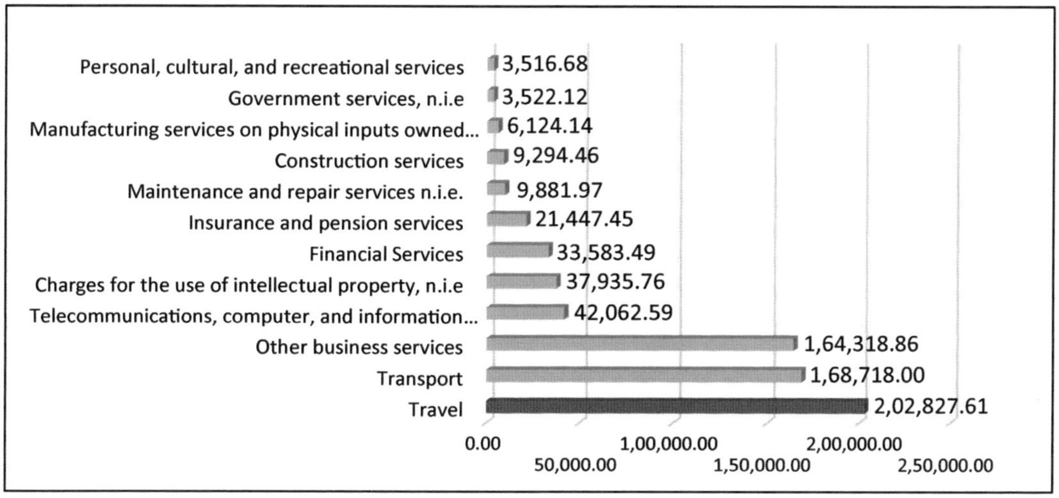

Source: Asia Competitiveness Institute based on ASEANstats.

Figure 1.9: Intra-ASEAN Trade in Services in 2017, by Major Service Category (in million US$)

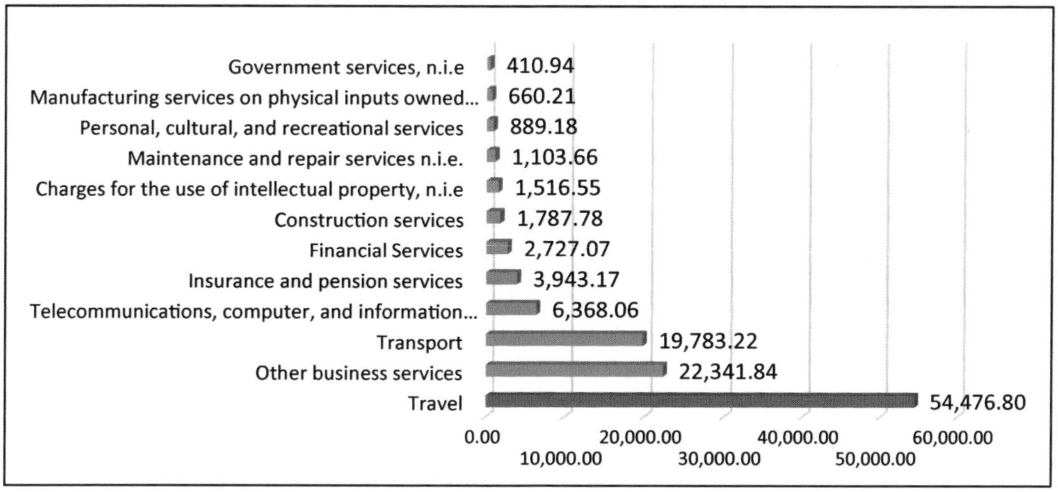

Source: Asia Competitiveness Institute based on ASEANstats.

In addition, the facilitation of easy intra-ASEAN access would fit into the larger roadmap of pursuing ASEAN Connectivity 2025 — an integrated ASEAN bloc is impossible without seamless transport infrastructure that enables the movement of people and goods. Thus, the development of the tourist sector goes hand in hand with the development of transport connectivity. To this end, various policy initiatives have been rolled out under the Master Plan for ASEAN Connectivity 2025,[24] including the ASEAN Agreement on the Facilitation of Inter-State Transport (AFAFIST), the ASEAN Highway Network (AHN) and the ASEAN Framework Agreement on

[24] See ASEAN Secretariat (2016).

Cross-Border Transport of Passengers (ASEAN CBTP). Furthermore, the moving around of human capital allows each country to further tap into their competitive advantages and reduce ASEAN's development divide in terms of differing population ages among countries. It is also significant to note the transport industry's large presence in the services sector, coming in second after travel in global ASEAN trade and third intra-ASEAN wise (see Figures 1.8 and 1.9), thereby underscoring the importance of developing transport services and infrastructure.

1.2.3 ASEAN and the Fourth Industrial Revolution

Other than trade and investment being pillars of growth, the increasingly fast-paced digitalisation of mediums across all fields also marks itself as a potential pathway for enormous growth and increasing quality of life. The rise of the Fourth Industrial Revolution can be seen in the significant increase in internet subscribers per 100 persons in ASEAN — from a low figure of 2.5 in 2000, it has now jumped to a high of 48.5 persons.[25]

The enhanced connectivity that the Fourth Industrial Revolution brings has multiple benefits. On the consumption side, technology encourages consumption through the easier linkage of consumers to product markets and vice versa. Furthermore, the simplified process of information dissemination allows for the alleviation of information asymmetry, which happens when sellers have a greater amount of information regarding their products than customers.[26] However, the widespread use of technology allows for customers to compare prices internationally and to have a greater amount of options. This is especially significant for the ASEAN bloc, where Micro, Small and Medium Enterprises (MSMEs) make up 88.8–99.9% of total establishments in the region. However, the share of its total exports remain low, hovering between 10.0% and 29.9% (ASEAN Secretariat, 2015a). Leveraging on the rise of technology would allow these businesses to be easily promoted through digital platforms — subsequently allowing for a wider consumer base, scale for lower cost, and boosting GDP and economic growth.

On the supply side, the growth of technology enables ASEAN to fill in vital gaps in existing infrastructure of various areas. For instance, ride-sharing technologies help to make up for poor public transport infrastructure in the developing economies, and also promotes consumption levels that feed back into the economy.

Digital transformation can also help to fill in the gaps in terms of educational infrastructure, giving citizens access to resources that were previously unavailable. As a result, the faster transmission of knowledge improves productivity and builds on ASEAN's growing adult literacy rate, increasing the quality of human capital in the region as well as building on the supply side of the economic growth equations.

Other pertinent examples of the benefits of the Fourth Industrial Revolution include improved accessibility to services, ranging from public provisions such as healthcare services and government e-portals to private sector banking. On the public sector side, the rise of telemedicine, generally defined as the provision of medicinal consultations and services via

[25] See ASEAN Secretariat (2018b).

[26] See Akerlof (1970).

telecommunication channels,[27] translates into less overcrowding in clinics, more convenience, and a greater accessibility to a wider audience of patients, among other benefits that run parallel to the increase in quality of living. While healthcare forms one of the priorities stated for liberalisation under the AFAS,[28] and a Healthcare Services Sectoral Working Group (HSSWG) has been established, ASEAN should consider looking further into the area of telemedicine. This is especially so given how the easy distribution of telemedicine provides opportunities for lower healthcare costs and alleviates doctor scarcity, both of which are prime concerns for the lesser developed CLMV countries. Singapore's considerable advancement in the telemedicine sector is evident in the various mobile applications available — from private companies such as MyDoc and Doctor Anywhere, to public renditions such as the Integrated Health Information Systems (IHiS) which recently rolled out the Smart Health initiative, a national platform for healthcare consultation.[29] This provides a strong base foundation for the other ASEAN member states to value-add and learn from.

Other technologically driven public-sector initiatives include the ASEAN e-Government Strategic Plan 2020 that strives to build two-way communication channels between citizens and governments. This will aid government accountability and transparency, reduce the costs of government operations and thus improve the overall standard of living. It also significantly boosts Cross-Border People and Goods movement between ASEAN member states.[30] For example, an easier process of applying for work permits and licensing in a neighbouring ASEAN state promotes the end goal of an integrated ASEAN and rolls into ASEAN's potential as a key services provider.

Lastly, the Fourth Industrial Revolution has also brought about digital transformations in the finance sector, where the growth of mobile money services and e-banking has increased the industry's efficiency. This has led to greater convenience and ease of use across country borders. For example, the linking of PromptPay from Thailand with PayNow from Singapore was announced on 14 November 2017.[31] The move would allow users of both PromptPay and PayNow to transfer money to each other through mobile phone numbers despite the difference in countries, with no need to go through the traditional banking network. This not only removes transaction costs but also increases intra-country consumption, incentivising entrepreneurship and developing SMEs — solidifying the economic growth of the ASEAN region. The same story also applies for other areas in the financial industry such as microfinancing, where reduced costs and increased efficiency translate into greater economic rewards. To this end, the ASEAN community has established the ASEAN Financial Innovation Network that serves as a collaborative platform for ASEAN microfinance institutions, banks, non-banking financial institutions, and FinTechs in the region.[32] Moreover, smooth financial transfers across ASEAN member

[27] See Pattichis *et al.* (2002) and Perednia and Allen (1995).

[28] See ASEAN Secretariat (2015b).

[29] See Smart Health Video Consultation at https://www.ihis.com.sg/vc.

[30] See ASEAN Secretariat (2015b).

[31] For full announcement speech see Ravi Menon (2017).

[32] For full press release see http://www.mas.gov.sg/News-and-Publications/Media-Releases/2017/ASEAN-Financial-Innovation-Network-to-support-financial-services-innovation-and-inclusion.aspx.

states' borders feed into improved intra-regional tourism, as currency exchange becomes less burdensome.

Overall, ASEAN has already put in place various policies aimed at building upon the rise of technologies, such as the all-encompassing e-ASEAN Framework Agreement. Measures like the ASEAN Digital Vision 2020, a World Economic Forum initiative that targets the training of over 20 million people by tech companies such as Cisco and Google,[33] will further solidify ASEAN's potential in building upon the Fourth Industrial Revolution to bring growth and prosperity to the region, especially through the boosting of the bloc as a key services provider in the global order.

1.3 ASEAN in 2018: Areas of Progress

During Singapore's Chairmanship of ASEAN in 2018, several initiatives were rolled out in response to the shared challenges facing the region. In a speech by the Prime Minister of Singapore at the 33rd ASEAN summit, he elaborated on how ASEAN's current and future initiatives demonstrate mutual benefits as well as support the message of unity and centrality, coherent economic engagement strategy, rule-based world order with adherence to international law, and an open, transparent and inclusive architecture.[34]

ASEAN in 2018 took the initiative to address disruptions brought about by the Fourth Industrial Revolution as well as continued its efforts to achieve higher economic integration both within and outside ASEAN. The upcoming Fourth Industrial Revolution rides on high internet connectivity and digital disruption to traditional industries that use physical labour and machineries for the production of goods. The emergence of new technologies such as Internet of Things, Artificial Intelligence, autonomous vehicles and 3D printing are already changing consumption behaviour and work efficiency.

Connectivity through the Internet not only changes the consumption patterns but also creates innovative and disruptive business ideas that lower costs and improve efficiency. Voice-activated smart home devices such as Google home and Alexa already help home owners to remotely control their home appliances, such as lighting and heating devices. Other innovations such as cashless transfer use internet platforms, thereby easing monetary transactions and reducing transaction time. Six countries in ASEAN are already working towards an integrated real-time cross-border payments system to ease cross-border financial transactions.[35]

2018 sees ASEAN following through several initiatives that may potentially enhance its competitiveness in the Fourth Industrial Revolution. These initiatives include ASEAN Smart Cities Network, ASEAN agreement on E-Commerce, ASEAN Financial Innovation Network, the

---

[33] See World Economic Forum (2018).

[34] See Lee (2018).

[35] Six payment system operators signed a Memorandum of Understanding in November 2017 to enable real-time cross-border payments. They are members of Asian Payment Network (APN) which consists of Payments Network Malaysia Sdn Bhd (PayNet), National ITMX Co. Ltd (ITMX) of Thailand, National Payment Corporation of Vietnam (NAPAS), Network for Electronic Transfers (Singapore) Pte Ltd (NETS), and PT Rintis Sejahtera (Rintis) of Indonesia. See http://www.asean.wcpss.org/aseanwcpss/pages/Asian Payment Network_APN.aspx

Master Plan on ASEAN Connectivity 2025, ASEAN-wide Self-Certification Scheme and the 10th Package of Commitments under the ASEAN Framework Agreement on Services.

ASEAN Smart Cities Network (ASCN)

One of the major leaps in ASEAN policies and initiatives this year is the ASEAN Smart Cities Network (ASCN). The growth in ASEAN is mostly driven by urban centres, and the urbanisation drive is likely to continue to drive future growth.[36] As more people move into cities, issues such as city congestion, poverty, inequality, security and safety can be challenges which impede growth. Digital and technological innovations can be utilised to resolve these issues to build a competitive economy, sustainable environment and high quality of life.

In view of rapid urbanisation in the region, cities from ASEAN states have collaborated to form the ASCN towards the achievement of sustainable urban development. ACSN provides a platform for cooperation between member states on smart city development, builds public–private partnerships on smart city projects and secures financial assistance and support from ASEAN's external partners. A total of 26 pilot cities were nominated by the governments in the respective ASEAN states to form the ASCN pioneer batch (see Table 1.2).[37]

The key focus areas to build competitiveness include building infrastructure as well as business innovation. These cities can invest in smart infrastructure that could improve mobility through improvements in the transportation systems. Businesses and industries can capitalise on new technologies and innovation to build their competitive advantage and enhance productivity. This is of particular importance for local Small and Medium Enterprises — global connectivity and other technological measures will aid their leap into the world market. Cities can

Table 1.2: List of Pilot Cities in the ASEAN Smart Cities Network

Brunei Darussalam • *Bandar Seri Bagawan*	**Cambodia** • *Battambang* • *Phnom Penh* • *Siam Reap*	**Indonesia** • *Banyuwangi* • *DKI Jakarta* • *Makassar*	**Lao PDR** • *Luang Prabang* • *Vientiane*
Malaysia • *Kota Kinabalu* • *Kuala Lumpur* • *Kuching* • *Johor Bahru*	**Myanmar** • *Mandalay* • *Nay Pyi Taw* • *Yangon*	**Philippines** • *Cebu City* • *Davao City* • *Manila*	**Singapore** • *Singapore*
Thailand • *Bangkok* • *Chonburi* • *Phuket*	**Vietnam** • *Da Nang* • *Hanoi* • *Ho Chi Minh City*		

Source: Asia Competitiveness Institute based on ASEAN Secretariat.

[36] See ASEAN Secretariat (2019a).

[37] *Ibid.*

also use these smart initiatives to upgrade the skills of the workforce to create a highly skilled labour force.

Some of the key enablers towards creating a smart city include smart infrastructure and regional partnerships. Smart infrastructure includes ICT networks, process automation, e-payments and digital platforms, and data analytics to increase the efficiency of city operations and innovations in the private sector. Regional partnerships between ASEAN and other countries, city networks or with the private sector will contribute to the development of ASCN through investment, knowledge sharing and capacity strengthening platforms.

ASEAN Agreement on E-Commerce

Across the globe today, growing accessibility to the internet and greater internet connectivity have contributed to the rise of electronic commerce (e-commerce). There are about 260 million internet users in Southeast Asia as of 2016 and more, predominantly the young, are joining the digital platform.[38] Online commerce in ASEAN is expected to reach US$200 billion by 2025.[39]

In view of e-commerce's potential to be the next driver of economic growth, ASEAN is committed to creating a conducive environment for e-commerce to grow and prosper. The ASEAN Agreement on E-Commerce facilitates the rules on e-commerce trade and builds greater digital connectivity in the region.[40] ASEAN Member States are committed to adopting laws and regulations related to electronic transactions that follow international standards. The Agreement aims to facilitate cross-border online transactions, create confidence and trust in the use of e-commerce and intensify intra-ASEAN cooperation in further development of the use of technology to drive economic growth.

The Agreement encourages cooperation that helps businesses to adopt e-commerce as the mode of transaction.[41] E-commerce enhances the economy through Information and Communications Technology (ICT) infrastructure, education and technology competency, online consumer protection, legal and regulatory framework, cybersecurity and intellectual property rights. This Agreement also extends to promote paperless trading between the private sector and government such as using electronic forms during custom clearance, invoice issuing and other business transactions. This is already taking place through the launch of the ASEAN Single Window that allows the electronic transaction of customs and trade-related documents to expedite cargo clearance. The Agreement includes the facilitation of the free flow of information through the ease of accessing and moving digital information across the border that drives the digital economy. The Agreement also contains clauses that protect consumer and privacy to bolster the confidence and trust of ASEAN consumers in electronic transactions. These initiatives will generate faster and more efficient transactions in the ASEAN region.

---

[38] See East-West Center (2017).

[39] *Ibid.*

[40] See Ministry of Trade and Industry (2018).

[41] See ASEAN Secretariat (2018a).

ASEAN Work Programme on Electronic Commerce 2017–2025

The accessibility and reliability of internet facilities are vital for smart cities and e-commerce. With regards to these aspects, the ASEAN Work Programme on Electronic Commerce 2017–2025 aims to provide region-wide accessibility to broadband infrastructure.[42] Under this programme, ASEAN identifies the key locations requiring broadband connectivity, promotes affordable access to international mobile roaming services, provides broadband access to rural and underserved areas, and develops mechanisms that enforce intellectual property rights.

Other areas of focus under this work programme include human capacity development programmes and consumer protection. Human capacity development programmes include capacity building initiatives that help develop skills and competency in e-commerce. Businesses are trained to use the internet as a tool to improve their business and train their workers. Educational materials and programmes are also put in place to educate the public with regard to the safe use of the internet and other technologies that could safeguard their privacy and protect their rights.

ASEAN Financial Innovation Network (AFIN)

ASEAN countries are currently lagging behind in financial inclusion, in both financial deepening and broadening. They own less-developed banks and financial institutions that limit the potential for capital market access, bond issuance, stock market investment and cash transfers.[43] The number of banks and financial institutions are low, financial services are limited, and the financial industry in ASEAN is not well integrated with the global financial system.[44]

ASEAN Financial Innovation Network (AFIN) was launched in 2018 to encourage financial inclusion and increase access to financial services.[45] As the world's first online, cross-border platform, it aims to connect financial institutions through a global digital marketplace and use digital connectivity to drive technological transformation in the region. This initiative is done in part with the collaboration between a network of banks, FinTechs and other non-bank institutions.[46]

The nucleus of AFIN comprises three main points of focus. First, AFIN aims to expand the access and consumption of financial services through support and IT infrastructure to banks, financial institutions and Fintech companies. Second, it supports regional and international financial market development and integration. Third, AFIN contributes to financial technology by providing a digital platform that increases the adoptability of the essential financial infrastructure. For instance, AFIN launched the online Global FinTech Marketplace that enables

---

[42] See ASEAN Secretariat (2017a).

[43] See Yang and Shimada (2011).

[44] See Yamanaka (2013).

[45] Please see the full details on the official website of ASEAN Financial Innovation Network, https://afin.tech/.

[46] *Ibid.*

financial institutions and FinTech firms to connect to one another through a global online marketplace.[47]

ASEAN-wide Self-Certification Scheme (AWSC) and the 10th Package of Commitments under the ASEAN Framework Agreement on Services

The ASEAN-wide Self Certification (AWSC) Scheme and the 10th Package of Commitments under the ASEAN Framework Agreement on Services (AFAS) allow the service providers in ASEAN to gain greater market access and enjoy more convenience. AWSC eases the process and lowers the cost for the authorisation of cross-border trade. Before AWSC, businesses needed to apply for a hardcopy Certificate of Origin Form from the trade ministry of the respective countries and pay an application fee. With the implementation of AWSC, exporters such as manufacturers and SMEs can self-certify the origin of their goods, need not go through administrative process and no longer need to pay for the application fees to get a hardcopy certification.

AFAS was first introduced in 1995 to progressively reduce restrictions on trade in services. The 10th Package of Commitments opens up the previously closed-off sectors to other ASEAN members, such as in logistics, tourism, maritime transport, telecommunications and professional services.[48] The package also allows ASEAN service providers to enjoy preferential services market access and face fewer trade barriers into ASEAN markets.

The Master Plan on ASEAN Connectivity 2025 (MPAC 2025)

ASEAN is one of the fastest growing economies in the world, driven by increases in trade and productivity in the region. Infrastructure development therefore must keep pace with economic growth for the region to continue its high pace of growth. Worryingly, ASEAN is experiencing low levels of access to and quality of infrastructure.[49] In particular, accessibility to electricity is low and is highly inefficient, caused by the loss of power during electrical transmission.[50] The roads in the region are also inaccessible and of low quality, due mostly to poor surface conditions.[51] High connectivity infrastructure that connects economic centres and transportation networks promotes growth and productivity by increasing access to producer and consumer markets as well as creating better access to the global value chain.[52]

ASEAN introduced the Master Plan on ASEAN Connectivity 2025 (MPAC 2025) to achieve a connected and integrated region that will promote competitiveness and inclusiveness. Three areas of connectivity are highlighted, among which are physical connectivity (roads),

[47] Please see the full details on the official website of ASEAN Financial Innovation Network, https://afin.tech/index.php/2018/09/20/worlds-first-cross-border-open-architecture-platform-to-improve-financial-inclusion/.

[48] See ASEAN Secretariat (2019b).

[49] See World Bank Group (2017).

[50] *Ibid.*

[51] *Ibid.*

[52] See World Bank Singapore Hub/Global Infrastructure Connectivity Alliance (2018).

institutional connectivity (laws and regulations) and people-to-people connectivity (human mobility).[53] Since the implementation of the previous master plan (Master Plan on ASEAN Connectivity 2010), a total of 39 initiatives have been completed.[54]

1.4 Obstacles and Challenges

The three pillars of the ASEAN community[55] are the key areas of focus for the development of ASEAN. The formation of the ASEAN community can be interpreted through the lens of providing Regional Public Goods (RPG).[56] Public goods are goods which have the two key properties of non-excludability and non-rivalry in consumption.[57,58] The exact extent to which different types of public goods express these properties varies. In general, these properties make the provision of public goods unattractive for private actors, resulting in undersupply, which governments need to remedy. RPGs can simply be thought of as goods which generate benefits that extend beyond national or geographic borders, and examples include transnational connectivity networks such as the ASEAN Highway Network and ASEAN Power Grid.

The recognition of such benefits underlies the pillars of the ASEAN community. While ASEAN has indeed made great achievements, the provision of regional public goods is subject to issues in provision, which include market failure and collective action problems. The following section will discuss some of the major challenges and problems ASEAN has and will continue to face.

1.4.1 Geopolitical Instability — Global and Regional

Situated in a geographically ideal junction between East and West, ASEAN's development strategy has been characterised by export-led growth and an emphasis on regional integration to better compete in global markets such as the AEC and MPAC. As demonstrated in Figure 1.10, ASEAN is economically tied to both the East and West and thus particularly exposed to geopolitical instabilities which threaten the viability of its export markets and hamper efforts to integrate. This concept of contagion is not alien to a region that faced major disruptions in the wake of the Asian Financial Crisis in 1998 and the Global Financial Crisis in 2008, which saw crisis in a single economy spread beyond its borders.

ASEAN's key initiatives such as RCEP, CPTPP and MPAC rely heavily on multinational agreement and participation, which have of late been subject to numerous disruptions. Notable disruptions include the withdrawal of the US from the TPP. While initially set to become the

---

[53] See ASEAN Secretariat (2016).

[54] Eighteen of the initiatives are related to physical connectivity, 15 to institutional connectivity, and six to people-to-people connectivity. See ASEAN Secretariat (2016).

[55] The three Pillars are the ASEAN Political-Security Community (APSC), the ASEAN Economic Community (AEC) and the ASEAN Socio-Cultural Community (ASCC).

[56] See Sandler (1998, 2013).

[57] A non-excludable good is a good which can be consumed even by non-paying consumers.

[58] A non-rival good is one which can be consumed without preventing another consumer from simultaneously consuming it.

Figure 1.10: Percentage Share of ASEAN Exports by Markets 2017

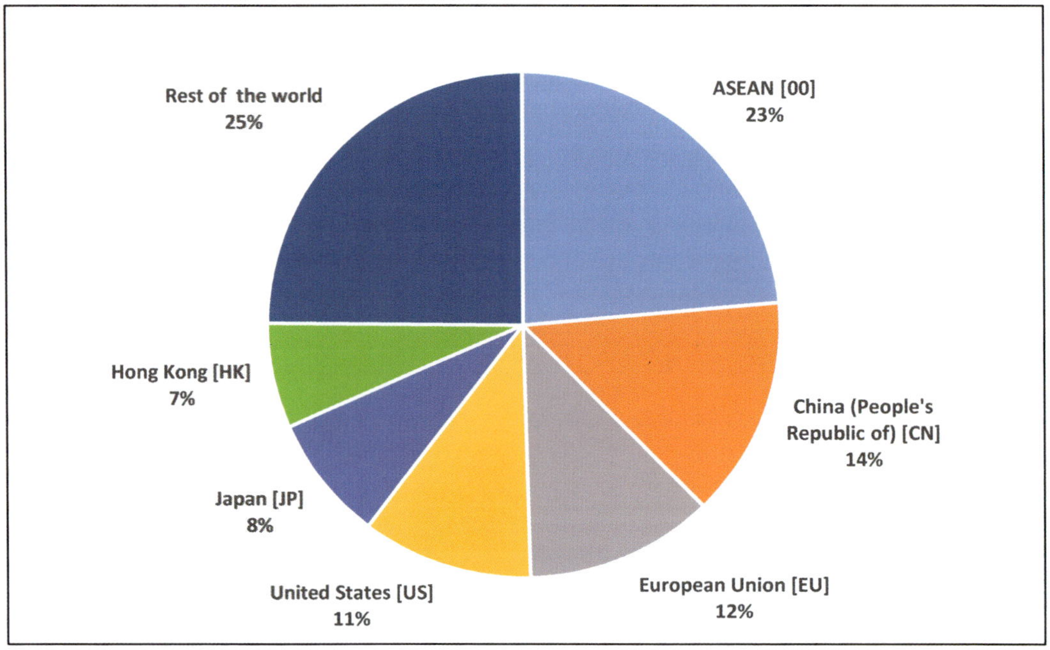

Source: Asia Competitiveness Institute based on ASEANstats.

world's largest trade deal, covering 40% of the global economy, the withdrawal in January 2017 by the US has forced a rework into the much diminished CPTPP. This new agreement covers 14% of the global economy and encompasses the following 11 economies — Australia, Brunei Darussalam, Canada, Chile, Japan, Malaysia, Mexico, New Zealand, Peru, Singapore and Vietnam. The agreement has been ratified and entered into force in the following seven countries as of February 2019 — Australia, Canada, Japan, Mexico, New Zealand, Singapore and Vietnam. There are strong indications that full adoption may be delayed as Malaysia, under new political leadership, signals that they are reevaluating the agreement.[59]

The RCEP, as previously discussed, is an ASEAN-led initiative which covers an impressive 30.16% of global output. While the Leaders of the participating economies have called for a conclusion in 2019 and agreed to intensify efforts, as of November 2018, negotiations on the RCEP launched in 2013 have thus far concluded on only seven of the 18 chapters. Domestic politics in the form of multiple upcoming elections will also weigh on the completion of this target. At the time of writing, within ASEAN, Thailand which holds the chairmanship of ASEAN in 2019, will be having general elections on 24 March, the first since the 2014 coup. Indonesia, the largest economy in ASEAN in terms of GDP, will be holding general elections in April. The Philippines will be holding mid-term general elections in May. India, Japan as well as Australia will also be holding elections in 2019.

[59] See Ministry of International Trade and Industry (2019).

Furthermore, the MPAC and the wider AEC that place heavy emphasis on improved connectivity are heavily reliant on all parties coordinating to realise the network in order to reap the full benefits from the positive externalities. Past failures to fully implement connectivity initiatives (e.g. MPAC 2010/AEC 2015) have now been compounded by increased tensions in the region, both between member states and with global parties. The newly elected government of Malaysia has thus far terminated or suspended several major connectivity infrastructure projects, including the East Coast Rail Link and the KL–Singapore High-Speed Rail which is a component of the Kunming–Singapore Railway. These actions have been enacted in response to the fiscal strain of these projects and the possibility of corruption. Concerns have been raised about the possibility of a Chinese Debt Trap when accepting Chinese funding for infrastructure development, following the Hambantota Port experience of Sri Lanka.[60]

The most notable point of tension between China and ASEAN stems from the territorial disputes surrounding the South China Sea involving multiple ASEAN member states and China.[61] The involvement of China presents a particularly prickly problem. China's importance in ASEAN's economy cannot be understated, as seen in Figure 1.2 and 1.11, China has been a major growing source of FDI inflow to ASEAN as well as a major export market. As Chapter 3 will discuss, China also has the second largest share of gross exports for ASEAN

Figure 1.11: ASEAN FDI Inflows (% Gross Fixed Capital Formation)

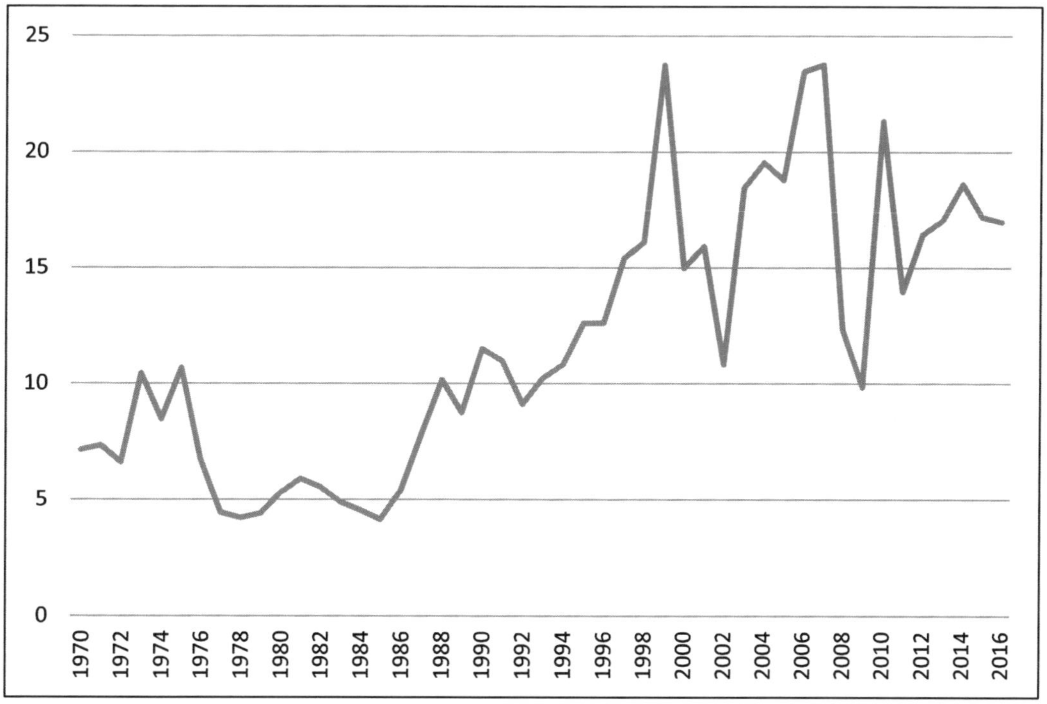

Source: Asia Competitiveness Institute based on UNCTAD.

[60] See Hurley *et al.* (2018).

[61] The claimants are Brunei, China, Taiwan (ROC), Malaysia, Indonesia, Philippines and Vietnam.

after intra-ASEAN trade. Further complicating the issue, the US, while not being a claimant, carries out freedom of navigation missions in the area in response to increased Chinese assertiveness.[62] Taken in the context of rising US–China tensions, the issue will likely remain a point of contention for the foreseeable future as China states its intention to conclude negotiations on the South China Sea Code of Conduct only by 2021.[63] The effects of US–China conflicts on ASEAN will be further elaborated upon in Chapter 4.

Geopolitical instability thus diminishes the potential benefits of the ASEAN Community agenda. First, through a collective action problem where parties fail to coordinate in order to gain the positive externalities. This can be thought of in the context of a classic Prisoner's Dilemma from game theory, and the failure of individual parties to cooperate or coordinate can cause large losses as in the case of the TPP.[64] Second, instabilities generate negative externalities, as in the case of the US–China trade war which has been demonstrated to cause external costs to parties beyond the US and China.[65] ASEAN member states now as ever need to ensure cooperation and resolve conflicts both within the bloc and with external partners.

1.4.2 Infrastructure Bottleneck

The provision of quality infrastructure is integral to economic growth and improved standards of living. Infrastructure such as electrical networks and transport networks underlie the economy, enabling the flow of goods, people and information. Additionally, the same set of infrastructure enables people to access better education, healthcare, goods, services and wider labour markets.[66] The benefits of infrastructure are often largely derived from the subsequent network of services. For example, consider the construction of highways: the economic value of a highway is largely attributable not to the act of constructing the highway, but to the usage of the highway to facilitate connectivity.[67] The setting up of infrastructure typically entails high initial costs and diminishing marginal costs of each additional customer; these properties result in infrastructure being monopolistic in nature.[68] The value and importance of quality infrastructure is not lost on the policy-makers of ASEAN, as reflected in the following speech by Mr. Lawrence Wong, Minister for National Development and Second Minister for Finance, at Asia Competitiveness Institute Annual Conference on "Infrastructure Development for Economic Competitiveness" at Grand Copthorne Waterfront Hotel as published by Ministry of Finance, Singapore on 23 November 2017.

As detailed in the speech by Minister Wong, what Asia needs is not simply infrastructure, there is also a dire need for quality infrastructure to achieve sustainable growth. The lack of quality infrastructure has repeatedly been identified and acknowledged as a key area of concern

---

[62] See Fravel (2016) and Yahuda (2013).

[63] See ISEAS — Yusof Ishak Institute (2018).

[64] See Asian Development Bank (2018).

[65] See United Nations Conference on Trade and Development (2019).

[66] See Conrad and Seitz (1994) and Rietveld (1989).

[67] See Boarnet (1997).

[68] See Asian Development Bank (2017).

Box 1.1: Speech by Mr. Lawrence Wong, Minister for National Development and Second Minister for Finance on "Infrastructure Development for Economic Competitiveness"

Excellencies and Distinguished Guests

Ladies and Gentlemen

I am very happy to join you this evening for this ACI conference on infrastructure development and I understand we have several guest who are from overseas, including a delegation from Indonesia. Let me take this opportunity to welcome all of you to Singapore.

We all know that infrastructure is a key pillar for sustainable economic growth. It can attract more investments; it can help create good jobs; and it can provide a quality living environment for people.

But at the same time, our approach to infrastructure development cannot be just about having more of the same. We should not be building for the sake of building. So it is vital that we get infrastructure right, and I think that includes developing infrastructure that is Sustainable, Inclusive, and Innovative.

Sustainable Infrastructure

First is the topic of sustainable infrastructure. How can we have more sustainable infrastructure?

The most obvious area for sustainability is in power generation where we would like to:

- Reduce coal and other carbon-intensive ways of power generation
- If there is a need for fossil fuels, use natural gas which is the least carbon intensive of fossil fuels.
- But beyond just fossil fuels, there is really a need to push for more renewable energy

This was difficult to do so in the past because the cost of renewables was more expensive than fossil fuels. But things have dramatically changed in recent years and the cost of renewable energy has come down sharply.

We feel and experience this in Singapore directly because we have been calling tenders for the deployment of solar panels on rooftops. When we first started calling the tenders, we had to pay money for people to put in place solar panels. These days when we call tenders, we do not have to pay a single cent because the solar panel operators can recover money from selling electricity into the grid, and that pays for the solar panels. So it is already great parity and it is cost effective.

(*Continued*)

Box 1.1: (*Continued*)

Of course, sustainability in power has to go beyond power and utilities; because it also applies to many other areas of infrastructure. It applies in buildings which are a major source of carbon emissions. So we need to push for green buildings. It applies in transport, where we need to push for cleaner vehicles.

There are also potential synergies across different fields and different sectors. So we do not have to necessarily look at it from a silo perspective but we have to look at integrated solutions. A good example is the way we do air conditioning in buildings. In Singapore there is high demand. Every building you go, lots of air condition usage. Even in our public housing, in our private condominiums, air condition is being used in almost every housing unit. So we see all these individual aircon compressors. They make the rooms very cool but they are emitting waste heat outside in the environment. And that is one reason why surface temperatures in Singapore are heating up.

So we have been putting in place solutions like district cooling; even underground district cooling where cooling is done across a whole network of buildings. There is no longer a need for individual aircon compressors. And the waste heat, or the heat that is generated from district cooling, can even be channelled into productive use — for industrial activities nearby, for example. So you are operating as a closed system.

Another good example is how we are now building a Water Treatment Plant and the Integrated Waste Management Facility co-located side by side. So the waste incinerator will generate electricity, it will reduce our dependence on landfills. The electricity generated from the waste facility will be used to power our water treatment plant. The water will then be piped back to the Waste treatment plan for cooling purposes. Again, an integrated solution that will reduce resource intensity, and will achieve more sustainable results.

So these are examples where even as we think about new infrastructure, there is tremendous work to design and make it more sustainable.

Inclusive Infrastructure

The second priority is to make infrastructure more inclusive.Because we want infrastructure that is accessible by everyone, and is built to serve people's needs. And this especially applies to urban infrastructure. It is an important priority for all of us especially given the stresses and fault lines that threaten to divide societies.

We don't want people to feel that a particular new infrastructure or a part of the city is beyond their reach or is catered only to the wealthy or to a particular group. So in designing

(*Continued*)

Box 1.1: (*Continued*)

infrastructure, inclusiveness must be an important priority and it must be built to serve a broader public purpose, and to serve the real needs of people.

That is something that we have been very careful about, even when we went about developing our city in Singapore. From the very start, we wanted to make Singapore a Garden City. Our founding Prime Minister Mr Lee Kuan Yew felt that this was not just a good to have, it was more than just a slogan. But it was about equal and public access to green and public spaces. It was nothing less than a matter of social equity.

As he puts it, "this is a priority that was very high up on my list…it's [about] a sense of equalness in society…Today, whether you are in a flat, executive condominium or landed property, it's clean…you are not excluded from the public spaces for everybody."

That speaks with an ethos of inclusiveness when we design and build infrastructure, and you see that today in the way that we design our city. It is reflected in our public housing scheme where we build public homes for the mass majority of Singaporeans and we ensure that this are affordable and quality homes for them. It is reflected in the way we do long term master planning for our city and our housing estates so that wherever you live, you are close to community and recreational spaces, including parks, water bodies and sports facilities. There is convenient access to public transport and convenient access to social facilities be it childcare, schools, hospitals or even elder care. And master planning, public housing, all these are important parts of building inclusive infrastructure that will make it accessible by everyone.

Innovative Infrastructure

Thirdly, we should try to make infrastructure innovative by leveraging on technology. There is tremendous scope to do this as technology is advancing rapidly with digitalisation, with data analytics, with new ways of building. So there is tremendous scope to not build the same thing in the same way but push the frontiers and do something different. And that is part of our process each time we think about investing in new infrastructure.

So the waste and water treatment plant I mentioned earlier is a good example. We could have just done a normal waste incinerator and a normal water treatment plant. But we looked at ways we can synergise, integrate and achieve greater resource efficiency.

Another example is the new Changi Airport Terminal 4 that was just opened recently. We are very proud of this terminal because it is a truly seamless automated terminal. Start-to-end, there is "self-service system". You can check-in, deposit baggage and clear immigration, all

(*Continued*)

Box 1.1: (*Continued*)

with automated systems. Highly productive and very convenient to use. And our friend for AirAsia, Mr Fernandes, which was on record said that this is one of the best airports in the world. It is very rare that he gives a compliment on airports but he knows and he has seen it. So AirAsia is there, and Cathay Pacific are some of the airlines that are using terminal 4 now.

In fact, in Singapore, besides these projects, we have a major pipeline of projects that are being built. We are looking at expanding our air and sea ports. We are looking at planning Changi Terminal 5. We are planning a new mega port in Tuas. We are building a high speed rail, linking Singapore and KL, and that will be at the heart of the new CBD in Jurong called Jurong Lake District. And we are building other regional centres around Singapore, in the North — in Woodlands; and in the Northeast — in Punggol. So these are all opportunities for us to experiment, to innovate and push for new frontiers for infrastructure.

Innovative infrastructure can also reinforce the other themes that we talked about earlier. Innovative infrastructure can enhance the inclusiveness of infrastructure too. For example, you talked about digital innovations in finance. I think there is tremendous scope, not just for innovation, but to make financial infrastructure more inclusive.

Today, nearly 30% of adults in developing Asia have a bank account. But many have smartphones and internet connection. So Fintech, perhaps can help them access cheaper and more efficient banking services. So that's one example where innovation can achieve new breakthroughs and can also make things more inclusive.

Another good example is remittance. Asia has experienced the fastest growth in remittance over the past decade in the world. We receive 55% of all global remittance inflows today. And that's because of the workers that around Asia, and they move from country to country and there is a significant remittance flow that is generated from their work.

The average remittance fees for them today, are more than 7 percent in South-East Asia. For every dollar that you remit, you have to pay 7 cents for remittance. These are hard-earned money that they worked for and that 7 percent eats into their savings. So if we can through Fintech, through innovations in financial infrastructure bring this down such a remittance fee, I think it will help tremendously. We should be aiming, for example, to cut remittance fees by half, to below 3%. If we can do that, it will save billions of dollars every year and it will help these workers remit more money and save more of their income.

So I think innovation is not just for innovation sake. Innovation can help enhance productivity, can help make infrastructure more sustainable and it can help make infrastructure more inclusive as well. These are the other themes that I highlighted just now.

(*Continued*)

Box 1.1: (*Continued*)

So overall, we all recognised that Asia's infrastructure needs are huge. And all of you would have heard statistics about how going forward, ASEAN need $200 billion dollars' worth of investment every year till 2030. And that is why, from Singapore's perspective, we fully support initiatives like the Belt & Road to help accelerate infrastructure development in the region.

This is the key message I want to leave you with. It is crucial also to get infrastructure right. We should not be building for the sake of building. We should not be going for bigger all the time. If there is a need to expand, of course we should expand, but it is not just about "more is necessarily better."

We also have to make sure that the infrastructure that we put in place going forward is sustainable, inclusive and innovative. And I believe that is the best way to achieve outcomes that we would like to see which is sustainable economic growth as well as environmental and social harmony.

Thank you.

Published on: 23 Nov 2017
Ministry of Finance, Singapore

for ASEAN, as reflected by the raft of related projects, from the setting up of the Asian Infrastructure Fund to the MPAC. In 2017, the Asian Development Bank (ADB) estimated that Southeast Asia requires US$147 billion in annual infrastructure investments from 2016 through 2030 and is currently investing an average of US$55 billion annually.[69] The region in aggregate underinvests by approximately 62.6%. This estimate by the ADB does not adjusts for the additional costs that climate change will necessitate. There is also a wide disparity in the quality of infrastructure in ASEAN as demonstrated by the WEF Global Competitiveness Index 4.0 Infrastructure rankings (Table 1.3).[70] There is an obvious gap between Singapore at first and the other countries in the region, Malaysia being the second best performer at 32nd.

Even with the emphasis on infrastructure development, ASEAN's infrastructure initiatives have been met with limited success; according to the executive summary of MPAC 2025, only 39 of the 125 initiatives in MPAC 2010 were completed. This presents a significant problem to the development of the region as a whole. The infrastructure initiatives are part of a wider regional connectivity networks, and the failure of a single section of the network thus jeopardises the viability of the whole network.

[69] See Asian Development Bank (2017).

[70] See World Economic Forum (2018a).

Table 1.3: GCI 4.0 Infrastructure Rankings

	Rank	Score
Brunei Darussalam	54	71.305651
Cambodia	112	51.671812
Indonesia	71	66.827515
Lao PDR	99	57.515473
Malaysia	32	77.888272
Philippines	92	59.423492
Singapore	1	95.703553
Thailand	60	69.658080
Viet Nam	75	65.441470

Source: Asia Competitiveness Institute based on World Economic Forum Global Competitiveness Index 4.0.

Table 1.4: Governance Indicators 2017

	Government Effectiveness	Regulatory Quality	Rule of Law	Control of Corruption
Brunei Darussalam	1.14	0.72	0.65	0.71
Indonesia	0.04	–0.11	–0.35	–0.25
Cambodia	–0.66	–0.50	–1.06	–1.29
Lao PDR	–0.36	–0.72	–0.88	–0.94
Myanmar	–1.05	–0.83	–0.95	–0.56
Malaysia	0.84	0.68	0.41	0.03
Philippines	–0.06	0.02	–0.41	–0.48
Singapore	2.21	2.12	1.82	2.13
Thailand	0.38	0.14	0.04	–0.39
Vietnam	0.00	–0.40	0.07	–0.58

Source: Asia Competitiveness Institute based on Worldwide Governance Indicators.

As previously stated, the benefits from infrastructure are often largely derived from the subsequent associated service flows. Given the monopolistic nature of infrastructure, there is a need to ensure that these services are well-regulated and efficient. This set of non-tangible supporting frameworks for hard infrastructure is broadly defined as soft infrastructure. The necessity of soft infrastructure has not gone unrecognised in ASEAN — the various initiatives discussed in earlier sections all include a law and regulation dimension to harmonize practices and improve efficiencies. Such soft infrastructure can go a long way in ensuring sustainable development, as highlighted in Minister Wong's point on planning for infrastructure to serve a broader purpose. However, the adoption of such practices remains unequal; the ASW for instance, touted as a key component of the AEC 2015 plan, only launched in January 2018, and at the time of writing only five of the ASEAN member states are ready. The remaining member states are still in various stages of readying national-level single windows. Of greater concern is the overall quality of governance in ASEAN, according to the Worldwide Governance Indicators, only three of the 10 ASEAN member states have across the board positive scores in terms of quality of government. This is indicative of a distinct lack of soft infrastructure (Table 1.4).

The lack of infrastructure in ASEAN can be presented in the form of a market failure. As described previously, the nature of infrastructure and public goods renders its unsuitable for provision through private sectors. In this instance, governments need to intervene to ensure adequate provision, and this is hampered by poor governance. ASEAN member states need to increase investments to meet infrastructure requirements; this however does not require that governments bear the entire load. As detailed in Section 1.1.1, ASEAN is attracting a large amount of FDI which can be channelled towards infrastructure projects. The role of governments here is thus to ensure that the proper soft infrastructure exists to facilitate and ensure maximum benefits.

1.4.3 Environmental Sustainability

Environmental sustainability forms a key component of sustainable development and is recognised in the ASEAN Community Vision 2025 and the UN 2030 Agenda for Sustainable Development, both of which ASEAN member states have committed to. Environmental issues in ASEAN member states are wide-ranging and differ from country to country.[71] The environmental agenda of ASEAN comprises two dedicated main work streams: environment and transboundary haze pollution (Figure 1.12). The ASEAN Social-Cultural Community Blueprint 2025 provides the guidelines for the ASEAN Cooperation on Environment. The measures for transboundary haze pollution are in accordance with the ASEAN Agreement on Transboundary Haze Pollution which entered into force in 2003 and has since been ratified by all member states.

While ASEAN has included environmental sustainability in its development agenda, the reality of the situation is that efforts are still lacking. The 2018 Environmental Performance Index[72] scores shown in Figure 1.13 compare the overall environmental performance of ASEAN member states out of 180 countries. We observe that the best performers are Singapore with a score of 64.23 (rank 49) and Brunei scoring 63.57 (rank 53). These are then followed by Malaysia scoring 59.22 (rank 75) and Philippines scoring 57.65 (rank 82). All other member states perform significantly worse. The overall environmental performance of ASEAN member states does not rate well globally.

As previously stated, the issue of transboundary haze holds a significant place in ASEAN's environmental agenda. The ASEAN Agreement on Transboundary Haze Pollution was established in 2002 following severe haze pollution in 1997–1998; it was only fully ratified by all member states in 2014, with Indonesia being the last member state to ratify the agreement. The effectiveness of this agreement remains questionable. In 2015, man-made fires and haze cost

[71] See Kojima (2016).

[72] See Wendling *et al.* (2018).

Figure 1.12: ASEAN Cooperation on Environmental Main Workstreams

ASEAN Strategic Plan on Environment	Transboundary Haze Pollution
• Nature Conservation and Biodiversity • Coastal and Marine Environment • Water Resource Management • Sustainable Cities • Climate Change • Chemicals and Waste • Environmental Education	• Management • Response • Monitoring • Prevention

Source: Asia Competitiveness Institute based on ASEAN Secretariat.

Figure 1.13: EPI Scores

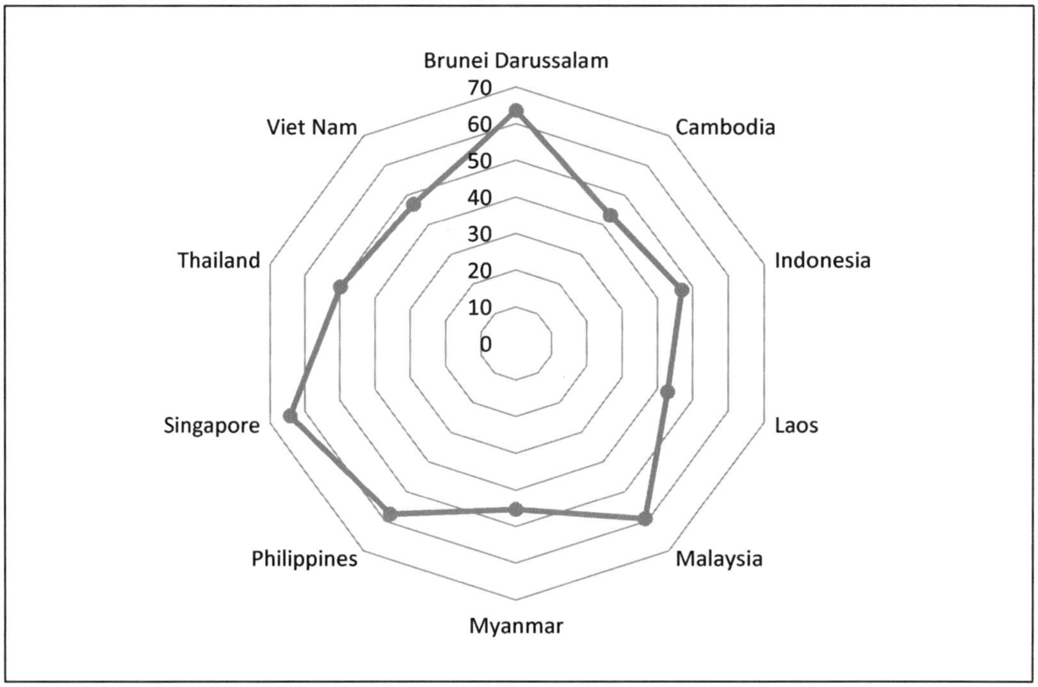

Source: Asia Competitiveness Institute based on Wending *et al*. (2018).

Figure 1.14: PM2.5 Air Pollution, Mean Annual Exposure (micrograms per cubic meter)

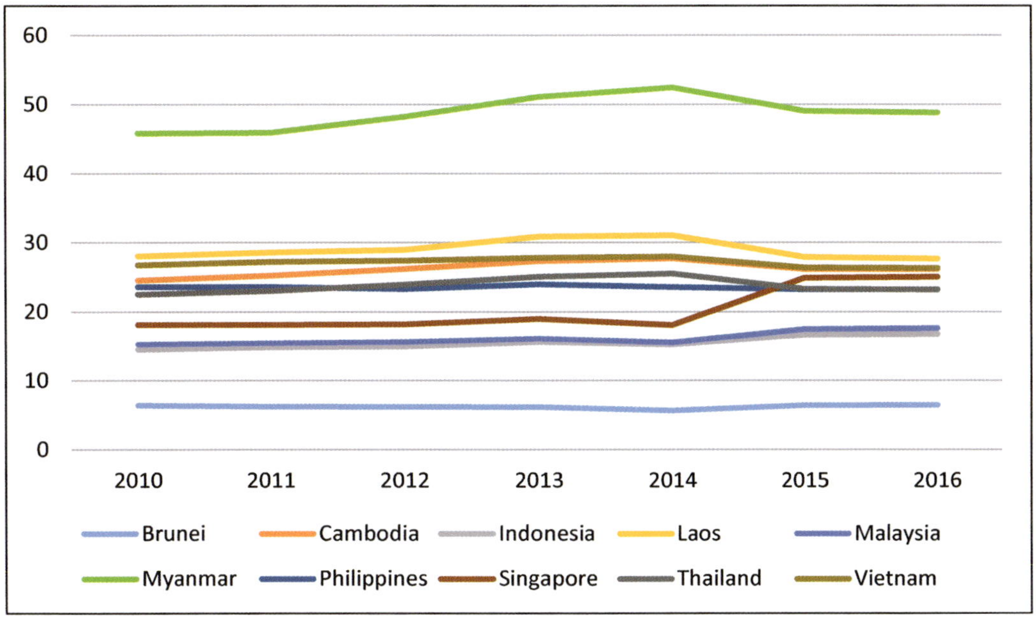

Source: Asia Competitiveness Institute based on data from World Bank, World Development Indicators.

Indonesia IDR 221 trillion (US$16.1 billion), exceeding the value-added for the country's oil palm production in 2014 according to World Bank estimates.[73] This figure does not include the regional costs which are still being studied at the time of writing. The Indonesian government has since taken steps to combat the issue. However, data from the World Bank on mean annual exposure to PM2.5 air pollution in Singapore, Malaysia and Indonesia shows that air pollution remains at the same elevated level in 2016. With the exception of Brunei, all ASEAN member states exceed the WHO guideline level of 10 micrograms per cubic meter for mean annual PM2.5 air pollution (Figure 1.14).

As expressed in the ASEAN Strategic Plan on Environment, one of the most pressing issues facing the region is the impact of climate change. An ADB study in 2015 estimates that Southeast Asia could lose 11% of GDP by 2100 to climate change if no response is taken, making the region one of the most vulnerable to the impacts of climate change.[74] The same study estimates the policy cost of emissions mitigation to be between 2.5% and 3.5% of regional GDP and generate benefits between five and 11 times the net mitigation costs from the period 2010–2100. It further finds that delays in implementation will increase the policy costs significantly over time.

The estimated climate-adjusted infrastructure requirements for the region is US$157 billion annually, up US$10 billion from the unadjusted estimate discussed in Section 1.4.2. The climate-

[73] See World Bank Group (2015, 2016).

[74] See Raitzer (2015).

Figure 1.15: CO2 Emissions in ASEAN, Annual

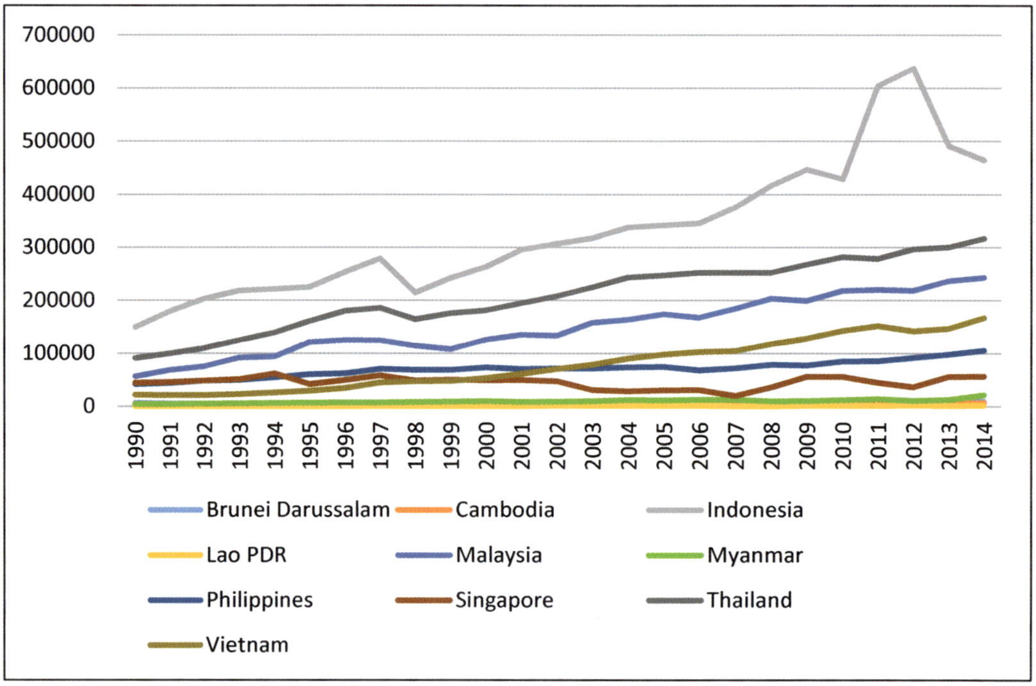

Source: Asia Competitiveness Institute based on data from World Bank, World Development Indicators.

Figure 1.16: Carbon Dioxide Damage (current US$)

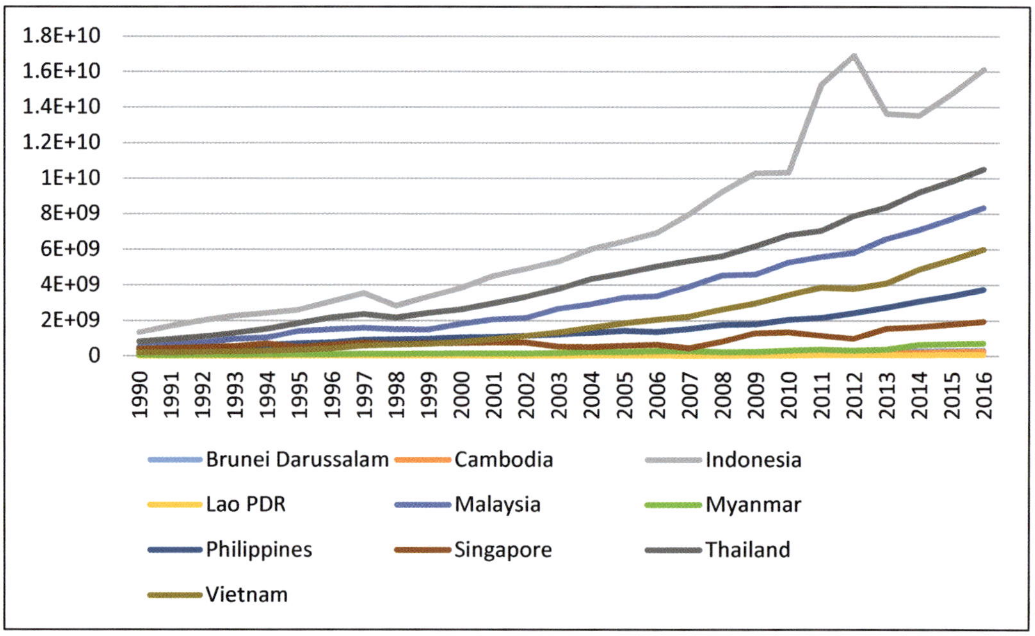

Source: Asia Competitiveness Institute based on data from World Bank, World Development Indicators.

adjusted investment gap is now approximately 65%.[75] As evidenced in Figures 1.15 and 1.16 which show the trajectory of CO2 emissions in ASEAN member states and the estimated cost of the emissions, there is an observable upward trend across time. The estimated total cost to ASEAN in 2016 is US$47.97 billion. These values are expected to increase as the region continues to grow and develop.

If we consider the environment as a shared resource, the market failure in this case, is most famously described by Hardin (1968) as the tragedy of the commons, also studied extensively by Nobel Prize-winning economist Ostrom.[76,77] Despite a stated recognition of environmental sustainability issues in ASEAN since 1977, it is evident from the data that ASEAN as a whole is lacking coordinated concrete action. The 2017 UN report on sustainable development in ASEAN highlights that economies in ASEAN are already placing considerable strain on the environment, which will likely worsen as the region continues to develop on its current trajectory.[78] While initiatives such as the ASEAN Cooperation on Environment, ASEAN Green Bonds Standards and individual national efforts such as Singapore's development of sustainable infrastructure do make some progress in addressing the severe underinvestment problem, ASEAN member states will likely have to take steps towards stronger collective action, given the transboundary nature of environmental pollution.

1.5 Concluding Remarks

The developments in ASEAN over the years show significant and steady progress. The potential for ASEAN to achieve the goal of becoming the fourth largest economy by 2030 remains within reach. The significance of ASEAN to the global economy continues to increase with the introduction of more initiatives, such as the RCEP, CPTPP and ASEAN Smart Cities Network that take advantage of global trends and opportunities by integrating the region further into the global economy.

Despite the obvious potential, ASEAN and its member states must remain aware that significant challenges remain. The issues discussed in Section 1.4 are but a brief discussion of some of the key challenges ASEAN faces. These challenges are a reminder that ASEAN needs to pay attention to the trade-offs and quality issues that accompany its remarkable economic growth. The emphasis on sustainable development in ASEAN does not appear to have translated into significant action as ASEAN remains lacking in terms of infrastructure and environmental sustainability, both of which have been demonstrated to present significant hurdles to future growth. This is further underpinned by the turbulent nature of geopolitics in the region.

The rest of the book is structured as follows: Chapter 2 provides the 2018 Update on Annual Competitiveness Analysis for ASEAN-10 Economies. On top of the annual rankings of economic competitiveness for the 10 ASEAN countries from 2000 to 2015 derived using ACI's

[75] See Asian Development Bank (2017).

[76] The tragedy of the commons describes the situation where a common resource is depleted as individuals driven by self-interest all simultaneously act to extract the highest possible value from the resource.

[77] See Ostrom (2015) Governing the Commons.

[78] See United Nations Economic and Social Commission for Asia and the Pacific (ESCAP) (2017).

comprehensive and rigorous methodological framework, we also present our breakthrough objective Shapley Weightage methodology. Moreover, through our assessments of each economy's relative strengths and weaknesses, we provide a constructive policy roadmap for domestic reforms in each member country.

Trade is one of the cornerstones of economic development in ASEAN, and understanding the nature of trade in ASEAN relative to the world is key to considerations of ASEAN's economic policies. Chapter 3 presents an empirical study of the impact of real effective exchange rates and integration into global value chains on exports of goods and services. The results enable us to draw a wide range of policy implications addressing issues such as exposure to external shocks, exchange rate management and investment environment.

Continuing in the vein of trade and ASEAN's role in the global value chain, Chapter 4 discusses the implications of the US–China Trade war on ASEAN. Here, we consider the US–China Trade war in the wider context of shifts in global production chains and how ASEAN and its various member states stand to benefit from production relocation, diversification and the potential pitfalls and challenges to be confronted in seeking these benefits.

The book concludes with a summary of key findings in Chapter 5. In addition, we discuss our findings in the context of the East Asian Development Model and its applicability to the various members states at different points of development. The chapter also outlines the potential impacts, on various segments of the economy as ASEAN moves to overcome development bottlenecks. Finally, we discuss the future research agenda regarding the ASEAN region.

References

Ahmad, Fayyaz, Muhammad Umar Draz, and Su-Chang Yang. 2018. "Causality Nexus of Exports, FDI and Economic Growth of the ASEAN5 Economics: Evidence from Panel Data Analysis." *The Journal of International Trade & Economic Development* 27 (6): 685–700.

Akerlof, George A. 1970. "The Market for 'Lemons': Quality Uncertainty and the Market Mechanism." *The Quarterly Journal of Economics* 84 (3): 488–500. https://doi.org/10.2307/1879431.

ASEAN Secretariat. 2015a. "ASEAN Strategic Action Plan for SME Development 2016–2025." Jakarta: ASEAN Secretariat. https://asean.org/wp-content/uploads/2015/12/SAP-SMED-Final.pdf.

ASEAN Secretariat. 2015b. "ASEAN Integration in Services." Jakarta: ASEAN Secretariat. https://www.asean.org/storage/2015/12/ASEAN-Integration-in-Services-(Dec%202015).pdf.

ASEAN Secretariat. 2016. "Master Plan on ASEAN Connectivity 2025." Jakarta: Association of Southest Asian Nations.

ASEAN Secretariat. 2017a. "2017–2015 ASEAN Work Programme on Electronic Commerce." Pasay City.

ASEAN Secretariat. 2017b. "Overview of ASEAN Plus Three Cooperation." ASEAN Secretariat Information Paper.

ASEAN Secretariat. 2018a. "Promoting Innovation and E-Commerce through the ASEAN Agreement on Electronic-Commerce." Factsheet. Association of Southest Asian Nations.

ASEAN Secretariat. 2018b. "ASEAN Key Figures 2018." Jakarta: ASEAN Secretariat. https://www.aseanstats.org/wp-content/uploads/2018/12/ASEAN-Key-Figures-2018.pdf.

ASEAN Secretariat. 2019a. "ASEAN Free Trade Area (AFTA Council)." ASEAN | ONE VISION ONE IDENTITY ONE COMMUNITY. March 8, 2019. https://asean.org/asean-economic-community/asean-free-trade-area-afta-council/.

ASEAN Secretariat. 2019b. "ASEAN Framework Agreement on services." Invest in ASEAN 2019. http://investasean.asean.org/index.php/page/view/asean-free-trade-area-agreements/view/757/newsid/870/asean-framework-agreement-on-services.html.

Asian Development Bank. 2017. *Meeting Asia's Infrastructure Needs*. Asian Development Bank. http://dx.doi.org/10.22617/FLS168388-2.

Asian Development Bank. 2018. *Toward Optimal Provision of Regional Public Goods in Asia and the Pacific: Conference Highlights*. Asian Development Bank. http://dx.doi.org/10.22617/TCS189599-2.

Baller, Silja, Soumitra Dutta, and Bruno Lanvin. 2016. "The Global Information Technology Report 2016: Innovating in the Digital Economy." Geneva: World Economic Forum.

Boarnet, Marlon G. 1997. "Infrastructure Services and the Productivity of Public Capital: The Case of Streets and Highways." *National Tax Journal* 50 (1): 39–57.

Branstetter, Lee. 2006. "Is Foreign Direct Investment a Channel of Knowledge Spillovers? Evidence from Japan's FDI in the United States." *Journal of International Economics* 68 (2): 325–344. https://doi.org/10.1016/j.jinteco.2005.06.006.

Bwalya, Samuel Mulenga. 2006. "Foreign Direct Investment and Technology Spillovers: Evidence from Panel Data Analysis of Manufacturing Firms in Zambia." *Journal of Development Economics* 81 (2): 514–526. https://doi.org/10.1016/j.jdeveco.2005.06.011.

Chow, Peter C.Y, and Mitchell H. Kellman. 1993. *Trade — The Engine of Growth in East Asia*. https://ideas.repec.org/b/oxp/obooks/9780195078954.html.

Conrad, Klaus, and Helmut Seitz. 1994. "The Economic Benefits of Public Infrastructure." *Applied Economics* 26 (4): 303–311. https://doi.org/10.1080/00036849400000077.

East-West Center. 2017. "ASEAN Matters for America." Washington DC.

Fravel, Taylor. 2016. "U.S. Policy Towards the Disputes in the South China Sea Since 1995." In *Power Politics in Asia's Contested Waters: Territorial Disputes in the South China Sea*, edited by Enrico Fels and Truong-Minh Vu, 389–402. Cham: Springer International Publishing. https://doi.org/10.1007/978-3-319-26152-2_18.

Gani, Azmat, and Michael D. Clemes. 2002. "Services and Economic Growth in ASEAN Economies." *ASEAN Economic Bulletin* 19 (2): 155–169.

Hardin, Garrett. 1968. "The Tragedy of the Commons." *Science* 162 (3859): 1243–1248. https://doi.org/10.1126/science.162.3859.1243.

Haskel, Jonathan E., Sonia C. Pereira, and Matthew J. Slaughter. 2007. "Does Inward Foreign Direct Investment Boost the Productivity of Domestic Firms?" *The Review of Economics and Statistics* 89 (3): 482–496.

Huang, Yiping. 2016. "Understanding China's Belt & Road Initiative: Motivation, Framework and Assessment." *China Economic Review* 40 (September): 314–321. https://doi.org/10.1016/j.chieco.2016.07.007.

Hurley, John, Scott Morris, and Gailyn Portelance. 2018. "Examining the Debt Implications of the Belt and Road Initiative from a Policy Perspective." 121. CGD Policy Paper. Washington, DC: Center for Global Development. https://www.cgdev.org/sites/default/files/examining-debt-implications-belt-and-road-initiative-policy-perspective.pdf.

ISEAS — Yusof Ishak Institute. 2018. "The 44th Singapore Lecture by His Excellency Li Keqiang, Premier of the State Council of the People's Republic of China — ISEAS-Yusof Ishak Institute." November 2018. https://www.iseas.edu.sg/events/singapore-lecture/item/8541-the-44th-singapore-lecture-by-his-excellency-li-keqiang-premier-of-the-state-council-of-the-people-s-republic-of-china.

Kojima, Michikazu. 2016. "Environmental Issues in Southeast Asia." In *Basic Studies in Environmental Knowledge, Technology, Evaluation, and Strategy: Introduction to East Asia Environmental Studies*, edited by Takayuki Shimaoka, Takahiro Kuba, Hirofumi Nakayama, Toshiyuki Fujita, and Nobuhiro Horii, 55–67. Tokyo: Springer Japan. https://doi.org/10.1007/978-4-431-55819-4_4.

Lee, Hsien Loong. 2018. "Prime Minister Lee Hsien Loong's Statement at the Press Conference by the ASEAN Chair on the 33rd ASEAN Summit." Speech, November 15.

Lee, Huay Huay, and Hui Boon Tan. 2006. "Technology Transfer, FDI and Economic Growth in the ASEAN Region." *Journal of the Asia Pacific Economy* 11 (4): 394–410. https://doi.org/10.1080/13547860600923593.

Ministry of International Trade and Industry. 2019. "Trans-Pacific Partnership Agreement (TPP) & Comprehensive and Progressive Agreement for Trans-Pacific Partnership (CPTPP)." Malaysia's Free Trade Agreements. March 2019. https://fta.miti.gov.my/index.php/pages/view/71?mid=40.

Ministry of Trade and Industry. 2018. "ASEAN Agreement on Electronic Commerce." Factsheet.

Ministry of Trade and Industry Singapore. 2018. "The CPTPP Enters into Force in December." https://www.mti.gov.sg/-/media/MTI/Newsroom/Press-Releases/2018/11/Press-release-The-CPTPP-Enters-Into-Force-in-December.pdf.

Page, John. 1994. "The East Asian Miracle: Four Lessons for Development Policy." *NBER Macroeconomics Annual* 9: 219–269. https://doi.org/10.2307/3585089.

Pattichis, C. S., Kyriacou, E., Voskarides, S., Pattichis, M. S., Istepanian, R., and Schizas, C. N. 2002. "Wireless Telemedicine Systems: An Overview." *IEEE Antennas and Propagation Magazine* 44 (2): 143–153. https://doi.org/10.1109/MAP.2002.1003651.

Perednia, Douglas A., and Ace Allen. 1995. "Telemedicine Technology and Clinical Applications." *JAMA* 273 (6): 483–488. https://doi.org/10.1001/jama.1995.03520300057037.

Ploberger, Christian. 2017. "One Belt, One Road — China's New Grand Strategy." *Journal of Chinese Economic and Business Studies* 15 (3): 289–305. https://doi.org/10.1080/14765284.2017.1346922.

Raitzer, David. 2015. *Southeast Asia and the Economics of Global Climate Stabilization*. Asian Development Bank. https://www.adb.org/publications/southeast-asia-and-economics-global-climate-stabilization.

Rammal, Hussain Gulzar, and Ralf Zurbruegg. 2006. "The Impact of Regulatory Quality on Intra-Foreign Direct Investment Flows in the ASEAN Markets." *International Business Review* 15 (4): 401–414.

Ravi Menon. 2017. "Singapore FinTech Journey 2." presented at the Singapore FinTech Festival, November 14. http://www.mas.gov.sg/News-and-Publications/Speeches-and-Monetary-Policy-Statements/Speeches/2017/Singapore-FinTech-Journey-2.aspx.

Rietveld, Piet. 1989. "Infrastructure and Regional Development." *The Annals of Regional Science* 23 (4): 255–274. https://doi.org/10.1007/BF01579778.

Sandler, Todd. 1998. "Global and Regional Public Goods: A Prognosis for Collective Action." *Fiscal Studies* 19 (3): 221–247. https://doi.org/10.1111/j.1475-5890.1998.tb00286.x.

Sandler, Todd. 2013. "Public Goods and Regional Cooperation for Development: A New Look." *Integration and Trade Journal* 17.

Sirgy, M. Joseph, Dong-Jin Lee, Chad Miller, and James E. Littlefield. 2004. "The Impact of Globalization on a Country's Quality of Life: Toward an Integrated Model." *Social Indicators Research* 68 (3): 251–298.

Taguchi, Hiroyuki, and Hak-Loh Lee. 2016. "ASEAN-plus-One Free Trade Agreements and Their Trade Effects." *MPRA Paper No. 72503*. https://mpra.ub.uni-muenchen.de/72503/.

Tan, Khee Giap, Le Phuong Anh Nguyen, Sasidaran Gopalan, and Trieu Duong Luu Nguyen. 2016. *2015 Annual Competitiveness Analysis, Agricultural Productivity and Development Vision for ASEAN-10*. Asia Competitiveness Institute — World Scientific Series. WORLD SCIENTIFIC. https://doi.org/10.1142/10219.

Tan, Khee Giap, Le Phuong Anh Nguyen, and Trieu Duong Luu Nguyen. 2017. *2016 Annual Competitiveness Analysis and Growth Slowdown Analysis for ASEAN-10*. Asia Competitiveness Institute — World Scientific Series. WORLD SCIENTIFIC. https://doi.org/10.1142/10617.

Tan, Khee Giap, Trieu Duong Luu Nguyen, Hui Yin Chuah, and Duy Nguyen. 2018. *2017 Annual Competitiveness Analysis and Impact of Exchange Rates on Foreign Direct Investment Inflows to ASEAN Economies*. Asia Competitiveness Institute — World Scientific Series. WORLD SCIENTIFIC. https://doi.org/10.1142/11065.

Tu, Yonghong, and Xiao Tan. 2012. "Technology Spillovers of FDI in ASEAN Sourcing from Local and Abroad." *China Finance Review International* 2 (1): 78–94. https://doi.org/10.1108/20441391211197465.

United Nations Conference on Trade and Development. 2019. "Key Statistics and Trends in Trade Policy 2018." United Nations Conference on Trade and Development. https://unctad.org/en/pages/PublicationWebflyer.aspx?publicationid=2345.

United Nations Economic and Social Commission for Asia and the Pacific (ESCAP). 2017. "Complementarites between the ASEAN Community Vision 2025 and the United Natons 2030 Agenda for Sustainable Development: A Framework for Acton." United Nations. https://www.unescap.org/sites/default/files/publications/UN%20ASEAN%20Complementarities%20Report_Final_PRINT.pdf.

Wendling, Z. A., Emerson, J. W., Esty, D. C., Levy, M. A., de Sherbinin, A., *et al*. 2018. "2018 Environmental Performance Index." New Haven, CT: Yale Center for Environmental Law & Policy. https://epi.envirocenter.yale.edu/.

World Bank Group. 2015. "December 2015 Indonesia Economic Quarterly." World Bank Group. http://www.worldbank.org/en/news/feature/2015/12/15/indonesia-economic-quarterly-december-2015.

World Bank Group. 2016. "The Cost of Fire : An Economic Analysis of Indonesia's 2015 Fire Crisis." 103668. The World Bank. http://documents.worldbank.org/curated/en/776101467990969768/The-cost-of-fire-an-economic-analysis-of-Indonesia-s-2015-fire-crisis.

World Bank Group. 2017. "The Status of Infrastructure Services in East Asia and the Pacific." Washington, D.C.: World Bank. https://openknowledge.worldbank.org/handle/10986/28954.

World Bank Group. 2019. "Belt and Road Initiative." Text/HTML. World Bank. March 8, 2019. http://www.worldbank.org/en/topic/regional-integration/brief/belt-and-road-initiative.

World Economic Forum. 2018a. "The Global Competitiveness Report 2018." World Economic Forum. https://www.weforum.org/reports/the-global-competitveness-report-2018/.

World Economic Forum. 2018b. "World Economic Forum Initiative Pledges to Equip 20 Million ASEAN Workers with Digital Skills by 2020." November 19, 2018. https://www.weforum.org/press/2018/11/world-economic-forum-initiative-pledges-to-equip-20-million-asean-workers-with-digital-skills-by-2020/.

Yahuda, Michael. 2013. "China's New Assertiveness in the South China Sea." *Journal of Contemporary China* 22 (81): 446–459. https://doi.org/10.1080/10670564.2012.748964.

Yamanaka, Takashi. 2013. "Integration of the ASEAN Banking Sector." Newsletter. Japan: Institute for International Monetary Affairs.

Yang, Ting, and Toshiyuki Shimada. 2011. "Challenges and Developments in the Financial Systems of the Southeast Asian Economies." *OECD Journal: Financial Market Trends* 2010 (2): 137–159. https://doi.org/10.1787/fmt-2010-5kggc0z277ln.

Chapter 2

2018 Update on Annual Competitiveness Analysis for ASEAN-10

2.1 Introduction

Ranked as the seventh largest economy in the world, the ASEAN bloc has experienced tremendous growth and has come a long way since its founding in 1967. Endowed with abundant natural resources, large human capital of a population over 630 million in 2016, and situated in a geographically advantageous position between the Asia-Pacific and Indian sub-continents, the region is poised for an even more prosperous future. As outlined in Chapter 1, the 10 members have put in place innumerable development agendas and policies aimed at pushing the region towards fulfilling its utmost potential of becoming the fourth largest economy by 2030.

However, the ASEAN-10 are still held back by various complications that pose great hurdles to its growth trajectory. Mentioned in Chapter 1 are internal struggles such as domestic instability, infrastructure bottlenecks and growing worries about how the region's economic growth might be taking place at the expense of environmental sustainability. Externally, global geopolitical conditions like trade disputes, as laid out in Chapter 4, and the rise of digitalisation further exacerbate the hurdles that the region will have to overcome.

ACI's competitiveness framework, methodology and analysis was thus developed with the aim of providing a dynamic and extensive growth roadmap for the ASEAN region. By going beyond rankings and assessing each ASEAN member country individually, ACI is able to provide personalised policy recommendations to each and every economy while taking into account both domestic and global contexts.

The following sections in this chapter hence detail ACI's competitiveness analysis that moves beyond a one-size-fits-all approach. Section 2.2 traces out ACI's competitiveness framework and methodology, as well as the simulation analysis undertaken that assesses the various dimensions of countries' competitiveness. This is followed by Section 2.3 that elaborates on the findings of ACI's competitiveness analysis, the top 20% strengths and weaknesses of the ASEAN economies, and ACI's *What-if* simulation. Subsequently, Section 2.4 explains the usage of the Shapley value as a robustness check for the index, while 2.5 concludes with an overall summary of total findings.

2.2 ACI Competitiveness Framework and Methodology

2.2.1 Literature Review on Competitiveness

The notion of regional or *in situ* competitiveness has been explored in various ways. Initially, in the 1980s, "competitiveness" was considered as part of the private sector domain, especially in relation to firm performance.[1] Over time, the discourse expanded onto the domain of

[1] See Porter (1980).

macroeconomics, as shown by the establishment of "Council on Competitiveness" or similar institutions in various advanced industrialised countries. Some scholars have argued that it was primarily firms that compete, not nations, regions, or places.[2] However, the performance of those firms depends on various factors that are embedded in the firm's location. These include quality of labour and infrastructure, governance, costs of doing business, as well as the performance of competing and complementary firms around the area.[3]

Two of the most highly cited cross-country competitiveness studies at the moment are the World Competitiveness Yearbook (WCY) by the IMD World Competitiveness Centre and the World Economic Forum's Global Competitiveness Report (GCR). The WCY defines competitiveness as composed of four factors: (i) economic performance, (ii) government efficiency, (iii) business efficiency, and (iv) infrastructure. Each factor is further made up of five criteria, so that there are 20 criteria in total. The WCY uses equal weights such that each criterion contributes 5% weight, and each factor contributes 25% weight to the overall competitiveness index.[4] Most of the data used are statistical indicators sourced from international, regional and national organisations. However, substantial perception data sourced from executive surveys supplement the statistical data.

The GCR breaks down its Global Competitiveness Index into three sub-indices: (i) basic requirements, (ii) efficiency enhancers, and (iii) innovation and sophistication factors.[5] Each of the three sub-indices has a different number of pillars. The basic requirements sub-index has four pillars: institutions, infrastructure, macroeconomic environment, and health and primary education. The efficiency enhancers sub-index is composed of six pillars: higher education and training, goods market efficiency, labour market efficiency, financial market development, technological readiness, and market size. Lastly, the sub-index on innovation and sophistication factors consists of two pillars: business sophistication and innovation. Most of the data that make up these pillars and sub-indices come from executive opinion surveys.

2.2.2 ACI Competitiveness Framework

While the notion of competitiveness has been defined in various ways, ACI's approach to competitiveness is eclectic and comprehensive as it takes into account different factors that collectively shape the ability of a nation or region to achieve substantial and inclusive economic development over a sustained period of time.

In line with this overarching thrust, ACI defines competitiveness through four environments: (i) Macroeconomic Stability (MS), (ii) Government and Institutional Setting (GIS), (iii) Financial, Businesses and Manpower Conditions (FBMC), and (iv) Quality of Life and Infrastructure Development (QLID). These four environments carry equal weightage (25%) in the computation of the Overall Competitiveness score. Following a nested approach, each environment comprises three sub-environments of the same weightage (33.3%) (see Figure 2.1). While giving different weights to different environments and sub-environments based on their

[2] See Krugman (1994).

[3] See Camagni (2002), Kitson, *et al.* (2004) and Bristow (2010).

[4] See IMD World Competitiveness Center (2014).

[5] See World Economic Forum (2014).

Figure 2.1: ACI Competitiveness Framework

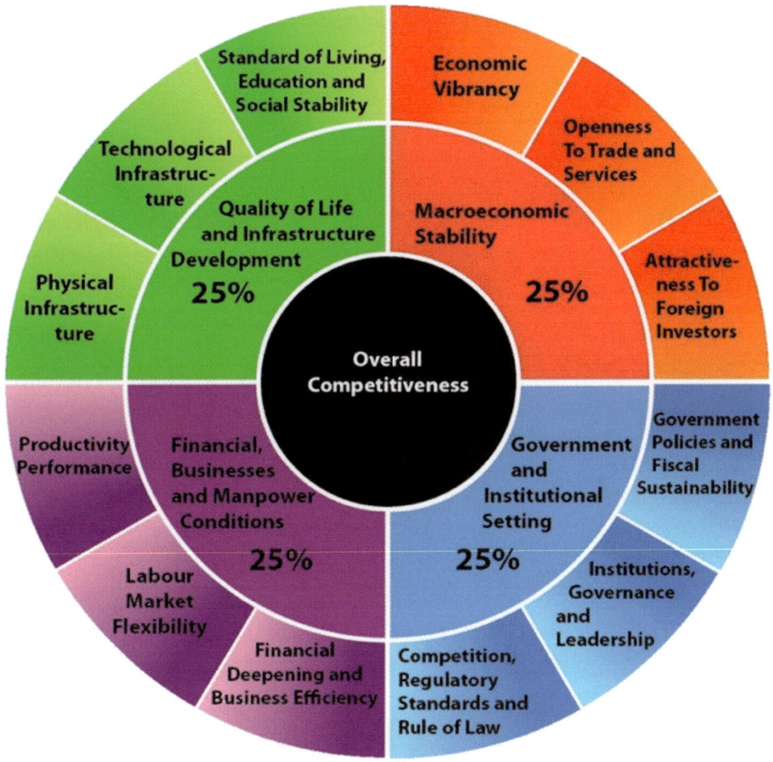

Source: Asia Competitiveness Institute.

importance seems more appropriate, the method is nonetheless arbitrary and contentious. Thus, equal distribution of weight reflects a balanced view towards the different factors that make up an overall notion of competitiveness.

ACI's framework provides a holistic, integrated and systematic way of examining national competitiveness. Two environments are specifically related to economic performance, namely Macroeconomic Stability (MS) and Financial, Businesses and Manpower Conditions (FBMC). MS encompasses aggregated macroeconomic conditions which include: (i) Economic Vibrancy, (ii) Openness to Trade and Services, and (iii) Attractiveness to Foreign Investors. FBMC, on the other hand, represents the microeconomy, particularly firms and factors that impact their performances. FBMC thus comprises: (i) Financial Deepening and Business Efficiency, (ii) Labour Market Flexibility, and (iii) Productivity Performance. The remaining two environments are institutional and social in character. Government and Institutional Setting (GIS) covers efficacy of government institutions and rule of law. This environment consists of: (i) Government Policies and Fiscal Sustainability, (ii) Institutions, Governance and Leadership, and (iii) Competition, Regulatory Standards and Rule of Law. Lastly, Quality of Life and Infrastructure Development (QLID) combines infrastructure, health and education services, environmental standards and social security. The three sub-environments are:

(i) Physical Infrastructure, (ii) Technological Infrastructure, and (iii) Standard of Living, Education and Social Stability.

There are in total 121 indicators in ACI's competitiveness rankings and simulations for ASEAN-10 economies in the period 2000–2015 (see Appendix 1). The extensive number of indicators ensures robust interpretation of each environment and sub-environment in the Overall Competitiveness score. Depending on data availability, some environments and sub-environments may have more indicators than others. Nonetheless, this is not an issue as they simply average out. This also allows a certain amount of flexibility in adding or removing indicators when updating the rankings in the future, so long as the overall structure of the four environments and 12 sub-environments remains unchanged.

2.2.3 Data Sources

The data for the 121 indicators used in this study are collected from various sources, of which the bulk come from official data sources such as the World Bank World Development Indicators, Asian Development Bank (ADB) and World Economic Forum Global Competitiveness Index (GCI). Other sources include Economist Intelligence Unit (EIU), Global Market Information Database (GMID), UNESCO Institute for Statistics, International Monetary Fund (IMF) World Economic Outlook Database, United Nations Conference on Trade and Development (UNCTAD), IMD WCY, International Telecommunication Union Information and Communications Technology (ICT) Indicators Database, United Nations Development Programme (UNDP), Reporters Without Borders, Freedom House, and The Pew Research Centre.

2.2.4 Computation of Standardised Scores Using Equal Weights

The next important question in terms of methodology is how to aggregate the different types of data into one coherent index. Given 121 different indicators in this research, all in different value or quantity terms, such as GDP in millions of US dollars, or population in number, how do we resolve these different units of measurement?

The ACI uses the statistical methodology of "standardised score". The standardised score is a relative comparison to see how well the performance of a certain economy is in comparison to the average economy. Therefore, the unit of measurement is no longer relevant. The standardised score has no unit of measurement because it simply measures relative performance among economies.

In statistical terms, it measures how many standard deviations away each economy is from the average economy (see Appendix 2 for technical explanation). If an economy has a standardised score of zero, it is an average performer in terms of that particular indicator. Having a negative score means the economy performs below average. Having a positive score, on the other hand, means above-average performance.

The farther away the score is from zero, the farther away is the performance of the said economy from the ASEAN average. If an economy has a high positive score, it means it is much above the average score. The standardised scores for each indicator are then aggregated at the sub-environment level and then reaggregated at the environment level, and finally aggregated again at the overall level. This allows the comparison of the performance of 10 ASEAN economies at different levels from the Overall Competitiveness to specific indicators in four environments.

2.2.5 *What-if* Competitiveness Simulation Analysis

A competitiveness ranking in itself is like a beauty contest; it merely identifies who are doing well and who are facing challenges but stops short of giving more constructive advice on improving the rankings. ACI's index goes one step further by tackling the "so what?" question. What is the policy implication of a competitiveness ranking result for a particular economy? The data used in the index allow us to do an in-depth analysis of the performance of each economy according to the different indicators, sub-environments, and environments. By analysing the data, we are able to identify not just the Overall Competitiveness ranking but also specific indicators for which the economy is doing well or struggling. This allows us to come up with policy recommendations for each economy.

ACI has come up with the *What-if* competitiveness simulation that is based on an improvement of each economy's top 20% weakest indicators,[6] and a recalculation of the standardised score based on such improvement. To do this, we first look at each economy and sort the different indicators for each economy from the highest to the lowest score. This allows us to identify the 24 weakest indicators, or the bottom 20% of the indicators, that each economy has.

Then, we raise the values of these 24 weakest indicators to the average level. This means their average score is raised to zero if it has been negative in the original ranking. For other economies which are already competitive, we leave their scores alone. Their scores are not discounted if they are already competitive. Once these scores are raised, we recalculate the ranking, assuming that other economies stay constant. We do this simulation one by one for each economy. Each economy would then have a new, improved standardised score. This allows us to answer the question: If a particular economy improves on its set of weakest indicators, and assuming other economies remain constant, how would that economy's competitiveness ranking improve?

2.3 Competitiveness Analysis of ASEAN-10 Economies, 2000–2015

In this section, we present the Overall Competitiveness rankings as well as the rankings for the four environments as derived from the standardised scores for each economy over the period 2000–2015. The scores for individual sub-environments are visualised in the median and maximum web analysis. Findings on the *What-if* competitiveness simulation are also discussed.

[6] In a list of 121 indicators, the weakest are listed at the bottom and the top 20% strongest are listed at the top.

2.3.1 Overall Competitiveness

Table 2.1 shows the Overall Competitiveness rankings along with the standardised scores of individual ASEAN member states over the period of 2000–2015. Singapore has demonstrated a consistent performance and maintained its first place in the region for the 15th consecutive year. More importantly, however, its increase in the overall competitiveness score from 2.0152 in 2014 to 2.1179 in 2015 has resulted in a wider "competitiveness gap" with Malaysia, which ranked second in 2015 with a score of 0.9387 (a small slip from 1.0568 in 2014).

One point worth highlighting here is that Brunei has overtaken Thailand and ranked third for the second time (its first being in 2014) throughout the study period. This is due to the persistent improvement in Brunei's scores, as seen in Table 2.1. On the other hand, Thailand has experienced a drop in its scores from 0.4477 in 2014 to 0.4099 in 2015. Meanwhile, despite being the largest economy in the region and maintaining its ranking at the fifth spot this year, Indonesia has experienced a drastic score decrease from 0.0412 in 2014 to –0.0762 in 2015. Philippines also kept its ranking of sixth place in 2015 with a slight improvement in its score as compared to 2014.

Table 2.1: Overall Competitiveness Rankings and Standardised Scores, 2000–2015

Overall Competitiveness										
	1		2		3		4		5	
Rank	Economy	Score	Economy	Score	Economy	Score	Economy	Score	Economy	Score
2000	Singapore	2.1621	Malaysia	0.9531	Thailand	0.5312	Brunei	0.3726	Indonesia	–0.1154
2001	Singapore	2.1217	Malaysia	0.9244	Thailand	0.6068	Brunei	0.4012	Philippines	–0.1615
2002	Singapore	1.9824	Malaysia	1.0491	Thailand	0.7477	Brunei	0.3706	Indonesia	–0.1851
2003	Singapore	1.9862	Malaysia	1.0605	Thailand	0.7429	Brunei	0.3786	Indonesia	–0.1185
2004	Singapore	1.9573	Malaysia	1.0743	Thailand	0.7228	Brunei	0.4158	Indonesia	–0.0784
2005	Singapore	1.9964	Malaysia	1.0657	Thailand	0.7177	Brunei	0.3724	Indonesia	–0.1784
2006	Singapore	1.9752	Malaysia	1.0799	Thailand	0.6692	Brunei	0.3891	Indonesia	–0.0500
2007	Singapore	2.0327	Malaysia	1.0678	Thailand	0.5723	Brunei	0.3339	Indonesia	0.0134
2008	Singapore	2.1041	Malaysia	0.9589	Thailand	0.5329	Brunei	0.3576	Indonesia	0.0719
2009	Singapore	2.1526	Malaysia	0.8578	Thailand	0.5334	Brunei	0.3588	Indonesia	0.0957
2010	Singapore	2.0811	Malaysia	0.9320	Thailand	0.5284	Brunei	0.4283	Indonesia	0.1185
2011	Singapore	2.0865	Malaysia	1.0434	Thailand	0.5002	Brunei	0.3939	Indonesia	0.0521
2012	Singapore	2.0839	Malaysia	1.0235	Thailand	0.4857	Brunei	0.4101	Indonesia	–0.0059
2013	Singapore	2.0924	Malaysia	0.9763	Thailand	0.5301	Brunei	0.4169	Indonesia	–0.0180
2014	Singapore	2.0152	Malaysia	1.0568	Brunei	0.5322	Thailand	0.4477	Indonesia	0.0412
2015	Singapore	2.1179	Malaysia	0.9387	Brunei	0.5575	Thailand	0.4099	Indonesia	–0.0762

(Continued)

Table 2.1: (*Continued*)

	Overall Competitiveness									
	6		7		8		9		10	
Rank	**Economy**	**Score**	**Economy**	**Score**	**Economy**	**Score**	**Economy**	**Score**	**Economy**	**Score**
2000	Philippines	–0.1844	Vietnam	–0.3895	Cambodia	–0.8558	Laos	–1.1893	Myanmar	–1.2845
2001	Indonesia	–0.1706	Vietnam	–0.3566	Cambodia	–0.8453	Laos	–1.1146	Myanmar	–1.4055
2002	Philippines	–0.2204	Vietnam	–0.3054	Cambodia	–0.8706	Laos	–1.1411	Myanmar	–1.4272
2003	Vietnam	–0.2882	Philippines	–0.3128	Cambodia	–0.9569	Laos	–1.1474	Myanmar	–1.3446
2004	Philippines	–0.2918	Vietnam	–0.3587	Cambodia	–0.9058	Laos	–1.0884	Myanmar	–1.4472
2005	Philippines	–0.2423	Vietnam	–0.3335	Cambodia	–0.9063	Laos	–1.0248	Myanmar	–1.4668
2006	Philippines	–0.2734	Vietnam	–0.3563	Cambodia	–0.9029	Laos	–1.0292	Myanmar	–1.5016
2007	Philippines	–0.2761	Vietnam	–0.3169	Cambodia	–0.9196	Laos	–1.0062	Myanmar	–1.5013
2008	Vietnam	–0.3073	Philippines	–0.3146	Cambodia	–0.9218	Laos	–1.0024	Myanmar	–1.4792
2009	Vietnam	–0.2047	Philippines	–0.4541	Laos	–0.8709	Cambodia	–0.9565	Myanmar	–1.5122
2010	Vietnam	–0.2180	Philippines	–0.4661	Cambodia	–0.9396	Laos	–0.9687	Myanmar	–1.4958
2011	Philippines	–0.3959	Vietnam	–0.4262	Cambodia	–0.8434	Laos	–0.8933	Myanmar	–1.5173
2012	Philippines	–0.3163	Vietnam	–0.4318	Cambodia	–0.6984	Laos	–0.9770	Myanmar	–1.5738
2013	Philippines	–0.3214	Vietnam	–0.4365	Cambodia	–0.7529	Laos	–0.8825	Myanmar	–1.6044
2014	Philippines	–0.3133	Vietnam	–0.3987	Cambodia	–0.9071	Laos	–0.9241	Myanmar	–1.5501
2015	Philippines	–0.2256	Vietnam	–0.3062	Cambodia	–0.9415	Laos	–1.0694	Myanmar	–1.4050

Source: Asia Competitiveness Institute.

The rest of the less-developed members in ASEAN remain at the bottom of the rankings in 2015. Vietnam, while still standing at the seventh place, seems to be gradually catching up through its narrowing score gap with the Philippines. Cambodia appears to have firmly overtaken Laos and Myanmar at the eighth position for the sixth year running. Laos, at the ninth place, continues to fare badly with a score of –1.0694 in 2015 compared to –0.9241 in 2015. On the other hand, Myanmar has seen a notable increase in its score from –1.5501 in 2014 to –1.4050 in 2015.

The development divide in the ASEAN region can be further seen in Figure 2.2, which depicts the 10 ASEAN economies' performances in 2000, 2014 and 2015. Uneven improvement in competitiveness within ASEAN can be observed as Philippines and Vietnam seem to be moving towards the regional average, while Cambodia, Indonesia, Laos, Malaysia and Thailand have all deteriorated in 2015 as compared to 2014. There seems to be an optimistic outlook for Brunei and Myanmar as their competitiveness scores have climbed up overall. Singapore, the top performer in the region, also enjoyed a slight increase in competitiveness from the previous year of 2014.

Figure 2.2: Overall Competitiveness — 2000, 2014 and 2015

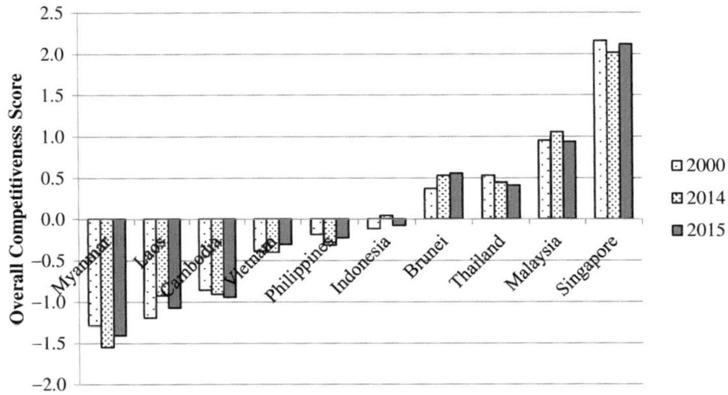

Source: Asia Competitiveness Institute.

2.3.2 Macroeconomic Stability

Table 2.2 presents the rankings and standardised scores for the first environment, Macroeconomic Stability, over the period 2000–2015. Singapore has once again remained at the top throughout the study period. However, the gap between Thailand and Malaysia has widened ever since 2013, where Thailand replaced Malaysia at second and third places respectively. The gap is expanded even further in 2015 as Indonesia hikes it score from 0.3968 in 2014 to 0.4801 in 2015. Indonesia thus overtakes Malaysia, hence putting Thailand, Indonesia and Malaysia in the second, third and fourth spots, respectively. Vietnam seems to have decidedly surpassed the Philippines, taking the sixth place for three consecutive years despite a slight improvement in Philippines' score from −0.5150 in 2014 to −0.4030 in 2015. Moreover, Cambodia's scores have been rising at a steady rate over the entire period of 2000–2015, thereby preserving its rank at the eighth place in 2015. On the other hand, Laos and Myanmar still remain stuck at the ninth and 10th places, respectively.

The relative performances of the 10 ASEAN member states as well as the evolution of competitiveness in the Macroeconomic Stability environment are illustrated in Figure 2.3. Laos appears to have made the most remarkable leap in its 2014 and 2015 scores, relative to 2000. Indonesia and Vietnam registered a moderate improvement in 2015 as compared to 2000, while the rest of the economies fluctuate in their performance over the same period. In particular, the performances of Malaysia, Myanmar and Thailand highlight a need for concern as they have experienced continuous drops in their scores for this environment.

Across the three sub-environments constituting Macroeconomic Stability, Laos and Indonesia achieved the most improvement in Economic Vibrancy between 2000, 2014 and 2015, whereas Malaysia, Myanmar and Singapore are showing worrying signs of decline (Figure 2.4). Meanwhile, Vietnam and Thailand have displayed a consistent improvement in terms of Openness to Trade and Services. In contrast, Brunei, Indonesia and Malaysia have been on a steady downward trend for this sub-environment (Figure 2.5). Singapore, Malaysia and Brunei

Table 2.2: Macroeconomic Stability Rankings and Standardised Scores, 2000–2015

	Macroeconomic Stability									
	1		2		3		4		5	
Rank	Economy	Score	Economy	Score	Economy	Score	Economy	Score	Economy	Score
2000	Singapore	2.1846	Malaysia	0.8498	Thailand	0.6423	Indonesia	0.3645	Brunei	–0.1940
2001	Singapore	2.0775	Malaysia	0.8187	Thailand	0.6765	Indonesia	0.3119	Brunei	0.0289
2002	Singapore	1.9981	Malaysia	0.8583	Thailand	0.7194	Indonesia	0.4046	Brunei	–0.0088
2003	Singapore	2.1469	Malaysia	0.8096	Thailand	0.6324	Indonesia	0.5578	Brunei	–0.1227
2004	Singapore	2.1565	Malaysia	0.8119	Thailand	0.7392	Indonesia	0.4439	Brunei	–0.1678
2005	Singapore	2.1525	Malaysia	0.8500	Thailand	0.7088	Indonesia	0.3852	Brunei	–0.1144
2006	Singapore	2.1087	Malaysia	0.8244	Thailand	0.7035	Indonesia	0.5099	Brunei	–0.1137
2007	Singapore	2.1002	Malaysia	0.8765	Thailand	0.6963	Indonesia	0.5527	Philippines	–0.2618
2008	Singapore	2.0978	Malaysia	0.7631	Indonesia	0.7401	Thailand	0.6948	Brunei	–0.1861
2009	Singapore	2.1904	Indonesia	0.7242	Thailand	0.7021	Malaysia	0.6173	Brunei	–0.1518
2010	Singapore	2.2118	Malaysia	0.6677	Indonesia	0.6528	Thailand	0.5624	Brunei	0.0404
2011	Singapore	2.2279	Malaysia	0.7262	Indonesia	0.6879	Thailand	0.4381	Brunei	0.0618
2012	Singapore	2.1837	Malaysia	0.6854	Thailand	0.6128	Indonesia	0.5869	Brunei	0.0683
2013	Singapore	2.2628	Thailand	0.6861	Malaysia	0.6019	Indonesia	0.4328	Brunei	0.0164
2014	Singapore	2.1709	Thailand	0.7317	Malaysia	0.6255	Indonesia	0.3968	Brunei	0.2478
2015	Singapore	2.2193	Thailand	0.6595	Indonesia	0.4801	Malaysia	0.4100	Brunei	0.2266

	Macroeconomic Stability									
	6		7		8		9		10	
Rank	Economy	Score	Economy	Score	Economy	Score	Economy	Score	Economy	Score
2000	Philippines	–0.3168	Vietnam	–0.4087	Cambodia	–0.5220	Myanmar	–1.2605	Laos	–1.3393
2001	Vietnam	–0.2531	Philippines	–0.3782	Cambodia	–0.5041	Laos	–1.1269	Myanmar	–1.6513
2002	Vietnam	–0.2814	Philippines	–0.2855	Cambodia	–0.6154	Laos	–1.1121	Myanmar	–1.6773
2003	Vietnam	–0.3652	Philippines	–0.4320	Cambodia	–0.6946	Laos	–1.2426	Myanmar	–1.2896
2004	Philippines	–0.3913	Vietnam	–0.5231	Cambodia	–0.5870	Laos	–1.0586	Myanmar	–1.4236
2005	Philippines	–0.4555	Vietnam	–0.4861	Cambodia	–0.5934	Laos	–0.9150	Myanmar	–1.5321
2006	Philippines	–0.3636	Vietnam	–0.5327	Cambodia	–0.6962	Laos	–0.8826	Myanmar	–1.5577
2007	Brunei	–0.2887	Vietnam	–0.5234	Cambodia	–0.7982	Laos	–0.8623	Myanmar	–1.4913
2008	Philippines	–0.4392	Vietnam	–0.5435	Cambodia	–0.7938	Laos	–0.9309	Myanmar	–1.4024
2009	Vietnam	–0.4429	Philippines	–0.6829	Laos	–0.7673	Cambodia	–0.8363	Myanmar	–1.3528
2010	Vietnam	–0.4667	Philippines	–0.5249	Cambodia	–0.8153	Laos	–1.0066	Myanmar	–1.3217
2011	Philippines	–0.4943	Vietnam	–0.6635	Cambodia	–0.7458	Laos	–0.9025	Myanmar	–1.3359
2012	Philippines	–0.3842	Vietnam	–0.5851	Cambodia	–0.7721	Laos	–0.9963	Myanmar	–1.3994
2013	Vietnam	–0.4568	Philippines	–0.5647	Cambodia	–0.6464	Laos	–0.8541	Myanmar	–1.4780
2014	Vietnam	–0.4130	Philippines	–0.5150	Cambodia	–0.8807	Laos	–0.9205	Myanmar	–1.4433
2015	Vietnam	–0.2743	Philippines	–0.4030	Cambodia	–0.8246	Laos	–0.9608	Myanmar	–1.5327

Source: Asia Competitiveness Institute.

Figure 2.3: Macroeconomic Stability — 2000, 2014 and 2015

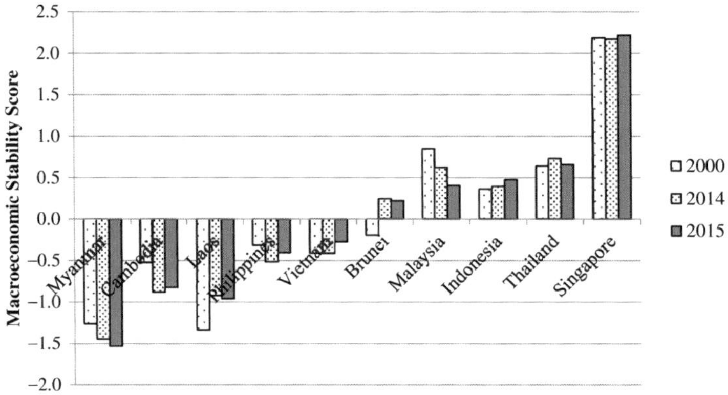

Source: Asia Competitiveness Institute.

Figure 2.4: Macroeconomic Stability (Economic Vibrancy) — 2000, 2014 and 2015

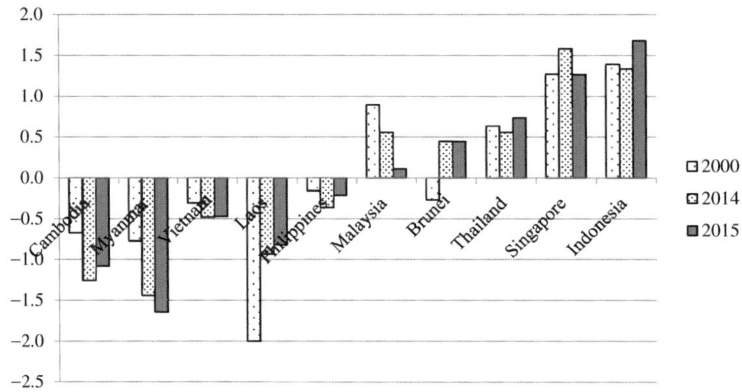

Source: Asia Competitiveness Institute.

Figure 2.5: Macroeconomic Stability (Openness to Trade and Services) — 2000, 2014 and 2015

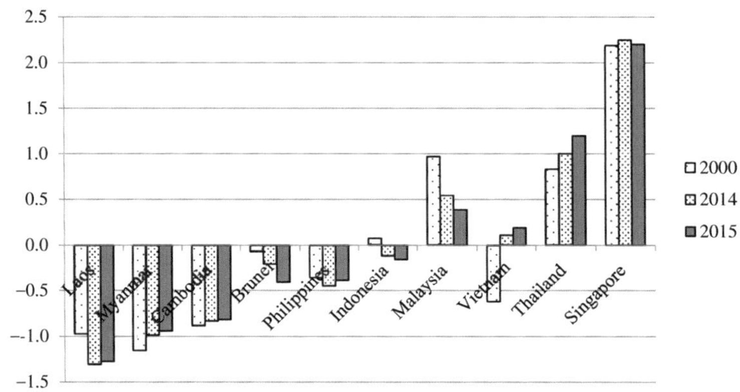

Source: Asia Competitiveness Institute.

Figure 2.6: Macroeconomic Stability (Attractiveness to Foreign Investors) — 2000, 2014 and 2015

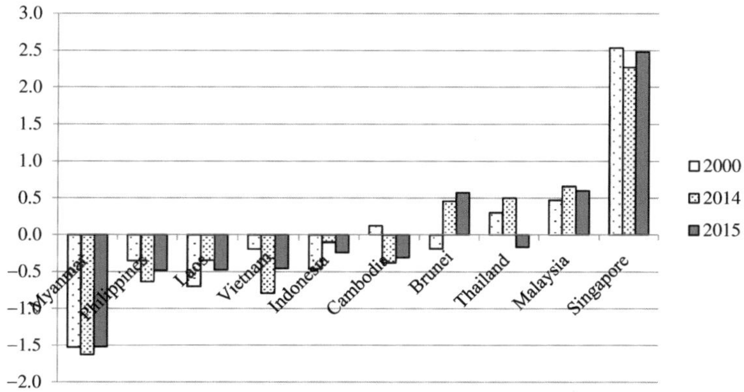

Source: Asia Competitiveness Institute.

performed the best in terms Attractiveness to Foreign Investors; however, Cambodia and Thailand had their scores substantially plunge to negative levels (Figure 2.6).

2.3.3 Government and Institutional Setting

Singapore and Malaysia have dominated the first and second place in the rankings for Government and Institutional Setting throughout the entire study period (see Table 2.3). Singapore, with its score jumping from 0.1916 in 2014 to 0.3084 in 2015, continues to be ahead of Malaysia and its other neighbours as the gap in their scores widen even further. Thailand's score in this environment has also significantly improved from 0.1916 (2014) to 0.3084 (2015), but it still remains stagnant at the fourth place, after Brunei. It is worth noting that Vietnam has exceeded Indonesia in 2015 to earn the sixth place. Interestingly, Myanmar overtook Cambodia to be ranked at the ninth, thus putting Cambodia in the last place.

As seen in Figure 2.7, among the four above-average performers, Brunei and Singapore have made steadfast improvements in Government and Institutional Setting in 2000, 2014 and 2015. Meanwhile, Malaysia and Thailand have had fluctuating scores. For those performing below average, Myanmar, Philippines and Vietnam showed encouraging signs of overall increase for this environment, while Cambodia, Indonesia and Laos have even worse performances in 2015.

Looking at the three sub-environments, Brunei, Cambodia, Malaysia and Myanmar dropped further throughout the period of 2000–2015 in terms of Government Policies and Fiscal Sustainability (Figure 2.8). Apart from Singapore, which has incessantly topped the list for all three sub-environments over the study period (Figures 2.8–2.10), the remaining ASEAN members demonstrate inconsistent performance. For instance, Thailand has experienced an upward

Table 2.3: Government and Institutional Setting Rankings and Standardised Scores, 2000–2015

	Government and Institutional Setting									
	1		2		3		4		5	
Rank	**Economy**	**Score**	**Economy**	**Score**	**Economy**	**Score**	**Economy**	**Score**	**Economy**	**Score**
2000	Singapore	2.2937	Malaysia	0.7786	Thailand	0.5409	Brunei	0.4489	Philippines	–0.0852
2001	Singapore	2.2819	Malaysia	0.7781	Thailand	0.5476	Brunei	0.3870	Philippines	–0.0453
2002	Singapore	2.1754	Malaysia	0.9528	Thailand	0.6567	Brunei	0.2602	Philippines	–0.1370
2003	Singapore	2.1470	Malaysia	0.9180	Thailand	0.8302	Brunei	0.2487	Vietnam	–0.1745
2004	Singapore	2.0646	Malaysia	1.0267	Thailand	0.7027	Brunei	0.4226	Philippines	–0.2498
2005	Singapore	2.0475	Malaysia	1.0893	Thailand	0.6890	Brunei	0.4037	Philippines	–0.1794
2006	Singapore	2.1149	Malaysia	0.9818	Thailand	0.6208	Brunei	0.4364	Philippines	–0.2331
2007	Singapore	2.1935	Malaysia	0.9685	Thailand	0.5390	Brunei	0.4345	Philippines	–0.2245
2008	Singapore	2.3680	Malaysia	0.7715	Thailand	0.4567	Brunei	0.4400	Vietnam	–0.2976
2009	Singapore	2.4651	Malaysia	0.5640	Thailand	0.4444	Brunei	0.4057	Indonesia	–0.2248
2010	Singapore	2.3205	Malaysia	0.7618	Brunei	0.5035	Thailand	0.4125	Indonesia	–0.1437
2011	Singapore	2.2518	Malaysia	0.9586	Brunei	0.5349	Thailand	0.3902	Indonesia	–0.3295
2012	Singapore	2.2843	Malaysia	0.9430	Brunei	0.4711	Thailand	0.2583	Philippines	–0.1923
2013	Singapore	2.2463	Malaysia	0.9417	Brunei	0.5178	Thailand	0.3499	Philippines	–0.1692
2014	Singapore	2.2851	Malaysia	1.0322	Brunei	0.4421	Thailand	0.1916	Philippines	–0.1345
2015	Singapore	2.4055	Malaysia	0.7034	Brunei	0.5216	Thailand	0.3084	Philippines	–0.1135

	Government and Institutional Setting									
	6		7		8		9		10	
Rank	**Economy**	**Score**	**Economy**	**Score**	**Economy**	**Score**	**Economy**	**Score**	**Economy**	**Score**
2000	Vietnam	–0.3486	Indonesia	–0.5787	Cambodia	–0.7935	Laos	–1.1262	Myanmar	–1.1300
2001	Vietnam	–0.2904	Indonesia	–0.5197	Cambodia	–0.8326	Laos	–1.0360	Myanmar	–1.2707
2002	Vietnam	–0.2176	Indonesia	–0.4675	Cambodia	–0.8424	Laos	–1.0618	Myanmar	–1.3188
2003	Philippines	–0.3251	Indonesia	–0.4147	Laos	–0.9875	Myanmar	–1.1182	Cambodia	–1.1238
2004	Vietnam	–0.2644	Indonesia	–0.4217	Laos	–0.9308	Cambodia	–0.9839	Myanmar	–1.3661
2005	Vietnam	–0.2849	Indonesia	–0.5316	Cambodia	–0.9385	Laos	–0.9565	Myanmar	–1.3386
2006	Indonesia	–0.2519	Vietnam	–0.3892	Laos	–0.9224	Cambodia	–0.9674	Myanmar	–1.3899
2007	Indonesia	–0.3602	Vietnam	–0.3925	Laos	–0.8848	Cambodia	–0.9496	Myanmar	–1.3239
2008	Philippines	–0.3246	Indonesia	–0.4261	Laos	–0.8640	Cambodia	–0.9674	Myanmar	–1.1564
2009	Vietnam	–0.2798	Philippines	–0.4877	Laos	–0.7624	Cambodia	–0.9228	Myanmar	–1.2016
2010	Vietnam	–0.3166	Philippines	–0.4025	Laos	–0.9295	Cambodia	–0.9779	Myanmar	–1.2282
2011	Philippines	–0.3429	Vietnam	–0.4744	Cambodia	–0.8101	Laos	–0.8756	Myanmar	–1.3031
2012	Vietnam	–0.3756	Indonesia	–0.4119	Cambodia	–0.7466	Laos	–0.7899	Myanmar	–1.4405
2013	Indonesia	–0.4125	Vietnam	–0.4429	Laos	–0.7919	Cambodia	–0.8484	Myanmar	–1.3909
2014	Indonesia	–0.3317	Vietnam	–0.4344	Laos	–0.8673	Cambodia	–0.9715	Myanmar	–1.2116
2015	Vietnam	–0.4074	Indonesia	–0.4209	Laos	–0.9697	Myanmar	–1.0117	Cambodia	–1.0157

Source: Asia Competitiveness Institute.

Figure 2.7: Government and Institutional Setting — 2000, 2014 and 2015

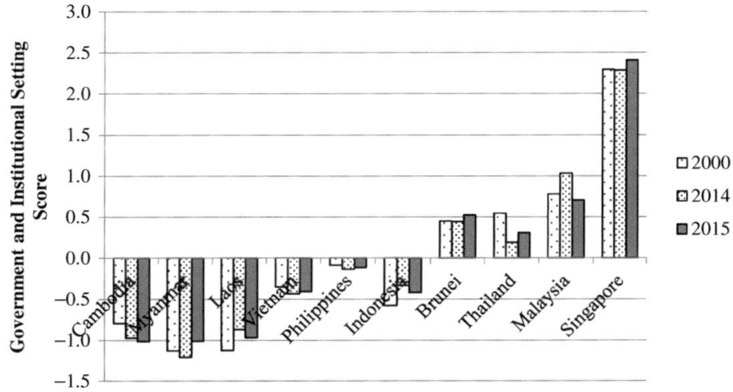

Source: Asia Competitiveness Institute.

Figure 2.8: Government and Institutional Setting (Government Policies and Fiscal Sustainability) — 2000, 2014 and 2015

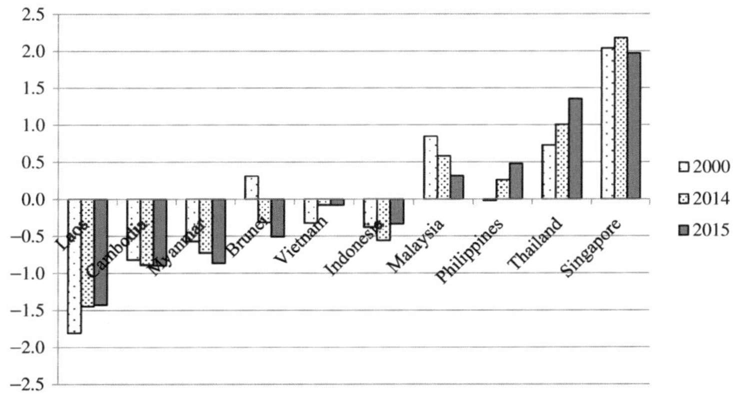

Source: Asia Competitiveness Institute.

Figure 2.9: Government and Institutional Setting (Institutions, Governance and Leadership) — 2000, 2014 and 2015

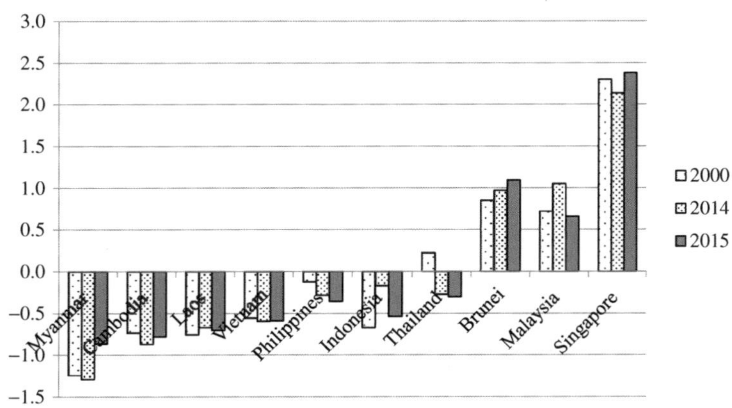

Source: Asia Competitiveness Institute.

Figure 2.10: Government and Institutional Setting (Competition, Regulatory Standards and Rule of Law) — 2000, 2014 and 2015

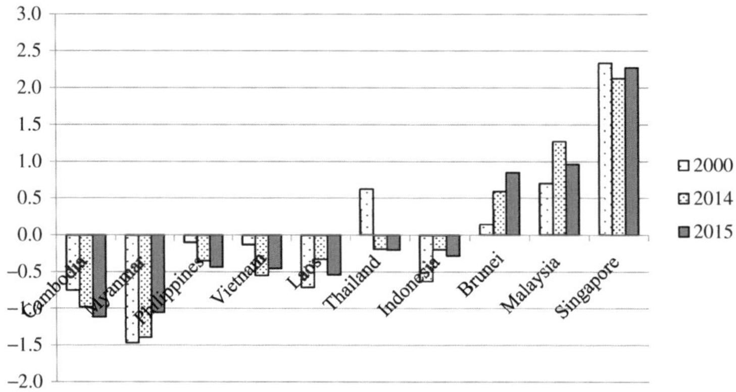

Source: Asia Competitiveness Institute.

trend for Government Policies and Fiscal Sustainability but fared below average for Institutions, Governance, and Leadership, as well as for Competition, Regulatory Standards, and Rule of Law. This inequality reflects room for improvement across these three sub-environments for the ASEAN member states.

2.3.4 Financial, Businesses and Manpower Conditions

Table 2.4 and Figure 2.11 show the rankings and standardised scores for Financial, Businesses and Manpower Conditions from 2000 to 2015. After being the champion in this environment for 14 consecutive years, Singapore has now been overtaken by Malaysia for two years. Although Singapore's score improved from 1.3232 in 2014 to 1.5518 in 2015, Malaysia's score improvement is more substantial, improving from 1.4985 in 2013, to 1.6273 in 2014, and finally to 1.6173 in 2015. Brunei has also replaced Thailand at the third place for the first time in 2015, as Thailand's score fell from 0.5671 (2014) to 0.5220 (2015). At the same time, Vietnam and Philippines, at the sixth and seventh positions, respectively, have tremendously shrunk the gap between them. Despite staying at the fifth place, Indonesia witnessed an immense decrease in its score to a figure below the average. Out of the bottom three economies, Myanmar improved in 2015 while Cambodia and Laos fared worse.

The standardised scores of the 10 ASEAN economies for the three sub-environments are illustrated in Figures 2.12–2.14. Interestingly, each sub-environment is championed by different economies. Singapore topped the Financial Deepening and Business Efficiency sub-environment, while Malaysia and Brunei took the top spots for Labour Market Flexibility and Productivity Performance, respectively. One point worth highlighting here is that in each sub-environment, there are only around three or four economies that performed above average, while the rest had negative scores. Further, only Singapore was able to pull up its negative score in 2014 to a positive level in 2015 for the sub-environment of Labour Market Flexibility. In terms of Productivity Performance, Brunei has surpassed all ASEAN

Table 2.4: Financial, Businesses and Manpower Conditions Rankings and Standardised Scores, 2000–2015

	Financial, Businesses and Manpower Conditions									
	1		2		3		4		5	
Rank	**Economy**	**Score**	**Economy**	**Score**	**Economy**	**Score**	**Economy**	**Score**	**Economy**	**Score**
2000	Singapore	1.8846	Malaysia	1.2700	Thailand	0.5267	Brunei	0.2646	Indonesia	–0.0210
2001	Singapore	1.9099	Malaysia	1.1592	Thailand	0.6945	Brunei	0.2699	Philippines	–0.0701
2002	Singapore	1.5633	Malaysia	1.4114	Thailand	0.9515	Brunei	0.3136	Vietnam	–0.1486
2003	Singapore	1.4880	Malaysia	1.4645	Thailand	0.8605	Brunei	0.4510	Vietnam	–0.0372
2004	Singapore	1.4765	Malaysia	1.4563	Thailand	0.8159	Brunei	0.4308	Indonesia	–0.0538
2005	Singapore	1.6562	Malaysia	1.2916	Thailand	0.8575	Brunei	0.2729	Vietnam	–0.0121
2006	Singapore	1.6281	Malaysia	1.4368	Thailand	0.7533	Brunei	0.3487	Vietnam	–0.1020
2007	Singapore	1.6275	Malaysia	1.4856	Thailand	0.5231	Brunei	0.3527	Indonesia	0.0364
2008	Singapore	1.7300	Malaysia	1.3656	Thailand	0.5240	Brunei	0.2364	Indonesia	0.1160
2009	Singapore	1.6908	Malaysia	1.3606	Thailand	0.5571	Brunei	0.2543	Vietnam	0.0946
2010	Singapore	1.5765	Malaysia	1.4394	Thailand	0.6897	Brunei	0.2934	Vietnam	0.0670
2011	Singapore	1.6336	Malaysia	1.5208	Thailand	0.7637	Brunei	0.1008	Indonesia	0.0579
2012	Singapore	1.6487	Malaysia	1.5194	Thailand	0.7009	Brunei	0.2392	Indonesia	0.0153
2013	Singapore	1.5693	Malaysia	1.4985	Thailand	0.7453	Brunei	0.2932	Indonesia	0.1363
2014	Malaysia	1.6723	Singapore	1.3232	Thailand	0.5671	Brunei	0.5261	Indonesia	0.2875
2015	Malaysia	1.6173	Singapore	1.5518	Brunei	0.5646	Thailand	0.5220	Indonesia	–0.0517

	Financial, Businesses and Manpower Conditions									
	6		7		8		9		10	
Rank	**Economy**	**Score**	**Economy**	**Score**	**Economy**	**Score**	**Economy**	**Score**	**Economy**	**Score**
2000	Vietnam	–0.1256	Philippines	–0.1602	Laos	–1.0766	Cambodia	–1.2395	Myanmar	–1.3232
2001	Indonesia	–0.1332	Vietnam	–0.2082	Laos	–1.1108	Cambodia	–1.2396	Myanmar	–1.2716
2002	Philippines	–0.2044	Indonesia	–0.2393	Laos	–1.1822	Cambodia	–1.1956	Myanmar	–1.2698
2003	Indonesia	–0.2712	Philippines	–0.2946	Cambodia	–1.1097	Laos	–1.1184	Myanmar	–1.4329
2004	Vietnam	–0.0710	Philippines	–0.3023	Cambodia	–1.1210	Laos	–1.1943	Myanmar	–1.4371
2005	Philippines	–0.0593	Indonesia	–0.2808	Laos	–1.1101	Cambodia	–1.1611	Myanmar	–1.4548
2006	Indonesia	–0.2168	Philippines	–0.2258	Cambodia	–0.9822	Laos	–1.1822	Myanmar	–1.4578
2007	Vietnam	–0.0207	Philippines	–0.3451	Cambodia	–0.9695	Laos	–1.1612	Myanmar	–1.5287
2008	Vietnam	–0.0560	Philippines	–0.2601	Cambodia	–0.9273	Laos	–1.0946	Myanmar	–1.6339
2009	Indonesia	0.0647	Philippines	–0.3845	Laos	–0.9285	Cambodia	–1.0215	Myanmar	–1.6877
2010	Indonesia	0.0625	Philippines	–0.5980	Laos	–0.9006	Cambodia	–0.9646	Myanmar	–1.6654
2011	Vietnam	–0.2562	Philippines	–0.3687	Cambodia	–0.9359	Laos	–0.9584	Myanmar	–1.5575
2012	Philippines	–0.4246	Vietnam	–0.4260	Cambodia	–0.6165	Laos	–1.0506	Myanmar	–1.6059
2013	Philippines	–0.3491	Vietnam	–0.5127	Cambodia	–0.7198	Laos	–1.0235	Myanmar	–1.6376
2014	Philippines	–0.4753	Vietnam	–0.4763	Cambodia	–0.8090	Laos	–0.9586	Myanmar	–1.6569
2015	Vietnam	–0.3223	Philippines	–0.4417	Cambodia	–0.9089	Laos	–1.1017	Myanmar	–1.4294

Source: Asia Competitiveness Institute.

Figure 2.11: Financial, Businesses and Manpower Conditions — 2000, 2014 and 2015

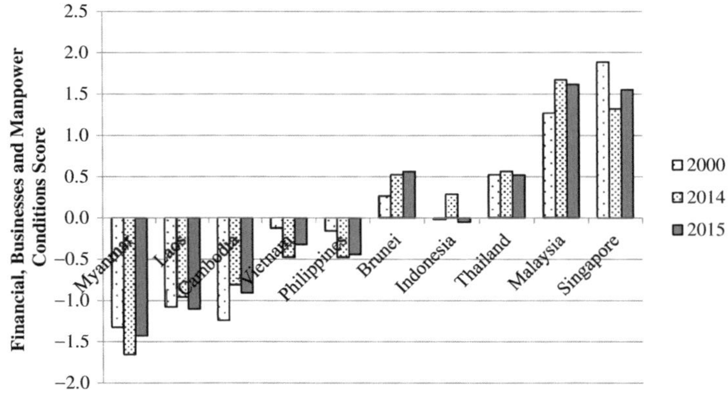

Source: Asia Competitiveness Institute.

Figure 2.12: Financial, Businesses and Manpower Conditions (Financial Deepening and Business Efficiency) — 2000, 2014 and 2015

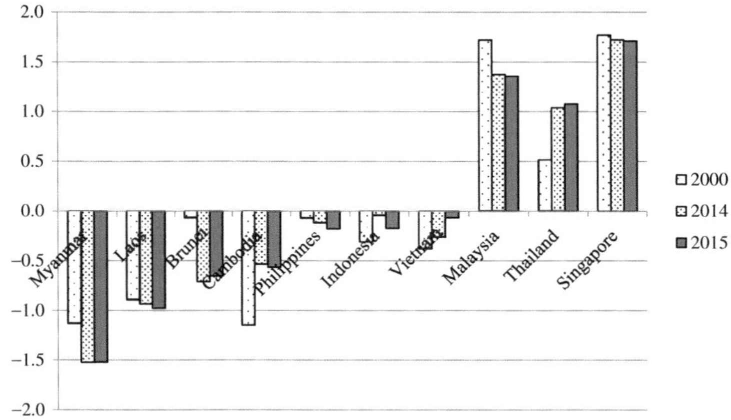

Source: Asia Competitiveness Institute.

Figure 2.13: Financial, Businesses and Manpower Conditions (Labour Market Flexibility) — 2000, 2014 and 2015

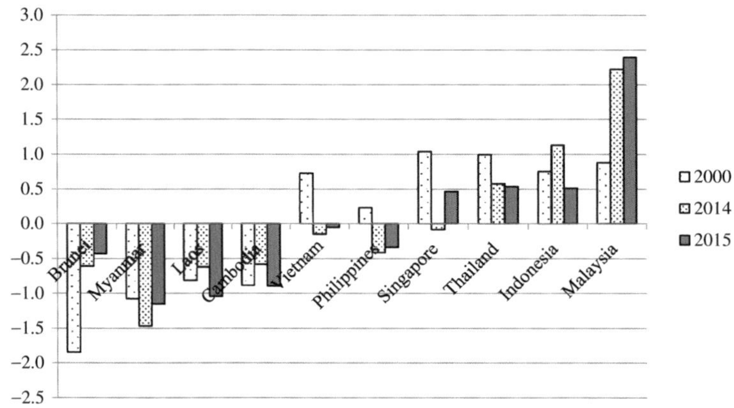

Source: Asia Competitiveness Institute.

Figure 2.14: Financial, Businesses and Manpower Conditions (Productivity Performance) — 2000, 2014 and 2015

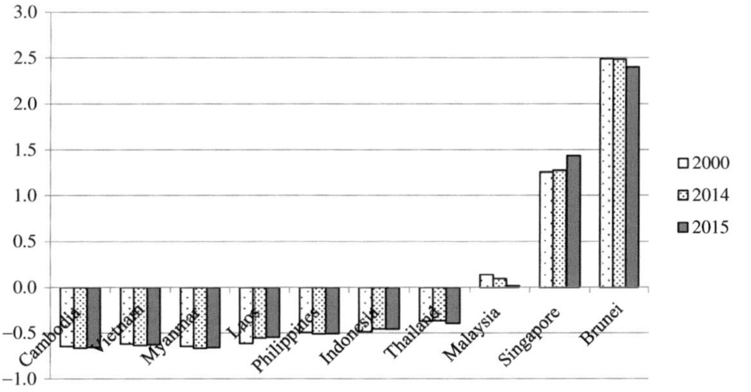

Source: Asia Competitiveness Institute.

economies by a large margin and has led the region throughout the study period. Yet, Singapore was the only country to see an improvement in Productivity Performance in 2015, while the rest — including Brunei — experienced a downward trend in labour productivity. This once again highlights the region's inequality and emphasises the difficulty of closing the development gap.

2.3.5 Quality of Life and Infrastructure Development

When it comes to Quality of Life and Infrastructure Development (Table 2.5), Singapore continues to top the ranking throughout the study period (2000–2015). Singapore is followed by Malaysia, which has managed to remarkably climb back to its second place after being overtaken by Brunei in 2013 and 2014. Despite a heavy drop in its score from 0.2476 (2014) to 0.0983 (2015), Thailand has maintained its ranking at the fourth place. Furthermore, Philippines has retained its fifth position after surpassing Indonesia in 2013, with a big hike in its score from –0.0913 (2014) to 0.0842 (2015). Notably, Vietnam has replaced Indonesia to become the sixth economy in 2015 for this environment, and Cambodia has managed to overtake Laos at the eighth spot. Despite an impressive rise in its score from –1.7047 in 2014 to –1.4699 in 2015, Myanmar still remains in last place.

As seen in Figure 2.15, all economies with the exception of Malaysia, Myanmar, Philippines and Vietnam fared worse between 2014 and 2015. This is especially so for Laos and Thailand. Overall, from 2000 to 2015, Malaysia, Philippines and Vietnam have witnessed the strongest improvement in their scores. Myanmar has experienced an overall decrease in this environment, and significant effort is required for improvement as it is the only state that scored near –1.5 in this environment.

As illustrated below, Singapore topped the rankings for all three sub-environments (see Figures 2.16–2.18), despite a continual fall in scores for Technological Infrastructure. Vietnam has also improved significantly in these three sub-environments as its score is gradually

Table 2.5: Quality of Life and Infrastructure Development Rankings and Standardised Scores, 2000–2015

	Quality of Life and Infrastructure Development									
	1		2		3		4		5	
Rank	**Economy**	**Score**	**Economy**	**Score**	**Economy**	**Score**	**Economy**	**Score**	**Economy**	**Score**
2000	Singapore	2.0777	Brunei	0.9353	Malaysia	0.8222	Thailand	0.3637	Philippines	–0.1579
2001	Singapore	2.0516	Brunei	0.8877	Malaysia	0.8693	Thailand	0.4612	Philippines	–0.1399
2002	Singapore	2.0129	Brunei	0.8840	Malaysia	0.8788	Thailand	0.5955	Philippines	–0.2349
2003	Singapore	1.9430	Malaysia	0.9324	Brunei	0.8956	Thailand	0.5664	Philippines	–0.1647
2004	Singapore	1.9374	Brunei	0.9364	Malaysia	0.8955	Thailand	0.5618	Philippines	–0.1949
2005	Singapore	1.9547	Malaysia	0.9385	Brunei	0.8949	Thailand	0.5528	Philippines	–0.2539
2006	Singapore	1.8983	Malaysia	0.9941	Brunei	0.8552	Thailand	0.5481	Indonesia	–0.2375
2007	Singapore	2.0227	Malaysia	0.8425	Brunei	0.8062	Thailand	0.4781	Indonesia	–0.1765
2008	Singapore	1.9860	Brunei	0.9001	Malaysia	0.8286	Thailand	0.3966	Indonesia	–0.1505
2009	Singapore	2.0038	Brunei	0.8836	Malaysia	0.7853	Thailand	0.3654	Vietnam	–0.1658
2010	Singapore	2.0169	Brunei	0.8351	Malaysia	0.7702	Thailand	0.3984	Indonesia	–0.1090
2011	Singapore	2.0175	Malaysia	0.8602	Brunei	0.8374	Thailand	0.3571	Indonesia	–0.2133
2012	Singapore	2.0236	Malaysia	0.8503	Brunei	0.8231	Thailand	0.3252	Indonesia	–0.2135
2013	Singapore	2.0835	Brunei	0.7987	Malaysia	0.7662	Thailand	0.2863	Philippines	–0.1707
2014	Singapore	2.0429	Brunei	0.8499	Malaysia	0.7720	Thailand	0.2476	Philippines	–0.0913
2015	Singapore	2.0289	Malaysia	0.9062	Brunei	0.8473	Thailand	0.0983	Philippines	0.0842

	Quality of Life and Infrastructure Development									
	6		7		8		9		10	
Rank	**Economy**	**Score**	**Economy**	**Score**	**Economy**	**Score**	**Economy**	**Score**	**Economy**	**Score**
2000	Indonesia	–0.2155	Vietnam	–0.6377	Cambodia	–0.7859	Laos	–1.1010	Myanmar	–1.3010
2001	Indonesia	–0.3280	Vietnam	–0.6469	Cambodia	–0.7388	Laos	–1.0975	Myanmar	–1.3186
2002	Indonesia	–0.4215	Vietnam	–0.5463	Cambodia	–0.7501	Laos	–1.1048	Myanmar	–1.3135
2003	Indonesia	–0.3325	Vietnam	–0.5440	Cambodia	–0.7934	Laos	–1.1140	Myanmar	–1.3887
2004	Indonesia	–0.2742	Vietnam	–0.5407	Cambodia	–0.8411	Laos	–1.0619	Myanmar	–1.4183
2005	Indonesia	–0.2709	Vietnam	–0.5219	Cambodia	–0.8530	Laos	–1.0278	Myanmar	–1.4134
2006	Philippines	–0.2503	Vietnam	–0.3743	Cambodia	–0.8966	Laos	–1.0508	Myanmar	–1.4862
2007	Philippines	–0.2474	Vietnam	–0.3018	Cambodia	–0.8766	Laos	–1.0240	Myanmar	–1.5231
2008	Philippines	–0.1994	Vietnam	–0.2979	Cambodia	–0.8959	Laos	–1.0083	Myanmar	–1.5592
2009	Indonesia	–0.1929	Philippines	–0.2063	Laos	–0.9199	Cambodia	–0.9297	Myanmar	–1.6236
2010	Vietnam	–0.1350	Philippines	–0.2947	Cambodia	–0.9109	Laos	–0.9458	Myanmar	–1.6252
2011	Vietnam	–0.2667	Philippines	–0.3367	Laos	–0.7445	Cambodia	–0.7948	Myanmar	–1.7161
2012	Philippines	–0.2343	Vietnam	–0.3000	Cambodia	–0.5929	Laos	–0.9796	Myanmar	–1.7020
2013	Indonesia	–0.2269	Vietnam	–0.2902	Cambodia	–0.7224	Laos	–0.7729	Myanmar	–1.7516
2014	Indonesia	–0.1925	Vietnam	–0.2237	Laos	–0.8404	Cambodia	–0.8597	Myanmar	–1.7047
2015	Vietnam	–0.1825	Indonesia	–0.3028	Cambodia	–0.8986	Laos	–1.1111	Myanmar	–1.4699

Source: Asia Competitiveness Institute.

Figure 2.15: Quality of Life and Infrastructure Development — 2000, 2014 and 2015

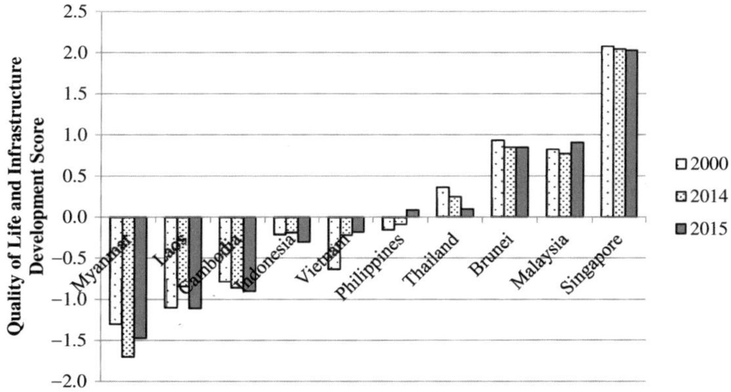

Source: Asia Competitiveness Institute.

Figure 2.16: Quality of Life and Infrastructure Development (Physical Infrastructure) — 2000, 2014 and 2015

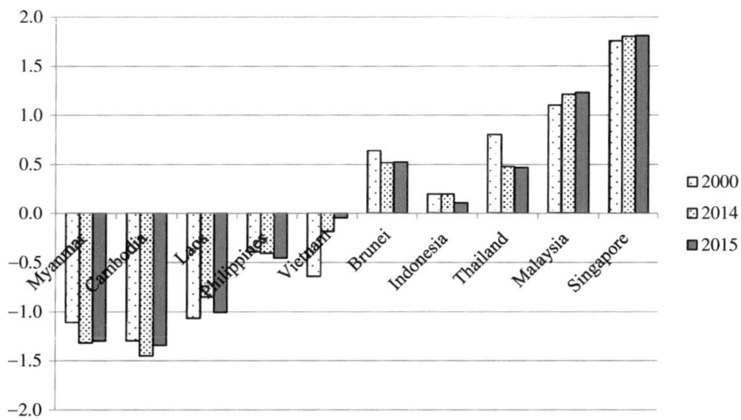

Source: Asia Competitiveness Institute.

Figure 2.17: Quality of Life and Infrastructure Development (Technological Infrastructure) — 2000, 2014 and 2015

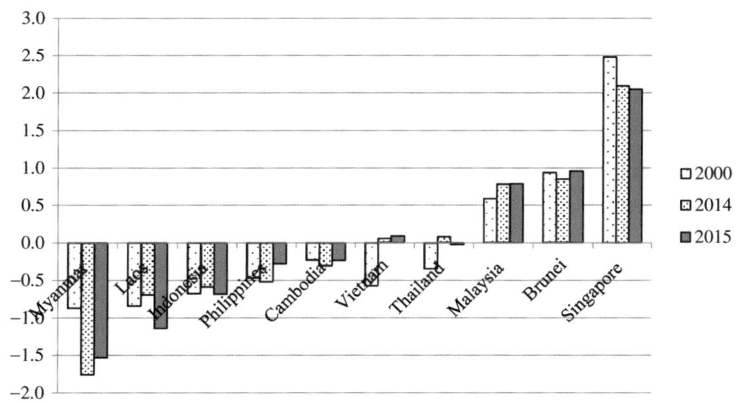

Source: Asia Competitiveness Institute.

Figure 2.18: Quality of Life and Infrastructure Development (Standard of Living, Education and Social Stability) — 2000, 2014 and 2015

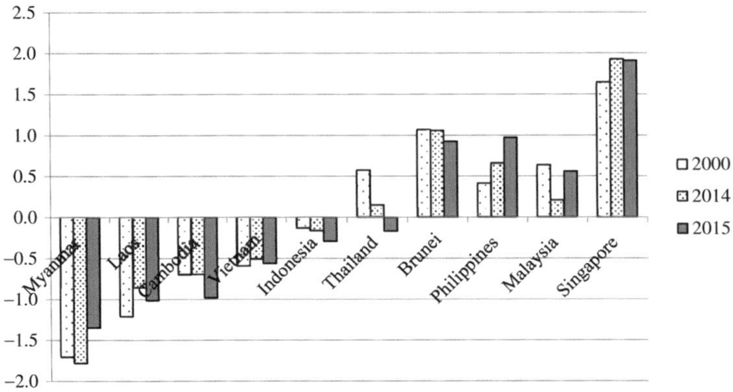

Source: Asia Competitiveness Institute.

converging to the regional average. On the flip side, Indonesia and Laos have shown decisive drops in 2015 relative to their performance in 2014 across all three sub-environments. The Philippines needs greater investments to be put into the Physical Infrastructure environment, but has increased its performance in the other two sub-environments of Technological Infrastructure and its Standard of Living, Education and Social Stability.

2.3.6 Competitiveness Over Time Analysis

For a better comparison of the competitive performances over time, we split the study period into two sub-periods, 2000–2007 (Period A) and 2008–2015 (Period B). Our Competitiveness Over Time (COT) analysis is conducted for Overall Competitiveness as well as each of the 12 sub-environments, which is instructive for policy-making as it reveals where individual economies are losing competitiveness. For all COT Figures 2.19–2.31, countries above the 45-degree line improved their competitiveness in Period B relative to Period A, below the line means the performance has worsened in Period B as compared to Period A, and on the line means no change over both sub-periods.

As Figure 2.19 shows, Singapore is located at the top of the 45-degree line measuring Overall Competitiveness, which is consistent with its top-notch performance highlighted in the preceding sections. Cambodia and Vietnam are on the 45-degree line, indicating constant competitiveness in both periods. Indonesia, Laos and Brunei have performed better in Period B than Period A, shown by their positions above the line. In contrast, the competitiveness of Malaysia, Myanmar, Philippines and Thailand have deteriorated in Period B relative to Period A as demonstrated by their positions below the line.

In Figure 2.20 for Economic Vibrancy, a sub-environment under Macroeconomic Stability, Indonesia not only stands at the top among all member states but also performs better in Period B than in Period A. This is followed by Singapore which takes the second place and also shows improvement in Period B relative to Period A. Among the bottom four economies, Laos

Figure 2.19: Competitiveness Over Time Analysis for Overall Competitiveness, Period B (2008–2015) Against Period A (2000–2007)

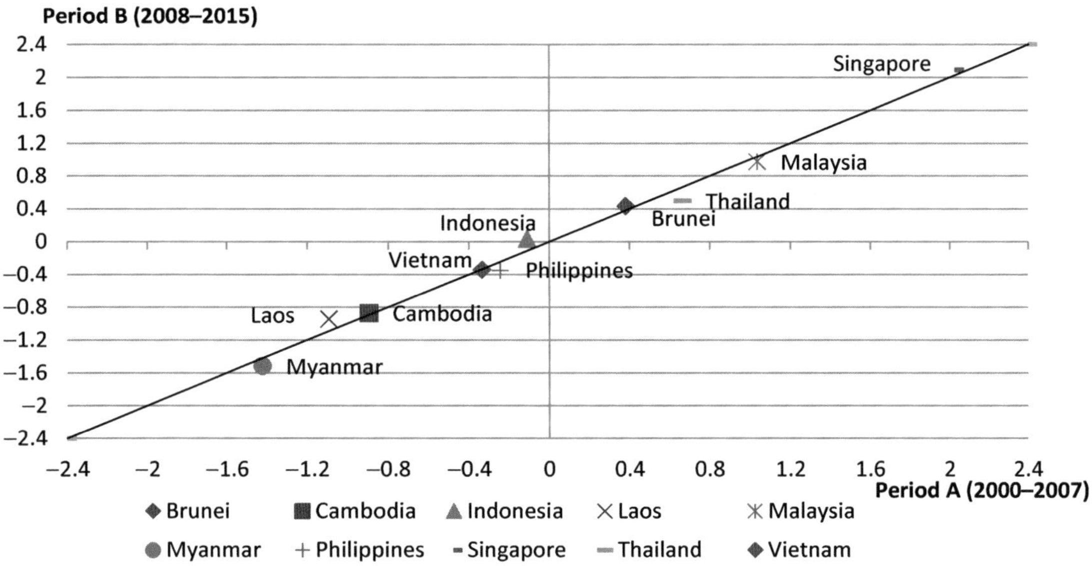

Source: Asia Competitiveness Institute.

Figure 2.20: Competitiveness Over Time Analysis for Economic Vibrancy, Period B (2008–2015) Against Period A (2000–2007)

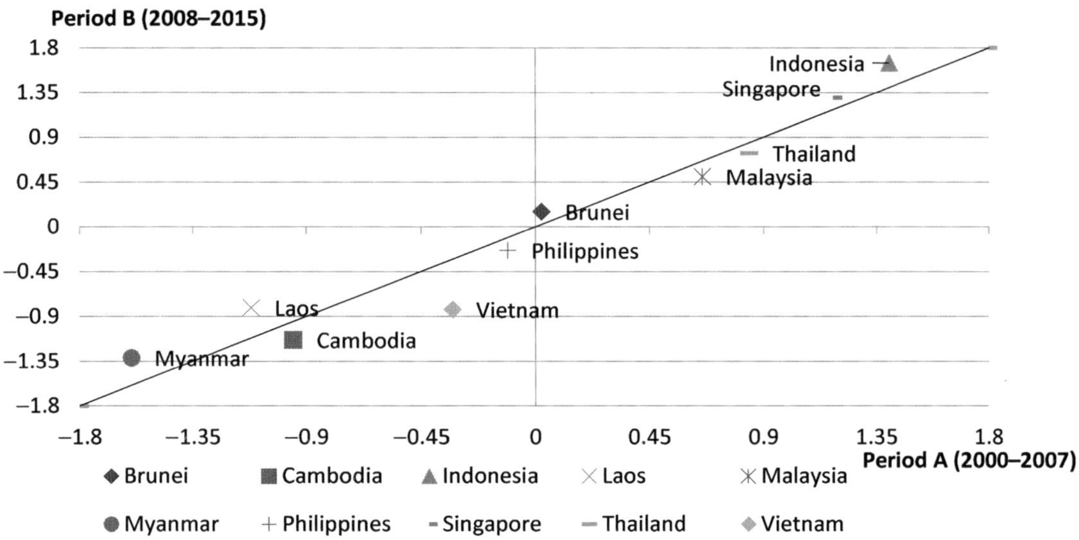

Source: Asia Competitiveness Institute.

and Myanmar show marked improvement over time, while Vietnam and Cambodia are losing in competitiveness in this sub-environment. Brunei makes a marked improvement in competitiveness in this sub-environment in Period B, whereas Philippines, Malaysia and Thailand all show a deterioration of competitiveness, as is evident from their positions below the 45-degree line.

In the remaining two sub-environments under Macroeconomic Stability, most ASEAN economies are clustered along the 45-degree line, which indicates little to no improvement in competitiveness, with the exception of Thailand and Vietnam lying above the line for Openness to Trade and Services (see Figure 2.21), and Brunei, Indonesia and Laos which fared better over time in terms of Attractiveness to Foreign Investors (see Figure 2.22).

As seen in Figures 2.23–2.25, Singapore remains at the top and far ahead of its peers for all three sub-environments under Government and Institutional Setting with improvement in Period B as compared to Period A. The performance of ASEAN economies is encouraging as shown by the improvement of Laos, Myanmar, Cambodia, Philippines and Thailand in terms of Government Policies and Fiscal Sustainability, while Brunei, Indonesia, Myanmar and Laos fared better in Competition, Regulatory Standards and Rule of Law in Period B as compared to Period A. Nonetheless, among the bottom three economies, only Laos shows significant improvement in all sub-environments in Period B relative to Period A, while Cambodia and Myanmar have only shown little or no improvement as they cluster around the 45-degree line. This signifies that more effort is required to catch up with the other economies in the region.

Among the three sub-environments under Financial, Businesses and Manpower Conditions, Singapore has maintained its top spot for Financial Deepening and Business Efficiency (Figure 2.26) while Malaysia and Brunei have been the most competitive in terms of Labour Market Flexibility (Figure 2.27) and Productivity Performance (Figure 2.28), respectively. However, while Singapore and Malaysia have become more competitive over time in terms of Financial Deepening and Business Efficiency, and Labour Market Flexibility, respectively, Brunei's competitiveness in Productivity Performance appears to be eroding as it fared worse in Period B relative to Period A. It is alarming to note that in the sub-environment of Productivity Performance, all ASEAN members except Singapore are clustered on the 45-degree line, signifying their stagnant productivity over the two sub-periods.

In Figures 2.29–2.31 illustrating the three sub-environments under Quality of Life and Infrastructure Development, Singapore's performance indicates a cause for concern when it comes to Technological Infrastructure, given its significant deterioration in Period B relative to Period A (Figure 2.30). On the bright side, Philippines and Laos have made big strides forward in Standard of Living, Education and Social Stability in Period B. Nonetheless, Malaysia and Thailand have fared significantly worse in the same sub-environment. Indonesia and Thailand have demonstrated improved competitiveness in Technological Infrastructure but a deterioration in Physical Infrastructure, which indicates challenges in balancing development in both sub-environments. It is also alarming to note a distinct gap between Myanmar and its peers in terms of Technological Infrastructure, and Standard of Living, Education and Social Stability. Moreover, Myanmar's competitiveness has deteriorated markedly in Period B relative to Period A for technical infrastructure. A standout, however, has been Vietnam's progress in all three sub-environments, where the economy performed better in Period B as compared to Period A, indicated by its presence above the 45-degree line.

Figure 2.21: Competitiveness Over Time Analysis for Openness to Trade and Services, Period B (2008–2015) Against Period A (2000–2007)

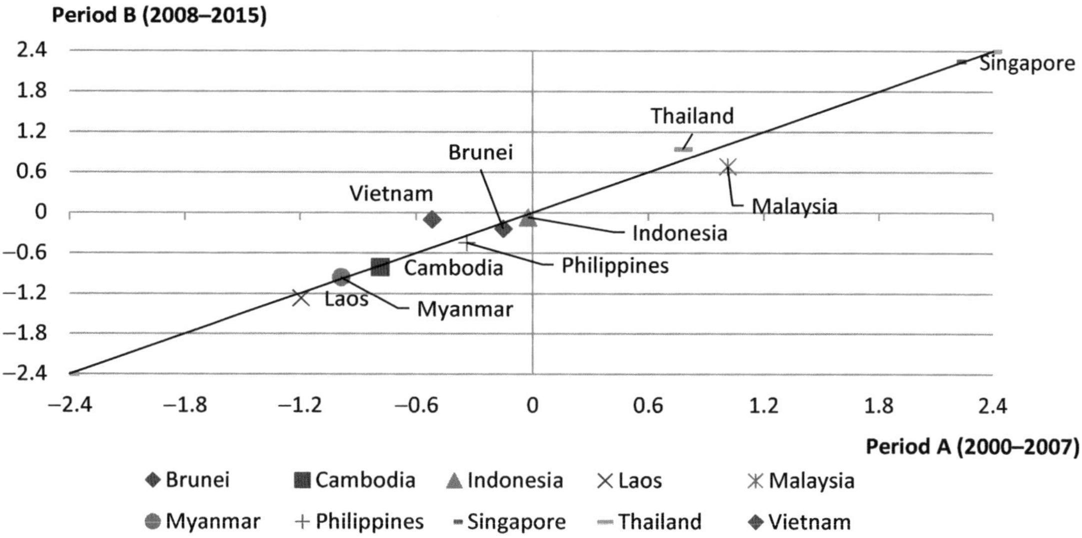

Source: Asia Competitiveness Institute.

Figure 2.22: Competitiveness Over Time Analysis for Attractiveness to Foreign Investors, Period B (2008–2015) Against Period A (2000–2007)

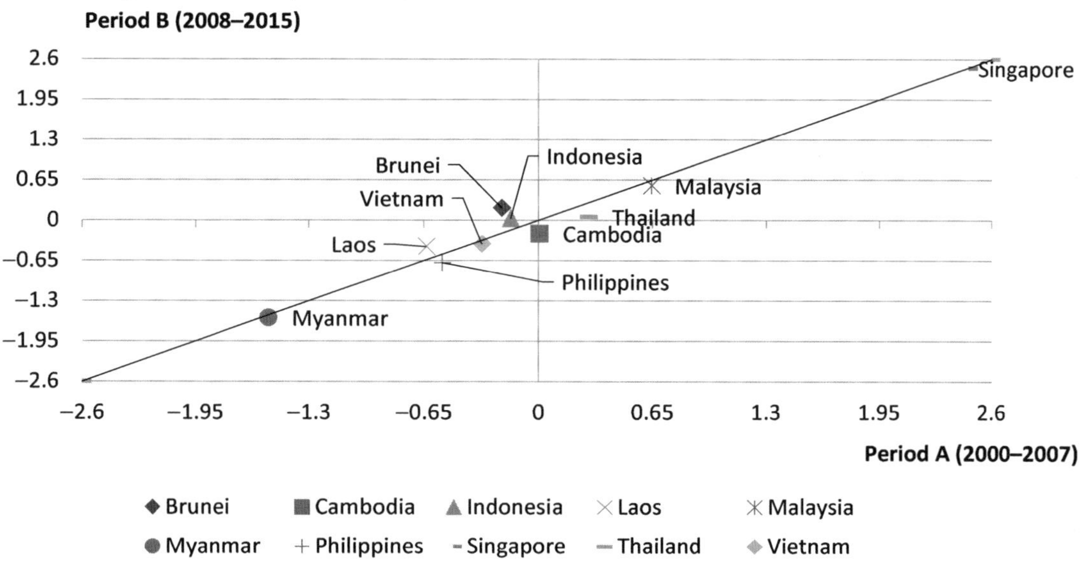

Source: Asia Competitiveness Institute.

Figure 2.23: Competitiveness Over Time Analysis for Government Policies and Fiscal Sustainability, Period B (2008–2015) Against Period A (2000–2007)

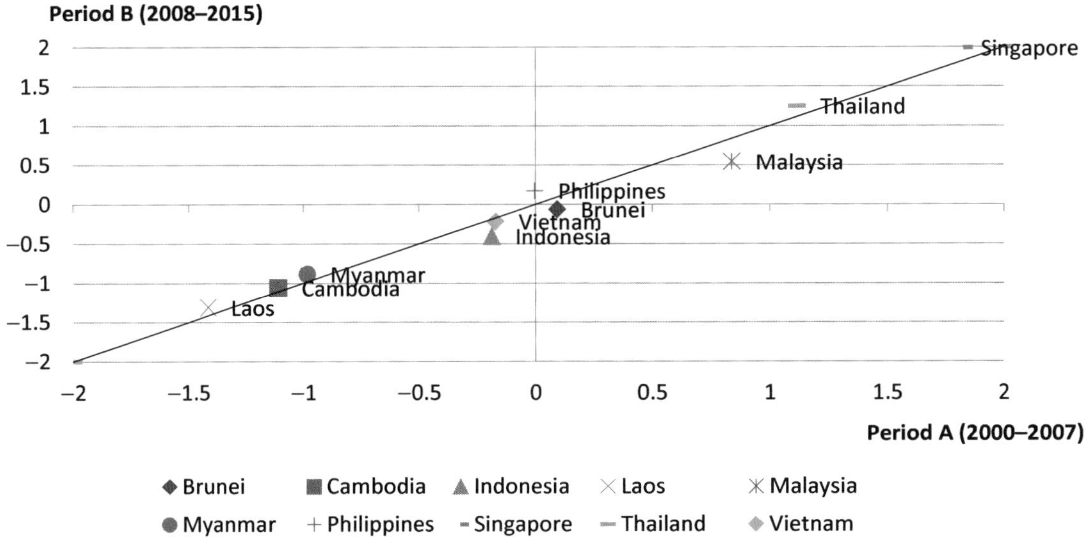

Source: Asia Competitiveness Institute.

Figure 2.24: Competitiveness Over Time Analysis for Institutions, Governance and Leadership, Period B (2008–2015) Against Period A (2000–2007)

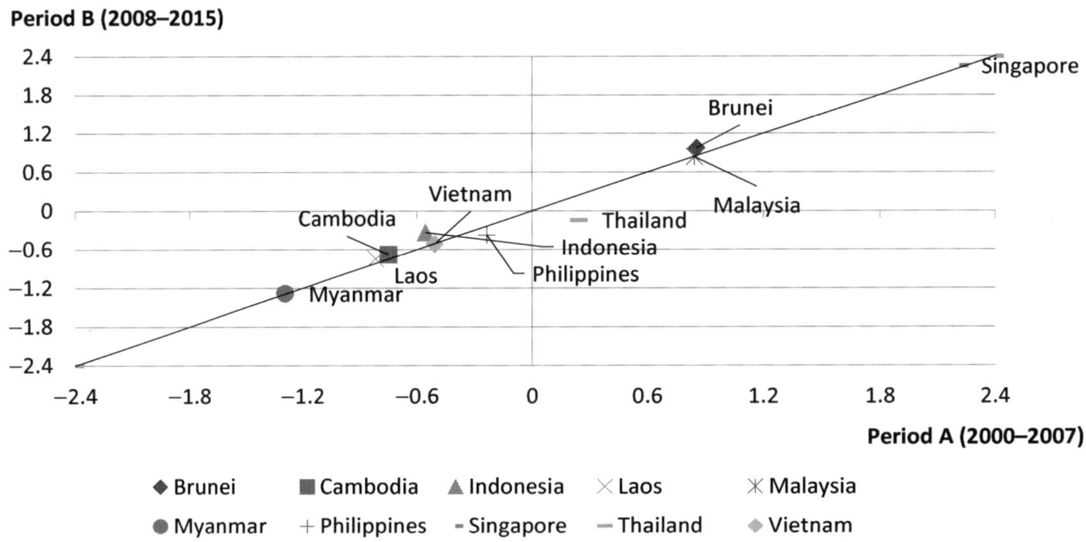

Source: Asia Competitiveness Institute.

Figure 2.25: Competitiveness Over Time Analysis for Competition, Regulatory Standards and Rule of Law, Period B (2008–2015) Against Period A (2000–2007)

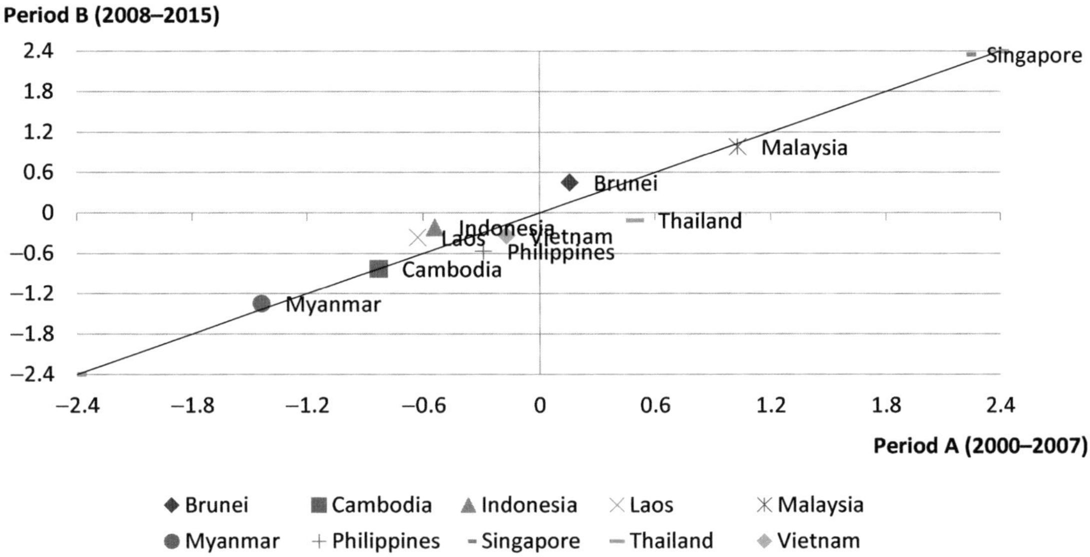

Source: Asia Competitiveness Institute.

Figure 2.26: Competitiveness Over Time Analysis for Financial Deepening and Business Efficiency, Period B (2008–2015) Against Period A (2000–2007)

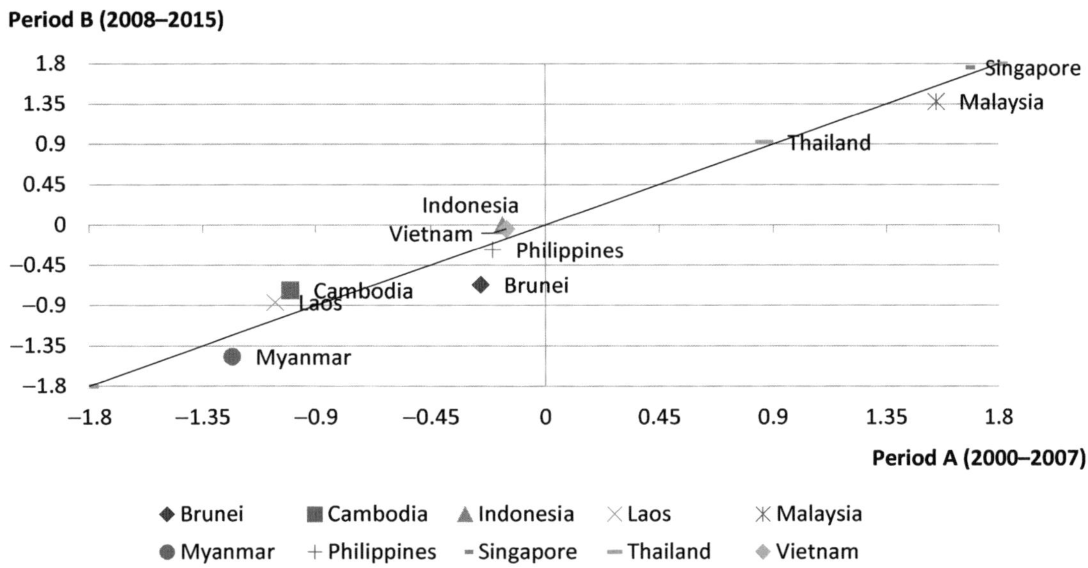

Source: Asia Competitiveness Institute.

Figure 2.27: Competitiveness Over Time Analysis for Labour Market Flexibility, Period B (2008–2015) Against Period A (2000–2007)

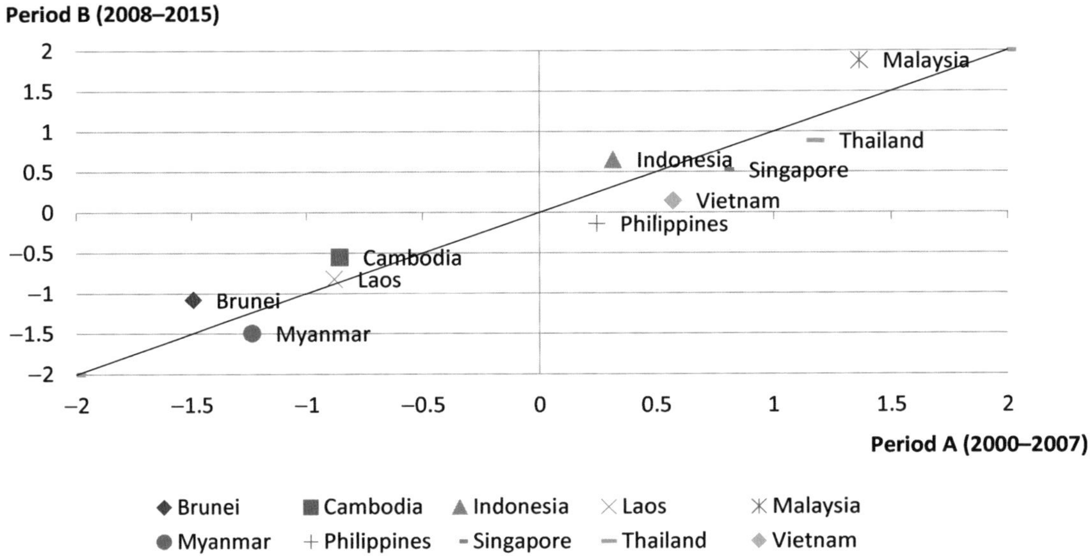

Source: Asia Competitiveness Institute.

Figure 2.28: Competitiveness Over Time Analysis for Productivity Performance, Period B (2008–2015) Against Period A (2000–2007)

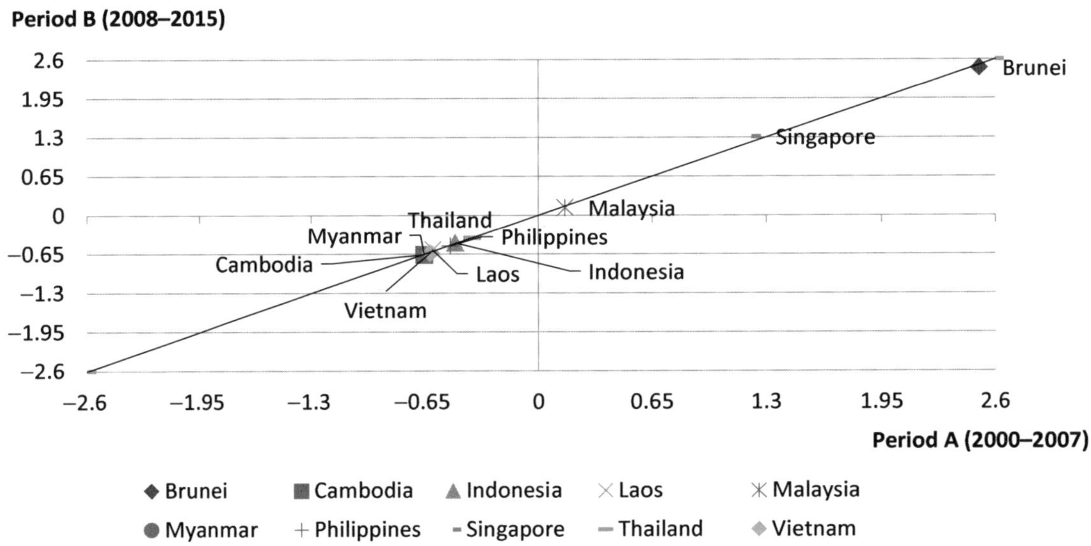

Source: Asia Competitiveness Institute.

Figure 2.29: Competitiveness Over Time Analysis for Physical Infrastructure, Period B (2008–2015) Against Period A (2000–2007)

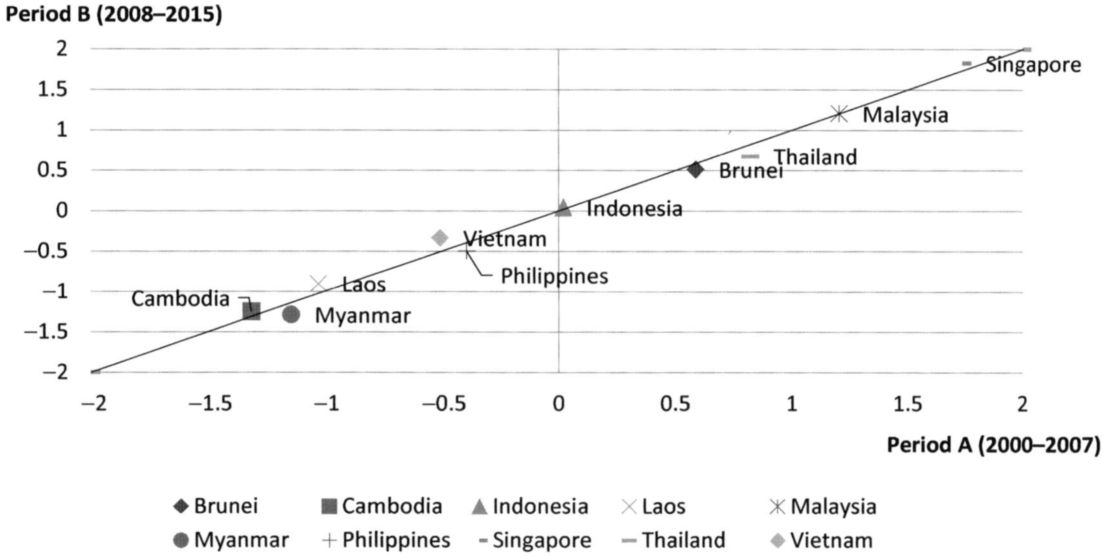

Source: Asia Competitiveness Institute.

Figure 2.30: Competitiveness Over Time Analysis for Technological Infrastructure, Period B (2008–2015) Against Period A (2000–2007)

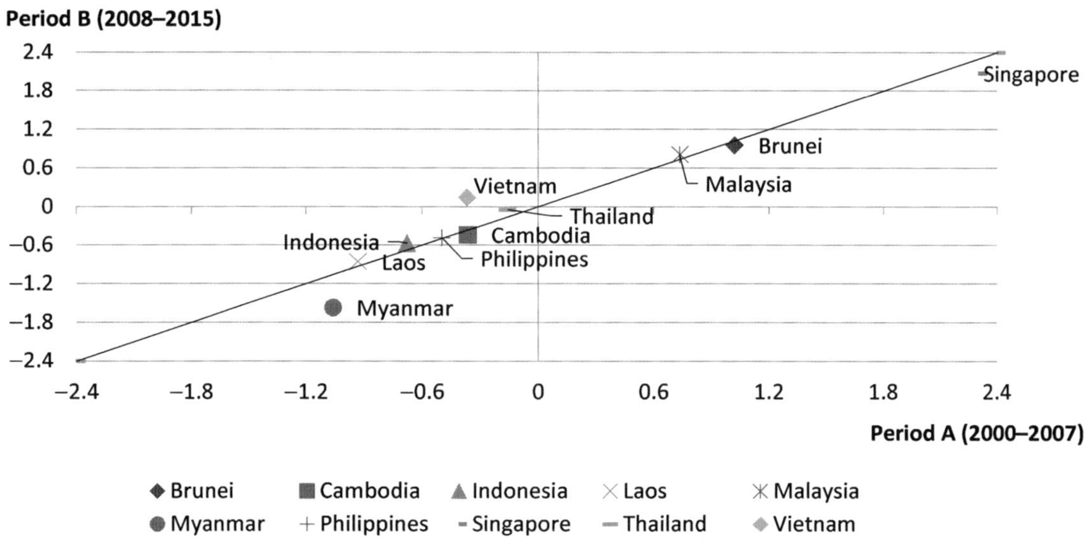

Source: Asia Competitiveness Institute.

Figure 2.31: Competitiveness Over Time Analysis for Standard of Living, Education and Social Stability, Period B (2008–2015) Against Period A (2000–2007)

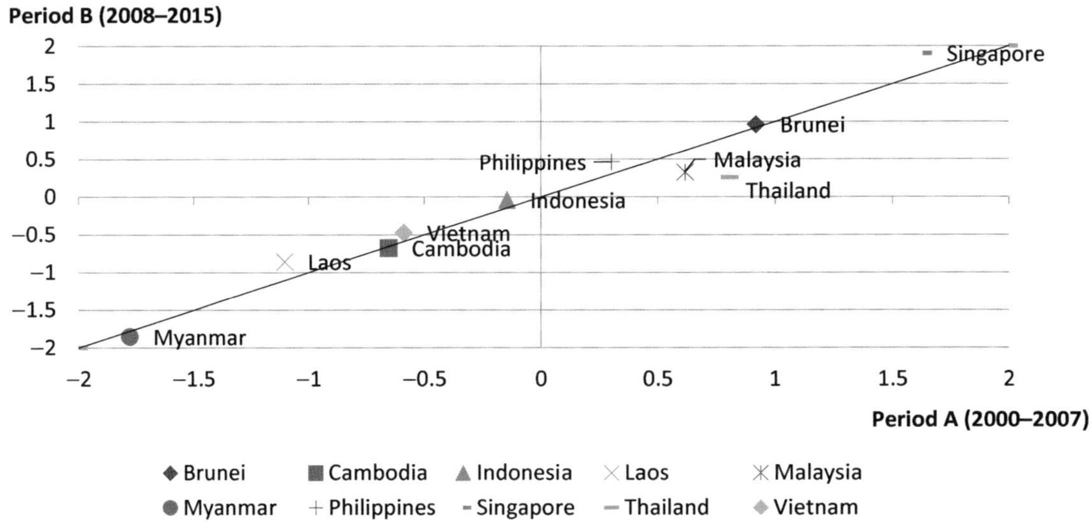

Source: Asia Competitiveness Institute.

Our COT analysis shows that the performance of ASEAN member states vary in different sub-environments over the study period. In line with its overall competitiveness performance in 2015, Singapore has topped most sub-environments by a large margin. Brunei and Malaysia are catching up with Singapore and have even overtaken the city-state in some sub-environments. However, the intensification of globalisation coupled with internal challenges has posed new threats to some of the ASEAN economies, particularly Philippines and Thailand. For the transitional economies in ASEAN, Vietnam in particular has stood out for making significant strides and emerging as a new investment spot among multinational corporations (MNCs) and other foreign investors. While Cambodia, Laos and Myanmar have shown optimistic signs of entering their take-off development stage, there remains a wide gap with other forerunners in the region in all sub-environments.

2.3.7 Maximising Strengths and Minimising Weaknesses

In this section, the top 20% strongest indicators and top 20% weakest indicators for individual ASEAN economies will first be discussed. This is followed by the analysis of spider web charts depicting each economy's competitiveness in each sub-environment *vis-à-vis* the ASEAN median and maximum (set by the regional top performer).

2.3.7.1 *Top 20% Strongest and Weakest Indicators*

Brunei's top 20% strongest and top 20% weakest indicators are listed in Tables 2.6 and 2.7, respectively. Being highly dependent on oil in its economy, Brunei is vulnerable to fluctuations in the unpredictable oil market. This makes venturing into new sources of growth a policy priority. Strong value added per worker in agriculture and industry (#1 and #2 in Table 2.6) can become

Table 2.6: Top 20% Strongest Indicators List for Brunei, 2015

Rank	20% Strongest Indicator	Score	Environment
1	Agriculture, Value Added Per Worker	2.9704	FBMC
2	Industry, Value Added Per Worker	2.5616	FBMC
3	Government Consumption Expenditure	2.2580	GIS
4	Government Environmental Protection Policies	2.1918	GIS
5	Access to Print Media	1.9828	QLID
6	Corporate Income Tax	1.9734	MS
7	Personal Computers	1.9151	QLID
8	Religious Unrest	1.8494	QLID
9	Sovereign Debt Risk	1.8093	FBMC
10	Gross Domestic Savings	1.7539	MS
11	Gross Fixed Capital Formation	1.5835	MS
12	Integrity of Legal System	1.5275	GIS
13	Public Security and Safety	1.5219	QLID
14	Air Quality	1.5127	QLID
15	Political Change	1.4930	GIS
16	Information and Communication Technology (ICT) Expenditure	1.4467	QLID
17	Current Account Balance	1.4138	MS
18	High Quality Management Staff	1.4078	FBMC
19	Quality of Judiciary	1.3447	GIS
20	Human Development Index	1.3286	QLID
21	Labour Market Rating	1.3195	FBMC
22	Quality of Police	1.2781	GIS
23	Money Supply Growth (M2)	1.2771	MS
24	Secondary Schooling	1.2708	QLID

Source: Asia Competitiveness Institute.

Table 2.7: Top 20% Weakest Indicators List for Brunei, 2015

Rank	20% Weakest Indicator	Score	Environment
98	Total Value of Stocks Traded	–0.7889	FBMC
99	International Tourism Receipts	–0.8309	MS
100	Population	–0.8518	QLID
101	Legislature/Parliament (Functioning of Government System)	–0.8647	GIS
102	Domestic Credit Provided by the Financial Sector	–0.8772	FBMC
103	Health Expenditure	–0.8868	QLID
104	Net Foreign Assets	–0.8912	GIS
105	International Reserves	–0.8919	GIS
106	Labour Force	–0.8949	FBMC
107	Exports of Goods and Services	–0.9035	MS
108	Market Capitalisation	–0.9438	FBMC
109	Output Services (Value Added)	–0.9575	MS
110	Tax Revenue/Government Revenue	–0.9673	GIS
111	Imports of Goods and Services	–0.9905	MS
112	Government Revenue (Including Grants)	–0.9944	GIS
113	Deposit Interest Rate	–1.0131	GIS
114	Listed Domestic Companies	–1.0300	FBMC
115	Gross Domestic Product	–1.0307	MS
116	Tax Revenue	–1.0332	GIS
117	Regional Competitiveness	–1.1580	GIS
118	Claims on Private Sector	–1.2589	FBMC
119	Cost of Management Staff	–1.7725	FBMC
120	Cost of Production Labour	–1.9651	FBMC
121	Budget Balance	–2.4894	GIS

Source: Asia Competitiveness Institute.

catalysts for the economic restructuring process. High Government Consumption Expenditure (#3) means that the government can provide the necessary impetus for these sectors to thrive. While economic growth matters, the government does not overlook the importance of environment as reflected in its fourth strongest indicator, government environmental protection policies.

On the other hand, high labour cost in terms of both management and production dimensions (#119 and #120 in Table 2.7) may hamper the economic development and restructuring in Brunei. Potential investors might also be turned away due to its poor claims on private sector (#118) and the absence of a robust domestic services market. This is clearly seen in Brunei's low scores in Output Services (#109) as well as Export and Import of Services (#107 and #111). Lack of regional competitiveness and dwindling tax revenues are also sources of potential concerns for the country. In addition to this, a weak financial sector as reflected in domestic credit provided by the financial sector and deposit interest rate (#102 and #113) might also hurt Brunei's overall attractiveness to investors.

For Cambodia, labour cost emerges as one of its top strengths at #12 and #17 in Table 2.8. Notable efforts have been made in strengthening the private sector, as shown in claims on private sector (#2) and corporate income tax (#13). While there are optimistic prospects in economic performance, development progress seems to be imbalanced as social indicators highlight a lack of public services provision, especially in education (#110, #111 and #120 in Table 2.9) and infrastructure (#112, #118 and #119), which are among the weakest indicators for Cambodia. Hence, more efforts are needed to channel the economic benefits towards improving social conditions for more comprehensive development in Cambodia.

Table 2.8: Top 20% Strongest Indicators List for Cambodia, 2015

Rank	20% Strongest Indicator	Score	Environment
1	Telecommunications System	2.8897	QLID
2	Claims on Private Sector	2.1973	FBMC
3	Real GDP Growth	1.1723	MS
4	Government Environmental Protection Policies	1.1503	GIS
5	Daily Organic Water Pollutant Emissions	1.1496	QLID
6	Unemployment Rate	1.1045	FBMC
7	Freedom of Religion	1.0752	QLID
8	Tax Revenue/Government Revenue	1.0737	GIS
9	Health Expenditure	1.0557	QLID
10	Freedom of Press	0.9598	QLID
11	Exchange Rate Appreciation	0.9135	GIS
12	Cost of Management Staff	0.7825	FBMC
13	Corporate Income Tax	0.7777	MS
14	International Monetary Fund Credit	0.7749	GIS
15	External Debt	0.7380	GIS
16	Traffic Congestion	0.7257	QLID
17	Cost of Production Labour	0.6371	FBMC
18	Cellular Mobile Telephone Subscribers	0.6123	QLID
19	Inflation	0.2903	MS
20	Urban Population Growth	0.2069	QLID
21	Budget Balance	0.1511	GIS
22	Openness to Trade	0.1195	MS
23	Foreign Owned Companies	0.0964	MS
24	Primary Schooling	0.0204	QLID

Source: Asia Competitiveness Institute.

Table 2.9: Top 20% Weakest Indicators List for Cambodia, 2015

Rank	20% Weakest Indicator	Score	Environment
98	Political System Risk	–1.0351	GIS
99	Gross Domestic Savings	–1.0469	MS
100	Ease of Starting Business	–1.0627	GIS
101	Internet Subscribers	–1.1027	QLID
102	Intellectual Property Rights Protection	–1.1036	GIS
103	Information and Communication Technology (ICT) Expenditure	–1.1084	QLID
104	Quality of Police	–1.1251	GIS
105	Interest Rate Spread	–1.1295	GIS
106	Current Account Balance	–1.1461	MS
107	Legislature/Parliament (Functioning of Government System)	–1.1521	GIS
108	Corporate Governance	–1.1660	GIS
109	Effectiveness of Legal System	–1.2045	GIS
110	Human Development Index	–1.2238	QLID
111	University and Post-Graduate Education	–1.2719	QLID
112	Electric Power	–1.2764	QLID
113	Availability of Scientists and Engineers	–1.2814	FBMC
114	Gross Fixed Capital Formation	–1.2991	MS
115	Government Consumption Expenditure	–1.3647	GIS
116	Urban Population	–1.3869	QLID
117	Quality of Judiciary	–1.5250	GIS
118	Access to Water	–1.5797	QLID
119	Access to Sanitation	–2.0952	QLID
120	Literacy Rate	–2.1634	QLID
121	Air Quality	–2.4260	QLID

Source: Asia Competitiveness Institute.

Being the largest economy in ASEAN, Indonesia's population size has contributed to abundant and low-cost labour supply (#3, #4, #13 and #22 in Table 2.10). The top two indicators, valued added in agriculture and industry (#1 and #2) show that Indonesia is dependent on a dualistic economic structure. In addition, Indonesia has also performed well in services sector (#5), which indicates a balanced development across three main sectors.

Nonetheless, a poor business-conducive environment may hinder economic activities in Indonesia. Improvement is needed in removing trade barriers (#114 in Table 2.11) in order to increase openness to trade (#107). Macroeconomic factors including quality of central bank, inflation, money supply, and external debt (#111, #116, #117 and #121) remain the top

Table 2.10: Top 20% Strongest Indicators List for Indonesia, 2015

Rank	20% Strongest Indicator	Score	Environment
1	Output Agriculture (Value Added)	2.8039	MS
2	Output Industry (Value Added)	2.7319	MS
3	Population	2.6478	QLID
4	Labour Force	2.5769	FBMC
5	Output Services (Value Added)	2.3189	MS
6	Deposit Interest Rate	1.8423	GIS
7	Freedom of Speech	1.5682	QLID
8	Gross Domestic Product	1.1581	MS
9	Tax Burden	1.1368	GIS
10	Gross Fixed Capital Formation	1.1108	MS
11	Freedom of Press	0.8702	QLID
12	Regional Competitiveness	0.8474	GIS
13	Cost of Management Staff	0.7825	FBMC
14	Market Capitalisation	0.7103	FBMC
15	Tax Revenue/Government Revenue	0.7022	GIS
16	Listed Domestic Companies	0.6989	FBMC
17	Political System Risk	0.6901	GIS
18	Availability of Scientists and Engineers	0.6601	FBMC
19	Tax Revenue	0.6377	GIS
20	Secondary Schooling	0.5952	QLID
21	Literacy Rate	0.5242	QLID
22	Cost of Production Labour	0.5209	FBMC
23	Cellular Mobile Telephone Subscribers	0.4944	QLID
24	Government Revenue (Including Grants)	0.4902	GIS

Source: Asia Competitiveness Institute.

Table 2.11: Top 20% Weakest Indicators List for Indonesia, 2015

Rank	20% Weakest Indicator	Score	Environment
98	High Quality Management Staff	–0.8133	FBMC
99	Policy Towards Private Enterprise Rating	–0.8385	GIS
100	Lending Rate	–0.8396	GIS
101	Government Stability	–0.8620	GIS
102	Lack of Discrimination Against Investors	–0.8714	MS
103	Labour Market Rating	–0.8797	FBMC
104	Domestic Credit to Private Sector	–0.8881	FBMC
105	Ease of Starting Business	–0.8975	GIS
106	Lack of Market Distortion due to State-Ownership	–0.9045	GIS
107	Openness to Trade	–0.9260	MS
108	Freedom of Religion	–0.9408	QLID
109	Government Effectiveness	–0.9533	GIS
110	Internet Subscribers	–0.9708	QLID
111	Quality of Central Bank/Monetary Authority	–1.0000	GIS
112	Lack of Corruption	–1.0451	GIS
113	Access to Sanitation	–1.0550	QLID
114	Barriers to Trade	–1.0614	GIS
115	Information and Communication Technology (ICT) Expenditure	–1.1084	QLID
116	Inflation	–1.1986	MS
117	Money Supply (M2)	–1.2700	GIS
118	Primary Schooling	–1.5665	QLID
119	Unemployment Rate	–1.7707	FBMC
120	International Monetary Fund Credit	–2.1697	GIS
121	External Debt	–2.3338	GIS

Source: Asia Competitiveness Institute.

weaknesses in Indonesia. While labour supply is a strength for Indonesia as discussed earlier, it is also crucial to not overlook the quality of the labour market (#103).

As commonly seen in most rapidly growing economies, Laos is also experiencing high urban population growth (#1 in Table 2.12). Among its top 20% strengths are manpower cost (#7 and #11), political stability (#10) and a relatively conducive business environment (#12, #15 and #17).

Macroeconomic indicators like Quality of Central Bank/Monetary Authority Gross Domestic Savings, Lending Rate and Interest Rate Spread, all feature in the 20% weakest indicators list (#98, #110, #119 and #121). In addition to this, Laos scores low on fiscal indicators like Government Revenue and Current Account Balance (#103 and #117). Connectivity advancement (#108, #113 and #120) should remain at the top of the priority list as this will not only encourage economic activity but also to facilitate the distribution of growth outcomes (Table 2.13).

Table 2.12: Top 20% Strongest Indicators List for Laos, 2015

Rank	20% Strongest Indicator	Score	Environment
1	Urban Population Growth	2.0683	QLID
2	Real GDP Growth	1.3606	MS
3	Daily Organic Water Pollutant Emissions	1.1496	QLID
4	Exchange Rate Appreciation	1.0295	GIS
5	International Monetary Fund Credit	0.8265	GIS
6	Traffic Congestion	0.7925	QLID
7	Cost of Management Staff	0.7825	FBMC
8	External Debt	0.7141	GIS
9	Government Environmental Protection Policies	0.6967	GIS
10	Political Change	0.6601	GIS
11	Cost of Production Labour	0.6371	FBMC
12	Claims on Private Sector	0.4947	FBMC
13	Unemployment Rate	0.4915	FBMC
14	Religious Unrest	0.4040	QLID
15	Corporate Income Tax	0.3597	MS
16	Telephone Main Lines	0.3451	QLID
17	Monopolies and Cartel	0.3038	GIS
18	Inflation	0.2744	MS
19	Government Consumption Expenditure	0.2148	GIS
20	Air Quality	0.1693	QLID
21	Gross Fixed Capital Formation	0.1280	MS
22	Electric Power	0.1031	QLID
23	Quality of Police	0.0729	GIS
24	Bureaucracy/Red Tape	0.0707	GIS

Source: Asia Competitiveness Institute.

Table 2.13: Top 20% Weakest Indicators List for Laos, 2015

Rank	20% Weakest Indicator	Score	Environment
98	Quality of Central Bank/Monetary Authority	−1.0000	GIS
99	Domestic Credit to Private Sector	−1.0220	FBMC
100	Human Development Index	−1.0294	QLID
101	Listed Domestic Companies	−1.0300	FBMC
102	Political System Risk	−1.0351	GIS
103	Government Revenue (Including Grants)	−1.0386	GIS
104	Tax Revenue	−1.0603	GIS
105	Ease of Starting Business	−1.0627	GIS
106	Gross Domestic Product	−1.0754	MS
107	Information and Communication Technology (ICT) Expenditure	−1.1084	QLID
108	Internet Subscribers	−1.1382	QLID
109	Freedom of Speech	−1.1625	QLID
110	Gross Domestic Savings	−1.2532	MS
111	Availability of Scientists and Engineers	−1.3546	FBMC
112	Health Expenditure	−1.3890	QLID
113	Port Facilities	−1.5009	QLID
114	Access to Water	−1.5586	QLID
115	Freedom of Press	−1.7513	QLID
116	Literacy Rate	−1.7647	QLID
117	Current Account Balance	−1.7667	MS
118	Regional Competitiveness	−1.8581	GIS
119	Lending Rate	−2.1174	GIS
120	Cellular Mobile Telephone Subscribers	−2.2094	QLID
121	Interest Rate Spread	−2.4827	GIS

Source: Asia Competitiveness Institute.

Despite being the second most competitive economy in ASEAN, Malaysia still lags far behind the top-performing economy, that is Singapore. As Malaysia surpassed Singapore for the first time throughout the study period in the environment of Financial, Businesses and Manpower Conditions, it is imperative for Malaysia to tap into its rich talent pool (#2, #8 and #11 in Table 2.14) in order to expedite the catching-up process. Furthermore, its sound institutional capacity (#3, #5, #9, #16 and #17) and well-functioning financial system (#13, #15, #19 and #21) also make it an attractive investment destination for local and foreign investors.

However, several indicators like External Debt and high IMF Credit (#112 and #115 in Table 2.15) have exposed fiscal vulnerabilities in Malaysia which pose a credible threat to the macroeconomic

Table 2.14: Top 20% Strongest Indicators List for Malaysia, 2015

Rank	20% Strongest Indicator	Score	Environment
1	Listed Domestic Companies	1.9300	FBMC
2	Availability of Scientists and Engineers	1.7303	FBMC
3	Legislature/Parliament (Functioning of Government System)	1.6700	GIS
4	Rail Facilities	1.5908	QLID
5	Integrity of Legal System	1.5275	GIS
6	Extent of Staff Training	1.4733	FBMC
7	Monopolies and Cartel	1.4659	GIS
8	High Quality Management Staff	1.4078	FBMC
9	Bureaucracy/Red Tape	1.3855	GIS
10	Local Road System	1.3613	QLID
11	Labour Market Rating	1.3195	FBMC
12	Intellectual Property Rights Protection	1.3150	GIS
13	Domestic Credit to Private Sector	1.2994	FBMC
14	Barriers to Trade	1.2965	GIS
15	Transparency of Processes for Investors	1.2679	MS
16	Transparency of Government	1.2679	GIS
17	Government Responsiveness	1.2648	GIS
18	Money Supply (M2)	1.2509	GIS
19	Domestic Credit Provided by the Financial Sector	1.2463	FBMC
20	Corporate Governance	1.2236	GIS
21	Quality of Banking and Financial System	1.2212	FBMC
22	Internet Subscribers	1.2058	QLID
23	Primary Schooling	1.1754	QLID
24	Labour Unrest	1.1704	QLID

Source: Asia Competitiveness Institute.

Table 2.15: Top 20% Weakest Indicators List for Malaysia, 2015

Rank	20% Weakest Indicator	Score	Environment
98	Foreign Direct Investment Inflows	–0.0770	MS
99	GDP Per Capita	–0.1394	MS
100	Traffic Congestion	–0.1434	QLID
101	Tax Burden	–0.2137	GIS
102	University and Post-Graduate Education	–0.2139	QLID
103	Industry, Value Added Per Worker	–0.2196	FBMC
104	Claims on Private Sector	–0.2442	FBMC
105	Gross Fixed Capital Formation	–0.2925	MS
106	Government Environmental Protection Policies	–0.2932	GIS
107	Unemployment Rate	–0.3408	FBMC
108	Population	–0.4403	QLID
109	Labour Force	–0.4960	FBMC
110	Lack of Corruption	–0.7312	GIS
111	Corporate Income Tax	–1.0693	MS
112	External Debt	–1.1267	GIS
113	Freedom of Religion	–1.1328	QLID
114	Daily Organic Water Pollutant Emissions	–1.1495	QLID
115	International Monetary Fund Credit	–1.1849	GIS
116	Real GDP Growth	–1.3340	MS
117	Quality of Government Policies	–1.3630	GIS
118	Political Change	–1.3668	GIS
119	Quality of Regulatory Environment	–1.3704	GIS
120	Exchange Rate Appreciation	–1.4991	GIS
121	Government Effectiveness	–1.5194	GIS

Source: Asia Competitiveness Institute.

environment of the country. An expanding urban population has also led to problems such as traffic congestion (#100) and water pollution (#114) which policy-makers need to be heedful of.

Myanmar possesses immense potential in becoming the next investment hub in ASEAN (#1, #2 and #3 in Table 2.16), albeit being a latecomer in the region. It should leverage on its large pool of low-cost labour (#6, #11 and #24) as well as high literacy rate (#20) in attracting new investment. This coupled with a sound regulatory environment (#7, #9, #10 and #16) and fiscal strength (#8, #14 and #23) are other strong features in Myanmar which will play a crucial role in attracting investors and fuelling sustainable growth.

The list of weakest indicators in Table 2.17 reveals a lack of basic infrastructure (#105, #106 and #107), socio-political instability (#101 and #113) and macroeconomic and financial stability

Table 2.16: Top 20% Strongest Indicators List for Myanmar, 2015

Rank	20% Strongest Indicator	Score	Environment
1	Tax Burden	1.9303	GIS
2	Deposit Interest Rate	1.7220	GIS
3	Gross Fixed Capital Formation	1.4910	MS
4	Daily Organic Water Pollutant Emissions	1.3627	QLID
5	Unemployment Rate	0.7973	FBMC
6	Cost of Management Staff	0.7825	FBMC
7	Government Effectiveness	0.7773	GIS
8	External Debt	0.7679	GIS
9	Quality of Regulatory Environment	0.6982	GIS
10	Quality of Government Policies	0.6899	GIS
11	Cost of Production Labour	0.6371	FBMC
12	Traffic Congestion	0.5922	QLID
13	Freedom of Press	0.5401	QLID
14	International Monetary Fund Credit	0.5236	GIS
15	Government Consumption Expenditure	0.5188	GIS
16	Lack of Corruption	0.4620	GIS
17	Claims on Private Sector	0.4207	FBMC
18	Political Change	0.3246	GIS
19	Interest Rate Spread	0.2165	GIS
20	Literacy Rate	0.1846	QLID
21	Urban Population Growth	0.1064	QLID
22	Access to Sanitation	0.0079	QLID
23	Gross Domestic Savings	0.0055	MS
24	Labour Force	–0.0835	FBMC

Source: Asia Competitiveness Institute.

Table 2.17: Top 20% Weakest Indicators List for Myanmar, 2015

Rank	20% Weakest Indicator	Score	Environment
98	Transparency of Government	–1.3763	GIS
99	Quality of Judiciary	–1.3979	GIS
100	Secondary Schooling	–1.3982	QLID
101	Labour Unrest	–1.4031	QLID
102	Cellular Mobile Telephone Subscribers	–1.4073	QLID
103	Lack of Cronyism	–1.4085	GIS
104	Real GDP Growth	–1.4253	MS
105	Local Road System	–1.5288	QLID
106	Electric Power	–1.6077	QLID
107	Airport Facilities	–1.6504	QLID
108	Levelness of Playing Field	–1.7131	MS
109	Business Impact of Rules on FDI	–1.7358	MS
110	Quality of Stock Market Regulatory Authority	–1.7451	FBMC
111	Networked Readiness Index	–1.7584	QLID
112	Strength of Auditing and Reporting Standards	–1.7852	GIS
113	Religious Unrest	–1.8290	QLID
114	Extent of Staff Training	–1.9470	FBMC
115	Exchange Rate Appreciation	–1.9923	GIS
116	Monopolies and Cartel	–1.9958	GIS
117	Quality of Banking and Financial System	–2.1699	FBMC
118	Tax Revenue/Government Revenue	–2.2122	GIS
119	Money Supply Growth (M2)	–2.3770	MS
120	Foreign Owned Companies	–2.3944	MS
121	Inflation	–2.4844	MS

Source: Asia Competitiveness Institute.

(#110, #115, #117, #119 and #121) in Myanmar. It is imperative to curb these weaknesses which may derail Myanmar from its development trajectory.

Philippines has an abundance of high-quality and cheap labour (#4, #10, #16 and #21). High Labour Activism (#3) also means the market is organised (Table 2.18). However, high unemployment (#121 in Table 2.19) is hampering the country's growth prospects.

Looking through Table 2.19, we find that list is marred by institutional ineffectiveness and bureaucratic inefficiencies (#98, #110, #111, #113 and #114). This has led to a reduced openness to trade and ease of setting-up businesses (#99 and #117). Poor connectivity (#101, #104, #107 and #112) is another major hindrance to Philippines' development which needs to be overcome in order for the country to move forward.

Table 2.18: Top 20% Strongest Indicators List for Philippines, 2015

Rank	20% Strongest Indicator	Score	Environment
1	Freedom of Religion	2.3232	QLID
2	Freedom of Speech	1.9583	QLID
3	Labour Activism	1.8697	QLID
4	High Quality Management Staff	1.0582	FBMC
5	Real GDP Growth	0.9665	MS
6	Tax Revenue/Government Revenue	0.9658	GIS
7	Daily Organic Water Pollutant Emissions	0.9449	QLID
8	Exchange Rate Appreciation	0.8758	GIS
9	Lending Rate	0.7954	GIS
10	Literacy Rate	0.7014	QLID
11	Corporate Governance	0.6872	GIS
12	Primary Schooling	0.6864	QLID
13	Freedom of Press	0.6121	QLID
14	Lack of Market Distortion due to State-Ownership	0.6030	GIS
15	Traffic Congestion	0.5882	QLID
16	University and Post-Graduate Education	0.5746	QLID
17	Strength of Auditing and Reporting Standards	0.5731	GIS
18	Quality of Stock Market Regulatory Authority	0.5594	FBMC
19	Budget Balance	0.5395	GIS
20	Population	0.5236	QLID
21	Cost of Production Labour	0.4823	FBMC
22	Interest Rate Spread	0.4747	GIS
23	Health Expenditure	0.4361	QLID
24	Internet Subscribers	0.4359	QLID

Source: Asia Competitiveness Institute.

Table 2.19: Top 20% Weakest Indicators List for Philippines, 2015

Rank	20% Weakest Indicator	Score	Environment
98	Integrity of Legal System	–0.6547	GIS
99	Openness to Trade	–0.6684	MS
100	Cost of Management Staff	–0.6732	FBMC
101	Port Facilities	–0.6793	QLID
102	Domestic Credit to Private Sector	–0.6817	FBMC
103	Institutional Sophistication	–0.6975	GIS
104	Local Road System	–0.6983	QLID
105	Personal Computers	–0.7058	QLID
106	Access to Print Media	–0.7107	QLID
107	Airport Facilities	–0.7133	QLID
108	Lack of Cronyism	–0.7153	GIS
109	Money Supply (M2)	–0.7243	GIS
110	Government Responsiveness	–0.7357	GIS
111	Effectiveness of Legal System	–0.7370	GIS
112	Telephone Main Lines	–0.7600	QLID
113	Government Environmental Protection Policies	–0.9362	GIS
114	Bureaucracy/Red Tape	–0.9779	GIS
115	Political Change	–0.9993	GIS
116	Gross Fixed Capital Formation	–1.1821	MS
117	Ease of Starting Business	–1.1952	GIS
118	Gross Domestic Savings	–1.2535	MS
119	Corporate Income Tax	–1.3513	MS
120	Urban Population Growth	–1.3802	QLID
121	Unemployment Rate	–1.9191	FBMC

Source: Asia Competitiveness Institute.

Having evolved from a port city to one of the most important global hubs, Singapore stands out with its open economic policies. This is reflected among its strongest indicators such as FDI inflows (#1), openness to trade (#7 in Table 2.20), and export and import (#10 and #11). High integrity and efficiency of governing institutions (#3, #6, #13, #16, #18, #19 and #22) have contributed to a transparent and conducive business environment, which in turn reinforces the competitiveness of the city state. Its top-notch ICT infrastructure (#8 and #21) further strengthens its position as host to many MNC headquarters in Southeast Asia.

Despite dominating the top spot in the rankings of Overall Competitiveness as well as the majority of sub-environments for over a decade, Singapore is not without its weaknesses (Table 2.21). Its small population (#112 and #114) and rising manpower costs (#119 and #120)

Table 2.20: Top 20% Strongest Indicators List for Singapore, 2015

Rank	20% Strongest Indicator	Score	Environment
1	Foreign Direct Investment Inflows	2.9005	MS
2	Services, Value Added Per Worker	2.7778	FBMC
3	Quality of Political Leadership	2.6758	GIS
4	GDP Per Capita	2.6731	MS
5	Social Unrest	2.5556	QLID
6	Lack of Corruption	2.5311	GIS
7	Openness to Trade	2.5242	MS
8	Telephone Main Lines	2.4999	QLID
9	Lack of Discrimination Against Investors	2.4645	MS
10	Exports of Goods and Services	2.3828	MS
11	Imports of Goods and Services	2.3228	MS
12	Policy Towards Private Enterprise Rating	2.3059	GIS
13	Quality of Government Policies	2.3027	GIS
14	Business Impact of Rules on FDI	2.2987	MS
15	Barriers to Trade	2.2969	GIS
16	Quality of Regulatory Environment	2.2774	GIS
17	International Reserves	2.2719	GIS
18	Transparency of Processes for Investors	2.2300	MS
19	Transparency of Government	2.2300	GIS
20	Institutional Sophistication	2.2087	GIS
21	Networked Readiness Index	2.1918	QLID
22	Government Effectiveness	2.1290	GIS
23	Lack of Market Distortion due to State-Ownership	2.1106	GIS
24	Net Foreign Assets	2.0612	GIS

Source: Asia Competitiveness Institute.

Table 2.21: Top 20% Weakest Indicators List for Singapore, 2015

Rank	20% Weakest Indicator	Score	Environment
98	Interest Rate Spread	0.1699	GIS
99	Freedom of Speech	0.1638	QLID
100	Tax Burden	0.0393	GIS
101	Exchange Rate Appreciation	0.0278	GIS
102	Freedom of Press	–0.1166	QLID
103	Output Industry (Value Added)	–0.2002	MS
104	Gross Fixed Capital Formation	–0.3158	MS
105	Agriculture, Value Added Per Worker	–0.3559	FBMC
106	Government Consumption Expenditure	–0.4001	GIS
107	Telecommunications System	–0.4240	QLID
108	Real GDP Growth	–0.4389	MS
109	Freedom of Religion	–0.4608	QLID
110	Output Agriculture (Value Added)	–0.7535	MS
111	Daily Organic Water Pollutant Emissions	–0.7600	QLID
112	Population	–0.7823	QLID
113	Tax Revenue/Government Revenue	–0.7860	GIS
114	Labour Force	–0.8135	FBMC
115	Government Environmental Protection Policies	–0.8271	GIS
116	Deposit Interest Rate	−1.0734	GIS
117	Claims on Private Sector	−1.2357	FBMC
118	Urban Population Growth	−1.5722	QLID
119	Cost of Management Staff	−1.7725	FBMC
120	Cost of Production Labour	−1.9651	FBMC
121	Traffic Congestion	–2.6429	QLID

Source: Asia Competitiveness Institute.

threaten to erode its attractiveness to MNCs as newcomers with large, young and increasingly educated workforce emerge.

Thailand manages to work past its internal political struggles (#114, #118 and #119 in Table 2.23) when it comes to the tourism sector and continues to receive a high number of international tourists (#1). Attention to public services including education (#5 and #9) is also not compromised (Table 2.22). However, basic education still lags behind as compared to secondary and tertiary education (#121 in Table 2.23). Easily available financial access (#3 and #11), coupled with sound macroeconomic fundamentals (#13, #15 and #17), highlights substantial potential for attracting foreign companies to provide competition to domestic players (#10), and for future economic growth.

Table 2.22: Top 20% Strongest Indicators List for Thailand, 2015

Rank	20% Strongest Indicator	Score	Environment
1	International Tourism Receipts	2.7018	MS
2	Total Value of Stocks Traded	1.8419	FBMC
3	Domestic Credit Provided by the Financial Sector	1.7907	FBMC
4	Tax Revenue	1.7221	GIS
5	University and Post-Graduate Education	1.6422	QLID
6	Government Revenue (Including Grants)	1.3945	GIS
7	Net Foreign Assets	1.3883	GIS
8	Gross Domestic Product	1.3205	MS
9	Secondary Schooling	1.1137	QLID
10	Listed Domestic Companies	1.0904	FBMC
11	Domestic Credit to Private Sector	1.0834	FBMC
12	International Reserves	1.0572	GIS
13	Money Supply (M2)	1.0213	GIS
14	Regional Competitiveness	0.9892	GIS
15	Inflation	0.9031	MS
16	Tax Revenue/Government Revenue	0.8783	GIS
17	Unemployment Rate	0.8636	FBMC
18	Exports of Goods and Services	0.8305	MS
19	Government Consumption Expenditure	0.8271	GIS
20	Access to Water	0.7751	QLID
21	Policy Towards Private Enterprise Rating	0.7686	GIS
22	Access to Sanitation	0.7655	QLID
23	Imports of Goods and Services	0.7305	MS
24	Market Capitalisation	0.6894	FBMC

Source: Asia Competitiveness Institute.

Table 2.23: Top 20% Weakest Indicators List for Thailand, 2015

Rank	20% Weakest Indicator	Score	Environment
98	Levelness of Playing Field	–0.4888	MS
99	External Debt	–0.4974	GIS
100	Government Responsiveness	–0.5935	GIS
101	International Monetary Fund Credit	–0.6013	GIS
102	Gross Fixed Capital Formation	–0.6126	MS
103	Freedom of Speech	–0.6163	QLID
104	Deposit Interest Rate	–0.6273	GIS
105	Quality of Political Leadership	–0.6283	GIS
106	Integrity of Legal System	–0.6547	GIS
107	Bureaucracy/Red Tape	–0.6865	GIS
108	Lack of Cronyism	–0.7194	GIS
109	Claims on Private Sector	–0.7502	FBMC
110	Intellectual Property Rights Protection	–0.7770	GIS
111	Social Unrest	–0.7778	QLID
112	High Quality Management Staff	–0.7955	FBMC
113	Public Security and Safety	–0.8013	QLID
114	Government Stability	–0.8620	GIS
115	Quality of Police	–0.8869	GIS
116	Tax Burden	–0.9718	GIS
117	Religious Unrest	–0.9726	QLID
118	Political System Risk	–1.0351	GIS
119	Political Change	–1.1641	GIS
120	Daily Organic Water Pollutant Emissions	–1.2375	QLID
121	Primary Schooling	–1.4797	QLID

Source: Asia Competitiveness Institute.

However, Thailand's political instability, which is exacerbated by religious and social unrest (#111 and #117 in Table 2.23), may still pose challenges to its economic recovery and deter investors. It is imperative for Thailand to also tackle its deteriorated fiscal health (#99 and #101).

Vietnam, being the leader among the four transition economies (Cambodia, Laos, Myanmar and Vietnam) in ASEAN has demonstrated its strengths in the provision of public services and infrastructure such as healthcare (#1 in Table 2.24), education (#3), access to water (#12), and ICT (#14). Moreover, the availability of large pool of low-cost workforce (#10, #15 and #16) is another key factor in attracting investors.

In Vietnam, while primary education is being given importance (#3), the quality and availability of secondary education has deteriorated (#119 in Table 2.25). Despite market reforms through

Table 2.24: Top 20% Strongest Indicators List for Vietnam, 2015

Rank	20% Strongest Indicator	Score	Environment
1	Health Expenditure	1.9484	QLID
2	Money Supply (M2)	1.4129	GIS
3	Primary Schooling	1.1805	QLID
4	Domestic Credit to Private Sector	0.9848	FBMC
5	Real GDP Growth	0.9433	MS
6	Claims on Private Sector	0.9212	FBMC
7	Domestic Credit Provided by the Financial Sector	0.9131	FBMC
8	Interest Rate Spread	0.8862	GIS
9	Traffic Congestion	0.7952	QLID
10	Cost of Management Staff	0.7825	FBMC
11	Openness to Trade	0.7624	MS
12	Access to Water	0.7540	QLID
13	Exchange Rate Appreciation	0.7484	GIS
14	Information and Communication Technology (ICT) Expenditure	0.7452	QLID
15	Urban Population Growth	0.6937	QLID
16	Regional Competitiveness	0.6485	GIS
17	Cost of Production Labour	0.6371	FBMC
18	Labour Force	0.6311	FBMC
19	Deposit Interest Rate	0.5615	GIS
20	Cellular Mobile Telephone Subscribers	0.4982	QLID
21	Lending Rate	0.4400	GIS
22	International Monetary Fund Credit	0.4164	GIS
23	Literacy Rate	0.3913	QLID
24	Inflation	0.3896	MS

Source: Asia Competitiveness Institute.

Table 2.25: Top 20% Weakest Indicators List for Vietnam, 2015

Rank	20% Weakest Indicator	Score	Environment
98	Local Road System	–0.6621	QLID
99	Institutional Sophistication	–0.6975	GIS
100	Market Capitalisation	–0.7009	FBMC
101	Government Responsiveness	–0.7357	GIS
102	Labour Market Rating	–0.7639	FBMC
103	Labour Activism	–0.7660	QLID
104	Daily Organic Water Pollutant Emissions	–0.7709	QLID
105	Barriers to Trade	–0.7802	GIS
106	Air Quality	–0.7806	QLID
107	Bureaucracy/Red Tape	–0.7946	GIS
108	Strength of Auditing and Reporting Standards	–0.8095	GIS
109	High Quality Management Staff	–0.8133	FBMC
110	Urban Population	–0.8295	QLID
111	Sovereign Debt Risk	–0.8943	FBMC
112	Lack of Market Distortion due to State-Ownership	–0.9045	GIS
113	Government Environmental Protection Policies	–0.9248	GIS
114	Labour Unrest	–0.9340	QLID
115	Corporate Income Tax	–1.0110	MS
116	Government Consumption Expenditure	–1.1924	GIS
117	Freedom of Speech	–1.2405	QLID
118	Corporate Governance	–1.3179	GIS
119	Secondary Schooling	–1.3982	QLID
120	Tax Burden	–1.7142	GIS
121	Freedom of Press	–1.9875	QLID

Source: Asia Competitiveness Institute.

the *Doi Moi* (renovation) policy that has been implemented since 1986, inertia as a result of a centrally planned economy and the dominance of an inefficient state sector continues to prevail (#113 in Table 2.25). Low government responsiveness and high levels of red-tape/bureaucracy (#101 and #107) further add to this. Another point to note is that economic development in Vietnam seems to come at the expense of the environment (#104, #106 and #113).

2.3.7.2 *Median Competitiveness Web Analysis*

As another instructive roadmap for policy-makers, the spider web charts are employed to show how competitive individual ASEAN economies are in each of the 12 sub-environments relative to the ASEAN-10 median and the ASEAN-10 maximum.

As shown in Figure 2.32, Brunei's Institutions, Governance and Leadership, Standard of Living, Education and Social Stability, and in particular, Productivity Performance, exceed the ASEAN-10 median by a large margin. This also indicates the important role of Brunei's productivity level in spurring competitiveness. Nonetheless, Brunei lags behind the regional median in other areas such as Labour Market Flexibility, and Financial Deepening and Business Efficiency, hence implying the need for more improvement in these two aspects. In addition, the prominent oil supplier's proximate position to the median level for Openness to Trade and Services, and Government Polices and Fiscal Sustainability calls for more attention in order to prevent Brunei from falling below the median.

Cambodia's performance in all 12 sub-environments are below the regional median (Figure 2.33). Physical Infrastructure and Economic Vibrancy are particularly of great concern since they are farthest away from the median scores. Fortunately, the lack of Physical

Figure 2.32: Median Competitiveness Web Analysis for Brunei, 2015

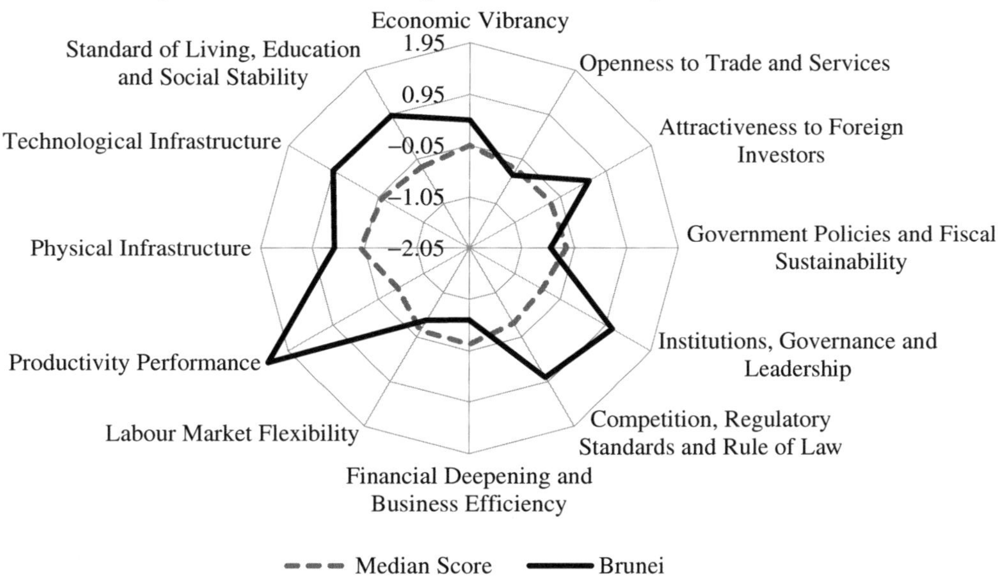

Source: Asia Competitiveness Institute.

Figure 2.33: Median Competitiveness Web Analysis for Cambodia, 2015

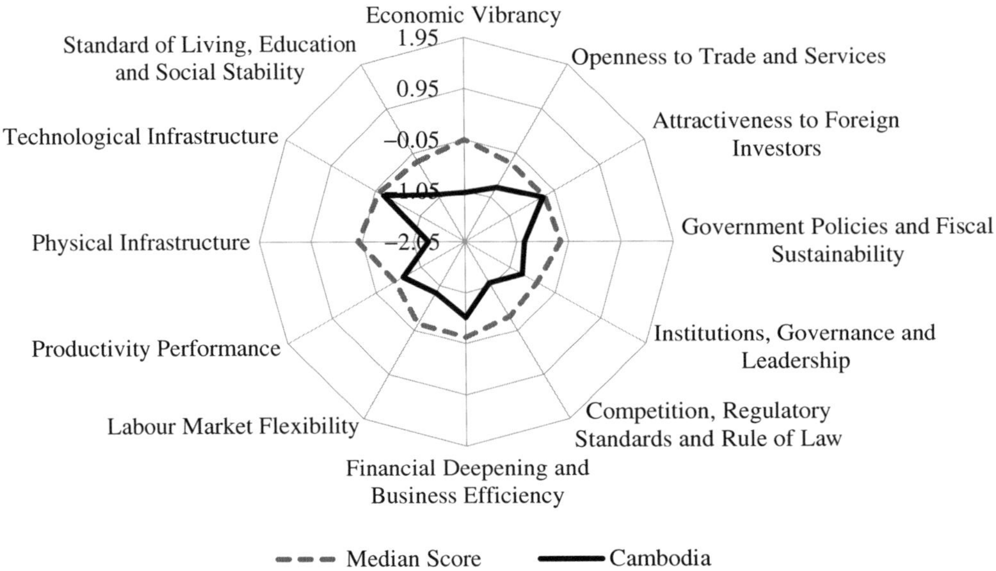

Source: Asia Competitiveness Institute.

Infrastructure seems to be complemented by moderate Technological Infrastructure which is close to the median level. The relatively poor institutional capacity as illustrated in the web analysis below, however, does not seem to deter foreign investors from investing in Cambodia given the proximity of Attractiveness to Foreign Investors to the median score.

Being a country with the largest population in ASEAN, Indonesia has performed remarkably well for Economic Vibrancy and Labour Market Flexibility as reflected in the well-above median scores in Figure 2.34. For most of the remaining sub-environments, Indonesia performs at a satisfactory level as the scores lie close to the ASEAN-10 median. In order to make a significant leap in the region, more efforts are needed especially in terms of Technological Infrastructure, and Government Policies and Fiscal Sustainability, which are below the regional median.

Laos, albeit remaining far below other ASEAN members in majority of the sub-environments, has shown some heartening performance in terms of Attractiveness to Foreign Investors, Competition, Regulatory Standards and Rule of Law, and Productivity Performance, of which the scores for these three aspects lie closely to the regional median scores. Meanwhile, the sub-environments of Openness to Trade and Services, and Government Policies and Fiscal Sustainability which have the lowest scores among all sub-environments highlight the need to intensify trade liberalisation and to improve fiscal capacity so as to bring Laos on par with the regional median (Figure 2.35).

Figure 2.34: Median Competitiveness Web Analysis for Indonesia, 2015

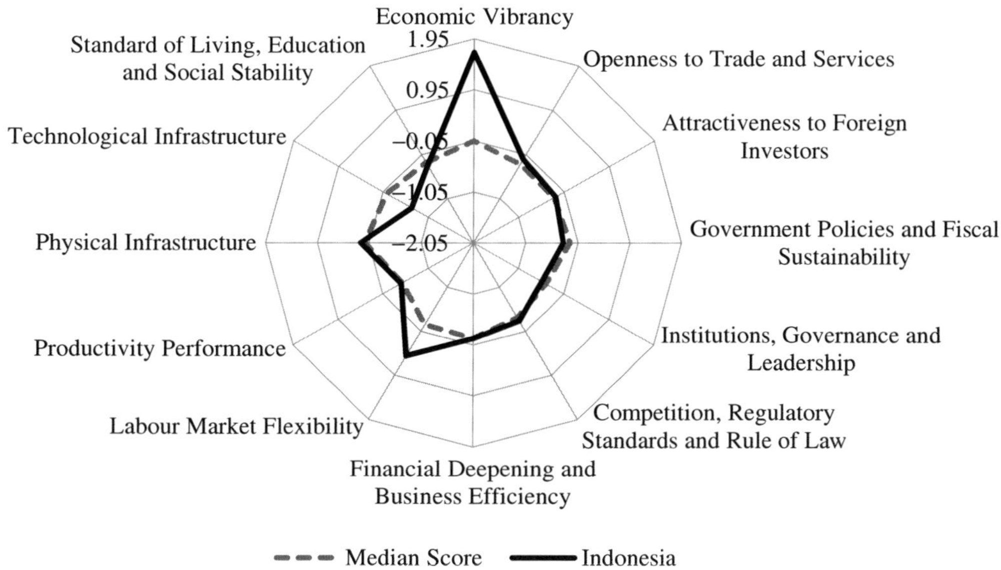

Source: Asia Competitiveness Institute.

Figure 2.35: Median Competitiveness Web Analysis for Laos, 2015

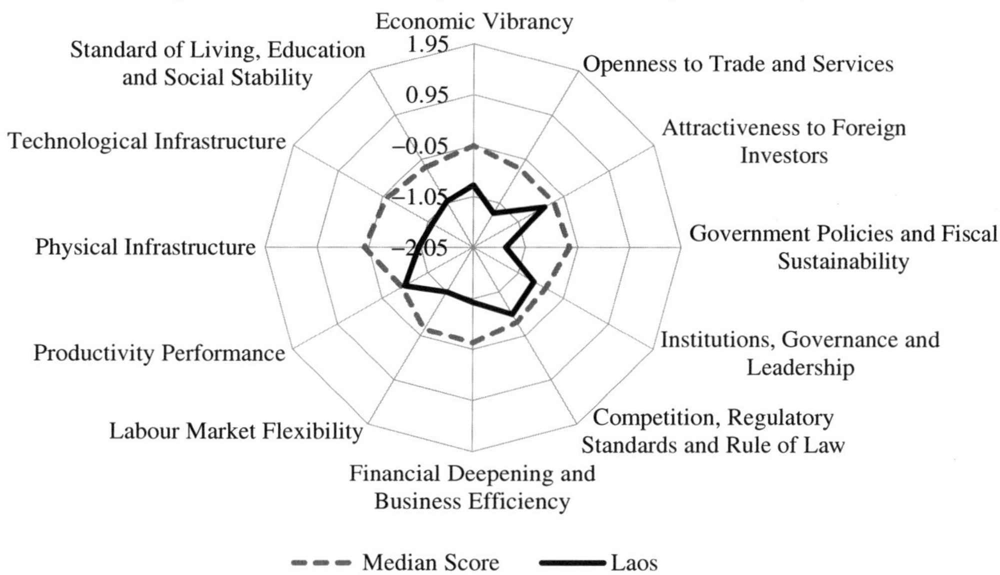

Source: Asia Competitiveness Institute.

Figure 2.36: Median Competitiveness Web Analysis for Malaysia, 2015

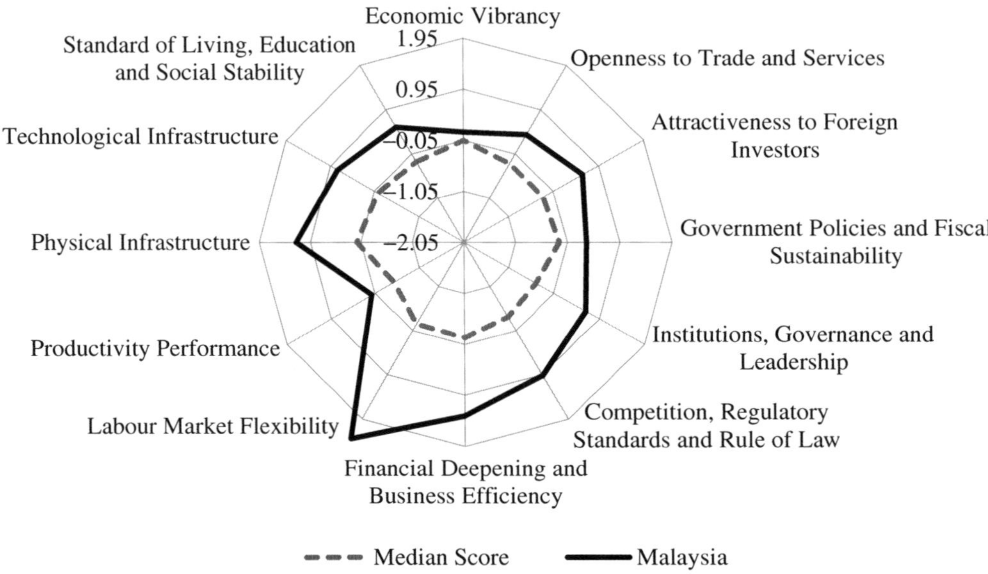

Source: Asia Competitiveness Institute.

Standing as the second most competitive country in ASEAN, Malaysia has exceeded the ASEAN-10 median for all sub-environments as depicted in Figure 2.36. Labour Market Flexibility stands out among all as it exceeds the median score by the largest margin. This is aligned with its top rank in that particular sub-environment. While the existing strengths in Competition, Regulatory Standards and Rule of Law, and Financial Deepening and Business Efficiency have placed Malaysia far ahead of the regional medians, areas such as Productivity Performance, and Standard of Living, Education and Social Stability should not be overlooked to further boost Malaysia's competitiveness level.

As expected, Myanmar, the lowest ranked country in overall competitiveness, scores below median level for all sub-environments as illustrated in Figure 2.37. Among all, Productivity Performance shows some extent of potential in catching up with the regional median, while Standard of Living, Education and Social Stability lies below the median score by the largest margin. Concerted efforts in improving multiple aspects is essential to increase the competitiveness of Myanmar and hence to narrow the score gap between each sub-environment and the regional median.

Figure 2.38 shows that the Philippines has performed strongly in terms of Government Policies and Fiscal Sustainability, and Standard of Living, Education and Social Stability at which the scores exceed the regional median by the largest margin. Despite this, it lags behind its regional peers in most sub-environments, particularly Openness to Trade and Services, and Physical Infrastructure which have the lowest scores. The Philippines should leverage on its

Figure 2.37: Median Competitiveness Web Analysis for Myanmar, 2015

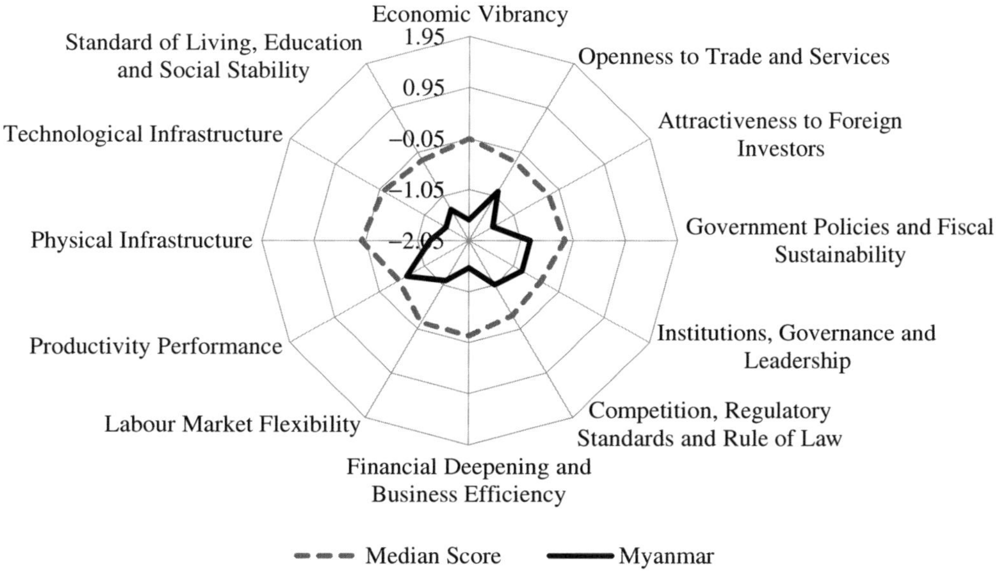

Source: Asia Competitiveness Institute.

Figure 2.38: Median Competitiveness Web Analysis for Philippines, 2015

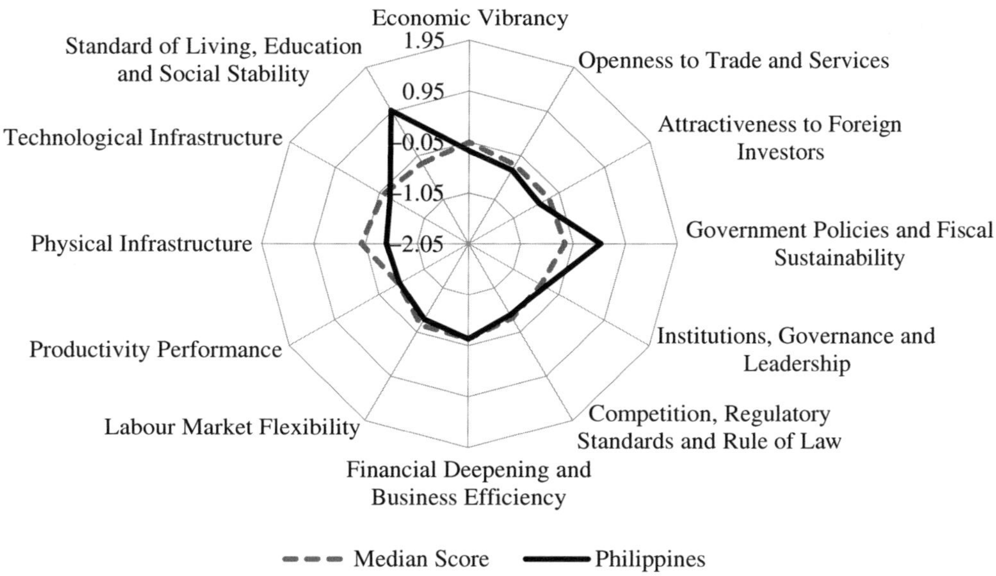

Source: Asia Competitiveness Institute.

Figure 2.39: Median Competitiveness Web Analysis for Singapore, 2015

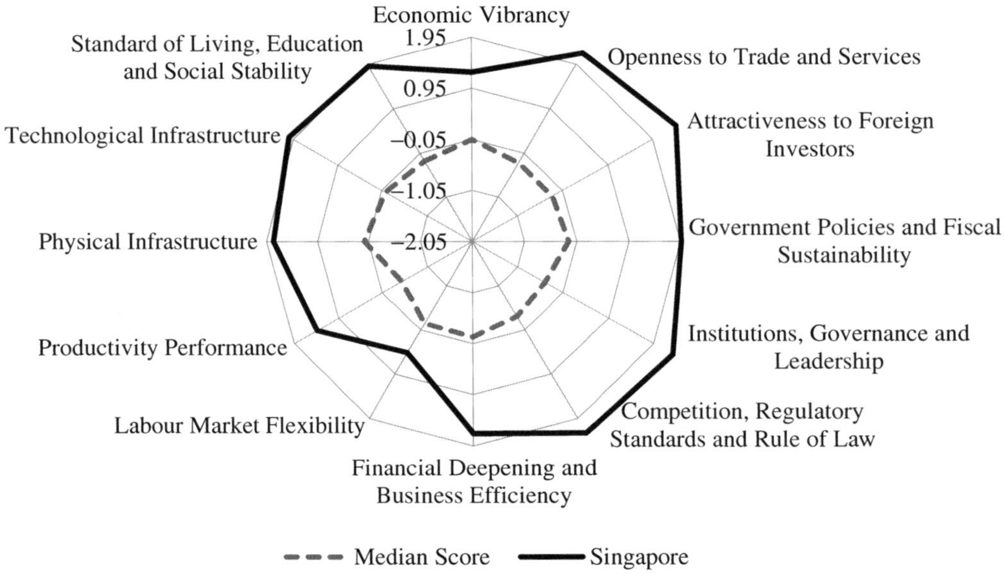

Source: Asia Competitiveness Institute.

strengths in fiscal capacity as well as social development in making significant strides in other dimensions including infrastructural development, Economic Vibrancy, and Attractiveness to Foreign Investors.

In line with its outstanding ranking in Overall Competitiveness throughout the study period of 2000–2015, Figure 2.39 depicts significant gaps between Singapore's scores and ASEAN-10 medians in all sub-environments except for Labour Market Flexibility. Singapore's weakest performance in the Labour Market Flexibility sub-environment should serve as a nudge to policy-makers to put more focus in this particular area, so as to retain Singapore's position as a regional champion, particularly against the backdrop of rising global uncertainties.

Standing at the third place after Singapore and Malaysia, Thailand lies well above ASEAN-10 median in most sub-environments. The sub-environments of Institutions, Governance and Leadership; Competition, Regulatory Standards and Rule of Law; Standard of Living, Education and Social Stability (Figure 2.40) coincide with the median scores. This indicates some room for improvement in these areas and should be prioritised by policy-makers in order to lift the overall competitiveness level of Thailand.

The performance of Vietnam relative to ASEAN-10 median is rather mixed (Figure 2.41). On one hand, the scores of the transitional economy exceed the regional median, albeit by a small margin in terms of Openness to Trade and Services, Government Policies and Fiscal Sustainability, Labour Market Flexibility, Financial Deepening and Business Efficiency and Technological Infrastructure. On the other hand, Vietnam lies below the median level for the remaining sub-environments except Physical Infrastructure, which coincides with the median score. More improvement in these areas is paramount to fuel further reform in Vietnam.

Figure 2.40: Median Competitiveness Web Analysis for Thailand, 2015

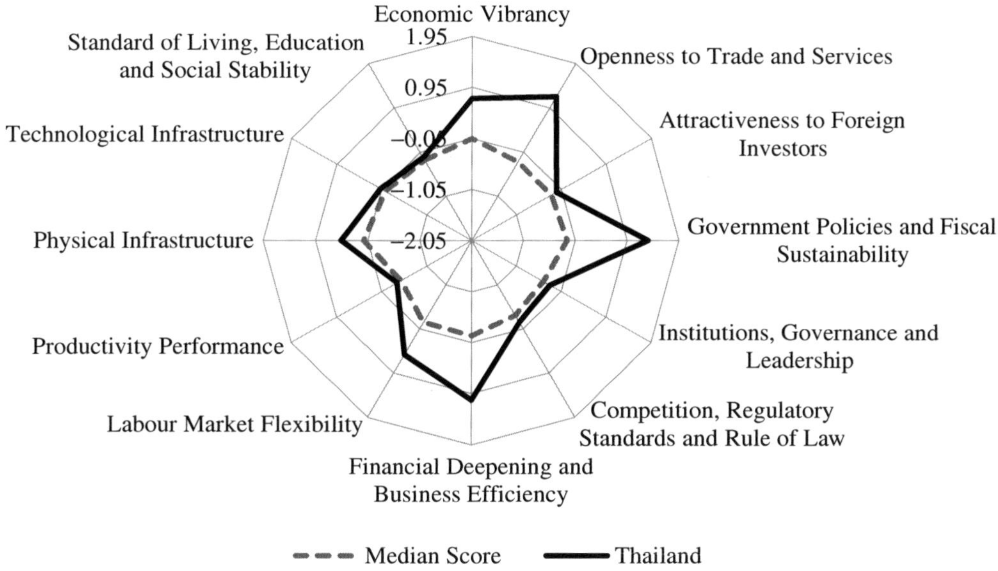

Source: Asia Competitiveness Institute.

Figure 2.41: Median Competitiveness Web Analysis for Vietnam, 2015

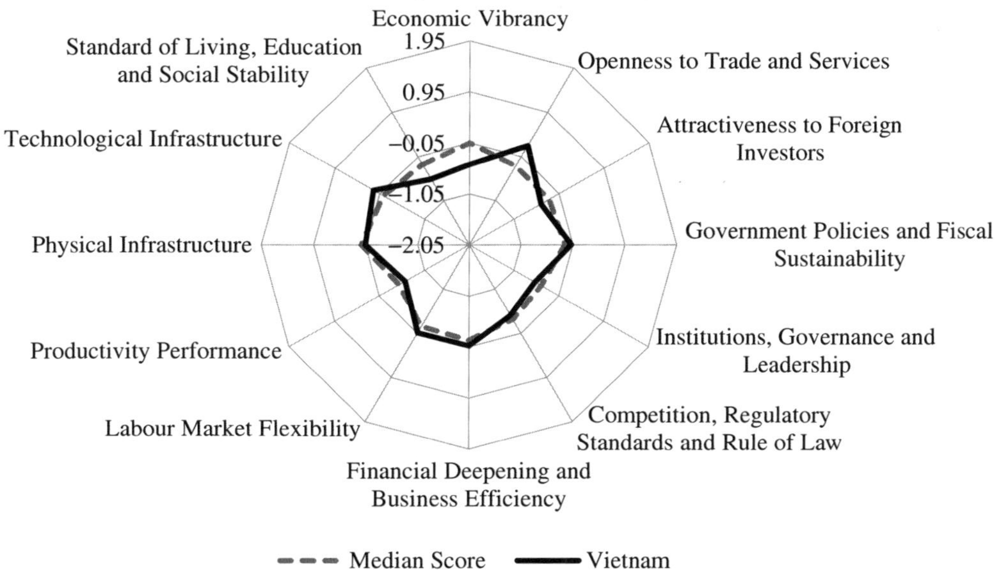

Source: Asia Competitiveness Institute.

2.3.7.3 Maximum Competitiveness Web Analysis

Maximum competitiveness web analysis presented in this sector reveals how far individual ASEAN economies are from the highest scores for each of the 12 sub-environments in the region.

As shown in Figure 2.42, Brunei has set a high standard in the region in terms of Productivity Performance. Nonetheless, more needs to be done for the oil-dependent nation in multiple aspects of competitiveness, particularly Openness to Trade and Services, Government Policies and Fiscal Sustainability, and Labour Market Flexibility, which fall far below the regional maximum.

Figure 2.43 illustrates the significant gaps between Cambodia and ASEAN maximum in all sub-environments. In view of resource and capacity constraints, the policy-makers may prioritise improvement in terms of Physical Infrastructure which scored the lowest among all, followed

Figure 2.42: Maximum Competitiveness Web Analysis for Brunei, 2015

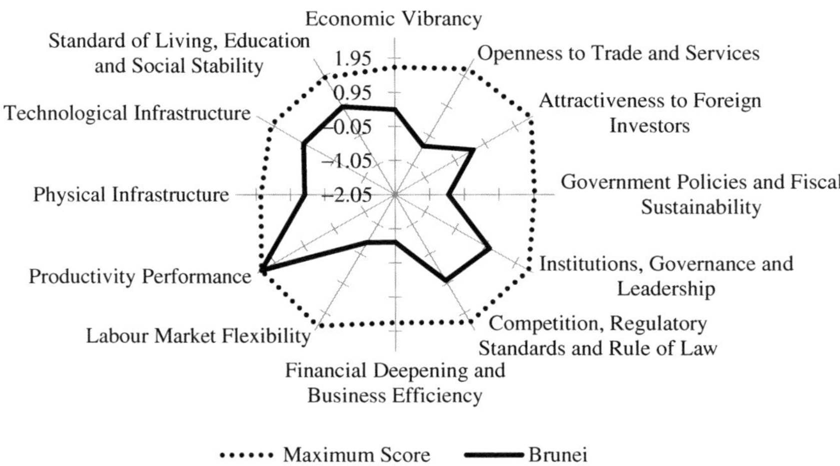

Source: Asia Competitiveness Institute.

Figure 2.43: Maximum Competitiveness Web Analysis for Cambodia, 2015

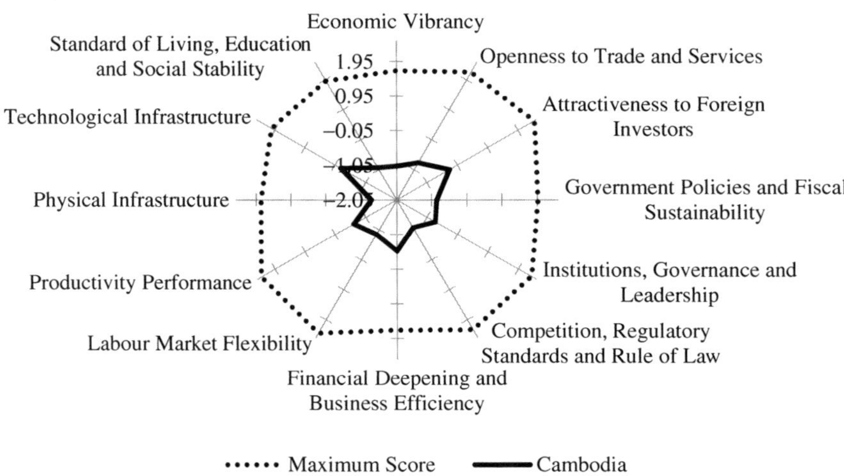

Source: Asia Competitiveness Institute.

closely by Economic Vibrancy and Competition, Regulatory Standards and Rule of Law. This, in turn may generate spill-over effects in stimulating foreign investments and upgrading standard of living in Cambodia.

Indonesia has demonstrated that it is on par with the regional top performer in the sub-environment of Economic Vibrancy (Figure 2.44). Besides that, Labour Market Flexibility and Physical Infrastructure also register positive outlook with smaller gap from the ASEAN maximum. However, more needs to be done in catching up with the regional champions in the rest of the sub-environments.

As shown in Figure 2.45, Laos unsurprisingly remains below the ASEAN maximum in all sub-environments given its weak ranking in the overall competitiveness throughout the study period. However, smaller gaps between the regional maximum and Attractiveness to Foreign

Figure 2.44: Maximum Competitiveness Web Analysis for Indonesia, 2015

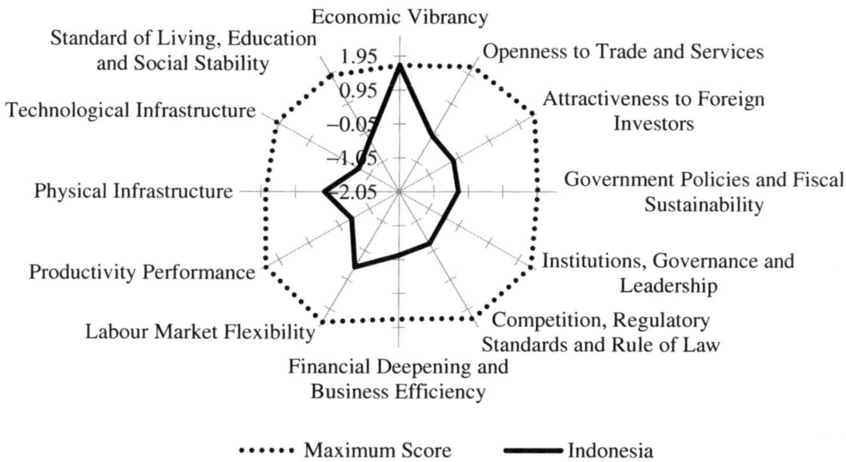

Source: Asia Competitiveness Institute.

Figure 2.45: Maximum Competitiveness Web Analysis for Laos, 2015

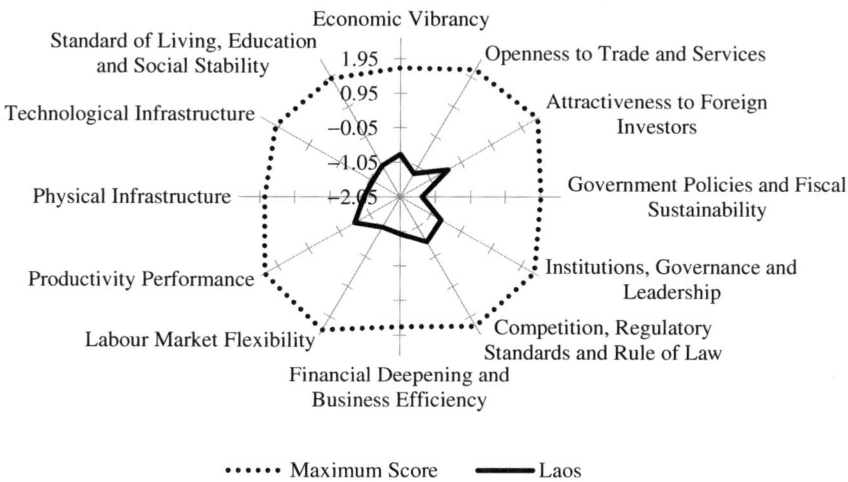

Source: Asia Competitiveness Institute.

Investors, and Competition, Regulatory Standards and Rule of Law provide grounds for hope for Laos to catch up with its peers in the region.

Malaysia (Figure 2.46), the second most competitive economy in ASEAN, has set the regional maximum for Labour Market Flexibility. Nevertheless, it remains below regional maximum for the majority of the remaining sub-environments. The largest gap between the score and median can be found in the sub-environment of Productivity Performance. Hence, improving productivity on the back of sound macroeconomic stability can be a good starting point for the country to catch up with Singapore.

Myanmar (Figure 2.47) lags far behind the ASEAN maximum for all sub-environments. Opening up the economy as well as promoting good governance should come in tandem in order to improve the country's Attractive to Foreign Investors and Competition, Regulatory Standards and Rule of

Figure 2.46: Maximum Competitiveness Web Analysis for Malaysia, 2015

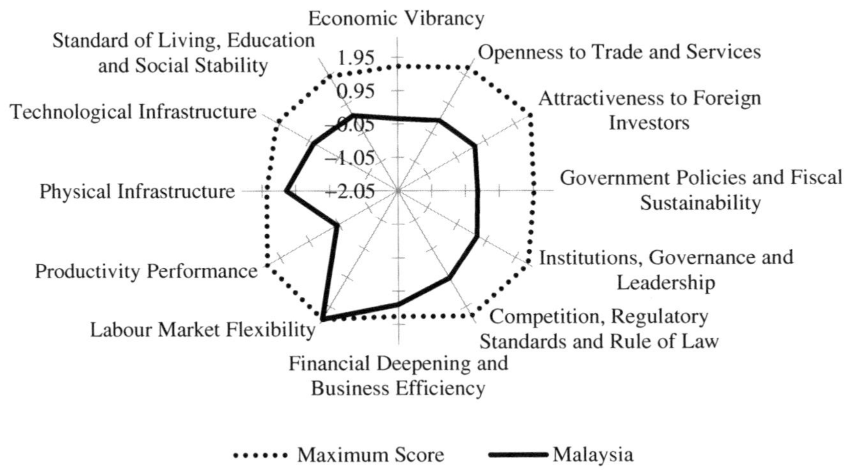

Source: Asia Competitiveness Institute.

Figure 2.47: Maximum Competitiveness Web Analysis for Myanmar, 2015

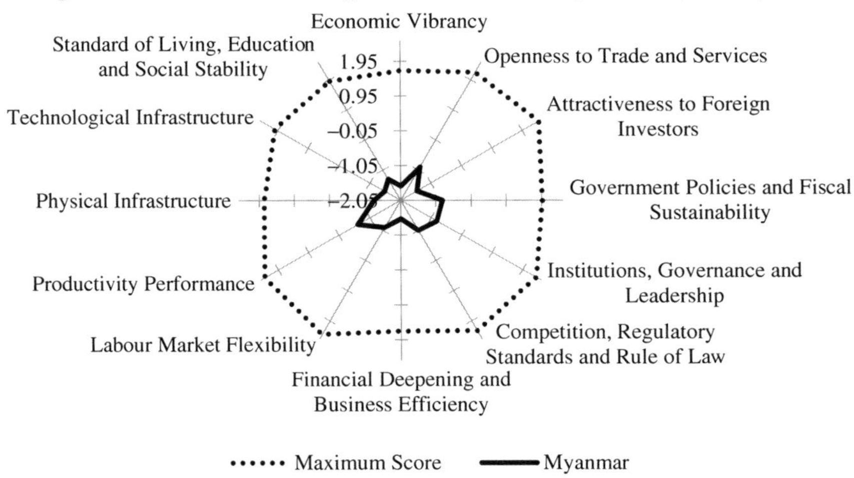

Source: Asia Competitiveness Institute.

Law. Financial Deepening and Business Efficiency, Labour Market Flexibility, and Technological Infrastructure are also important elements in fostering a favourable business environment.

Philippines (Figure 2.48) falls far behind the regional maximum for all sub-environments. Sub-environments of Openness to Trade and Services, Attractiveness to Foreign Investors, and Productivity Performance, in particular, have the largest gaps with the maximum scores. Reforms in these sub-environments are essential against the backdrop of an increasingly integrated market. Infrastructural development should also be included in the policy agenda to support the reforms.

Being the top performer in the region, Singapore has set high benchmarks in the majority of sub-environments as illustrated in Figure 2.49. Nonetheless, it has lost domination in Labour Market Flexibility and Productivity Performance. With growing competition, especially from Malaysia and Brunei in these two sub-environments, Singapore needs to expedite its reform in

Figure 2.48: Maximum Competitiveness Web Analysis for Philippines, 2015

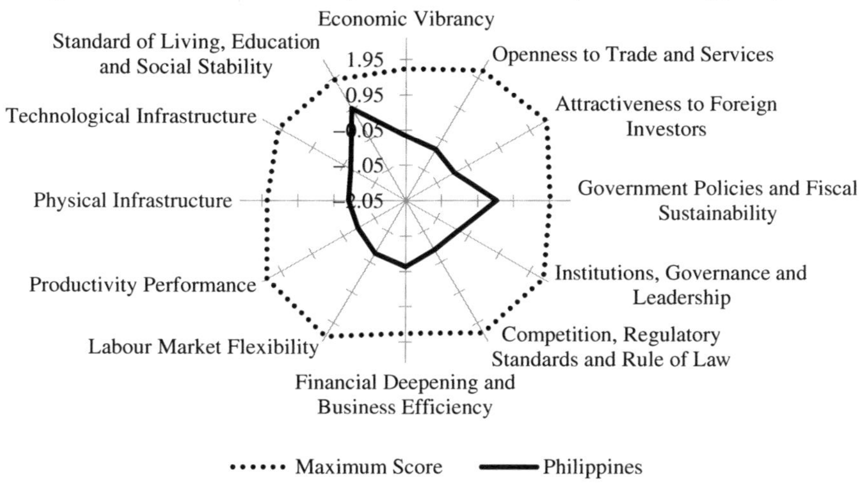

Source: Asia Competitiveness Institute.

Figure 2.49: Maximum Competitiveness Web Analysis for Singapore, 2015

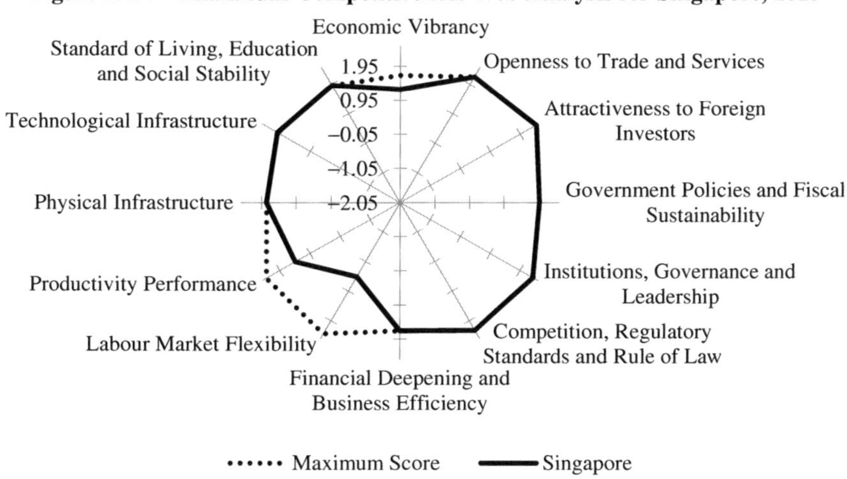

Source: Asia Competitiveness Institute.

the labour market as well as its transformation to a knowledge economy in order to retain its top position in the region.

Despite lying below ASEAN-10 maximum for all sub-environments (Figure 2.50), the performance of Thailand shows some encouraging signs in terms of Government Policies and Fiscal Sustainability, Openness to Trade and Services as well as Financial Deepening and Business Efficiency. Nevertheless, evident gaps with the regional maximum in Institutions, Governance and Leadership, Attractiveness to Foreign Investors and Competition, Regulatory Standards and Rule of Law call for more heed in order to restore confidence levels in Thailand's institutional capacity.

Figure 2.51 shows that Vietnam lies below the regional maximum in all 12 sub-environments with the smallest gaps in terms of Openness to Trade and Services, Government Policies and

Figure 2.50: Maximum Competitiveness Web Analysis for Thailand, 2015

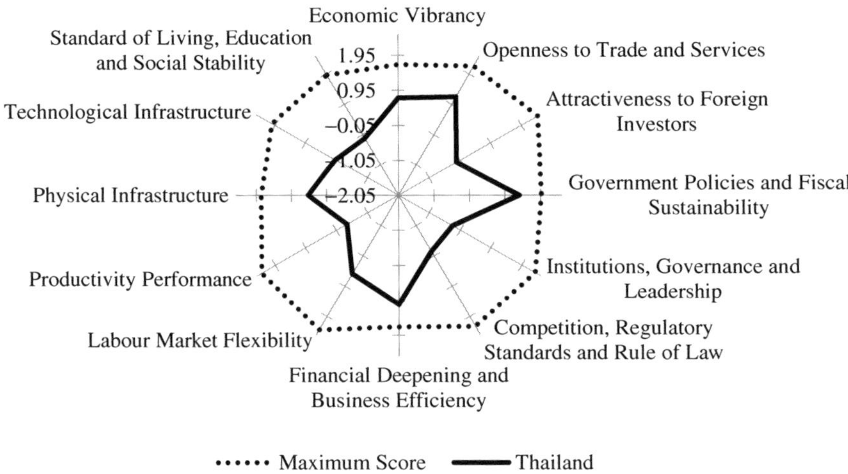

Source: Asia Competitiveness Institute.

Figure 2.51: Maximum Competitiveness Web Analysis for Vietnam, 2015

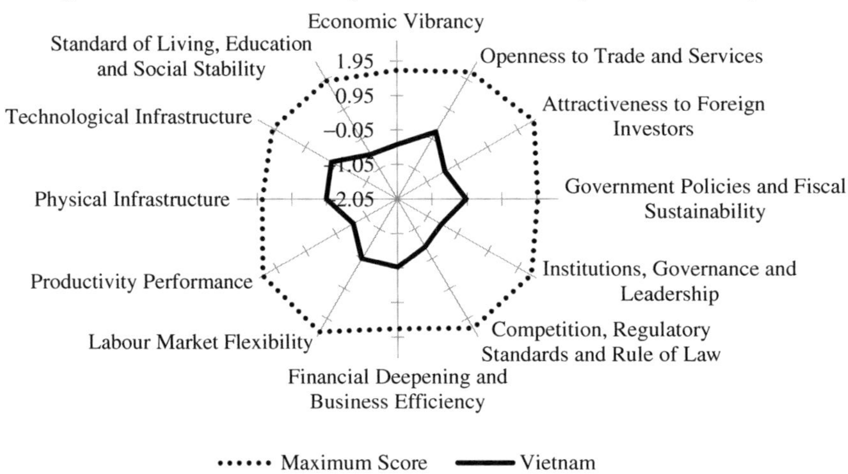

Source: Asia Competitiveness Institute.

Fiscal Sustainability, Labour Market Flexibility, Financial Deepening and Business Efficiency and Technological Infrastructure. As the rapid emergence of other transition economies including Cambodia, Laos and Myanmar pose new challenges and competition to the country, it is important to expedite its catching up process, particularly for its Attractiveness to Foreign Investors and Productivity Performance.

2.3.8 Upgrading Competitiveness through *What-if* Simulation Analysis

This section lays out the *What-if* simulation analysis as detailed in the methodology discussion in Section 2.2.5. The simulation analysis is conducted for Overall Competitiveness as well as each environment. The comparison of standardised scores and rankings of individual ASEAN-10 economies before and after simulation is shown in Tables 2.26–2.30.

Table 2.26 illustrates the simulation analysis for Overall Competitiveness in ASEAN. After simulation, most of the ASEAN states show an improvement in rankings, with the exception of Singapore, Malaysia and Cambodia. While the rankings of these economies stay consistent at the first, second and eighth places, respectively, they still experience an increase in scores. For example, despite Cambodia's ranking staying consistent at eighth place its score has jumped to –0.5445 as compared to its previous score of –0.9415. On the other hand, with a score advancement of 0.5835 and a leap from the last position to the eighth, Myanmar demonstrates the largest improvement out of all 10 ASEAN member states. Vietnam also shows considerable advancement, rising from seventh place to become the fifth, while all other economies improve by one rank after having the top 20% of their weakest indicators raised to the regional average level.

Table 2.27 showcases the results of the simulation on the Macroeconomic Stability environment. Brunei and Myanmar improve the most, increasing their rankings by two spots, while the rankings of Cambodia, Singapore, Thailand and Vietnam remain the same. However, they still

Table 2.26: *What-if* Competitiveness Simulation Analysis on Overall Competitiveness, 2015

	Rank		Score	
Economy	**Before**	**After**	**Before**	**After**
Brunei	3	2	0.5575	1.0288
Cambodia	8	8	–0.9415	–0.5445
Indonesia	5	5	–0.0762	0.3286
Laos	9	8	–1.0694	–0.5957
Malaysia	2	2	0.9387	1.1286
Myanmar	10	8	–1.4050	–0.8215
Philippines	6	5	–0.2256	0.1082
Singapore	1	1	2.1179	2.3072
Thailand	4	3	0.4099	0.6119
Vietnam	7	5	–0.3062	–0.0129

Source: Asia Competitiveness Institute.

Table 2.27: *What-if* Competitiveness Simulation Analysis on Macroeconomic Stability, 2015

	Rank		Score	
Economy	**Before**	**After**	**Before**	**After**
Brunei	5	3	0.2266	0.5602
Cambodia	8	8	–0.8246	–0.5833
Indonesia	3	2	0.4801	0.6490
Laos	9	8	–0.9608	–0.6689
Malaysia	4	3	0.4100	0.5888
Myanmar	10	8	–1.5327	–0.8373
Philippines	7	6	–0.4030	–0.1083
Singapore	1	1	2.2193	2.2790
Thailand	2	2	0.6595	0.7248
Vietnam	6	6	–0.2743	–0.2171

Source: Asia Competitiveness Institute.

Table 2.28: *What-if* Competitiveness Simulation Analysis on Government and Institutional Setting, 2015

	Rank		Score	
Economy	**Before**	**After**	**Before**	**After**
Brunei	3	2	0.5216	0.9921
Cambodia	10	8	–1.0157	–0.6124
Indonesia	7	5	–0.4209	0.1766
Laos	8	7	–0.9697	–0.4456
Malaysia	2	2	0.7034	1.0720
Myanmar	9	8	–1.0117	–0.5644
Philippines	5	5	–0.1135	0.1423
Singapore	1	1	2.4055	2.4588
Thailand	4	2	0.3084	0.6510
Vietnam	6	5	–0.4074	–0.0393

Source: Asia Competitiveness Institute.

experience an increase in scores. The rest of the ASEAN economies' rankings move up by one spot after the simulation.

For Government and Institutional Setting in Table 2.28, Cambodia, Indonesia and Thailand show the biggest improvement after the simulation and increase their positions by two ranks. Singapore, Malaysia and the Philippines retain their spots as the first, second and fifth economies, respectively, but experience an increase in scores, while the other ASEAN member states increase their ranks by one place.

Table 2.29: *What-if* Competitiveness Simulation Analysis on Financial, Businesses and Manpower Conditions, 2015

	Rank		Score	
Economy	**Before**	**After**	**Before**	**After**
Brunei	3	1	0.5646	1.4983
Cambodia	8	8	–0.9089	–0.6989
Indonesia	5	4	–0.0517	0.4780
Laos	9	8	–1.1017	–0.7603
Malaysia	1	1	1.6173	1.7059
Myanmar	10	8	–1.4294	–0.8882
Philippines	7	5	–0.4417	0.0329
Singapore	2	1	1.5518	2.1166
Thailand	4	3	0.5220	0.6847
Vietnam	6	5	–0.3223	0.0321

Source: Asia Competitiveness Institute.

Table 2.30: *What-if* Competitiveness Simulation Analysis on Quality of Life and Infrastructure Development, 2015

	Rank		Score	
Economy	**Before**	**After**	**Before**	**After**
Brunei	3	2	0.8473	0.9172
Cambodia	8	6	–0.8986	–0.2069
Indonesia	7	6	–0.3028	–0.0262
Laos	9	8	–1.1111	–0.4267
Malaysia	2	2	0.9062	1.0174
Myanmar	10	8	–1.4699	–0.8914
Philippines	5	4	0.0842	0.3528
Singapore	1	1	2.0289	2.1845
Thailand	4	4	0.0983	0.3151
Vietnam	6	4	–0.1825	0.1741

Source: Asia Competitiveness Institute.

As seen in Table 2.29, Malaysia and Cambodia experience an increase in scores in the Financial, Businesses and Manpower Conditions, but retain their rankings of first and eighth place, respectively. Brunei, Myanmar and the Philippines advance two spots in their rankings, while the rest of the ASEAN member states move up one rank after the simulation.

Table 2.30 shows the results of the simulation on the Quality of Life and Development environment. Cambodia, Myanmar and Vietnam show the biggest improvements as they move up two places in rankings. As before, Malaysia, Singapore and Thailand retain their rankings but experience an increase in their scores. The rest of the ASEAN member states improve by one rank each post-simulation.

2.4 Shapley Weightage Methodology as Robustness Check

2.4.1 Shapley Value

The Shapley value is the most commonly used solution concept in cooperative game theory. Formally, a coalition game (N, v) in cooperative game theory is defined by a set of players N and a characteristic function $v(S)$: $2^N \rightarrow R$, where it maps coalition S (or subset of players) to a real number. The function describes the expected payoffs the S players can obtain by cooperation. The Shapley value of the coalition game is an n-vector, denoted by $\Phi(v)$, satisfying a set of axioms, i.e. Individual Rationality, Efficiency, Symmetry, Additivity and Null Player.

The i-th component of $\Phi(v)$ can be determined by

$$\Phi(v) = \sum_{S \subseteq N \setminus \{i\}} \frac{|S|!\,\left(N - |S| - 1\right)!}{N!}(v(S \cup i) - v(S)).$$

In this context, the players will be the indicators used for the construction of the index. The coalition will be the sub-environments and environments which the indicators belong to. The desirable properties, i.e. the axioms, are meaningful for general index ranking. Individual Rationality ensures that each indicator has a positive contribution to the index score. An indicator must satisfy the Null Player axiom, so that it is economically meaningful for that indicator to be considered relevant to the index. Symmetry guarantees that if two indicators carry the same value, they are equally important in the index scoring. Efficiency and Additivity are also important mathematical properties for the construction of the index.

The application of Shapley value has been well studied in various strands of literature. The concept has been used to solve the taxation and redistribution problem, as described by Aumann and Kurz (1977). It is also used in voting for public goods problems. Aumann and Myerson (1988), for instance, have studied the link or coalition formation among players using the Shapley value. Moulin (1992) studies the application of the Shapley value in fair division of unproduced goods under monetary transfer and quasi-linear utilities. Petrosjan and Zaccour (2003) study the Shapley value cost allocation in a pollution reduction setting. More recently, Hougaard *et al.* (2017) have applied the Shapley value concept to licensing under FRAND terms.[7] However, the Shapley value has not, to our knowledge, been applied to index ranking analysis before.

As a robustness check to the Equal Weightage approach, we would like to propose an objective weighting method based on Shapley value — the "Bottom-Up" approach.

2.4.2 Shapley Weightage — The "Bottom-Up" Approach

The Shapley value of each indicator is first computed based on the standardised value of the indicator for every economy. By ACI's definition, it measures the aggregate dispersion of the

[7] FRAND is a short notation for Fair Reasonable and Non-Discriminatory.

indicator, thus reflecting the inequality among the cities. More weights are assigned to those indicators with a higher Shapley value. The weights of sub-environments are computed based on both the absolute performance (standardised score) and the relative performance (weights) of indicators under that particular sub-environment. The weights of environments are computed in a similar way by considering the relevant absolute performance and the relative performance of sub-environments. The detailed description of the methodology can be found in Appendix 3.

2.4.3 Comparison between the Shapley Method and the Entropy Method

Yet another objective weight assignment method, commonly applied in the area of decision science, is entropy (Zeleny, 1982). The entropy for the indicator i is defined as

$$Entropy_i = -\frac{1}{\ln(E)}\sum_{e=1}^{E} p_{ei}\ln(p_{ei}),$$

where E is the number of economies, $p_{ei} = \frac{v_{ei}}{\sum_{e=1}^{E} v_{ei}}$ and v_{ei} is the characteristic of the raw data x_{ei}. The weightage of indicator i is, then, defined by

$$W_i = 1 - Entropy_i.$$

The interpretation of the entropy of an indicator concerns the information that the particular indicator transmits. The higher the entropy, the less the information carried, implying a lower weight assigned to that indicator.

While this method appears to be an improvement over a subjective weighting scheme, one of the important reasons why the entropy method cannot be used for ACI's analysis is its inability to handle negative values due to the use of logarithm operator. Thus, the alternative standardisation method, other than *z-score*, is required.

In the report *Assessing Provincial Development under the Five Development Concepts*, Institute of Applied Economics Shanghai Academy of Social Sciences has applied the entropy method to assign weights to indicators. To avoid negative values, they deploy the *max–min standardisation* method, where

$$v_{ei} = \frac{x_{ei} - \min(x_i)}{\max(x_i) - \min(x_i)}.$$

The reason the entropy method is less appropriate than the Shapley method is that when applied to the field of index construction, the former method is very sensitive to indicators containing outliers.

Consider the following example. There are 11 economies and three indicators with different measurement units (see Table 2.31). Indicator 1 contains an outlier. All the economies perform equally in Indicator 2. There is a clear divergence of performance among all the economies in Indicator 3. We will use *z-score* standardisation for the Shapley method and *max–min* standardisation for the entropy method.

Table 2.31: Example to Compare the Shapley and Entropy Weight Methods

Economy	Indicator 1	Indicator 2	Indicator 3
A	10	2	1
B	1	3	2
C	1	2	3
D	1	2	4
E	1	2	5
F	1	2	6
G	1	2	7
H	1	1	8
I	1	2	9
J	1	2	10
K	1	2	11

Source: Asia Competitiveness Institute.

Under the entropy method, the weights of indicators are

$$w_1^{Entropy} = 0.866, \quad w_2^{Entropy} = 0.045, \quad w_3^{Entropy} = 0.089.$$

Due to the presence of an outlier under Indicator 1, i.e. Economy A, the entropy method predicts that Indicator 1 carries the most information, thus assigning it a much higher weight relative to the rest.

Under the Shapley method, the weights of indicators are

$$w_1^{Shapley} = 0.308, \quad w_2^{Shapley} = 0.229, \quad w_3^{Shapley} = 0.463.$$

As observed, similar to the entropy method, the Shapley weights assign a relatively higher weight to Indicator 1 than Indicator 2 because of the presence of the outlier. However, the highest weight is assigned to Indicator 3 because of the dispersion observed, overcoming the bias that the entropy method generates due to its inability to handle outliers.

To summarise the foregoing discussion, the derivation of the final index score must be done with the help of aggregation of all relevant information, implying that all the indicators are the determinants. Important indicators which show that the economies are unequally developed (e.g. Indicator 3) should be reflected upon. However, as noted earlier, the entropy method fails to capture this feature due to the fact that such indicators convey less information than those with an outlier (e.g. Indicator 1). The Shapley method, on the other hand, offers a better alternative as it captures both the fact that economies are most unequally developed under Indicator 3 as well as the existence of the outlier in Indicator 1.

2.4.4 Findings based on the Shapley Weightage Methodology

Figure 2.52 shows the weight of each environment in the Overall Competitiveness Index under the Shapely methodology based on data in 2015. As shown, Macroeconomic Stability makes up 24.6% of the overall index; Government and Institutional Setting 24.4%; Financial, Businesses and Manpower Conditions 26.4%; and finally, Quality of Life and Infrastructure Development 24.5%.

The Shapley Weightage of an environment measures the degree of unequal development among the economies in that particular environment: the more divergent the performances of the economies, the higher the Shapley weight. Hence, seeing as how the Shapley weight for the Financial, Businesses and Manpower Conditions environment was the greatest, this was where ASEAN member states differed from each other the most in 2015. Further, at a more nuanced level, an economy will receive a higher score under the Shapley Weightage methodology if it performs well in an environment where there is higher inequality across all assessed economies. This adds another layer of sophistication as compared to the Equal Weightage methodology.

However, the newly calculated 2015 Shapley weights are not significantly different from the equal weightage of 25%. Mathematically, there are two possible reasons that can account for this phenomenon. The first is that every surveyed economy has become equally developed in all aspects — across all indicators, all sub-environments, and thus, all environments. But as regional inequality still exists deeply within the ASEAN region, this is clearly not the case in reality. Therefore, we can turn to the second explanation, which is that the aggregate dispersion, i.e. the Shapley value, of each indicator, sub-environment, and hence environment, for all the

Figure 2.52: Weight for Each Environment by the Shapley Weightage Methodology

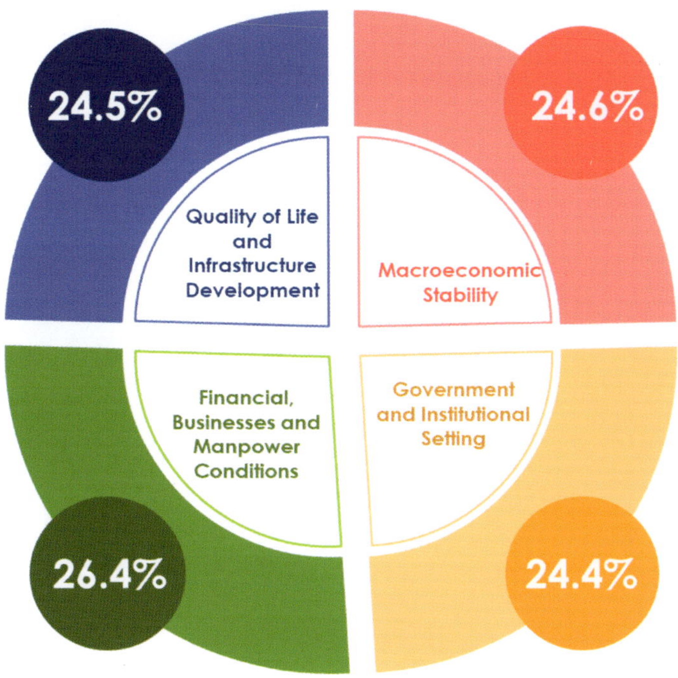

Source: Asia Competitiveness Institute.

economies, is rather similar across all indicators. In other words, the frontrunner economies excel while the less-developed economies lag behind for majority of the indicators. Hence, notwithstanding these nuances in the underlying explanations for the observed results, it is safe to say that the original results based on equal weightage are robust. Tables 2.32–2.36 show that ranking and index results derived from the equal weightage and Shapley Weightage

Table 2.32: Comparison of Ranking and Index Results between Equal Weightage and Shapley Weightage Methodologies — Overall Competitiveness in 2015

Economy	Equal Weightage-Based Ranking	Shapley Weightage-Based Ranking	Equal Weightage-Based Score	Shapley Weightage-Based Score
Singapore	1	1	2.1179	2.1114
Malaysia	2	2	0.9387	0.9414
Brunei	3	3	0.5575	0.5782
Thailand	4	4	0.4099	0.4161
Indonesia	5	5	–0.0762	–0.1056
Philippines	6	6	–0.2256	–0.2172
Vietnam	7	7	–0.3062	–0.3109
Cambodia	8	8	–0.9415	–0.9509
Laos	9	9	–1.0694	–1.0618
Myanmar	10	10	–1.4050	–1.4006

Source: Asia Competitiveness Institute.

Table 2.33: Comparison of Ranking and Index Results between Equal Weightage and Shapley Weightage Methodologies — Macroeconomic Stability in 2015

Economy	Equal Weightage-Based Ranking	Shapley Weightage-Based Ranking	Equal Weightage-Based Score	Shapley Weightage-Based Score
Singapore	1	1	2.2193	2.2039
Thailand	2	2	0.6595	0.6756
Indonesia	3	3	0.4801	0.5006
Malaysia	4	4	0.4100	0.3867
Brunei	5	5	0.2266	0.2489
Vietnam	6	6	–0.2743	–0.2863
Philippines	7	7	–0.4030	–0.3944
Cambodia	8	8	–0.8246	–0.8443
Laos	9	9	–0.9608	–0.9519
Myanmar	10	10	–1.5327	–1.5388

Source: Asia Competitiveness Institute.

Table 2.34: Comparison of Ranking and Index Results between Equal Weightage and Shapley Weightage Methodologies — Government and Institutional Setting in 2015

Economy	Equal Weightage-Based Ranking	Shapley Weightage-Based Ranking	Equal Weightage-Based Score	Shapley Weightage-Based Score
Singapore	1	1	2.4055	2.3754
Malaysia	2	2	0.7034	0.7306
Brunei	3	3	0.5216	0.5504
Thailand	4	4	0.3084	0.3237
Philippines	5	5	–0.1135	–0.1355
Vietnam	6	6	–0.4074	–0.3842
Indonesia	7	7	–0.4209	–0.4287
Laos	8	8	–0.9697	–0.9732
Myanmar	**9**	**10**	**–1.0117**	**–1.0438**
Cambodia	**10**	**9**	**–1.0157**	**–1.0147**

Note: Bold text shows instances where a country's rank based on Equal Weightage methodology is different from that based on Shapley Weightage methodology.
Source: Asia Competitiveness Institute.

Table 2.35: Comparison of Ranking and Index Results between Equal Weightage and Shapley Weightage Methodologies — Financial, Businesses and Manpower Conditions in 2015

Economy	Equal Weightage-Based Ranking	Shapley Weightage-Based Ranking	Equal Weightage-Based Score	Shapley Weightage-Based Score
Malaysia	**1**	**2**	**1.6173**	**1.5890**
Singapore	**2**	**1**	**1.5518**	**1.6152**
Brunei	3	3	0.5646	0.5777
Thailand	4	4	0.5220	0.5145
Indonesia	5	5	–0.0517	–0.1544
Vietnam	6	6	–0.3223	–0.3386
Philippines	7	7	–0.4417	–0.4142
Cambodia	8	8	–0.9089	–0.8998
Laos	9	9	–1.1017	–1.0871
Myanmar	10	10	–1.4294	–1.4023

Note: Bold text shows instances where a country's rank based on Equal Weightage methodology is different from that based on Shapley Weightage methodology.
Source: Asia Competitiveness Institute.

Table 2.36: Comparison of Ranking and Index Results between Equal Weightage and Shapley Weightage Methodologies — Quality of Life and Infrastructure Development in 2015

Economy	Equal Weightage-Based Ranking	Shapley Weightage-Based Ranking	Equal Weightage-Based Score	Shapley Weightage-Based Score
Singapore	1	1	2.0289	2.0286
Malaysia	2	2	0.9062	0.8963
Brunei	3	3	0.8473	0.8659
Thailand	**4**	**5**	**0.0983**	**0.0903**
Philippines	**5**	**4**	**0.0842**	**0.1179**
Vietnam	6	6	−0.1825	−0.1946
Indonesia	7	7	−0.3028	−0.3274
Cambodia	8	8	−0.8986	−0.9322
Laos	9	9	−1.1111	−1.1025
Myanmar	10	10	−1.4699	−1.4423

Note: Bold text shows instances where a country's rank based on Equal Weightage methodology is different from that based on Shapley Weightage methodology.
Source: Asia Competitiveness Institute.

methodologies are largely similar to each other except for minor differences in the last three tables, namely in the environments of Government and Institutional Setting; Financial, Businesses and Manpower Conditions; and Quality of Life and Infrastructure Development.

2.5 Concluding Notes

Generally, there have not been any stark changes to the competitiveness rankings of the ASEAN-10. The Shapley methodology used also solidifies the robustness of this year's results.

In terms of overall competitiveness, rankings still stay the same as last year's. Notably, Singapore and Malaysia have maintained their first and second ranks for the 15th year running. Brunei seems to be doing well in holding on to its position, now for the second consecutive year, as the third economy after overtaking Thailand's spot in 2014. In addition, Myanmar, Laos and Cambodia still rank as the bottom three economies — a phenomenon that has been carried on since 2000.

Moving into the sub-environments and other facets of competitiveness, Malaysia in particular seems to be on a downward trend in terms of macroeconomic stability, going from second place in 2012 to fourth place in 2015. Thailand and Indonesia now rank second and third, respectively. Again, Cambodia, Laos and Myanmar make up the bottom three economies.

While little movement has been made in the environment of government and institutional settings, Malaysia has overtaken Singapore for the second year running to clinch the top place in the environment assessing financial, businesses and manpower conditions. Brunei and Vietnam also move up in this environment to become the third and sixth economies, respectively. Yet again, Cambodia, Laos and Myanmar come in as the bottom three.

In the last environment analysing quality of life, rankings also stay similar, with Singapore coming in the first and Malaysia and Brunei having fluctuating rankings between themselves as they vie for second and third places, respectively. Unsurprisingly, Cambodia, Laos and Myanmar rank as the bottom three countries again.

An extremely apparent development divide is highlighted through the trend of the same few countries consistently making up the top and the bottom of the rankings. This issue must be urgently addressed in order to solidify the region's growth as a whole.

The section on each country's 20% strongest and weakest indicators thus presents an important takeaway. This is because, on the individual level, it can be utilised to directly assess how the ASEAN member countries can improve domestically. Regionally, it allows for the ASEAN-10 to adopt a sustainable growth approach that leverages on all their strengths and works on their weaknesses. They can thus work towards achieving the results released in the *What-if* policy simulation, and unleash the region's full potential.

References

Aumann, Robert J., and Mordecai Kurz. 1977. "Power and Taxes". *Econometrica*: *Journal of the Econometric Society*: 1137–1161.

Aumann, Robert J., and Roger Myerson. 1988. "Endogenous formation of links between players and coalitions: an application of the Shapley value". *The Shapley Value*: 175–191.

Bristow, Gillian. 2010. Critical Reflections on Regional Competitiveness: Theory, Policy, Practice (Routledge Studies in Human Geography). Oxon: Routledge.

Camagni, Roberto. 2002. "On the Concept of Territorial Competitiveness: Sound or Misleading?" *Urban Studies* 39 (13): 2395–2411.

Hougaard, Jens Leth, Chiu Yu Ko, and Xuyao Zhang. 2017. "A Welfare Economic Interpretation of FRAND". *IFRO Working Paper*. University of Copenhagen, Department of Food and Resource Economics.

IMD World Competitiveness Center. 2014. IMD World Competitiveness Yearbook. Lausanne: International Institute for Management Development.

Institute of Applied Economics Shanghai Academy of Social Sciences. 2016. "五大发展理念指标体系及省级区域评估报告 Assessing Provincial Development under the Five Development Concepts (in Chinese)". Shanghai Academy of Social Sciences.

Kitson, Michael, Ronald Martin, and Peter Tyler. 2004. "Regional Competitiveness: An Elusive yet Key Concept?" *Regional Studies* 38 (9): 991–999.

Krugman, Paul. 1994. "Competitiveness: A Dangerous Obsession". *Foreign Affairs* 73 (2): 28–44.

Moulin, Hervé. 1992. "An Application of the Shapley Value to Fair Division with Money". *Econometrica*: *Journal of the Econometric Society*: 1331–1349.

Petrosjan, Leon, and Georges Zaccour. 2003. "Time-Consistent Shapley Value Allocation of Pollution Cost Reduction". *Journal of Economic Dynamics and Control* 27 (3): 381–398.

Porter, Michael E. 1980. *Competitive Strategy*: *Techniques for Analyzing Industries and Competitors*. New York: Free Press.

World Economic Forum. 2014. *Global Competitiveness Report 2013–2014*. Geneva: World Economic Forum.

Zeleny, Milan. 1982. *Multiple Criteria Decision Making*. New York: McGraw-Hill.

Discussant Notes 2.1

Tan Sri Rastam Mohd Isa

Chairman and Chief Executive,
Institute of Strategic and International Studies (ISIS), Malaysia

Thank you very much. First of all, congratulations to Professor Tan Khee Giap for another successful study. I remember talking about this I think two years ago, making almost similar comments. Now, looking at both studies, there are some key takeaways from there that I think we can look at. One, of course, the first presentation has captured a wide range of parameters affecting the ASEAN member states' competitiveness, largely in the four main indicators. I do not have to go through them, really.

So if we look at the other one, of course it provides an in-depth analysis of particular sub indicators, particularly exchange rates and trade performances, and the findings which suggest that policies in managing exchange rates volatility is also crucial for export oriented economies, which in turn also affects overall competitiveness.

Now, if we look at ASEAN competitiveness, we know that, as has been said, ASEAN is a major global economy — if taken as a whole — 630 million people, 2.4–2.5 trillion dollars GDP — even larger than the Russian economy. Mentioning ASEAN as a single entity certainly remains a top priority for all ASEAN member states.

Now, if we look at the various member states in terms of competitiveness, there are of course significant differences in the level of development. This certainly is manifested also in the competitive rankings, as well as trade performances. For example, if you look at the top four exporters among the ASEAN-8, [this] constituted at least 83% of the ASEAN-8 total exports from 1995–2011. So, the question of looking at the ASEAN vision 2025, the various blueprints, I think are also very important perhaps in future studies.

Next, if we were to look at the competitiveness rankings, it seems that in terms of the overall rankings, they remain the same for ASEAN member states between 2014 and 2015. There is really no change. The ACI competitiveness ranking also showed somewhat similar results with the GCI, the global competitiveness index of the world economic forum, except that the latest GCI for 2017–2018; for example, Thailand and Indonesia have outperformed Brunei in ASEAN. Now, if you look at the rankings, and as has been said also by the presenters, I think what is important is to ensure that the development gap is really addressed here. So of course one of the issues related to the development gap within ASEAN is connectivity. I think this is also one of those issues that have been discussed in respect of infrastructure development and so on.

Since I come from Malaysia, I can't help but narrow down to Malaysia. I can see that Malaysia has maintained its position as the second most competitive ASEAN member state, but somehow the competitiveness scores have fallen slightly. Now, I will just move on quickly, it seems that Malaysia is moving in the right direction but there are certainly areas for improvement. What are these areas? Of course in terms of GDP growth, in terms of government and institutional settings (as stated there); in terms of ensuring regulatory environment and government effectiveness and of course there's a lot that has been done in respect of government transformation programmes and so on and so forth. Next, on enhancing labour productivity which is vital to ensure competitiveness. From that study it appears that Malaysia is the best performer among the ASEAN economies in the financial business and manpower conditions rankings. Yet Malaysia could do better in terms of labour force participation and employment rates and labour productivity. So, I do not think for the sake of brevity and time I need to go into so much detail on that.

Now, let me move on to exchange rate movements affecting export performances. Now, it appears that exchange rate movement affects export performances, but higher GVC integration mitigates this impact, and this study certainly has added valuable contributions to the existing literature on the impacts of exchange rates on export performance and in the context of deepening integration with GVCs. Now, for the ASEAN-8 — for example, the study has found negative associations between exchange rates appreciation and increased volatility with gross exports. However while high foreign value added share of gross exports helps to offset the effects of currency appreciation on exports, it has smaller cushioning impacts on the effect of exchange rate volatility. So, for ASEAN policy makers, this certainly indicates that the priority can be reoriented from competitive currency devaluation to managing exchange rate volatility, as well as making the most out of ASEAN's participation in GVCs.

Exchange rate volatility certainly increases uncertainty and business costs for both trading parties especially with regard to prices and cost of hedging, all of which are detrimental to trade performance. Flexibility of an exchange rate regime and certainty in the domestic economy has been identified as contributing factors to exchange rate volatility, and from a policy stand point there are limits to what governments can do to offset currency volatility.

Now, what we need of course is a stable policy environment as an essential recipe for managing exchange rate volatility. There are various policy environments that one can look at. For example, according to the IMF, there is evidence to suggest that high level of foreign currency reserves contribute to currency stability through signaling at greater potential for intervention in a crisis situation. Here is some thoughts on GVCs: The way we look at ASEAN is becoming more integrated in the GVC networks. However, one of the problems that needs to be addressed is the number of non-tariff measures that have unfortunately increased. NTMs have increased from 1634 measures to 5975 measures from 2000–2015, despite a fall in average tariffs from 8.9% to 4.9%. So, obviously, these are figures from ERIA and obviously, this is a major policy issue that needs to be addressed within ASEAN.

In summary, these are some of the things that I think we should be looking at. Obviously, the idea of one community for ASEAN requires further work, especially in closing the competitiveness gap, as well as the development gap. Next is about Malaysia, but I think the more important, two other issues is that managing exchange rate volatility remains important for export competitiveness, and this requires a stable monetary and fiscal policy environment. Imports are as important as exports in the global value chain, thus ASEAN has to continue its efforts in dismantling the rise of protectionist sentiments, or rather resist protectionist sentiments and dismantle NTMs and NTBs. And of course, all the ASEAN member countries should also devise sustainable policy tools to ensure that the benefits of participation in the global value chain are being enjoyed by the greater ASEAN population, because the eventual goal of the ASEAN community is to have people-oriented and people-centered ASEAN that also promotes inclusive growth. Thank you.

Discussant Notes 2.2

Dr. Hezri Adnan

Senior Director of Research,
Institute of Strategic and International Studies (ISIS), Malaysia

Introduction

Greetings of peace and solidarity. I would like to begin by thanking the Asia Competitiveness Institute — especially Professor Dr Tan Khee Giap for inviting the Institute of Strategic and International Studies Malaysia as a regular discussant in its Annual Update of ACI's Competitiveness Index.

1) Indicators and indices are here to stay
As a student of public policy, I appreciate the fact that we cannot run away from indicators and indices. Year after year, we see the development of all sorts of high-profile indices and league-table ranking such as Human Development Index, Corruption Perception Index, indices from the World Happiness Report, and the aggregated indicators associated with the Ecological Footprint measures, to name a few examples. There are also academic journals dedicated to the science of indicator development such as Social Indicators Research and the Ecological Indicators journal. In my area of research and policy advocacy, there are also less well-known one such as Index of Sustainable Economic Welfare and Sustainable Development Index. Among the development fraternity, the most fashionable discussion revolves around a suite of 244 indicators associated with the Sustainable Development Goals or the 17 SDGs and their 169 targets. Those who love indices would say 'What cannot get measured cannot get done', those critical of them would use terms like 'voodoo science' to raise doubt about the utility of the art and craft of indicator development. This can be avoided if we don't see indicator systems as a non-negotiable fact. They are meant to simplify a complex reality and they are tool to generate debate for better governance.

If we look back, the interest in indicator science is hardly new. In fact, indicator systems are a manifestation of an age-old societal desire to be rational and scientific. Charles Dicken is known for his satirical take on the early Industrial Revolution in Britain through his novel Hard Times. Let me quote the most memorable and most cited prose from Hard Times:

> 'NOW, what I want is, Facts. Teach these boys and girls nothing but Facts. Facts alone are wanted in life. Plant nothing else, and root out everything else. You can only form the minds of reasoning animals upon Facts: nothing else will ever be of any service to them!'

But if we read more into Dicken's message, we realize that the desire to be rational and to be scientific goes beyond the confine of school or university education. Just think about the rise of

Performance Management in public administration with the emphasis on Key Performance Indicators and the pros and cons that are associated with it. Dickens was a seer and visionary in anticipating the desire to institutional the rational approach in governance or the obsession of 'modernization' with indicators and indices:

> "We hope to have before long, a board of fact, composed of commissioners of fact, who will force the people to be a people of fact, and of nothing but fact"

This begs the question, how to we mobilize indicators and indices in public policy, and socialize them within the broader ambit of media and society to improve governance? By the same token, how do you track the influence of ACI Competitiveness Rankings and Simulation in media and in the policy circle? Collaborations with regional governments (through research under Aid-for-Trade) in Shandong China, Uttar Pradesh India, and East Java Indonesia — are a welcome strategy in mobilizing the instrumental use of indicators.

2) Usefulness of ACI's Competiveness: Relevance for the Region

With that introduction, let me go back to the 'competitiveness indices industry'. I say industry because there are many — I hope not too many — efforts in measuring competitiveness.

I echo the views of many past Discussants of ACI Competitiveness Index on its coverage and methodological strength when compared with other measures of competitiveness. Avoidance of 'beauty pageant contest' is commendable and reflects ACI's interest in analysis rather than media attraction, although this is also useful in its own right.

Its sub-national or regional measure of competitiveness is useful and unique. Imbalance in regional competitiveness has proven to cause many surprising political consequences:

- The results of the 14th General Election in Malaysia saw the so-called safe vote deposit of Sabah and Sarawak regions — lower in competitiveness than the Peninsular region — changing their preference for a new political Alliance
- Similarly, in Thailand — the much-neglected farmers from Isan or Northeastern Region have led to the rise of the Red Shirts which has changed the landscape of Thai politics

3) Usefulness of ACI Competitiveness: Link to Rankings Outside of Competitiveness Discourse viz Relevance to the Sustainable Development Goals

As we know since 2015 the Millennium Development Goals (MDGs) have evolved into the Sustainable Development Goals (SDGs). This makes sustainable development a top priority on policymakers' agendas. It was already made known at the ASEAN Foreign Ministers' Meeting in Singapore two months ago that the SDGs will feature prominently during the Chairmanship of Thailand next year. Among other things is the creation of ASEAN Center for Sustainable Development Studies and Dialogue (possibly at the Mahidol University).

The indicators in the SDGs now appear to be linked more closely to the competitiveness discourse than they used to be because most are prerequisites for job creation and long-term sustainable growth. This link is one of the reasons that policymakers find them attractive. In the list of 17 SDGs to be achieved by 2030, three are directly captured by ACI's Competitiveness Framework or 'environments':

- ACI's 'Financial, Business, and Manpower Conditions' is highly relevant with SDG 8 Decent Work and Economic Growth
- ACI's 'Quality of Life and Infrastructure Development' environment is highly resonant with SDG 9 Industry, Innovation and Infrastructure
- ACI's 'Government and Institutional Setting' environment strikes a chord with SDG 16 on Peace Justice and Strong Institutions and its many targets and indicators. Without peace, stability, human rights and effective governance, based on the rule of law — we cannot hope for neither sustainable development nor competitiveness

The SDGs key message is the indivisibility of the goals. So targets and indicators are highly interconnected. There are measures to unpack the form of interaction between two or more targets and to encourage the formulation of integrated policies:

- Consistent
- Enabling, Reinforcing, Indivisible
- Constraining, Counteracting, Cancelling

Chapter 3

Impact of Exchange Rates on Trade in Value-Added of ASEAN Economies

3.1 Introduction and Motivation

This chapter is based on the study by Tan *et al.* (2017a), an in-depth empirical study of the modern structure of trade which provides a grounded and evidence-based platform for evaluating current events in this time of growing anti-globalization and protectionist sentiment. This chapter provides an analysis of the trends and patterns of ASEAN trade flows during the period of 1995–2011 based on data from the 2016 edition of the OECD-WTO TiVA database; unfortunately, the data series has since been discontinued. However, the analysis of trends and patterns serves to supplement the findings in the empirical study found in Section 3.5 by Tan *et al.* (2017a) which uses the same set of data by providing context of the patterns of trade in ASEAN relevant to the period of analysis. A full discussion on data caveats can be found in Section 3.3.

This is a topic of interest as exports have long been posited to be an important engine of growth and development and has formed the cornerstone of development strategies in many economies. The classic literature on export-led growth suggests that growth in exports may propel economic growth as it facilitates the optimal reallocation of resources towards the highly productive export sectors, generate technological spillovers and enable specialisation and economies of scale.[1] Additionally, exports may also create positive externalities on non-exporters whereby increased competition spurs these firms to become more competitive, resulting in greater productivity gains for the entire economy.

A strong external sector is vital for the economic performance of many countries, especially in Asia. For instance, the remarkable growth of China over the past three decades with tens of millions lifted out of poverty was associated with the country's emergence as an export powerhouse and the "factory of the world". The transformative power of trade can also be illustrated through the growth experience of the Southeast Asian countries. Indonesia, Malaysia, Thailand and Singapore were counted among the High Performing Asian Economies (HPAEs) in the 1990s, a group of economies which had achieved high growth sustained over three decades from the 1960s to the early 1990s with significant decline in inequality and improvement in human welfare.[2] Their success has been attributed in part to the export-led industrialisation policy in these economies.[3] Drawing from the experience of their more developed counterparts, the transitional economies in Southeast Asia, namely Cambodia, Laos, Vietnam and Myanmar have also adopted the export-led growth model as their development strategy.[4]

[1] See Keesing (1967), Balassa (1978), Heller and Porter (1978), Feder (1983), Marin (1992), Bhagwati (1994), Krueger (1998), and Ang and Madsen (2013).

[2] See World Bank (1993).

[3] See Little (1981), World Bank (1993), Chow and Kellman (1993) and Song (2012).

[4] See Tan *et al.* (2017b).

Figure 3.1: Share of Exports of Goods and Services in Gross Domestic Product by Region, 1995–2015

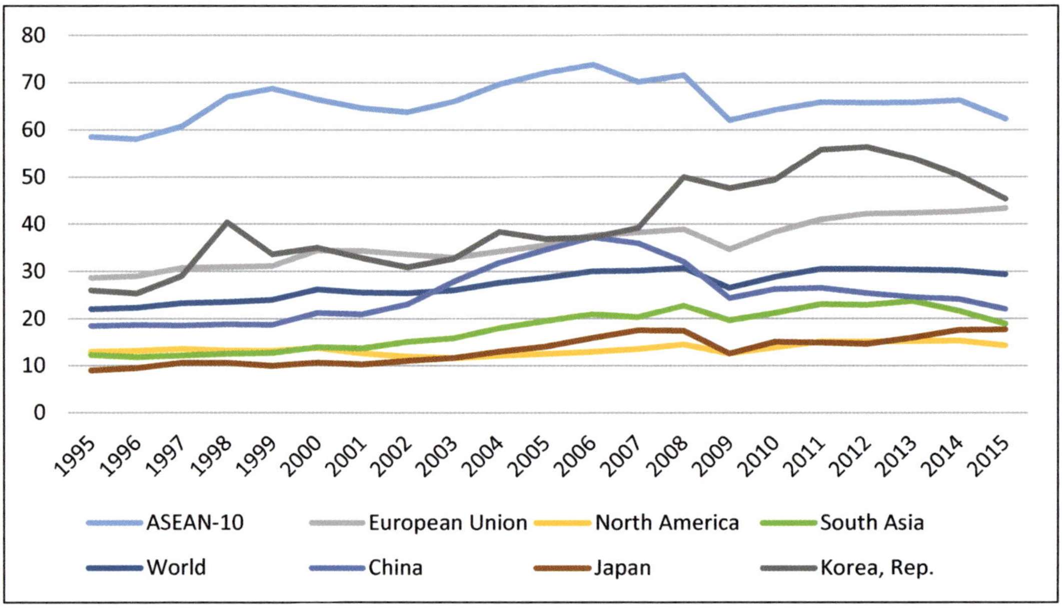

Source: Asia Competitiveness Institute based on data from World Bank, World Development Indicators.

Indeed, the 10 member countries of the Association of Southeast Asian Nations (ASEAN) are highly dependent on exporting activities. Exports of goods and services constitute on average 60% of their Gross Domestic Product (GDP) over the period 1995–2015. This is much higher than the world average and the shares of North America, the European Union, South Asia as well as that of China, Japan and South Korea (see Figure 3.1).

As exports continue to be vital to the economic future of Asia, particularly the ASEAN economies, it is worth noting that the patterns of trade and international production have changed over the past 20 years. Thanks to advancements in transportation and communication technologies, firms have found it increasingly profitable to split previously integrated production into two or more components located in different economies, in a phenomenon known as "production fragmentation".[5] This process has accelerated since the early 1990s, creating sequential production chains or complex production networks that stretch across multiple economies and regions.[6] Such mechanisms are commonly referred to as global value chains (GVCs). In East and Southeast Asia, global production chains have played an essential role in the expansion of trade.[7] In particular, Athukorala (2005) found that East and Southeast Asian economies are more dependent on production networks than their counterparts in North America and Europe. Going forward, ASEAN countries have shown a commitment to enhance their participation in GVCs, as seen by the adoption of the ASEAN Work Plan for Enhancing the GVC Agenda.[8]

[5] See Jones and Kierzkowski (2001).

[6] See Deardorff (2001), WTO (2008), Timmer *et al.* (2014) and Amador and Cabral (2016).

[7] See Ng and Yeats (2001), Wakasugi (2007), Ando (2006) and Yamano *et al.* (2011).

[8] See ASEAN Secretariat (2017).

The rise of GVCs means that exports are seldom produced in their entirety within a single country, using only domestic inputs. On the contrary, exports are likely to contain foreign value-added components. In fact, as Section 3.3 shall illustrate, almost 30% of the value content of ASEAN economies' gross exports is foreign. This has led to calls to reevaluate our understanding of trade, especially in the ways it is measured as well as its determinants.[9] One of the crucial factors determining export performance is movements of exchange rates both in terms of their levels and volatility. Recent research has recognised the role of GVC participation on the responses of exports to exchange rate adjustments,[10] but studies on the nexus between GVCs and exchange rates remain relatively few. In addition, current research in this vein has largely focused on the exchange rate elasticity of exports instead of volatility. It is reasonable to suspect that the trade effects of exchange rate in the presence of GVCs may differ from convention. This is because exchange rate fluctuations now not only affect the price competitiveness of exports but may also have a countervailing effect on production costs via its bearing on the costs of imported inputs.

This study seeks to empirically examine the effects of real effective exchange rate (REER) movements and volatility on exports of goods and services among ASEAN economies as well as whether integration into GVCs influences these impacts. The study relies on exports and GVC measurements from the Trade in Value-Added (TiVA) database, which is jointly published by the Organisation for Economic Co-operation and Development (OECD) and the World Trade Organization (WTO). We have used the December 2016 version of the database, which is the latest available at the time of the study and reports annual data for the 1995–2011 period, hence achieving better data coverage than previous similar studies. Moreover, our study is ASEAN-centric whereas existing ASEAN-related studies have subsumed these economies under larger samples. As a result, our findings provide ASEAN-specific insights and policy implications for policy-makers in the region.

The remainder of the chapter is organised as follows. Section 3.2 further elaborates on the emergence of GVCs and the conceptual framework used to understand and measure an economy's participation in production fragmentation. Section 3.3 discusses the trends and patterns of exports of goods and services in ASEAN economies. This is followed by Section 3.4, which reviews the existing theoretical and empirical literature on the nexus between exchange rates, exchange rate volatility and exports. Section 3.5 outlines the empirical methodology adopted in this study and details the data availability and selection. The empirical results and robustness checks are discussed in Section 3.6. The chapter concludes in Section 3.7 with a discussion on the policy implications derived from this study.

3.2 Understanding Production Fragmentation and GVCs

The need to account for inter-country linkages in analysing trade within the context of GVCs is often demonstrated through examples of production processes which utilise inputs from multiple

[9] See Amador and Cabral (2016).

[10] See Bems and Johnson (2012). Also, see related literature reviewed in Section 3.5.

countries. For instance, the case study on the iPhone 4 in OECD (2011) shows that by conventional measures of trade in final goods, the United States (US) records a trade deficit of almost US$170 *vis-à-vis* China per each iPhone. However, Chinese factories are involved mostly in the assembly segment of production, which only generates around US$6.5 in terms of value-added. The remaining value comes from imported inputs from South Korea, Germany, France, Japan and the rest of the world. In fact, South Korea accounts for the largest amount of value-added at US$80. Clearly, with the presence of GVCs, traditional gauges of gross trade may overstate or understate the actual value-added supplied by a country, which may lead to misleading policy implications.

GVCs have become increasingly prevalent globally. As reported in UNCTAD (2013), in 2013, over US$20 trillion or approximately 60% of global trade comprised trade in intermediate goods and services that are incorporated at multiple levels of the production networks for final consumption. Furthermore, the same report found that the share of global value-added trade captured by developing economies is expanding rapidly. It grew from about 20% in 1990 to 30% in 2000 and to over 40% in 2013.

Against this backdrop, there have been several attempts to reconceptualise the way we understand trade. Amador and Cabral (2016) provide a detailed survey of this literature which has culminated in the comprehensive framework by Koopman *et al.* (2010, 2014). As depicted in Figure 3.2, this framework decomposes gross exports into different value-added components. The Domestic Value-Added (DVA) component measures the value-added content by domestic

Figure 3.2: Decomposition of Gross Exports through the Koopman *et al.* (2010)'s Framework

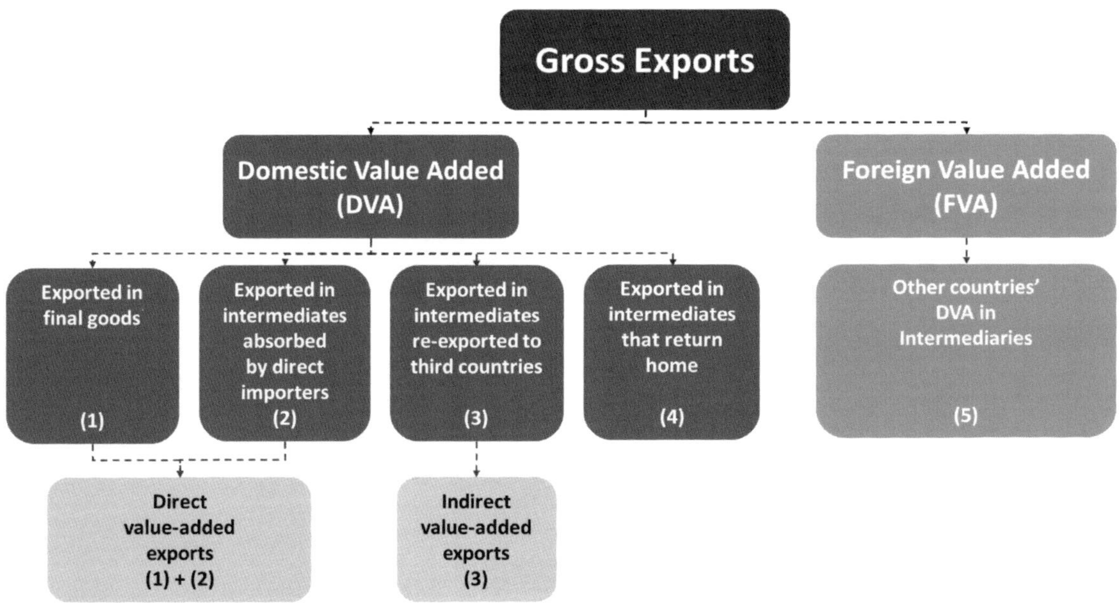

Note: Koopman *et al.* (2014) further broke down items (4) and (5) into sub-components. However, the basic framework presented is sufficient for our purpose.
Source: Adapted from Koopman *et al.* (2010).

Table 3.1: Summary on the Measures of GVCs

Measures	Trade in Parts and Components	Processing Exports	Input–Output (I–O)-Based Measures
Pros	Simple, high coverage and cross-country comparability.	Accurate and highly disaggregated data source.	Detailed tracking of value-added at each production stage. Reflects exports of value-added from both the manufacturing and service sectors.
Cons	Low accuracy due to sensitivity to goods classification systems. Explicit focus on trade in goods.	Low coverage (only for exported/imported goods for processing abroad/internally and then reimported/reexported). Explicit focus on trade in good.	High complexity and low data availability.

Source: Amador and Cabral (2016).

factors embodied in the exported output. The Foreign Value-Added (FVA) component measures the foreign value-added content embodied in intermediate inputs used in export production. Moreover, DVA can be broken down into that embodied in final goods and services which is item (1) and that embodied in intermediate exports which is the sum of items (2), (3) and (4). In turn, item (2) refers to the value-added exported in intermediates used to produce final goods consumed by the direct importers; item (3) denotes the value-added in intermediates which are processed and reexported to a third economy while item (4) represents the contents which are ultimately reimported by the economy from which they originate.

Together with the development of new frameworks to understand trade, the literature has also explored various means to measure participation in GVCs. Trade in parts and components, flows of processing exports and input–output (I–O)-based measures developed from the value-added frameworks of trade are the three most commonly used gauges of GVCs (Amador and Cabral, 2016). There has been a shift of focus among the recent literature to the I–O-based measures. As shown in Table 3.1, they are more comprehensive than the other two alternatives. I–O-based measures enable detailed tracking of value-added at each stage of the production process, accounting for value-added by both the manufacturing and service sectors.

Consistent with the recent literature, this study will use I–O-based measures of GVC participation.

3.3 Data Caveats

Before analysing the trends and patterns of trade for ASEAN, it is important to discuss the various concerns surrounding the choice of data for analysis. Among the available databases for I–O-based measures, we employ the OECD-WTO TiVA database given its extensive coverage of the ASEAN economies. Moreover, TiVA provides readily available breakdown of gross exports according to Koopman *et al.* (2010). The TiVA database reports annual data for eight ASEAN countries, namely Brunei, Cambodia, Indonesia, Malaysia, Philippines, Singapore, Thailand and Vietnam over the 1995–2011 period. These countries shall subsequently be

Table 3.2: Summary of Sources and Definitions of Variables Used in the Main Empirics

Variable	Unit	Definition	Source
Real Gross Exports	US$ Million (constant 2007 prices)	Gross exports data come from the row sum of the international trade flows in the OECD Inter-Country Input–Output (ICIO) tables. They are consistent with official (SNA93) National Accounts estimates of total exports and imports of goods and services, adjusted for reexports, as well as estimates for GDP. Real gross exports are obtained by deflating nominal gross exports with CPI data from the IMF World Economic Outlook (WEO), April 2017 edition.	OECD-WTO TiVA
REER	Index	REER is calculated from nominal effective exchange rate and a measure of the relative price or cost between the country under study and its trading partners.	Bruegel Institute
REER Volatility	Standard Deviation	Standard deviation of monthly changes of REER.	Bruegel Institute
Real FDI Stock	US$ Million (constant 2007 prices)	FDI is defined as an investment involving a long-term relationship and reflecting a lasting interest in and control by a resident entity in one economy of an enterprise resident in a different economy. FDI stock is the value of the share of their capital and reserves (including retained profits) attributable to the parent enterprise, plus the net indebtedness of affiliates to the parent enterprises. Real FDI stock is obtained by deflating nominal gross exports with GDP deflator data from the IMF WEO, April 2017 edition.	UNCTAD
Foreign Real GDP (FORGDP)	US$ Million (constant 2007 prices)	Weighted geometric average of real GDP of country *i*'s trading partners — all economies reported in OECD-WTO TiVA as well as rest of the world. Weights for trading partner *j* are its shares in country *i*'s total trade.	Calculated from IMF WEO, April 2017 edition and OECD-WTO TiVA
FVA Share in Gross Exports	Percent	The share of foreign value-added components in gross exports.	OECD-WTO TiVA

Source: Authors' compilation.

Table 3.3: Descriptive Statistics

Variable	Mean	Between Std. Dev.	Within Std. Dev.	Min	Max	Observations	Number of Countries
Real Gross Exports (2007p US$ million)	79,147	62,655	35,179	1,259	249,794	135	8
REER (index value)	102.15	5.3	9.37	71.16	124.93	135	8
REER Volatility (standard deviation of monthly REER changes)	1.59	0.69	1.3	0.25	9.27	135	8
Real FDI Stock (2007p US$ million)	65,413	87,839	70,097	545	661,290	134	8
FORGDP (2007p US$ million)	1,356,117	169,392	201,663	438,287	1,787,103	135	8
FVA Share in Gross Exports (%)	28.9	12.8	4.9	2.3	47.7	135	8

Note: The observation for Indonesia in 1998 was dropped because the REER value was a clear outlier.
Source: Authors' compilation.

referred to as ASEAN-8 for the rest of this chapter. Laos and Myanmar were excluded due to data availability. Gross exports computed by TiVA have been adjusted for entrepot trade.

Table 3B.1 in Annex B compares the different databases of I–O-based measures of GVCs. As seen from the table, Eora Multi-Region Input–Output (MRIO) and OECD-WTO TiVA have the most comprehensive coverage of ASEAN economies. However, detailed decompositions of gross exports are not readily available from EORA MRIO. In contrast, OECD-WTO TiVA allows easy decomposition of exports according to Koopman *et al.* (2010)'s framework. Hence, it is most suitable for our purpose.

As for REER data, among the sources which compute conventional REER based on gross trade, Bruegel and UNCTAD have the best coverage of our economies of interest (see Table 3B.2, in Annex B). However, UNCTAD only reports annual data while our measures of REER volatility require monthly data. Hence, we use Bruegel data instead of UNCTAD. Meanwhile, the availability of value-added REER data is still rather limited. As shown in Table 3B.3 in Annex B, only Bayoumi *et al.* (2013) provide monthly data for four ASEAN economies, namely Indonesia, Singapore, Thailand and Vietnam. Therefore, as outlined in Section 3.5.1, Bruegel's conventional REER data is used for the main empirics whereas Bayoumi *et al.* (2013)'s value-added REER series are used for robustness checks.

In brief, Table 3.2 summarises the definitions and sources of the variables used to estimate the main results of the study while Table 3.3 shows their descriptive statistics. The observation for Indonesia in 1998 has been dropped from the sample as it is an outlier in terms of the REER value. This is likely associated with the disruption caused by the Asian Financial Crisis and should not be considered typical behaviour.

3.4 Trends and Patterns of Trade: ASEAN

As previously described in Section 3.1, trade is an important driver of ASEAN's economy. As shown in Figure 3.3, the shares of trade of goods and services in the GDP in the region were consistently much higher than the global average throughout the period 1995–2015. ASEAN's shares were also higher than other major economies such as China, Japan and South Korea as well as the European Union. Generally, shares of trade of goods and services as a percentage of GDP grew between 1995 and 2008. However, the Global Financial Crisis in 2009 caused a dip in the trend across all geographical regions. ASEAN had tried to recover since, showing a general upward trend from 2010 onwards.

The same observations can also be made of ASEAN's shares of gross exports to GDP over the same time period in Figure 3.1. On average, ASEAN's shares were significantly higher than the world average and those of other regions. The share of exports also dipped during the Global Financial Crisis in 2009, but showed a recovering trend in the years that followed.

Zooming into ASEAN-8's data from the TiVA database, gross exports of ASEAN-8 grew from US$313.5 million in 1995 to US$1.2 trillion in 2011 — an annualised rate of about 8.7% per annum (see Figure 3.4). Among the eight countries, Philippines' growth rate was the lowest at 6.6% per annum, while Vietnam's annualised growth rate was the highest at 17.8%. There were also noticeable dips in gross exports during the three major financial crises in the region:

Figure 3.3: Shares of Trade of Goods and Services in GDP, 1995–2015

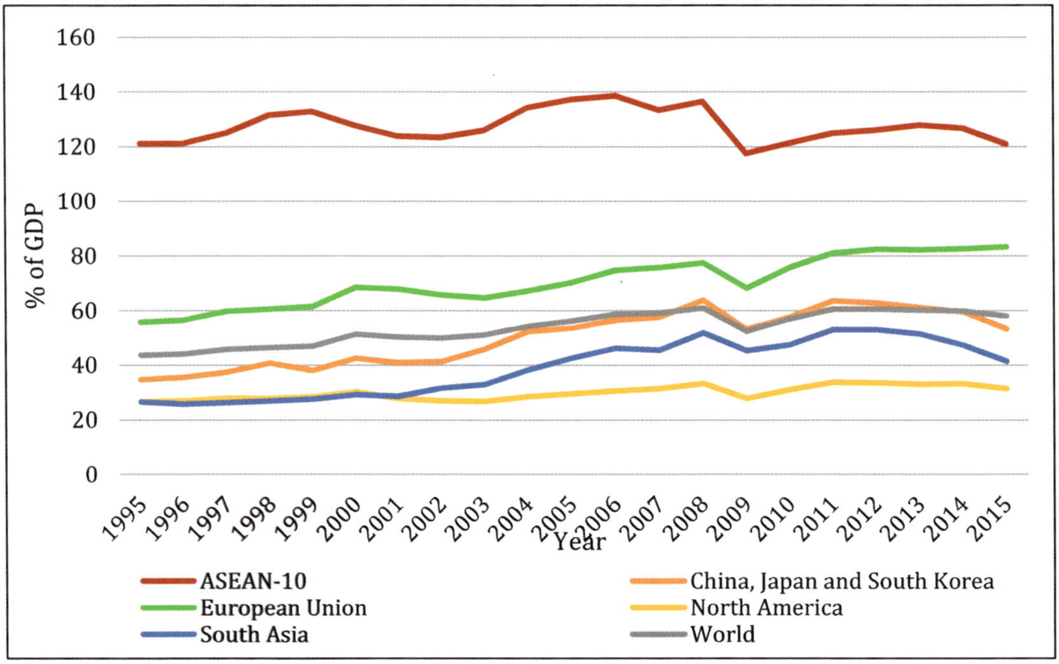

Source: Asia Competitiveness Institute based on data from World Bank, World Development Indicators.

Figure 3.4: Gross Exports of Goods and Services of ASEAN-8, 1995–2011

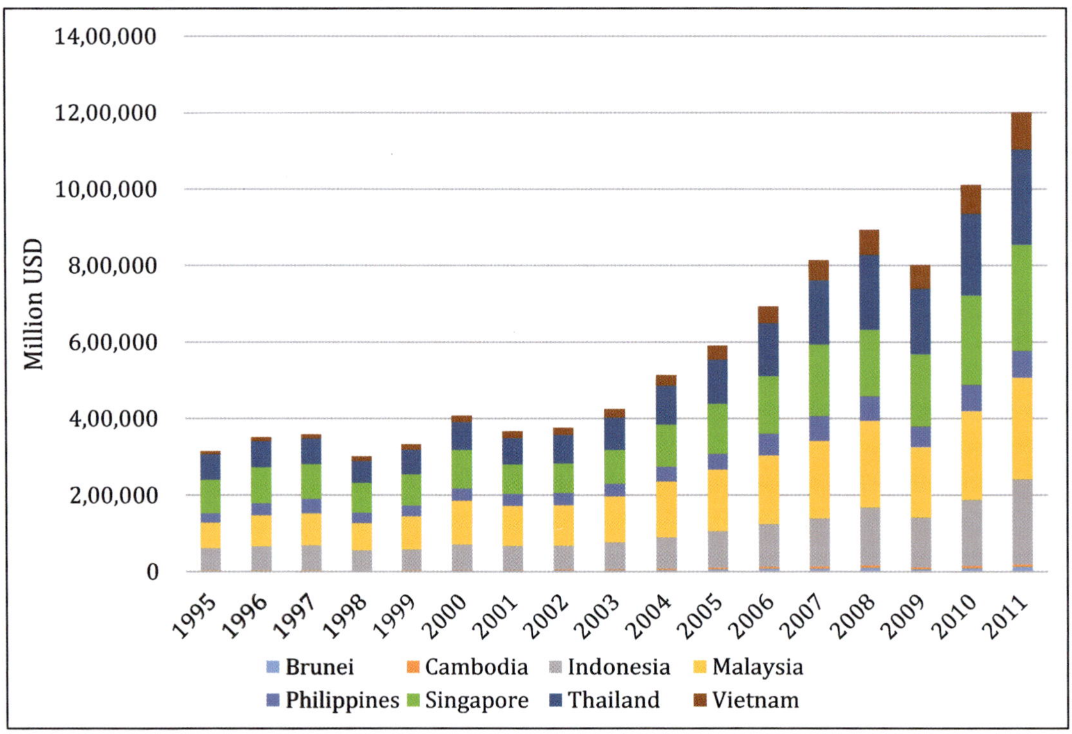

Source: Asia Competitiveness Institute based on data from OECD-WTO TiVA.

Figure 3.5: Share of Gross Exports of ASEAN-8 in Total World Exports, 1995–2011

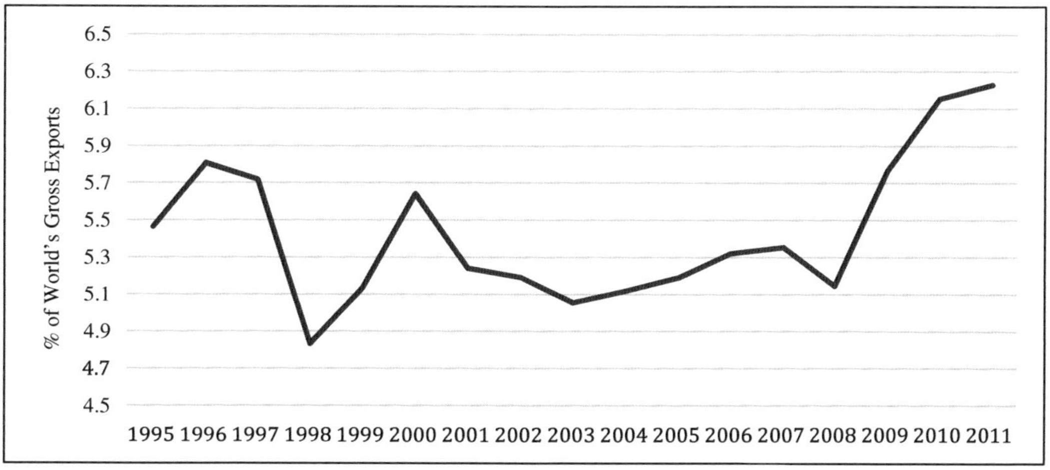

Source: Asia Competitiveness Institute based on data from OECD-WTO TiVA.

first during the Asian Financial Crisis in 1998, second during the Dot-Com Bubble Burst in 2001–2002, and third during the Global Financial Crisis in 2009. Despite these crises, exports had generally been growing, with total gross exports in 2011 being the highest in recent years.

Collectively as a region, ASEAN-8's share of gross exports in total world exports had generally showed an increasing trend between 1995 and 2011 (see Figure 3.5). In 1995, the share of ASEAN-8 was a mere 5.4%. Similar to the region's total gross exports, the share of ASEAN-8's gross exports to total world exports also showed noticeable dips during the three financial crises, with the 1998 data being the lowest at 4.8% due to the Asian Financial Crisis. Despite the dips, the share of ASEAN-8's exports in 2011 was also of a historic high — standing at more than 6.2%.

When ASEAN-8's gross exports are broken down into individual economies, we can also observe that between 1995 and 2011, the major exporters in the region were consistently Singapore, Malaysia, Thailand and Indonesia (see Figure 3.6). Collectively, these four economies contributed to at least 83% of total exports in the region throughout the period. Vietnam also showed a consistent increasing trend from 2.2% in 1995 to 8% in 2011. However, certain economies such as Cambodia and Brunei still retained low percentages over the years. Cambodia's share of exports, in fact, never exceeded 0.8%.

In absolute values, gross exports of individual economies of ASEAN-8 had increased between 1995 and 2011 (see Figure 3.7). The four major exporters in the region — Singapore, Malaysia, Thailand and Indonesia — were also the countries that experienced the most significant increase in exports over the period. Despite being the second smallest country in terms of population in ASEAN, Singapore's exports had consistently topped the region, with a historic high of about close to US$280,000 million in 2011. As the biggest economy in the region both in terms of nominal GDP and population, Indonesia came third, with a gross exports value of about US$220,000 million. On the other hand, although exports generally grew across all economies,

Figure 3.6: Share of Individual Economies in ASEAN-8's Gross Exports, 1995–2011

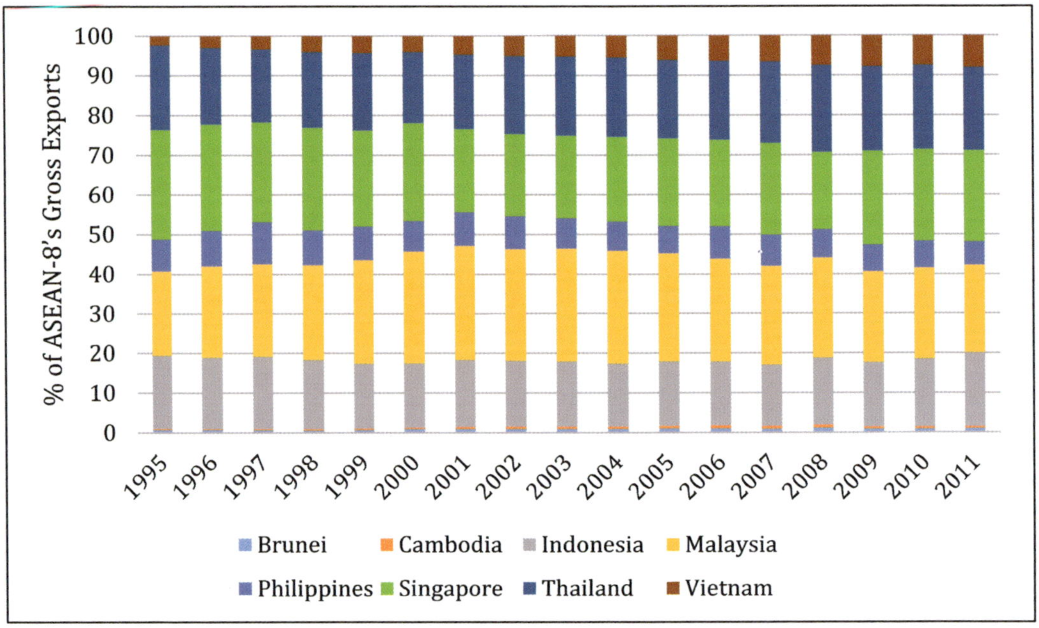

Source: Asia Competitiveness Institute based on data from OECD-WTO TiVA.

Figure 3.7: Gross Exports of Goods and Services of ASEAN-8, 1995–2011

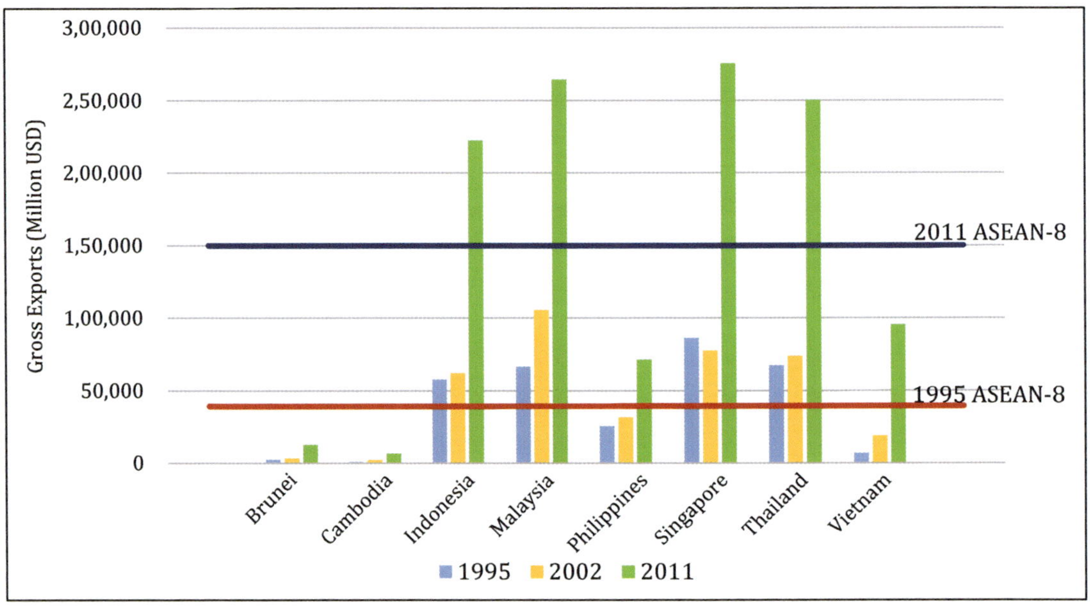

Source: Asia Competitiveness Institute based on data from OECD-WTO TiVA.

Figure 3.8: ASEAN-8's Gross Exports by Broad Sectors, Period Average, 1995–2011

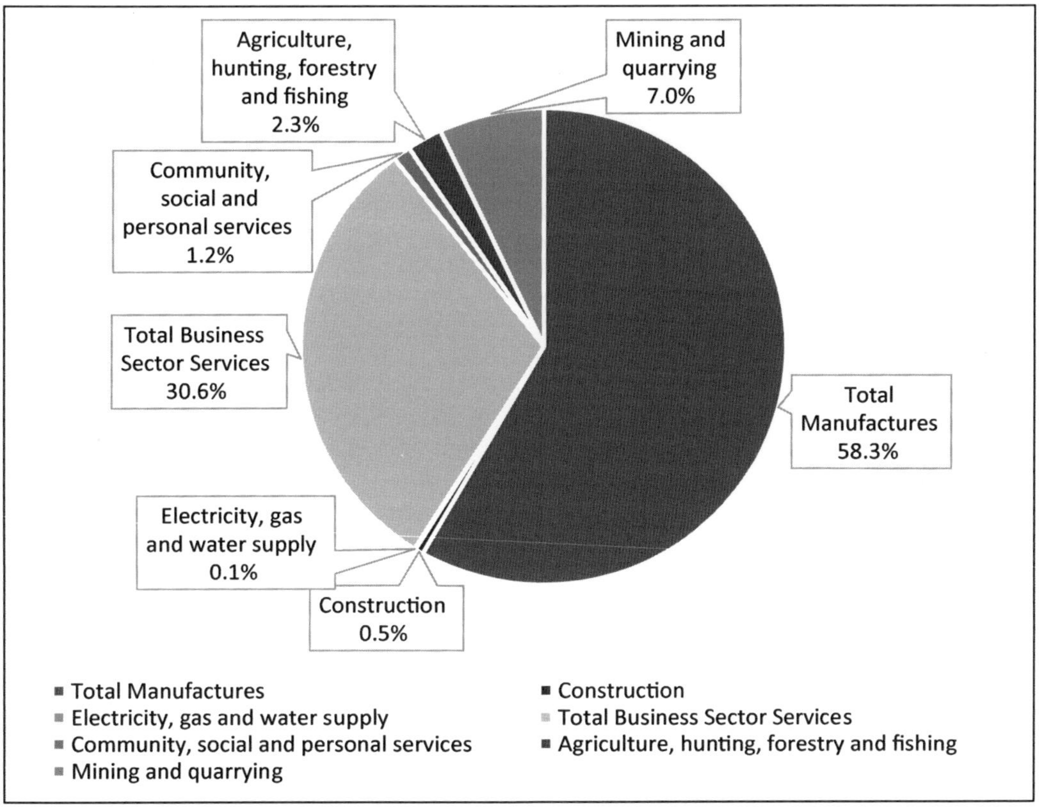

Source: Asia Competitiveness Institute based on data from OECD-WTO TiVA.

there was still a significant gap between the exports of Brunei and Cambodia compared to other economies in the region.

The types of exports originating from ASEAN-8 have, however, remained consistent over the years. As shown in Figure 3.8, between 1995 and 2011, the exports of the region came from two primary sectors: manufacturing (averaging to about 58.3%) and services (averaging to about 31.8%). These two sectors together made up close to an average of 90% of the region's total exports. Exports from the mining and quarrying as well as agriculture, hunting, forestry and fishing sectors were surprisingly low, averaging to only about 7% and 2.3%, respectively. Exports from other sectors were almost negligible.

Figures 3.9 and 3.10 show how the relative importance of ASEAN's trading partners has evolved over the years. In 1995, the United States, European Union and Japan were key trading partners to ASEAN-8 as ASEAN-8 exported close to 55% of its goods and services to these economies (see Figure 3.10). However, the importance of these economies had slowly diminished. Their share of ASEAN's exports almost halved to around 30% in 2011. Instead, intra-regional trade and trade with China have become very significant. Exports among ASEAN-8 and to China made up close to 35% of ASEAN-8's gross exports in 2011 (see Figure 3.10).

Figure 3.9: Partners' Shares of ASEAN-8's Gross Exports, 1995

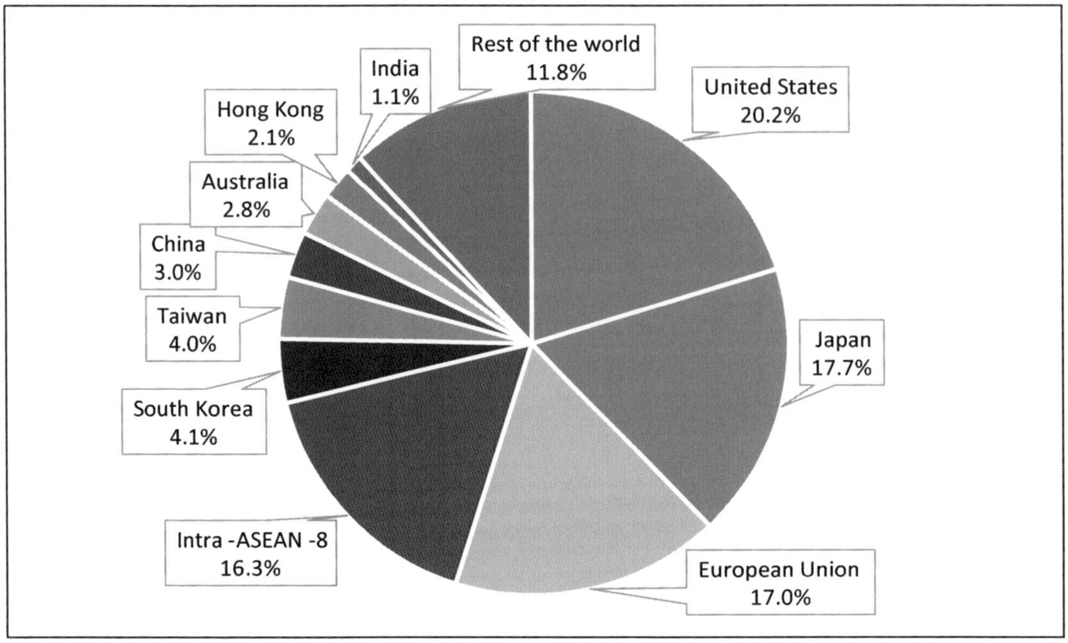

Source: Asia Competitiveness Institute based on data from OECD-WTO TiVA.

Figure 3.10: Partners' Shares of ASEAN-8's Gross Exports, 2011

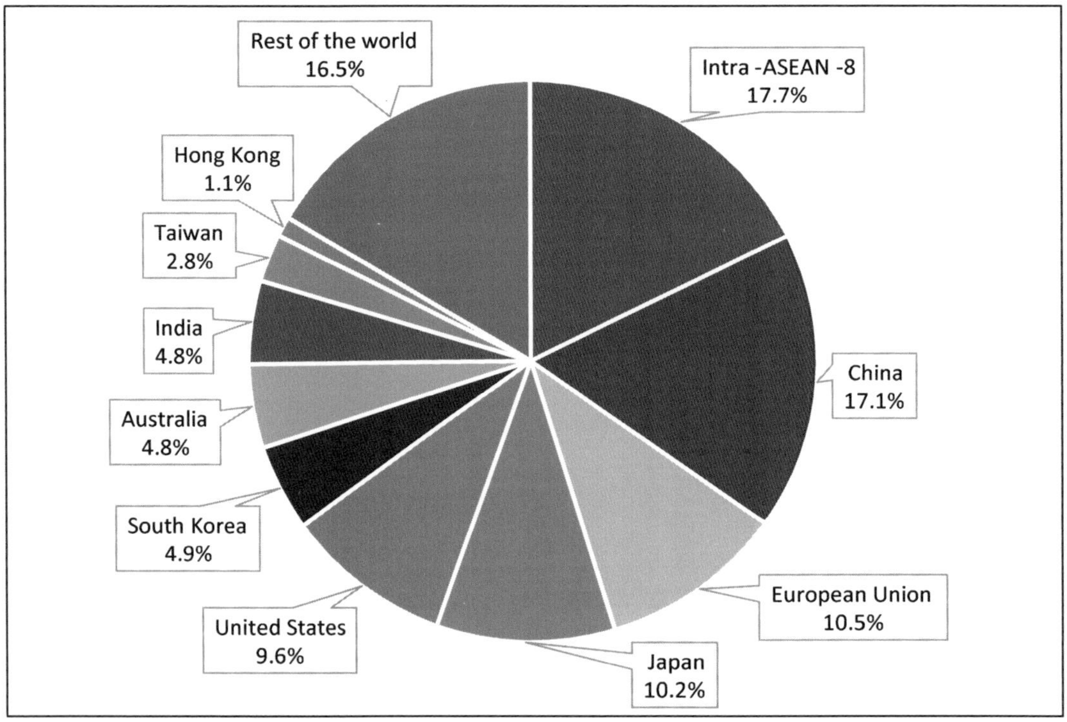

Source: Asia Competitiveness Institute based on data from OECD-WTO TiVA.

Figure 3.11: ASEAN-8's Average Share of Value-Added Components of Gross Exports, 1995–2011

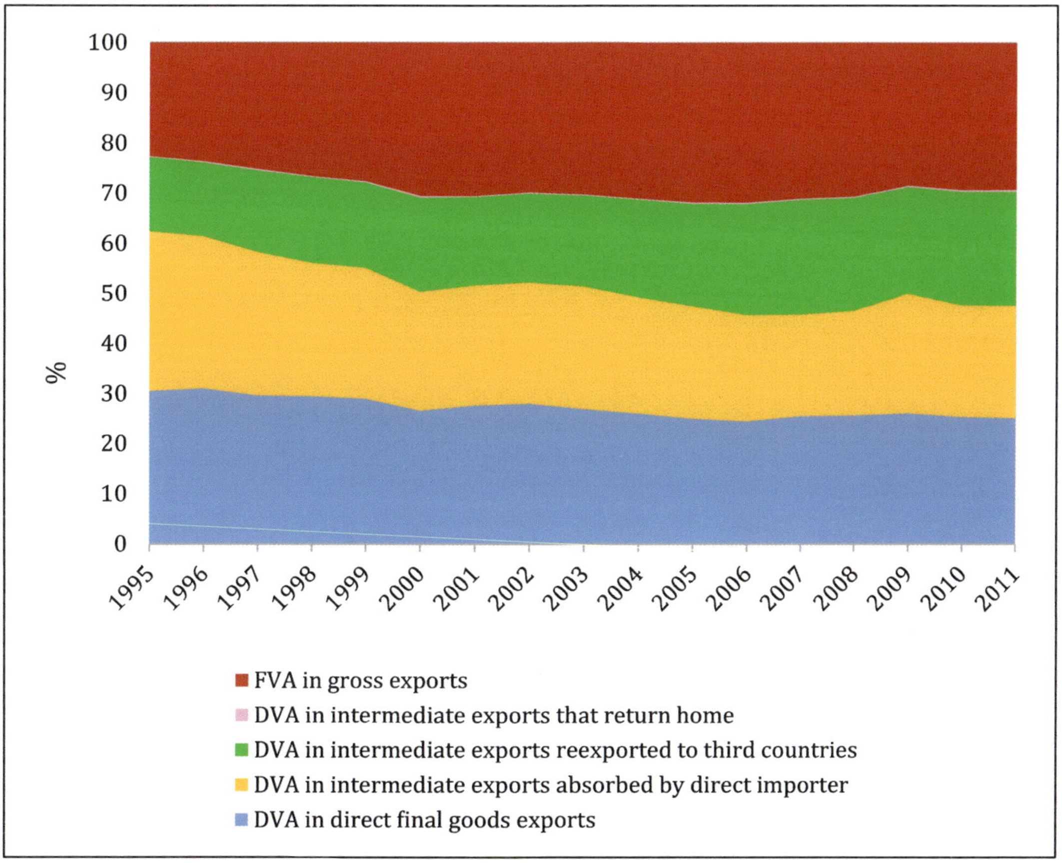

Source: Asia Competitiveness Institute based on data from OECD-WTO TiVA.

When decomposing ASEAN-8's gross exports into the different components according to Koopman *et al.* (2010)'s framework, it can be observed that the average share of FVA in the region's gross exports has slowly gained significance (see Figure 3.11). In fact, almost a third of ASEAN's total value of exports in 2011 consisted of FVA. A significant portion of ASEAN's exports therefore comprised imported contents from other economies. Higher participation of ASEAN-8 in the GVC can also be demonstrated by the growing importance of exports of DVA embodied in intermediate goods and services as compared to exports of DVA embodied in final goods and services over the years.

Interestingly, if FVA in the exports of ASEAN-8 was excluded, the share of the gross exports of the individual economies changed (see Figure 3.12). Most notably, Singapore no longer occupied the largest share in the region, although its share was still significant at around 20.9%. Indonesia contributed to the largest share of gross exports in DVA at 22.9% in 2011. This is not too surprising as Indonesia is a major commodity exporter. Furthermore, being a large, well-endowed economy also means that Indonesia's other export sectors would rely more on domestic resource factors of production rather than imported inputs.

Figure 3.12: ASEAN-8's Share of Gross Exports in Domestic Value-Added, 2011

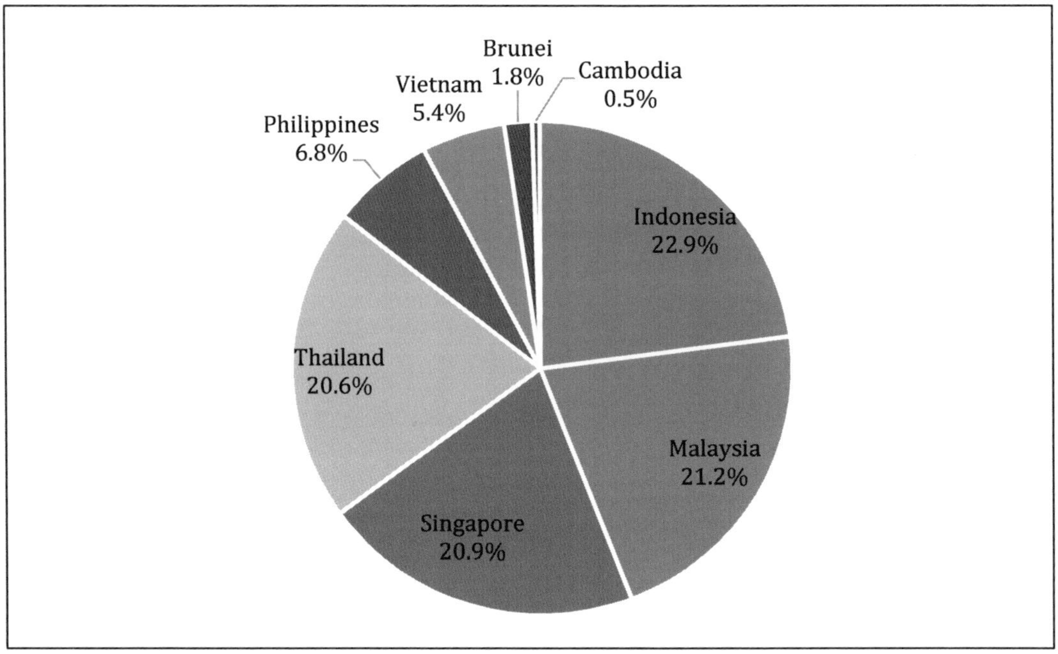

Source: Asia Competitiveness Institute based on data from OECD-WTO TiVA.

Indeed, when breaking down individual ASEAN-8's exports into DVA and FVA, we can observe that a significant portion of Singapore's, Malaysia's and Thailand's exports in 2011 consisted of imported inputs (see Figure 3.13). Countries that primarily export commodities such as Indonesia and Brunei, however, were shown to have considerably fewer imported contents in their exports.

Exports are a significant driver of growth in the ASEAN economies, as shown by their high contribution to the region's GDP. The region's shares of trade and exports to GDP generally showed an increasing trend, despite the dip that took place during the Global Financial Crisis in 2009. Although the types of goods and services exported remain unchanged, China had become an important export destination to the region. An increasing number of countries in ASEAN were also exporting among themselves.

Singapore, Malaysia, Indonesia and Thailand remained as major exporters of the region, while the less developed countries such as Cambodia and Vietnam still lagged behind. There continued to exist a huge gap between these economies. Given the purported link between economic growth and trade, this gap must be addressed in order to bridge the development gap. Continuous efforts to boost international trade in these economies therefore need to be sustained.

Moreover, a new approach to trading has emerged; ASEAN countries are now integrated into larger GVCs. Quite a significant portion of ASEAN's exports today contains imported inputs from other economies. This reliance on imported inputs subsequently has implications for exchange rate policies. If traditionally exchange rate depreciation would results in more

Figure 3.13: Breakdown of ASEAN-8's Gross Exports, 2011

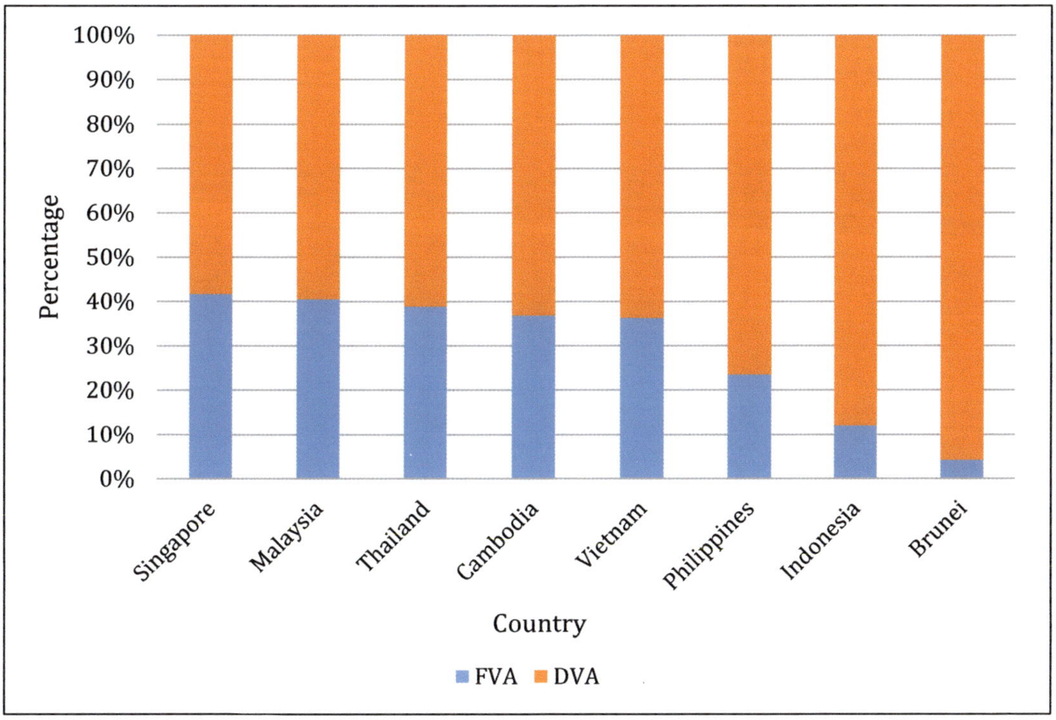

Source: Asia Competitiveness Institute based on data from OECD-WTO TiVA.

price-competitive exports, such positive effects may be dampened because imported inputs would also become costlier. Policy-makers thus need to take into account this possible dampening effect in when crafting their respective exchange rate policies.

3.5 Literature Review

3.5.1 Theoretical Literature

There have been large bodies of literature investigating the relationship between exchange rate and exports. The literature has outlined some broad theoretical priors about the trade impacts of movements in exchange rate levels and its volatility. With respect to exchange rate levels, the conventional hypothesis is that depreciation of the exporting country's currency will boost its exports. In particular, Freund and Pierola (2012) argued that a large real depreciation should stimulate both the intensive and the extensive margins, as it lowers the foreign prices of exports while also making it more profitable to expand to new markets or export new products. However, much depends on the exchange rate pass-through, or the degree to which fluctuations in the exporting country's exchange rate manifest in changes in local-currency import prices in the destination market. In a comprehensive survey, Ghosh and Rajan (2007) pointed out that exchange rate pass-through among Asian economies generally depended on the level development: developing economies tended to exhibit greater pass-through than developed economies.

Determinants of pass-through may be broadly categorised into micro- and macro-factors. The first group relates to the industrial structure of the economy while the latter highlights the macroeconomic environment, particularly the role of monetary policy.[11] In addition, Ahmed *et al.* (2017) suggested that deeper integration into GVCs and greater utilisation of foreign content in producing exports could be expected to dampen the effects of exchange rate movements on export performance. As the exchange rate depreciates, the cost of imported inputs rises, thus reducing competitive gains from depreciation as compared to the conventional case without GVCs.

In terms of exchange rate volatility, the literature, as summarised in McKenzie (1999) and Auboin and Ruta (2013), suggests that high exchange rate volatility may deter exports. This can come about through two channels: the direct effect and the cost effect. The first refers to the case whereby producers are discouraged to export because of the high uncertainty of profits associated with increased exchange rate volatility. Meanwhile, the latter views greater volatility as equivalent to higher transaction costs on exports.

However, there are certain caveats. First and foremost, the trade effects of exchange rate volatility depend critically on the degree of risk aversion of the traders.[12] Second, the presence of hedging instruments further complicates the picture. Baron (1976) suggested that perfect forward markets may reduce, if not eliminate, the effects of exchange rate volatility on exports. Nevertheless, later studies have nuanced this conclusion by pointing out that hedging is not always available for all categories of firms. Even if it is, it may generate costs which translate into higher export prices.[13] Third, sunk costs in setting up exporting operations may also make firms less responsive to rising exchange rate volatility.[14]

Despite this rich literature, the role of GVCs in shaping the relationship between exchange rate volatility and exports remains relatively unexplored. Synthesising existing arguments in this budding literature, Sato and Zhang (2017) suggest that the effects of GVC participation may be ambiguous. On the one hand, the countervailing effects of exchange rate fluctuations on cost of imported inputs and prices of exports mean that the variance of profit to exporting firm may only rise to a lesser degree in the GVC context as compared to the conventional case. In this sense, GVC participation dampens the effects of exchange rate volatility on exports. On the other hand, trade costs due to uncertainty may be more relevant in supply chain trade (Hayakawa and Kimura, 2009). In other words, GVC participation may also amplify the adverse effects of exchange rate volatility on export performance. The net impact of GVCs therefore depends on which effect dominates.

3.5.2 Empirical Literature

In line with the theory, the existing empirical literature generally shows that in the conventional context, exchange rate depreciation (appreciation) has a positive (negative) effect on real exports.

[11] See Bussière (2007) and Shambaugh (2008) and the literature reviewed therein, especially Goldberg and Knetter (1997) as well as Campa and Goldberg (2002).

[12] See De Grauwe (1998) and Broll and Eckwert (1999).

[13] See Caporale and Doroodian (1994) and Obstfeld and Rogoff (1998).

[14] See Dixit (1989), Krugman (1989) and Franke (1991).

In addition, empirical estimations also tend to suggest a negative relationship between exchange rate volatility and exports although heterogeneities between different studies remain profound.[15]

In ASEAN-related studies, exchange rate appreciation and increased volatility have often been found to adversely affect export performance. Table 3A.1 in Annex A lists notable empirical studies on the trade impacts of exchange rate movements and volatility in the conventional context which either focus on ASEAN economies or include them as parts of larger samples.

Table 3A.2 in Annex A summarises the ASEAN-related empirical studies on the trade effects of exchange rate movements and volatility in the GVC context. These papers have only emerged over the past 10 years and most have subsumed ASEAN countries under regional or global samples. Exports are still found to be negatively related to exchange rate appreciation and increased volatility, though findings on the impact of GVC participation on these relationships are still mixed. For instance, Ahmed *et al.* (2017) suggested that participation in GVCs lowered the exchange rate elasticity of manufactured goods exports. However, their results were disputed by Leigh *et al.* (2017). Using data from the TiVA database, IMF (2015) and Cheng *et al.* (2016) have generalised the conclusion of Ahmed *et al.* (2017) for gross exports.

In terms of volatility, Thorbecke (2008) found that trade flows of electronic components within East and Southeast Asia were sensitive to exchange rate volatility but not bilateral exchange rate movements. Echoing this finding, Hayakawa and Kimura (2009) and Tang (2014) found that trade in intermediate goods was more responsive to exchange rate volatility than other types of trade flows. Thus, they concluded that integration into GVCs might make economies more susceptible to risks from exchange rate uncertainties. However, in a recent study using I–O-based measures of trade in value-added, Sato and Zhang (2017) came to a contrary finding that GVC participation might dampen the effects of exchange rate volatility on exports.

3.5.3 Gaps in the Literature

The review in this section shows that there are gaps in the literature on the role of GVCs with respect to the effects of exchange rate on exports. First, papers in this literature have primarily zoomed in on movements in exchange rate levels whereas volatility has been less well studied. Second, the earlier papers on exchange rate movements as well as most of the few studies on volatility were based on trade in parts and components or specific types of goods exports. Therefore, the data used in these papers are sensitive to the goods classification system employed by the authors and uncomprehensive in their coverage of goods exports. In addition, these studies also leave out exports of services which is an important component of trade in GVCs. I–O-based trade in value-added data, which accounts for both goods and service exports, has only begun to be utilised in a handful of very recent papers such as IMF (2015), Cheng *et al.* (2016), Sato and Zhang (2017) as well as Ahmed *et al.* (2017). Third, there are very few ASEAN-centric papers which yield ASEAN-specific policy implications. This chapter seeks to address these gaps in the literature.

[15] See McKenzie (1999) and Ćorić and Pugh (2010) as well as Auboin and Ruta (2013) for detailed surveys.

3.6 Empirical Methodology

The export demand equation to estimate the impacts of REER movements and volatility on real gross exports is specified as follows. The baseline model expresses real gross exports as a function of the stock of Foreign Direct Investment (FDI) to represent production capacity and trade-weighted geometric average of trading partners' real GDP (FORGDP) to measure foreign demand for exports. This is consistent with the related literature (see, for example, Cheng *et al.*, 2016). Lagged FDI stock is used to avoid endogeneity. Real gross exports are obtained by deflating nominal gross exports by the consumer price index (CPI). In other words, the baseline equation is as follows:

$$\ln Y_{i,t} = \beta_0 + \beta_1 \ln \text{FDI}_{i,t-1} + \beta_2 \ln \text{FORGDP}_{i,t} + u_i + \mu_t + \epsilon_{i,t} \quad (1)$$

where

$\ln Y_{i,t}$: Log of real gross exports of country i in year t;
$\beta_1 \ln \text{FDI}_{i,t-1}$: Lagged log of real FDI stock of country i;
$\ln \text{FORGDP}_{i,t}$: Log of trade-weighted geometric average real GDP of trading partners;
u_i and μ_t : Country and time fixed effects.

A priori, β_1 and β_2 are expected to be positive as increases in FDI stock and FORGDP represent upward shifts in supply capacity and foreign demand for exports, respectively. The model is then augmented with REER levels and volatility. In the main empirics, REER enters as the yearly average of monthly REER while REER volatility is measured as the standard deviation of the monthly changes in REER. Lag values are used to guard against endogeneity. The augmented model is expressed in equation (2) as follows:

$$\begin{aligned}\ln Y_{i,t} = {} & \beta_0 + \beta_1 \ln \text{FDI}_{i,t-1} + \beta_2 \ln \text{FORGDP}_{i,t} + \beta_3 \ln \text{REER}_{i,t-1} \\ & + \beta_4 \ln \text{VREER}_{i,t-1} + u_i + \mu_t + \epsilon_{i,t}\end{aligned} \quad (2)$$

The coefficients β_3 and β_4 reflect the effects of exchange rate movements and volatility on real gross exports. We then interact REER and REER volatility with the FVA share in Gross Exports, while also incorporating the latter into the model. The coefficients on the interaction terms β_6 and β_7 are the key coefficients of interest. They capture the effects of intensive utilisation of imported inputs in export production on the relationships between exports, REER and REER volatility. *A priori*, the signs of these coefficients are ambiguous.

$$\begin{aligned}\ln Y_{i,t} = {} & \beta_0 + \beta_1 \ln \text{FDI}_{i,t-1} + \beta_2 \ln \text{FORGDP}_{i,t} + \beta_3 \ln \text{REER}_{i,t-1} \\ & + \beta_4 \ln \text{VREER}_{i,t-1} + \beta_5 \text{FVA}_{i,t-1} + \beta_6 \text{FVA}_{i,t-1} * \ln \text{REER}_{i,t-1} \\ & + \beta_7 \text{FVA}_{i,t-1} * \ln \text{VREER}_{i,t-1} + u_i + \mu_t + \epsilon_{i,t}\end{aligned} \quad (3)$$

The model is estimated through panel regression with controls for country and time-fixed effects on a sample containing eight ASEAN economies over the period 1995–2011. Data on exports and the FVA share in Gross Exports for each country are obtained from WTO-OECD TiVA. As for REER data, we collect the REER138 series published by the Bruegel Institute for the main empirics. This is a conventional REER series computed based on gross trade data. Although the literature has increasingly promoted the use of REER adjusted for value-added trade, limitations in the computation of such data mean that it can only be employed as a robustness check. Section 3.5.2 discusses our choices of data serie in more detail.

In addition, a variety of robustness checks were conducted. Though meta-regression studies such as Ćorić and Pugh (2010) have found that the specification of exchange rate volatility generally does not have a significant effect on empirical findings, our main results were tested against different measures of REER volatility and various REER series, including Bruegel's REER41 and the two value-added REER series computed by Bayoumi *et al.* (2013). Finally, checks were conducted to see if the results remain robust when real gross exports are deflated by GDP deflators instead of CPI.

3.7 Empirical Results and Robustness Checks

Table 3.4 presents our main findings. Real gross exports are positively associated with FDI stock and FORGDP. Furthermore, these relationships are statistically significant across all specifications. This is in line with theoretical priors. Meanwhile, REER and REER volatility are negatively associated with real gross exports. However, the relationships only become statistically significant when the FVA share and the interaction terms are incorporated into the model. This points to a need to account for GVC participation when estimating the effects of REER and REER volatility on exports.

As shown in the last column of Table 3.4, the interaction terms of FVA with REER and REER volatility enter the regression equation positively and both coefficients are statistically significant at the 1% threshold. This indicates that GVC participation has offsetting effects on the trade impacts of exchange rate. The coefficients on these terms are both statistically significant at the 1% threshold and economically significant. Using the estimated coefficients, the dampening effect of FVA on the impact of REER on real gross exports at the average FVA share may be calculated as follows:

$$\frac{0.0455 * \text{average FVA share}}{-1.415} * 100\% \approx -93\% \qquad (4)$$

Similarly, the dampening effect of FVA on the impact of REER volatility on real gross exports at the average FVA share may be calculated as

$$\frac{0.00893 * \text{average FVA share}}{-0.342} * 100\% \approx -75\% \qquad (5)$$

In other words, FVA helps to reduce the effect of exchange rate appreciation (depreciation) on real gross exports by 93% and offset the effect of increased volatility by about 75%.

These findings have important implications for exchange rate policies in ASEAN countries. Our result on the dampening effect of FVA share on the trade impact of REER movements serve to nuance the view put forth in Freund and Pierola (2012) that competitively valued exchange

Table 3.4: Summary of Empirical Results

Dependent Variable: ln(Real Gross Exports)	Model 1a: Baseline	Model 1b: Augmented with REER	Model 1c: Augmented with REER Volatility	Model 1d: Augmented with FVA and FVA Interactions
Lag of ln(Real FDI Stock)	**0.105****	**0.109****	**0.105****	**0.160*****
	(0.0454)	(0.0457)	(0.0457)	(0.0453)
ln(FORGDP)	**1.126*****	**1.128*****	**1.096*****	**0.897*****
	(0.160)	(0.161)	(0.162)	(0.202)
Lag of ln(REER138)	—	–0.186	–0.226	**–1.415*****
	—	(0.224)	(0.226)	(0.435)
Lag of ln(Volatility)	—	—	–0.0640	**–0.342*****
	—	—	(0.0517)	(0.0970)
Lag of Share of FVA in Gross Exports	—	—	—	**–0.212***** (0.0731)
Lag of FVA Share × Lag of ln(REER138)	—	—	—	**0.0455***** (0.0159)
Lag of FVA Share × Lag of ln(Volatility)	—	—	—	**0.00893***** (0.00290)
Constant	**–6.239*****	**–5.425****	**–4.739***	3.083
	(2.136)	(2.354)	(2.413)	(3.573)
Country fixed effect	Yes	Yes	Yes	Yes
Time fixed effect	Yes	Yes	Yes	Yes
Observations	126	126	126	126
R-squared	0.814	0.816	0.818	0.846

Note: *, ** and *** represent statistical significance at the 1%, 5% and 10% thresholds, respectively.
Source: Authors' computation.

rates are crucial to promote exports. As our findings imply, competitive devaluation may not yield the desired export-boosting effect in countries with high share of FVA embodied in export production. However, managing volatility remains an important priority for ASEAN policy-makers as increased volatility may still reduce exporting activities despite the cushioning impact from GVC participation.

Table 3.5 summarises the results for REER, REER volatility and the interaction terms in our robustness checks. As can be seen from the table, the main results are largely robust across different specifications. One thing to note is that using value-added REER greatly reduces the sample size. In these regressions, the coefficients on REER and the interaction terms lose their significance, but retain their respective signs.

Lastly, although it is not a variable of interest, calculate the marginal effect of FVA share on real gross exports at average levels of REER and REER volatility. To do this, we differentiate Equation (3) with respect to FVA. This results in the following:

Table 3.5: Summary of Key Results in Robustness Checks

Variations		REER	REER Volatility	Interaction between FVA Share and REER	Interaction between FVA Share and REER Volatility	Notes on Sample Size for Robustness Checks
Different measures of REER volatility	Volatility measured as standard deviation of monthly REER	Negative & Significant	Negative & Significant	Positive & Significant	Positive & Significant	126 observations
	Volatility measured as coefficient of variations of monthly REER	Negative & Significant	Negative & Significant	Positive & Significant	Positive & Significant	126 observations
	Use REER Volatility without log	Negative & Significant	Negative & Significant	Positive & Significant	Positive & Significant	126 observations
Different REER Series	Bruegel's REER41	Negative & Significant	Negative & Significant	Positive & Significant	Positive & Significant	126 observations
	Bayoumi *et al.* (2013)'s REER in Goods	Negative & Insignificant	Negative & Significant	Positive & Insignificant	Positive & Insignificant	62 observations
	Bayoumi *et al.* (2013)'s REER in Tasks	Negative & Insignificant	Negative & Significant	Positive & Insignificant	Positive & Insignificant	62 observations
Real Gross Exports deflated by GDP Deflator		Negative & Significant	Negative & Significant	Positive & Significant	Positive & Significant	126 observations

Source: Authors' calculation and compilation.

$$\frac{d\ln Y_{i,t}}{d\mathrm{FVA}_{i,t-1}} = \beta_5 + \beta_6 * \ln \mathrm{REER}_{i,t-1} + \beta_7 * \ln \mathrm{VREER}_{i,t-1} \quad (6)$$

We then substitute in the coefficients from Table 3B.2, Model 1d and the mean values for REER and REER volatility in Table 3B.1. This generates an interesting result; note that despite the negative sign on the coefficients of the FVA term in Table 3B.2, the marginal effect of FVA share on real gross exports at the average levels of REER and REER volatility is positive: raising the FVA share by one percentage point will increase gross exports by 0.26%.

3.8 Policy Implications and Concluding Notes

International trade has evolved from exchanges of final goods and services produced mostly within national borders — the stylised "Portuguese wine" or "English cloth" in the traditional Ricardian model — to exchanges of value-added intermediate goods in complex GVCs spanning multiple countries. The expansion of trade among ASEAN countries over the past two to three decades is closely linked to their integration into regional and global value chains. Rising prevalence of production fragmentation has opened a host of interesting research questions, among which are issues related to fluctuations in exchange rate levels and its volatility.

This chapter has shed light on the extent of ASEAN's integration into GVCs and the effects of GVC participation, conceptualised as the greater utilisation of foreign content in export production, on the trade impacts of exchange rate. Despite the rich bodies of theoretical and empirical research on the nexus between exchange rate and exports, there are few studies which account for the role of GVCs. Our study contributes to this budding literature by investigating the trade effects of both exchange rate levels and volatility in the GVC context. Using annual data from the OECD-WTO TiVA, we obtain a measure of the FVA share in gross exports for eight ASEAN countries between 1995 and 2011. We then employ the panel fixed effects model to estimate the effects of REER and REER volatility on real gross exports and their interactions with the FVA share. Past similar papers based on older vintages of the TiVA database such as Ahmed *et al.* (2017) and Cheng *et al.* (2016) have only focused on exchange rate elasticity and could only use data points which were available at five-year intervals.

Through this empirical exercise, we find that there is still evidence of a negative relationship between exchange rate appreciation and gross exports for ASEAN-8. However, integration into GVCs almost completely offsets this relationship. On average, high FVA share in gross exports reduces the effect of exchange rate appreciation/depreciation on exports by 93%. Thus, competitive devaluation may not boost exports in the presence of GVCs. However, exchange rate volatility still matters. We find that increased volatility negatively impacts export performance. Additionally, its impacts are not fully offset by high FVA share. As such, ASEAN economies cannot rely on FVA as a natural hedge and managing exchange rate volatility remains important for these export-oriented economies to thrive.

Taken as a whole, the study provides several key policy insights to ASEAN as a trade-reliant region. First, the positive relationship established between Gross Exports and FDI demonstrates a need to maintaining a positive investment environment conducive to attracting investments. Second, the positive relationship between Gross Exports and Foreign Real GDP highlights a possible risk factor arising from exposure to external shocks to the world economy. Lastly and no less importantly, based on the innovation of this study in analysing the impact of exchange rates and exchange rate volatility in the context of GVCs, we find that FVA share offsets the positive impact of exchange rate depreciations and does not offset the negative impact of exchange rate volatility. If the goal of monetary policy is to encourage export-oriented growth, policy-makers should be careful of devaluing the exchange rates and introducing volatility.

References

Ahmed, Swarnali, Maximiliano Appendino, and Michele Ruta. 2017. "Global Value Chains and the Exchange Rate Elasticity of Exports." *The B.E. Journal of Macroeconomics* 17 (1): 1–24.

Amador, João, and Sónia Cabral. 2016. "Global Value Chains: A Survey of Drivers and Measures." *Journal of Economic Surveys* 30 (2): 278–301. doi:10.1111/joes.12097.

Ando, Mitsuyo. 2006. "Fragmentation and Vertical Intra-Industry Trade in East Asia." *North American Journal of Economics and Finance* 17 (3): 257–281. doi:10.1016/j.najef.2006.06.005.

Ang, James B, and Jakob Madsen. 2013. "International R&D Spillovers and Productivity Trends in the Asian Miracle Economies." *Economic Inquiry* 51 (2): 1523–1541.

Arize, Augustine C., Thomas Osang, and Daniel J. Slottje. 2000. "Exchange-Rate Volatility and Foreign Trade: Evidence from Thirteen LDCs." *Journal of Business & Economic Statistics* 18 (1): 10–17.

ASEAN Secretariat. 2017. *ASEAN Economic Community 2025 Consolidated Strategic Action Plan*. Jakarta: ASEAN Secretariat.

Athukorala, Prema-chandra. 2005. "Product Fragmentation and Trade Patterns in East Asia." *Asian Economic Papers* 4 (3): 1–27.

Auboin, Marc, and Michele Ruta. 2013. "The Relationship between Exchange Rates and International Trade: A Literature Review." *World Trade Review* 12 (3): 577–605.

Baak, Saang Joon, M. A. Al-Mahmood, and S. Vixathep. 2007. "Exchange Rate Volatility and Exports from East Asian Countries to Japan and the USA." *Applied Economics* 39 (8): 947–959.

Balassa, Bela. 1978. "Exports and Economic Growth". *Journal of Development Economics* 5 (2): 181–189.

Baron, David P. 1976. "Flexible Exchange Rates, Forward Markets, and the Level of Trade." *American Economic Review* 66 (3): 253–266.

Bayoumi, Tamim, Mika Saito, and Jarkko Turunen. 2013. "Measuring Competitiveness: Trade in Goods or Tasks?" *IMF Working Paper No.* 13(100). International Monetary Fund (IMF): Washington DC.

Bems, Rudolfs, and Robert C. Johnson. 2012. "Value-Added Exchange Rates." *NBER Working Paper No.* 18498. National Bureau of Economic Research (NBER): Massachusetts.

Bems, Rudolfs, and Robert C. Johnson. 2015. "Demand for value added and value-added exchange rates." IMF Working Paper, September 8, 2015. Academic OneFile.

Bhagwati, Jagdish N. 1994. "Free Trade: Old and New Challenges". *Economic Journal* 104 (423): 231–246.

Broll, Udo, and Bernhard Eckwert. 1999. "Exchange Rate Volatility and International Trade." *Southern Economic Journal* 66 (1): 178–185.

Campa, Jose Manuel, and Linda S. Goldberg. 2002. "Exchange Rate Pass-Through into Import Prices: A Macro or Micro Phenomenon?" *NBER Working Paper* 8934. National Bureau of Economic Research (NBER): Massachusetts.

Caporale, Tony, and Khosrow Doroodian. 1994. "Exchange Rate Variability and the Flow of International Trade". *Economic Letters,* 46–1 (September): 49–54.

Chaudhary, Ghulam Mujtaba, Shujahat Haider Hashmi, and Muhammad Asif Khan. 2016. "Exchange Rate and Foreign Trade: A Comparative Study of Major South Asian and South-East Asian Countries." *Procedia — Social and Behavioral Sciences*, 230: 85–93.

Cheng, Kevin C., Gee Hee Hong, Dulani Seneviratne, and Rachel van Elkan. 2016. "Rethinking the Exchange Rate Impact on Trade in a World with Global Value Chains." *International Economic Journal* 30 (2): 204–216.

Chit, Myint Moe. 2008. "Exchange Rate Volatility and Exports: Evidence from the ASEAN–China Free Trade Area." *Journal of Chinese Economic and Business Studies* 6 (3): 261–277.

Chow, Peter C. Y., and Mitchell H. Kellman. 1993. *Trade — The Engine of Growth in East Asia*. New York: Oxford University Press.

Ćorić, Bruno, and Geoff Pugh. 2010. "The Effects of Exchange Rate Variability on International Trade: A Meta-Regression Analysis." *Applied Economics* 42 (20): 2631–2644.

Deardorff, Alan V. 2001. "Fragmentation in Simple Trade Models." *The North American Journal of Economics and Finance* 12 (2): 121–137. doi:10.1016/S1062-9408(01)00043-2.

De Grauwe, Paul. 1988. "Exchange Rate Variability and the Slowdown in Growth of International Trade." *Staff Papers (International Monetary Fund)* 35 (1): 63–84.

Dixit, Avinash. 1989. "Entry and Exit Decisions under Uncertainty." *Journal of Political Economy* 97 (3): 620–638.

Doğanlar, Murat. 2002. "Estimating the Impact of Exchange Rate Volatility on Exports: Evidence from Asian Countries." *Applied Economics Letters* 9 (13): 859–863.

Doroodian, Khosrow. 1999. "Does Exchange Rate Volatility Deter International Trade in Developing Countries?" *Journal of Asian Economics* 10 (3): 465–474.

Fang, Wenshwo, Yihao Lai, and Stephen M. Miller. 2005. "Export Promotion through Exchange Rate Policy: Exchange Rate Depreciation or Stabilization?" *Department of Economics Working Paper No*. 2005-07. University of Connecticut: Connecticut.

Feder, Gershon. 1983. "On Exports and Economic Growth." *Journal of Development Economics* 12 (1–2): 59–73. doi:10.1016/0304-3878(83)90031-7.

Franke, Günter. 1991. "Exchange Rate Volatility and International Trading Strategy". *Journal of International Money and Finance* 10 (2): 292–307.

Freund, Caroline, and Martha Denisse Pierola. 2012. "Export Surges." *Journal of Development Economics* 97 (2): 387–395.

Ghosh, Amit, and Ramkishen S. Rajan. 2007. "A Survey of Exchange Rate Pass-Through in Asia." *Asian-Pacific Economic Literature* 21 (2): 13–28. https://doi.org/10.1111/j.1467-8411.2007.00199.x-i1.

Goldberg, Pinelopi Koujianou, and Michael M. Knetter. 1997. "Goods Prices and Exchange Rates: What Have We Learned?" *Journal of Economic Literature* 35 (3): 1243–1272.

Hall, Stephen, George Hondroyiannis, P.A.V.B. Swamy, George Tavlas, and Michael Ulan. 2010. "Exchange-Rate Volatility and Export Performance: Do Emerging Market Economies Resemble Industrial Countries or Other Developing Countries?" *Special Issue: P.A.V.B Swamy* 27 (6): 1514–1521.

Hayakawa, Kazunobu, and Fukunari Kimura. 2009. "The Effect of Exchange Rate Volatility on International Trade in East Asia." *Journal of the Japanese and International Economies* 23 (4): 395–406.

Heller, Peter S., and Richard C. Porter. 1978. "Exports and Growth: An Empirical Re-Investigation." *Journal of Development Economics* 5 (2): 191–193. doi:10.1016/0304-3878(78)90007-X.

IMF. 2015. "Reaping the Benefits from Global Value Chains" In *Regional Economic Outlook: Asia and Pacific*. Chapter 2. Washington DC: IMF.

Jones, Ronald W., and Henryk Kierzkowski. 2001. "Fragmentation: New Production Patterns in the World Economy." In *Fragmentation: New Production Patterns in the World Economy*, edited by Sven Arndt and Henryk Kierzkowski. Oxford: Oxford University Press.

Johnson, Robert C., and Guillermo Noguera. 2012. "Accounting for Intermediates: Production Sharing and Trade in Value Added." *Journal of International Economics* 86 (2): 224–236. doi:10.1016/j.jinteco.2011.10.003.

Keesing, Donald B. 1967. "Outward-Looking Policies and Economic Development." *The Economic Journal* 77 (306): 303–320.

Koopman, Robert, Shang-Jin Wei, Zhi Wang, and William Powers. 2010. "Give Credit Where Credit Is Due: Tracing Value Added in Global Production Chains". *NBER Working Paper No*. 16426. National Bureau of Economic Research (NBER): Massachusetts.

Koopman, Robert, Zhi Wang, and Shang-Jin Wei. 2014. "Tracing Value-Added and Double Counting in Gross Exports". *American Economic Review* 104 (2): 459–494.

Krueger, Anne O. 1998. "Why Trade Liberalisation Is Good for Growth." *The Economic Journal* 108 (450): 1513.

Krugman, Paul. 1989. "Differences in Income Elasticities and Trends in Real Exchange Rates." *European Economic Review* 33 (5): 1031–1046.

Little, Ian Malcolm David. 1981. "The Experience and Causes of Rapid Labour-Intensive Development in Korea, Taiwan Province, Hong Kong, and Singapore, and Possibilities for Emulation." In *Export-Led Industrialization and Development*, edited by M. K. Datta-Chaudhuri and Eddy Lee, 23–45. Geneva: ILO. https://scholar.google.com/scholar_lookup?publication_year=1982&author=I.+M.+D.+Littleauthor=E.+Lee&title=Export-Led+Industrialization+and+Development.

Leigh, Daniel, Weicheng Lian, Marcos Poplawski-Ribeiro, Rachel Szymanski, Viktor Tsyrennikov, and Hong Yang. 2017. "Exchange Rates and Trade: A Disconnect?" *IMF Working Paper No.* 17/58. International Monetary Fund (IMF): Washington DC.

Manzur, Meher, and Kenneth Khoo. 1996. "Real Exchange Rates and ASEAN Trade: A New Approach." *Journal of Asia-Pacific Business* 1 (3): 81–96.

Marin, Dalia. 1992. "Is the Export-Led Growth Hypothesis Valid for Industrialized Countries?" *The Review of Economics and Statistics* 74 (4): 678–688.

McKenzie, Michael D. 1999. "The Impact of Exchange Rate Volatility on International Trade Flows." *Journal of Economic Surveys* 13 (1): 71–106.

Ng, Francis, and Alexander Yeats. 2001. "Production Sharing in East Asia: Who Does What for Whom, and Why?" in *Global Production and Trade in East Asia*, 63–109. Boston, MA: Springer. doi:10.1007/978-1-4615-1625-5_5.

Obstfeld, Maurice and Kenneth Rogoff. 1998. "Risk and Exchange Rates." *NBER Working Paper No.* 6694. National Bureau of Economic Research (NBER): Massachusetts.

Sato, Kiyotaka, and Shajuan Zhang. 2017. "Exchange Rate Volatility, Exports and Global Value Chains." Presented at the RIETI-IWEPP-CESSA Joint Workshop: "Exchange Rates and International Currency: Perspective from China and Japan," Beijing, 19 November.

Sauer, Christine, and Alok K. Bohara. 2001. "Exchange Rate Volatility and Exports: Regional Differences between Developing and Industrialized Countries." *Review of International Economics* 9 (1): 133–152.

Savvides, Andreas. 1992. "Unanticipated Exchange Rate Variability and the Growth of International Trade." *Weltwirtschaftliches Archiv* 128 (3): 446–463.

Shambaugh, Jay. 2008. "A New Look at Pass-Through." *Journal of International Money and Finance* 27 (4): 560–591.

Soleymani, Abdorreza, Soo Y. Chua, and Abdul Fatah Che Hamat. 2017. "Exchange Rate Volatility and ASEAN-4's Trade Flows: Is There a Third Country Effect?" *International Economics and Economic Policy* 14 (1): 91–117.

Song, H. 2012. "New Challenges to the Export Oriented Growth Model." In *Moving Toward a New Development Model for East Asia-the Role of Domestic Policy and Regional Cooperation*, edited by Y Zhang, Fukinari Kimura, and S Oum. Jakarta: ERIA.

Tan Khee Giap, Luu Nguyen Trieu Duong, Chuah Hui Yin, and Diamanta Vania Lavi. 2017a. "Assessing the Impact of Real Exchange Rates on ASEAN's Trade Flows in the Context of Global Value Chains."

ACI Technical Working Paper #08–2017. Singapore: Asia Competitiveness Institute, Lee Kuan Yew School of Public Policy, National University of Singapore.

Tan, Khee Giap, Le Phuong Anh Nguyen, and Trieu Duong Luu Nguyen. 2017b. *2016 Annual Competitiveness Analysis and Growth Slowdown Analysis for ASEAN-10*. Asia Competitiveness Institute — World Scientific Series. Singapore: World Scientific. https://doi.org/10.1142/10617.

Tang, Hsiao Chink. 2014. "Exchange Rate Volatility and Intra-Asia Trade: Evidence by Type of Goods." *The World Economy* 37 (2): 335–352.

Timmer, Marcel P., Abdul Azeez Erumban, Bart Los, Robert Stehrer, and Gaaitzen J. de Vries. 2014. "Slicing Up Global Value Chains." *The Journal of Economic Perspectives* 28 (2): 99–118.

Thorbecke, Willem. 2008. "The Effect of Exchange Rate Volatility on Fragmentation in East Asia: Evidence from the Electronics Industry." *Journal of the Japanese and International Economies* 22 (4): 535–544.

UNCTAD. 2013. "Global Value Chains: Investment and Trade for Development." *World Investment Report 2013*. Geneva: UNCTAD.

World Bank. 1993. "The East Asian Miracle: Economic Growth and Public Policy." Washington DC: World Bank.

WTO. 2008. "Trade, the Location of Production and the Industrial Organization of Firms." In *Trade in a Globalizing World*, 81–122. World Trade Report 2008. Geneva: WTO. https://www.wto.org/english/res_e/publications_e/wtr08_e.htm.

Wakasugi, Ryuhei. 2007. "Vertical Intra-Industry Trade and Economic Integration in East Asia." *Asian Economic Papers* 6 (1): 26–45.

Yamano, Norihiko, Meng Bo, and Kiichiro Fukasaku. 2011. "Fragmentation and Changes in the Asian Trade Network." 2011-01. *ERIA Policy Brief*. ERIA. http://www.eria.org/publications/policy_briefs/fragmentation-and-changes-in-the-asian-trade-network.html.

Discussant Notes 3.1

Dr. Lee Jae Young

Group Head and Lead Economist,
ASEAN+3 Macroeconomic Research Office (AMRO) Management

The presented studies are timely and relevant, in particular, when globalization has been facing strong headwinds in several advanced economies recently. For decades, trade and investment have been the engines of global growth, but we should admit that our understanding about how trade and investment were shaping our economies not only in growth but also in other parts of our lives remain limited. Surge of protectionism in major advanced economies might simply reflect our lack of understanding about globalization and limited policy actions thereafter. While globalization and, in particular, the development of global value chain was analysed and studied by many researchers, we did not clearly understand how the medium-term consequences could be. A few comments are provided.

First, while it is broadly agreed among economists that trade and investment are the key pillars of globalization, the relationship between trade and investment remains an issue. Inward foreign direct investment (FDI) has been broadly seen positive for growth and employment in a host economy, but outward FDIs has been often viewed as stolen jobs and lost growth by some policymakers. How to understand FDI and trade in this globalized world remains crucial.

In the study of "impact of real effective exchange rates on trade in goods and services", FDI stock was used as proxy for production capacity. There are different types of FDIs that would have different implications on exports and other outcomes. Relationship between trade and FDI stock may need to be further elaborated which may affect the efficiency of the model. For instance, market-seeking type of FDI does involve reduced imports and may not have big impacts on export of the host country. In contrast, efficiency-seeking type of FDI which may integrate a host country into the global value chain would require importing intermediary goods or exporting final products.

Many Japanese companies expanded their investments in several ASEAN countries in response to rising cost of production in Japan due to appreciation of its currency and in search for markets as well. In many cases, these companies imported intermediary goods from Japan which in turn put into assembly with varying degrees. Recent survey by JETRO shows that Japanese overseas subsidiaries have rapidly increased their local sales in Asia but exports to other countries have been limited. In particular, as for transportation equipment, local sales accounted for about over 80 percent. Meanwhile, local contents in those FDI companies' products continued to increase, reaching around 50 to 60 percent in many sectors. Data also shows that imports and exports of these FDI companies fluctuated over years depending on degree of local content and situation of the target markets. These types of dynamics of FDI companies' activities may cause biases in model estimation.

Second, a few emerging markets and developing economies have large energy or commodity sectors in their exports and thus energy or commodity prices, which largely depend on global growth, have had significant impacts on such economies. Exchange rates of these energy or commodity exporting countries were heavily influenced by global growth that affects global demand on commodities and energy and commodity prices. By the same token, exchange rates of energy or commodity importing countries would be also affected by global energy or commodity prices in the opposite direction. Given that growth and exchange rate would be closely related, the model estimation could be inefficient. For example, in commodity-exporting countries like Indonesia and Malaysia, policymakers were concerned about losses in competitiveness in manufacturing sector due to real exchange rate appreciation during commodity boom period. Incorporating the energy or commodity price into the model could be challenging.

Third, one of the policy implications from the study, which is "competitive devaluation may not yield the desired export-boosting effect in a world of global value chains" may need to be qualified a bit, if we consider medium-term consequences. Set aside the feasibility of maintaining a medium-term competitive devaluation, if a country has succeeded in maintaining a prolonged period of cheap currency, the country might continue to have larger inflows of efficiency-seeing type of FDI which in turn might increase exports. Consequent current account surplus might result in currency appreciation of the country which may self-correct the imbalances. However, this may not apply to a prolonged period of appreciation due to surge in oil or other commodity exports that happened in many oil or other commodity-exporting countries in the past. Should the country lose competitiveness in manufacturing exports, due to commodity-boom-driven currency appreciation, the country might lose ground in manufacturing sector. In such a case, even a significant competitive devaluation might not help the country regain its prowess in manufacturing sector. This is the so-called, "Dutch Disease".

Lastly, it is true that the establishment of the AEC in 2015 shows that ASEAN is on the right track in their efforts to strengthen regional integration. However, ironically, the fact that there seems like not much resistance to economic integration which is seen in the U.S. and in Europe also implies that there is a long way to go for ASEAN integration. While it is true that ASEAN is getting more intensively integrated into the global value chain, but at the same time intra-regional integration among ASEAN members themselves remain pretty limited as often compared to the case of Europe. How to enhance economic complementarity and mutual benefits among ASEAN economies themselves remains the key task.

Discussant Notes 3.2

Dr. Frederico Gil Sander

Lead Country Economist, Macroeconomics & Fiscal Management, The World Bank Group

Thank you. Tan Sri already stole my most important point, which is that actually one of the things that GVCs really kind of put into focus is how you need to import in order to export. So countries, if you are thinking about global competition, the focus is all on exports, and you want to protect your domestic industries, so that you move up the value chain, so that they can actually export more. But I think that what is sometimes lost in this, and what I think the discussion on global value chains helps focus, is that you need to be able to import and import effectively and easily, in order to actually be a player in the global value chain. If you are doing just in time production, the logistics, the facility that you have, trade facilitation, the facility of goods moving through imports, the kind of tariff regime — all of these things are going to be very important for someone who is going to decide to build part of the global value chain in a particular country, so I think that this is actually the most important point, and thank you Tan Sri for making it.

One of the things that ASEAN really needs to look at is how to actually dismantle this protectionism, which is actually not helping its own competitive position as an exporter into the broader global market. I think that the second point, which is very closely related to that, is on the importance of investment, in order for trade in a world of GVCs, that openness to investment, including investment in things which may seem unrelated, such as services and manufacturing related services, as well as other complementary services to the well-functioning of a manufacturing sector, is also going to be brought into focus by global value chain analysis. What we see in the global value chain analysis, is that a lot of the value added that is exported actually comes from services, and it actually comes from services that are embedded into the manufacturing exports.

So, if you think that I am only going to have FDI for manufacturing because I want to increase my manufacturing exports and I am going to retain a very close very restrictive services sector — actually what the GVC literature helps you see is that these things are connected, and you are actually undermining the competitiveness of your manufacturing sector when you have a lot of restrictions on foreign investment in the services sector as well. So, imports are needed to exports, and services are needed for manufacturing, and the technology that comes with FDI in manufacturing is important, but so is the technology that comes with FDI into services. Now, going to the issue of the exchange rate, I think that here it is important to take a step back, and think and remember why do we find this relationship and why do we talk about competitive exchange rates and non-competitive exchange rates.

That actually has to do one with the fact that the price level is related to the level of wages. Right, so if you have an appreciated exchange rate, presumably what this is saying in short, is that you have very high labour costs, very high operating costs in the domestic currency, compared to the cost that you can get for the products that you export, and therefore if your exchange rate was devalued, you would actually be more competitive. But what should always be kept in mind, is that the extent that wages play an important part in this: What matters is really not the wage level, but it is the unit labour cost, which is the wage level divided by the productivity of those workers which are earning those wages. So you could actually have — and it is natural to have — in a sense appreciating exchange rates over time, because wages are growing, but that will only make the country less competitive if the labour productivity is not growing in tandem. And of course, there are a lot of pressures as the economy goes richer through various mechanisms for wages to rise above productivity. And this is why it is a tough job of policy makers to try to make sure that productivity is always growing in tandem with wages. What it takes for the productivity to continue growing, to go back to my earlier comments, is precisely to be involved in global trade — even for large countries like Indonesia, even for large countries like India, where I worked before.

I am from Brazil. All these large countries, they might think that they do not need the external demand. But I think that what China shows — China also doesn't need the external demand — but what they did is that they use the external demand to actually drive productivity growth by creating these centers of excellence in the coast — they were doing the exports and they were bringing and learning, by doing a lot of the technology in a lot of the different managerial techniques — all the little kind of micro elements that drives to higher productivity growth. So, this issue of dismantling barriers and really looking out for more in order to drive productivity growth — I think that it is something very important for the small economies that require the external markets to get economies of scale, but it is also important for the larger economies, which have the economies of scale, but who need the external market to drive productivity growth.

And I just want to make one final point in thinking about this trade agenda — which is maybe a little bit provocatively: What is the role of national champions in terms of driving growth of trade and growth in global value chains? I think that we have seen that Japan created its national champions, certain recognized company names that became very well known in external markets, that was followed by Korea. And now I mentioned that many of us have Samsung phones here, so that Korea has developed its own brand names and its own champions.

Now, we are starting to see China create its own brand names. You know HUAWEI; even in the e-commerce sector there many kind of Chinese company names which are starting to become household names. But what about in ASEAN? What would it take? I mean there are many companies that are kind of household names domestically. But what would it take to actually take some of those domestic household names, who have become quite accommodated in each of their respective economies, and tell them that they should actually go abroad- maybe starting within the ASEAN market itself? I think that one of the good examples of something that happened in Malaysia is the Transformation Programme for the government-linked companies. Among all the Transformation Programmes that Malaysia has experienced over the last few years, this perhaps is the least publicized, but I think it is actually a very effective Transformation Programme, and one of the key elements in my view is that one of the many elements of the transformation Programme was to tell some of the government-linked companies that they should go and become regional players within ASEAN. So you go to Indonesia, you have CIMB present in Indonesia, you have Maybank. You go to Thailand, CIMB is now present in Thailand. So at least regionally, you see a lot of these government-linked companies actually going and trying to export their services at the regional market and trying to become at least regional names. But I think that ASEAN can aspire and can have larger ambitions. Right, why shouldn't CIMB or Maybank be like Citibank and as recognized globally as some of these Western banks? I mean HSBC has already done it, starting from Hong Kong. Thinking about the role of national champions — national champions which become household names within ASEAN and globally, I think that can also be something that helps drive trade growth.

So with that, thank you very much.

Annex A Literature Tables

Table 3A.1: ASEAN-Related Empirical Studies on the Relationship between Exchange Rate and Exports in the Conventional Context

Paper	Methodology	Country	Period	Dependent Variable	Independent Variable	Controls	Findings
Arize *et al.* (2000)	Time series regression (Johansen method of co-integration)	13 less developed countries (LDCs) including four ASEAN economies: Indonesia, Malaysia, Philippines and Thailand	1973–1996	Real export volume	REER volatility	Income, Relative prices	Negative impact of exchange rate volatility on exports in both the short and long run.
Baak *et al.* (2007)	Time series regression (co-integration and error-correction model)	Hong Kong, South Korea, Singapore and Thailand	1981–2004	Bilateral export volume from the five countries to Japan and US	Real exchange rate volatility	Income, real bilateral exchange rate	In the case of exports to the US, the paper found a negative long-run relationship between exports and exchange rate volatility in South Korea and Singapore, but no such relationship in Hong Kong and Thailand. Short-run impacts were not detected for Singapore and Thailand, but for Hong Kong and South Korea. When exports to Japan were considered, positive long-run relationship was found for Hong Kong and Singapore while negative long-run relationship was found for South Korea and Thailand. Statistically significant negative short-run dynamics were found for all economies except for Hong Kong.
Chaudhary *et al.* (2016)	Time series regression (co-integration and error-correction model)	Pakistan, India, Bangladesh, Sri Lanka and four ASEAN economies: Indonesia, Malaysia, Singapore and Thailand	1979–2010	Exports and imports	Nominal exchange rate levels	NA	Statistically significant long-run relationship between exchange rate and exports for Indonesia but no significant result was found for Malaysia, Singapore and Thailand.

Chit (2008)	Fixed and random effects models for panel data	China, Indonesia, Malaysia, Philippines, Thailand	1982–2005	Real export volume	Bilateral real exchange rate volatility	Income, Relative prices	Negative relationship between bilateral real exchange rate volatility and bilateral exports.
Doğanlar (2002)	Time series regression (Granger method of co-integration)	Turkey, South Korea, Pakistan and two ASEAN economies: Malaysia and Indonesia	1980–1996	Real export volume	Real exchange rate volatility	Income, Relative prices	Negative relationship between exchange rate volatility and exports.
Doroodian (1999)	Time series regression (ARMA-GARCH model)	India, South Korea and an ASEAN economy: Malaysia	1973–1996	Real export volume	Real exchange rate volatility	Income, Relative prices	Negative relationship between exchange rate volatility and exports.
Fang *et al.* (2005)	Dynamic conditional correlation bivariate GARCH-M model	Eight Asian economies including four ASEAN economies: Indonesia, Malaysia, Philippines and Singapore	1979–2003	Bilateral export revenue with US	Real exchange rate levels	Real foreign income	Negative relationship between exchange rate depreciation and exports.
Hall *et al.* (2010)	Panel regression with generalised method of moments estimation and time-varying-coefficient estimation	21 economies including three ASEAN economies: Philippines, Singapore and Thailand	1980–2005	Real export volume	Real exchange rate volatility	Income, relative prices, oil exporters export earnings, exporters	Negative relationship between exchange rate volatility and exports.

(*Continued*)

Table 3A.1: *(Continued)*

Paper	Methodology	Country	Period	Dependent Variable	Independent Variable	Controls	Findings
Manzur and Khoo (1996)	Ordinary Least Square (OLS)	Indonesia, Malaysia, Singapore, Thailand	1973–1990	Export volume	Real exchange rate levels	Income elasticity, price elasticity	A real appreciation (depreciation) might diminish (enhance) export growth. However, the exchange rate effect was found to be relatively minor.
Sauer and Bohara (2001)	Fixed and random effects models for panel data	91 economies, including five ASEAN economies: Indonesia, Malaysia, Myanmar, Philippines, and Thailand	1973–1993	Real export volume	REER levels and volatility	Income, Relative prices	Negative relationship between exchange rate volatility and real exports. However, the trade effects of exchange rate were found to be heterogeneous across different geographical regions.
Savvides (1992)	OLS	62 economies, including six ASEAN economies: Indonesia, Malaysia, Myanmar, Philippines, Singapore and Thailand	1973–1986	Real export growth	REER volatility	Openness, terms of trade, productivity shocks	Negative relationship between the unanticipated exchange rate variability and real export growth.
Soleymani *et al.* (2017)	Gravity model	Indonesia, Malaysia, Singapore, Thailand, China, Hong Kong, Japan, Korea, US	1980–2012	Export and import volume	Real exchange rate volatility	Income and real exchange rate movements	Negative relationship between exchange rate volatility and export performance.

Source: Authors' compilation.

Table 3A.2: ASEAN-Related Empirical Studies on the Relationship between Exchange Rate and Exports in the GVCs Context

Paper	Methodology	Country	Period	Dependent Variable	Independent Variable	Controls	Findings
Ahmed *et al.* (2017)	Panel regression with country and time fixed effects	46 economies including four ASEAN economies: Indonesia, Malaysia, Singapore and Thailand	1996–2012	Real export growth for total exports, merchandise exports and manufacturing exports and value-added export growth	Growth of REER, REER levels in Goods Value-Added and REER levels in Tasks Value-Added	Lagged GDP, foreign demand, interaction between growth of REER and indicators of GVC participation and position	Participation in GVCs was found to lower exchange rate elasticity of manufactured goods exports. Results remained consistent when the analysis was conducted on sectoral data.
Cheng *et al.* (2016)	Panel regression with country and time fixed effects	57 economies including six ASEAN economies: Indonesia, Malaysia, Philippines, Singapore, Thailand and Vietnam	1995–2011	Volumes of foreign value-added (FVA) and domestic value-added (DVA), Gross imports and exports, Volumes of non-GVC trade	Value-added REER levels	Foreign demand, interaction between lagged value-added REER and share of foreign value-added in exports, real FDI stock, tariff, output gap, share of foreign value-added REER	Positive relationship between exchange rate depreciation and FVA and DVA of GVC-related exports. The exchange rate elasticity of exports was found to depend on the FVA content, in which higher FVA led to lower elasticity.
Hayakawa and Kimura (2009)	Gravity model	60 economies including five ASEAN economies: Indonesia, Malaysia, Philippines, Singapore and Thailand	1992–2005	Real export volume	Real exchange rate volatility	Income, distance, language, population, adjacency	Negative relationship between exchange rate volatility and exports. The negative impact was larger for Intra-East Asian trade and trade in intermediate goods.

(*Continued*)

Table 3A.2: ***(Continued)***

Paper	Methodology	Country	Period	Dependent Variable	Independent Variable	Controls	Findings
IMF (2015)	Panel regression with country and time fixed effects	57 economies including six ASEAN economies: Indonesia, Malaysia, Philippines, Singapore, Thailand and Vietnam	Not clearly stated	Exports and imports of non-GVC final goods and GVC-related goods	REER levels weighted by domestic value-added of exports	Demand, measure of position in GVC participation, real FDI stock, tariff, output gap	Exchange rate depreciation was found to have a negative effect on non-GVC exports, GVC-related exports and GVC-related imports. Positive relationship between exchange rate depreciation and non-GVC imports. The effect of exchange rate movements on GVC-related trade varied across regions and depended on the technological content of manufacturing.
Leigh *et al.* (2017)	Panel regression with country and time fixed effects	60 economies including all ASEAN economies except Laos and Myanmar	1980–2014	Export and import volume in aggregate and sectoral levels	Sectoral REER levels	Time trend, dummy for global financial crisis, foreign demand	Negative relationship between exchange rate depreciation and exports. Limited evidence supporting the argument that GVC participation has changed the discourse.
Sato and Zhang (2017)	Dynamic panel model with two-step generalised method of moments estimator	29 economies including six ASEAN economies: Indonesia, Malaysia, Philippines, Singapore, Thailand and Vietnam	1997–2012	Real exports of manufacturing industry	Bilateral nominal exchange rate volatility	Foreign demand, bilateral real exchange rate, GVC participation, an interaction term between bilateral real exchange rate and GVC participation, exporter–importer sector-specific effect, time fixed effect	Negative relationship between exchange rate volatility and exports but the effect was found to be dampened by GVC participation.

Thorbecke (2008)	Gravity model estimated through panel DOLS	China, Japan, Korea, five ASEAN economies: Indonesia, Malaysia, Philippines, Singapore and Thailand	1985–2005	Bilateral exports of electronic components and electronic final goods	REER volatility	Country pair and time fixed effects	Negative relationship between exchange rate volatility and electronic components flow in East Asia.
Tang (2014)	Gravity model estimated through panel DOLS	18 Asian economies including all ASEAN economies except Myanmar	1980–2009	Bilateral exports of primary, intermediate, equipment and consumption goods	Bilateral exchange rate volatility	Country pair and time fixed effects	Negative relationship between exchange rate volatility and exports with stronger impacts for intermediate goods.

Source: Authors' compilation.

Annex B Data Sources, Coverage and Definitions

Table 3B.1: Input–Output-Based Measures of GVCs

Database	Publishing Institution	Period	Countries
EORA MRIO	University of Sydney	1990–2012	187 (ASEAN-10)
OECD-WTO TiVA	OECD, WTO	1995–2011	63 (ASEAN-8 excluding Laos and Myanmar)
World Input–Output Database (WIOD)	European Commission	2000–2014	43 (Indonesia)
ADB MRIO	Asian Development Bank	2000, 2005–2008 and 2011	45 (ASEAN-5)
Global Trade Analysis Project (GTAP)	Purdue University	2004, 2007, 2011	140 (ASEAN-9 excluding Myanmar)
Asian International I–O Table	Institute of Developing Economies (IDE-JETRO)	1975, 1980, 1985, 1990, 1995, 2000, 2005	10 (ASEAN-8)

Source: Authors' compilation.

Table 3B.2: Sources of Conventional REER Data

Indicator	Price Index	Source	Definition	Coverage	Time Period	Data Frequency
REER	GDP deflator (2005 = 100)	UNCTAD	Each of the country's exchange rates against other major currencies (i.e. nominal exchange rates) is deflated by the price indices of the country and the corresponding partner countries to calculate real exchange rates. The weighted average (geometric mean) of real exchange rates is then calculated using the annual value of country's trade with the respective countries as its weights. It is then converted into an index and aggregated into various trade and economic country groups.	ASEAN-10	1998–2014	Annual
	CPI (2007 = 100)	Bruegel Institute	The REER is calculated from nominal effective exchange rate and a measure of the relative price or cost between the country under study and its trading partners. Bruegel provides two versions of the REER series: REER 138 and REER 41. The former calculates REER for a country with respect to 138 trading partners while the latter does so for 41 trading partners.	ASEAN-9 (Myanmar excluded) for annual series, ASEAN-10 for monthly series	1960–2015 (Annual) 1992–2015 (Annual) January 1995– December 2016 (Monthly)	Annual, Monthly

(*Continued*)

Table 3B.2: (*Continued*)

Indicator	Price Index	Source	Definition	Coverage	Time Period	Data Frequency
	CPI (2010 = 100)	Bank for International Settlements (BIS)	REERs are geometric weighted averages of bilateral exchange rates adjusted by relative consumer prices. The weighting pattern is time-varying.	Indonesia, Malaysia, Philippines, Singapore, Thailand	January 1994–July 2017	Monthly
	CPI (2010 = 100)	IMF	REER is the nominal effective exchange rate (a measure of the value of a currency against a weighted average of several foreign currencies) divided by a price deflator or index of costs.	Malaysia, Philippines, Singapore	January 1975–June 2017	Annual, Quarterly, Monthly
	Unit Labour Cost (2010 = 100)			Singapore	January 1995–June 2017	Annual, Quarterly, Monthly

Source: Authors' compilation.

Table 3B.3: Sources of Value-Added REER Data

Indicator	Series	Price Index	Source	Definition	Coverage	Time Period	Data Frequency
Value-Added REER	REER in Tasks REER in Goods	GDP deflator	Bayoumi *et al.* (2013)	REER in Tasks is the first-order approximation of Bems and Johnson (2012)'s VAREER. REER in Goods includes adjustments for shares of foreign country's value-added and domestic value-added in total cost.	Indonesia, Thailand, Singapore and Vietnam	January 1990–December 2011	Monthly
	VAREER based on Johnson and Noguera (2012) data	GDP deflator	Bems and Johnson (2015)	The authors used GDP deflators instead of CPI. REER to measure changes in relative prices and bilateral trade in value-added to construct country trade weights. The modelled intermediate input demand and consumption demand by assuming a production function with a global supply chain structure.	Indonesia, Thailand and Vietnam	1970–2009	Annual
	VAREER based on WIOD data				Indonesia	1995–2011	

Source: Authors' compilation.

Chapter 4
Impact of the US–China Trade War on ASEAN

4.1 Introduction

4.1.1 Global Trade Tensions

As the ASEAN bloc surges forward with its economic strategies aimed at opening up their markets and ensuring integration,[1] countries around the world are experiencing extensive "tensions in the global trading environment" and a widespread "proliferation of trade restrictive measures".[2]

Outlined in the World Trade Organization's (WTO) 2018 annual report on trade-related developments, WTO members imposed 137 new trade-restrictive measures during a one-year period from October 2017 to October 2018.[3] While this only forms 17% of total trade measures taken by WTO members, it is crucial to consider the trade coverage of the measures imposed, which the WTO defines as "the annual imports of the products concerned from economies affected by the measures".[4]

As expressed in Figure 4.1, attempts at trade-facilitating measures have amounted to a substantial US$295.6 billion, making up 30% of total trade coverage valued at US$996 billion. However, this falls far from trade-restrictive measures that ultimately stand at a larger sum of US$588.3 billion, making up the bulk of total trade coverage at 59%. Notably, this amount is also seven times larger than that of the previous year.

The development of trade-restrictive measures comes hand in hand with significant geopolitical developments playing out on the world stage, such as Brexit, the European Union's (EU) labelling of China as a "systemic rival" and "economic competitor",[5] as well as the United States' (US) "America First" strategy. The latter alone has resulted in consequential outcomes such as the US' withdrawal from the Trans-Pacific Partnership (TPP) agreement, renegotiations of the North American Free Trade Agreement (NAFTA) and the United States–Mexico–Canada Agreement (USMCA), as well as an upsurge of US tariffs with China, Mexico, Canada, Turkey, India and the EU. Most significant of all is the rapid, two-way escalation of tariffs between US and China, where friction between the two key contenders signals the possibility of a looming, full-blown trade war.

---

[1] See Chapter 1 for further details.

[2] See Azevedo (2018) for the 11 December 2018 speech by Roberto Azevêdo, Director General of World Trade Organization.

[3] See World Trade Organization (2019).

[4] Amount does not refer to the cost of trade measures.

[5] See European Commission (2019a).

Figure 4.1: Trade Coverage of Import Measures Taken by WTO Members, October 2017–October 2018

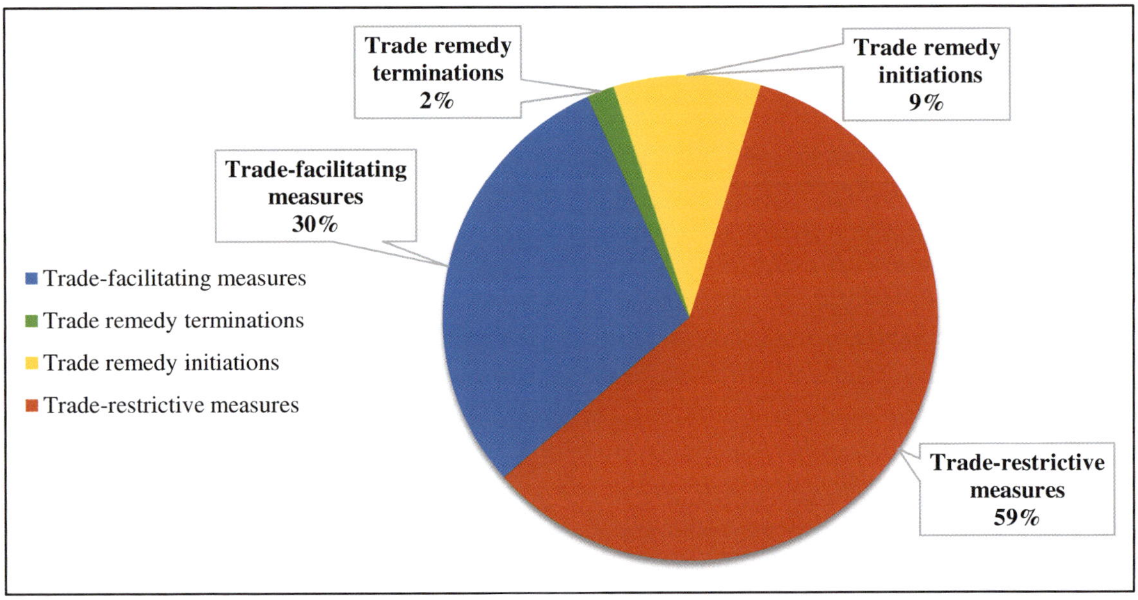

Source: Asia Competitiveness Institute based on WTO 2018 Annual Report.

4.1.2 Background of US–China Dispute

With the International Monetary Fund's projected 2019 GDP growth rate of 6.2% in comparison to the US' 2.5%, China's enormous potential for further growth has earned its status as a "superpower" that is soon to be potentially on par with the US.[6] Already, it is ranked the second largest economy in the world in terms of Gross Domestic Product (GDP). In 2017, China's GDP exceeded US$12 million, only slightly behind the US at US$19 billion.[7] If this figure is translated into Purchasing Power Parity (PPP) terms, China becomes the number one economy in the world, with a GDP (PPP) of 23.3 million international dollars in comparison to United States' 19.4 million international dollars.[8]

Trade-wise, according to the US Census Bureau, China replaced Canada's position as the US' top goods trading partner in September 2015, with China contributing to 15.7% of US' total goods trade versus Canada's 15.5%.[9] Since then, China has maintained its position as the US' largest trading partner in merchandise goods and has accounted for a growing amount of trade in merchandise goods — tellingly, in December 2017, it contributed 16.4% of US' total goods trade.

In sum, total merchandise goods trade between US and China amounted to US$635.4 million in 2017. This is also supplemented by a large total trade in services amounting to US$75 billion. However, while the US experienced a services trade surplus with China valued at US$40.2 billion,

[6] See Buzan (2004).

[7] See The World Bank (2019).

[8] *Ibid.*

[9] See U.S. Census Bureau Foreign Trade Division (2019a).

Figure 4.2: US Trade in Goods with China (million US$)

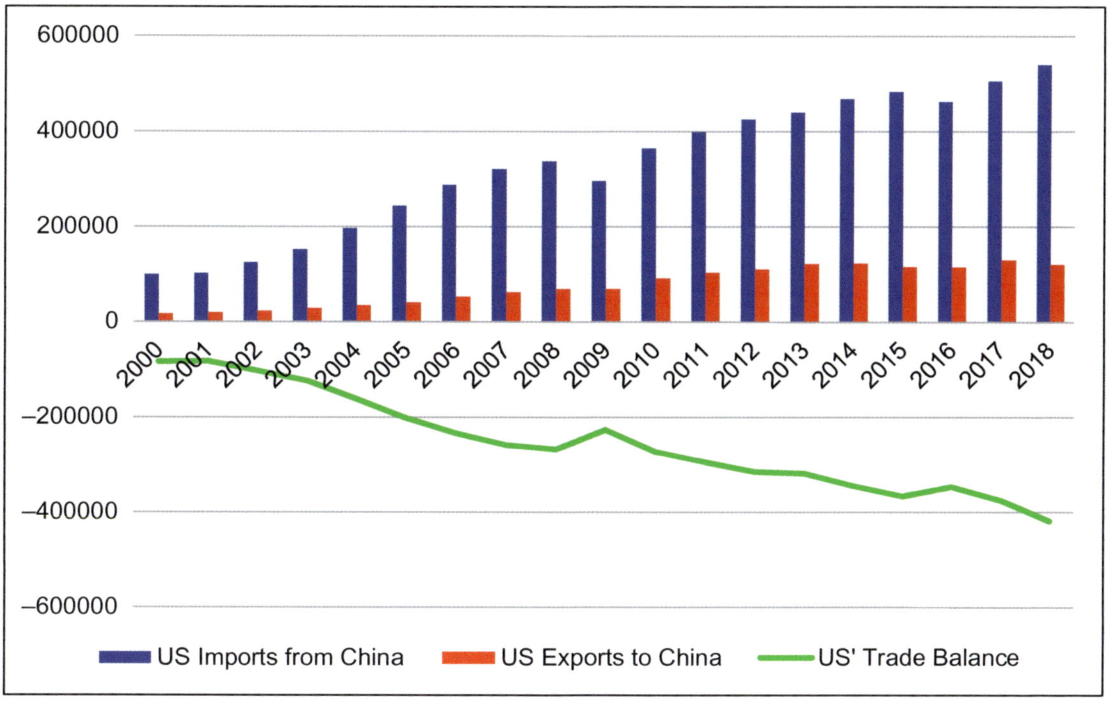

Source: Asia Competitiveness Institute based on data from US Census Bureau.

China's status as the number one exporter of merchandise goods resulted in the US having a goods trade deficit of US$375.6 billion — a far cry from the deficit of US$0.6 billion in 1985.[10] The trend of US' increasing goods trade deficit with China is further expressed in Figure 4.2.

Overall, this left the US with a more-than-substantial goods and services trade deficit of US$335.4 billion in 2017 — an 8.2% increase from 2016.[11] Other than the tensions caused by a growing trade deficit, clashes over the protection of technology, intellectual property rights and national security have become the core of ongoing US–China disputes today.

Frictions leading up to the trade stand-off between the two economies first gained momentum with the United States Trade Representative's (USTR) "Section 232 Investigation" on the impact of steel and aluminium imports on its national security in April 2017,[12] as well as the "Section 301 Investigation" targeted at scrutinizing "China's Acts, Policies, and Practices Related to Technology Transfer, Intellectual Property, and Innovation" in August 2017.[13] "Global safeguard tariffs" were then applied by the US on all solar panel, washing machine, steel and aluminium imports. In return, China retaliated by placing tariffs on fruit, wine, seamless steel pipes, pork and recycled aluminium, as well as anti-dumping tariffs on US imports of sorghum.

[10] See U.S. Census Bureau Foreign Trade Division (2019b).

[11] See Office of the United States Trade Representative (2019).

[12] See U.S. Department of Commerce (2019b).

[13] See Office of the United States Trade Representative (2017).

While there have been multiple attempts at trade talks and trade deals, there is still no end of dispute in sight.[14] In total, there have been three rounds of tariffs implemented by both countries and various WTO complaints lodged against each other. The third round of retaliatory tariffs implemented by both countries consist of US tariffs on US$200 billion worth of Chinese goods,[15] and the Chinese tariffs of US$60 billion on US imports[16] in September 2018. This brings the total amount of US tariffs applied to China to be US$250 billion, while total Chinese tariffs applied to the US stand at US$110 billion.

The US still threatens tariffs on US$267 billion more of Chinese goods, and the Chinese have held up their "tit for tat" retaliatory strategy by promising the use of "all measures including quantitative and qualitative tools to strike back."[17] Conflict between the two has been further antagonized by a host of various other events, such as US measures in January 2018 targeted at banning government use of Huawei and ZTE technology, both of which are the two largest Chinese telecommunication firms, stating that "Chinese Government-supported tele-communications equipment on US networks may be exploited through Chinese cyber activity, with China's intelligence services operating as an advanced persistent threat to US networks".[18] This was followed by a US-led detainment of the Chief Financial Officer of Huawei, in December 2018, on the grounds that the firm had violated US sanctions with Iran.[19] Subsequently, given the alleged violation of sanctions with Iran, a potential bipartisan bill was announced in January 2019 with intention to reinstate bans on US technological imports to Chinese firms.[20] This also comes in conjunction with a US anti-dumping probe into steel imports from Canada, China, and Mexico[21] — all of which have added fuel to the fire, leading to unresolved relations with neither side backing down.

Notably, relations between the two economies have long been complex and fraught with precariousness. In 2000, China's ascension to the WTO was hotly debated over the grounds of human rights violations.[22] Following that, incidences of friction that continued to occur between the two include: the US–China plane collision in 2001,[23] a 2007 WTO dispute lodged by the US against China for violating intellectual property rights,[24] China becoming the largest US foreign creditor in 2008,[25] another WTO dispute in 2012 regarding China's restrictions on rare earth metal exports,[26] and the 2014 charge of five Chinese hackers for cyber espionage.[27] Further, as mentioned above, contentions surrounding intellectual property rights and national security have been long-lasting since they were first raised in 2007.

---

[14] As of March 2019.

[15] See Press Release by Office of the United States Trade Representative (2018b).

[16] See Kim (2018).

[17] See Press Release by Ministry of Commerce, People's Republic of China (2018).

[18] See bill by U.S. Congress (2018).

[19] See Horowitz (2018).

[20] See The Straits Times (2019).

[21] See U.S. Department of Commerce (2019a).

[22] See Jendrzejczyk (2000) for statement by Mike Jendrzejczyk, Washington Director of Human Rights Watch.

[23] See Congressional Research Service (2001).

[24] See WTO Dispute Settlement case DS360 at World Trade Organization (2010).

[25] See Sharma (2010).

[26] See WTO Dispute Settlement case DS431 at World Trade Organization (2015).

[27] See Press Release by U.S. Department of Justice (2014).

Given the humongous value and size of these two economies in the global market, this has led to a flurry of economic uncertainty around the world. Stating that "there are signs that escalating trade tensions may already be affecting business confidence and investment decisions", the WTO has also consistently anticipated a fall in global merchandise trade volume growth, from a high of 4.7% in 2017 to 4.4% in 2018, and finally, to 4.0% in 2019.[28] Similarly, this has also led the International Monetary Fund (IMF) to revise its latest global growth forecasts downwards for 2019 and 2020 by 0.2% and 0.1%, respectively, thereby cutting projected growth rates to 3.5% in 2019 and 3.6% in 2020.[29]

While macroeconomic uncertainty spells trouble for all, the spillover effects of the US–China tensions will have a considerable impact in the ASEAN region. This is because its relative open-market economy[30] means that it is extremely dependent on external macroeconomics conditions. To this end, the following article titled "Can ASEAN Cope with the 'Trade War'?" by Mr. Bilahari Kausikan, Chairman of the Middle East Institute at the National University of Singapore, and former Permanent Secretary at the Ministry of Foreign Affairs of Singapore, can shed some light on the issue. This article first appeared in the January 2019 issue of ASEANFocus, a publication of the ASEAN Studies Centre at ISEAS-Yusof Ishak Institute, Singapore.

4.1.3 ASEAN and the Trade War

Box 4.1: Can ASEAN Cope with the "Trade War"?

ASEAN is facing a prolonged period of heightened US–China competition and hence of greater uncertainty. The most obvious manifestation of this new phase in US–China relations is the so-called "trade war". The term is something of a misnomer: trade is only the instrument; the objective is strategic competition. From 1972, when the US and China re-established relations, to the global financial crisis of 2009, the overall emphasis of US–China relations was on engagement. The US and China will continue to work together selectively. But as Vice-President Mike Pence's speech of 4 October 2018, the National Security Strategy of December 2017, and the National Defense Strategy of January 2018 clearly signaled, the overall emphasis of the relationship is now on strategic competition.

China was clearly caught on the back-foot by the new approach. Towards the end of the Hu Jintao administration and far more shrilly under Xi Jinping's leadership, Chinese foreign policy took on a triumphalist tone. Beijing seems to have over-estimated its own capabilities and began to believe its own propaganda about the US being in inevitable decline. ASEAN should not make the same mistake.

The new US approach of robust competition will not end with the Trump Administration. Nor will the agreement that Presidents Donald Trump and Xi Jinping reached in Argentina

(*Continued*)

[28] See Press Release by Azevedo (2018).

[29] See International Monetary Fund (2019).

[30] See Chapter 1.

Box 4.1: (*Continued*)

substantially change the situation. The new trend had been developing over many years. It was President George W. Bush that first dubbed China a "strategic competitor" almost twenty years ago. The mood of American businesses towards China on intellectual property (IP) and technology theft began to turn sour during the Bush '43 administration. 9/11 was a distraction. The subsequent wars in the Middle East gave China a virtually free hand in East Asia. President Barack Obama's "pivot" or "rebalance" was intended to refocus on China. But Obama had little stomach for competition and his rhetoric was hardly matched by action.

Trump has successfully positioned his administration's approach to China as an overdue correction to the perceived failures of his predecessors. Even if they do not always agree with his methods, this has resonated positively across the security and defense community, American businesses, as well as human rights and religious freedom advocates. This broad bipartisan consensus is a new paradigm that no American politician can ignore. Any subsequent presidential candidate will find it difficult to soften China policy without being accused of weakness. In any case, the new legislation that has been put in place with strong bipartisan support to make it difficult for China to acquire US technology defines a new framework for the relationship that any successor administration will find difficult to change, even if it is so inclined.

The Argentina deal is only a 90-day tactical pause in the implementation of new tariffs. It makes the US look reasonable. The 90-day deadline — not reported within China — dials-up the pressure on Beijing to demonstrate that it is serious about addressing US complaints about IP violations and other unfair economic policies. China has made some gestures. It has introduced a new foreign investment law with better protection for intellectual property that prohibits forced technology transfer. It has released a 'negative list' of sectors that are off-limits to foreign businesses to provide greater transparency. China may offer further concessions. But these gestures have generally been received with skepticism. If a deal is reached at the end of the 90-day pause, it will probably only address tariffs, not technology. Fundamental changes to the Chinese way of doing business and to the Chinese economy are not likely.

The core of the problem is a fact so obvious as to be often over-looked: China is a communist country — not in its ideology, but in the structure of its political system that is built around a Leninist Party that claims absolute dominance over every facet of the economy and society. Party dominance gives any Chinese business connected to the Chinese Communist Party (CCP) a privileged position — in effect this means every Chinese business because no Chinese business can succeed against the will of the Party. It is precisely that privilege that the US and other countries deem unfair. No Chinese leadership will ever compromise on the dominance of the CCP, and Xi Jinping has placed greater emphasis on CCP control. The probability therefore is that whatever China is willing or able to do to assuage US concerns will fall short of US expectations and that after this pause, US pressures on

(*Continued*)

Box 4.1: (*Continued*)

China will resume. Action has already been taken against Huawei and other Chinese technology companies. More action can be expected.

Xi is already facing some internal criticism for having mismanaged the relationship with the US. This does not immediately threaten his position, but is also not a factor that he can ignore. For now, Xi has adopted a conciliatory approach towards the US and its allies. This is unlikely to last. Since the current conciliatory attitude is probably not going to end US pressures, sooner or later, Xi must act tough. He cannot afford to appear weak by continuing to be conciliatory with no substantive result. The crucial question is what China will do. Not responding is not an option, and the response is not necessarily only on trade.

At least for now, China is hurting, particularly on the technology front. Growth has slowed as Chinese economic policy is pulled in contradictory directions. The Chinese private sector, which provides more than half of GDP growth, is facing great uncertainty. The Trump Administration's bilateral approach towards trade seems to be working — the FTA with South Korea has been tweaked, the renegotiated North America Free Trade Agreement (NAFTA) gives the US a veto over its partners' trade relationships with China, Japan has apparently been persuaded to discuss a bilateral trade agreement. Europe shares many US concerns and is incapable of dealing with a resurgent Russia on its own. Europe must therefore ultimately accommodate US concerns no matter how distasteful it finds the Trump Administration. There is thus no incentive for the US to change tack, and every reason for the US to pressure its partners to follow its approach towards China. Why should ASEAN be exempted?

Some analysts have speculated that ASEAN could benefit from the diversion of investments from China. This is possible, but is a short-sighted view that only provides cold comfort. The extent of diversion remains to be seen and may well be less than anticipated. New investments may be postponed. But no serious business can afford to foreswear the China market, as Japan's unsuccessful decades long search for a viable 'China plus one' investment strategy demonstrates. In so far as investment diversion occurs, ASEAN must expect greater scrutiny. ASEAN economies will be closely monitored to ensure that they do not act as a backdoor for China into the US market. The US will demand that sophisticated economies like Singapore put in place credible and robust safeguards to ensure that sensitive technology does not leak into China. The harsh fact is that the definition of what is "credible", "robust", and "sensitive" will be primarily American.

Technology is already eroding the cost advantage of widely distributed supply chains. Heightened US–China competition could accelerate such shifts in supply chains and derail ASEAN's project of making Southeast Asia a common market and common production platform unless we move more decisively. Concerns over the security of supply chains also implies that the scrutiny of ASEAN's relationship with China will go beyond the purely economic and will involve judgements on the overall autonomy of member states' foreign and domestic policies.

(*Continued*)

Box 4.1: (*Continued*)

Since trade is only the instrument of strategic competition, it will become increasingly difficult for ASEAN member states to neatly separate the economic dimensions of their relationships with China from political and security dimensions. Their ability to attract high quality western investments and keep access to advanced western technologies will, at least in some measure, be influenced by perceptions of their positions on non-economic issues such as the South China Sea, and their ability to resist Chinese influence. This is particularly so with regard to defense technologies, which are crucial to Singapore. There is no viable alternative to American (and more generally, western) defense technology.

All this is a counsel of realism, not of despair. During the Cold War, ASEAN successfully navigated even more intense and dangerous periods of major power competition when the possibility of war was ever present. The possibility of conflict can never be entirely discounted, but war is currently highly unlikely. ASEAN thus ought to be able to cope with the new complexities. We succeeded during the Cold War because ASEAN did not then lack ambition and courage. The last decade or so has, however, seen a narrowing of ASEAN's strategic imagination and a lack of bold leadership. We must understand that the greatest risk under present circumstances is unwillingness to take risks.

Mr. Bilahari Kausikan is Chairman of the Middle East Institute at the National University of Singapore, and former Permanent Secretary at the Ministry of Foreign Affairs of Singapore.

As detailed by Mr. Kausikan, the US–China trade war and the effects it will have on ASEAN goes beyond simple issues of trade and enters the geopolitical realm of "strategic competition". It is hence of essence for the ASEAN bloc to find a comfortable middle ground for themselves between the major powers in the market.

Also mentioned was the diversion of investments from China to ASEAN. Indeed, in response to the increasing geopolitical tussles and trade disruptions, there have been promising signs that countries and companies alike have begun to diversify their economies, with many looking towards Asia and the ASEAN region as attractive destinations. For example, the EU has been striding forward with its efforts in deepening economic relations with new markets. Developments include the EU–Singapore Free Trade Agreement (EUSFTA) and the EU–Singapore Investment Protection Agreement (EUSIPA) in October 2018,[31] as well as the 2019 Economic Partnership Agreement (EPA) between EU and Japan that marks the largest trade zone in the world.[32]

On the private-sector side, companies like Dyson[33] and Nissan[34] have announced the moving and relocation of their headquarters to Singapore and Thailand, respectively. Malaysian Finance Minister, Lim Guan Eng, has even been quoted in the news as saying that there have been various

[31] See Press Release by Ministry of Trade and Industry, Singapore (2018).

[32] See Press Release by European Commission (2019b). Also see Tan, *et al.* (2015) for growth drivers for ASEAN-5.

[33] See Seow (2019).

[34] See Nissan (2019).

inquiries into Malaysia's economy from those "who wish to be in the right position" given an escalation of the trade war, and that Malaysia's problem is thus not business demand, but rather "a problem of capacity — whether [it] can ramp up capacity in the shortest possible time."[35]

The reorganization of global trade chains and the diversification of economies is even more amplified given China's rapid economic growth, as its movement up the value chain points to an eventual shift of its labour-reliant, low-cost manufacturing bases outwards to the rest of the world. For instance, China has become Myanmar's largest FDI contributor, pouring US$18 billion into the country, most of which has gone into the oil and gas as well as manufacturing sectors.[36]

This comes as part and parcel of "Made in China 2025", China's development plan which is geared at upgrading and transforming the Chinese industry into one that occupies a major position in advanced manufacturing. Its main thrust is hence tailored towards 10 main high-tech, capital-intensive industries, such as information technology as well as automated machines and robotics.[37]

Added to China's rise in the global value chain is also the rise in its wage costs, which has resulted in greater investment into lower cost environments.[38] As elaborated by Biswas (2018), major beneficiaries of this in the ASEAN region have been low-cost, labour-intensive environments such as Vietnam. For instance, Vietnam's industrial production has experienced a 10% year-on-year average growth rate increase from 2013 to 2017. This is largely due to the hike in its electronics manufacturing industry, with its share of total GDP going from 5.2% in 2010 to contribute about one-quarter of GDP in 2016. Production dislocation is hence already underway, with or without the happenings of a full-blown US–China trade war.

The benefits of production diversion to ASEAN have been and will potentially be even more tremendous. The influx of FDI and increased demand for exports naturally provides a strong boost for economic growth. As seen in Figure 1.1 in Chapter 1, ASEAN-10's GDP growth rate stood at a robust 5.3% in 2017, an increase from the figure of 4.8% in 2016.[39] This entails increases in employment opportunities, technological transfer, skills-sharing and boosts in financing. All in all, it works towards allowing the ASEAN region to, moving forward, unlock its infrastructure and production bottlenecks, thus giving its residents a higher quality of life.

However, going back to Mr. Kausikan's article, the conviction that the ASEAN region will definitely stand to gain is "short-sighted" and must be subject to "greater scrutiny." The ASEAN bloc still faces various obstacles to overcome, such as how it will grapple with the rise of other competing, emerging markets like Latin America and Brazil. It is therefore of paramount importance to analyse how exactly ASEAN members can work towards effectively paving their way to become the principal beneficiary of the diverging geopolitical landscape.

4.2 Windows of Opportunity and Potential Pitfalls

As firms consider relocating and diversifying from China amid escalating trade tension between US and China, firms may not necessarily choose ASEAN as their next investment destination.

[35] See Huang (2018).
[36] See International Monetary Fund (2018).
[37] See U.S. Chamber of Commerce (2017).
[38] See Biswas (2018).
[39] See ASEAN Secretariat (2018b).

ASEAN must capitalize on its comparative advantages and curb its weaknesses to capture the opportunity for investment influx. Here, we will discuss how regional cooperation and diversity, labour market landscape, the rise of middle-class consumers, infrastructure development, rule of law and quality of governance will affect ASEAN as the next investment destination.

4.2.1 Regional Cooperation and Diversity

The strength of ASEAN lies in it being a platform that fosters regional cooperation through dialogue and economic cooperation. Regional cooperation such as Free Trade Agreements, AEC and various initiatives outlined earlier in the book facilitate greater movement of goods and services across borders by decreasing tariff rate and reducing the time taken for the movement of goods.[40] ASEAN as an economic bloc also improves the relationship between the countries that are diverse in terms of economic development, political institutions and socio-cultural background.

Due to its cooperative structure, ASEAN member states have come together to implement key reforms and policies that bridge its development gap. One such example is the establishment of the Asian Infrastructure Fund (AIF) that helps less-developed countries in ASEAN to build physical infrastructure such as roads and railways.[41] The diversity of the region is also an advantage for ASEAN as each country has different sets of comparative advantages such as its abundance in labour force and natural resources. The regional integration may be one of its biggest advantage when it comes to capturing the trade dislocation from China, capturing both labour-intensive manufacturing processes as well as higher value production. This practice is already in place for some of the companies that had set up branches or production plants in the region. Multinational corporations are already tapping on this advantage through their production strategies that involve horizontal and vertical integration in more than one ASEAN country. This creates a production network that forms a regional value chain, tapping on each country's comparative advantages.

An example of a firm that conducts this strategy is Procter & Gamble (P&G), one of the largest Fast-Moving Consumer Goods (FMCG) companies in the world.[42] It employs over 4000 employees across ASEAN in its manufacturing plants, distribution centres and service centre. Singapore acts as P&G's Asia Pacific headquarter and houses its Innovation Centre for Research and Development. P&G business service centre is in Philippines whereas the marketing hub is operating in Thailand. It's manufacturing plants span over six countries, namely Singapore, Philippines, Thailand, Malaysia, Indonesia and Vietnam. These plants are part of the integrated supply chain in ASEAN. For instance, the feedstock from Indonesia is processed into chemicals in Malaysia, and these chemicals are exported to other P&G manufacturing plants in ASEAN and other parts of the world as raw materials.

However, companies that are planning their relocation strategy may be dissuaded from ASEAN as a potential destination due to the conflicts among the countries. Even though ASEAN

---

[40] Refer to Chapter 1 for discussion on the various initiatives.

[41] See Asian Development Bank (2016).

[42] See ASEAN Secretariat (2013).

as an integrated platform fosters a cooperative relationship among the member states, there are territorial and ideological disputes among these countries that strain their relationship and cause uncertainty in future policy-making. For instance, the recent tension between Singapore and Malaysia has caused uncertainty in the High-Speed Rail project that dampens investor's confidence and decreases the economic prospect of both countries to engage in regional integration. These differences and disputes could be remedied by closer integration and understanding among the leaders of the ASEAN states through dialogue. Besides that, regional agreements such as the FTAs, ASW, CPTPP and the impending RCEP are evidence that ASEAN countries can reconcile for economic gain despite their differences.

Besides that, the diversity of ASEAN can also be its weakness. As ASEAN is diverse, policies and regulations differ from country to country. This made integration difficult as companies with manufacturing plants and headquarters in different countries are subjected to different sets of regulations and law and order. While multinational companies with experience and resources may be able to benefit from the comparative advantage of the countries in the region, smaller companies and factories that do not have legal expertise or experience to handle multiple jurisdictions at any one point may not benefit from the horizontal and vertical integration.

The AEC attempts to bridge this regulatory difference through building ASEAN as a single market and production base. The AEC has initiated various deliverables such as ASEAN Trade in Goods Agreement (ATIGA) and ASEAN Consultative Committee for Standards and Quality (ACCSQ) to build a common framework and an integrated supply chain in ASEAN.[43]

4.2.2 Labour Market Landscape

The population of ASEAN has reached 642.1 million in 2017, 50.4% of which belongs in the working age group of 20–54 years.[44] The rise in the working age population is attractive for labour-intensive firms that had flocked to China for its abundance of low-cost labour.[45] Labour force can be divided into low-skilled labour and high-skilled labour. The availability of low-skilled labour in a country is attractive for firms that required labour-intensive and low-skilled operations, while high-skilled labour is required for higher value-added and knowledge-based tasks.[46]

Due to its high growth and economic development, the wage of Chinese workers has been increasing. This is one of the factors initiating the shift of the production chain out of China, and into other low labour cost countries such as ASEAN.[47] The abundance of low-cost labour in Cambodia, Vietnam, Malaysia and Indonesia enables the region to absorb labour-intensive firms that are moving out of China. Evidence shows that South Korean and Japanese firms are moving away from China and are attracted to cheaper labour in parts of ASEAN such as Cambodia and Vietnam.[48]

---

[43] See ASEAN Economic Community (2017) for more initiatives and strategies by AEC.

[44] See ASEAN Secretariat (2018c).

[45] See Wei *et al.* (1999) for effective wage rate against FDI inflows in China.

[46] See Maurer (2017).

[47] *Ibid.*

[48] See Aseanup (2018), Saleh *et al.* (2017) and Ujikane (2016).

The apparel and garment industry is one example of relocation of low-skilled production out of China. In the last few years, firms in low-end apparel and Ready-Made Garments manufacturing are moving out of China and into other parts of the world with lower labour cost such as Vietnam, Bangladesh and India.[49] This is a result of additional tariffs that will be imposed on US$200 billion worth of Chinese goods including goods in the apparel and clothing categories.[50] Vietnam is in a good position to benefit from such an event since its economy is largely driven by labour-intensive and low-wage garment and footwear industries.[51] On top of that, the country itself has strong trade ties with the US and had exported more than US$12 billion worth of garments to the US in 2017, or about a quarter of all Vietnamese exports to the US.[52] Other than Vietnam, countries such as Indonesia and the Philippines are also strong in labour-intensive manufacturing and services industries.[53]

Besides that, there is a significant portion of the workforce in these countries that are working in the informal sector, and these workers have not integrated into the growing manufacturing industry. The informal employment in Thailand is as high as 62.4% with 40% of them in the agricultural sector.[54] There is a huge talent pool that has not been tapped into, and this creates availability of labour for manufacturing plants or new businesses.

As ASEAN is diverse as a region, the type of labour available in each of the country is also different. Some of the countries in ASEAN have a better educated workforce than others. The average years of schooling in China is 7.8 years whereas it is only 4.8 years in Cambodia, 4.9 years in Myanmar and 5.2 years in Laos.[55] For instance, Singapore, Thailand, Malaysia and Indonesia have a well-educated labour force and a more established manufacturing sector.[56] ASEAN can capitalize on the diversity of its labour force where some parts of ASEAN can support low wage and low-skilled industry while other parts can support higher skilled production. For instance, *Singapore* has a skilled and highly educated workforce that is highly capable of attracting high value chain production.[57] Singapore houses many multinational companies and global banks such a Bank of America Merrill Lynch, Salesforce.com and the Asia-Pacific headquarters of Coca-Cola Company. There is an opportunity for Singapore to absorb knowledge-intensive production sectors from the Chinese market.

While Singapore, Malaysia, Thailand and Indonesia are attempting to develop their workforce to move up the production value chain, there is a shortage of skilled labour in their economies.[58] The lack of skilled labour is a challenge for ASEAN to tap into the higher value-added production chain such as in areas of science and engineering. According to a report by International

[49] See The Economist Intelligence Unit (2018).
[50] See Office of the United States Trade Representative (2018b).
[51] See International Labour Organization (2019e).
[52] See The Economist intelligence Unit (2018) and United Nations (2019a).
[53] See International Labour Organization (2018, 2019a, 2019d).
[54] See International Labour Organization (2019c).
[55] See United Nations Development Programme (2016).
[56] See International Labour Organization (2018, 2019a, 2019b, 2019c)
[57] See International Labour Organization (2018).
[58] See Tan and Tang (2016).

Labour Organization (ILO), *Singapore* is facing the challenges of fostering innovation in its schools and technical training institutes. Singapore should strengthen its existing skills development programme to improve innovation and the productivity of its workforce to benefit from technological disruption from the fourth industrial revolution.

About 60% of the workforce in *Malaysia* is working in middle-skilled occupations.[59] Malaysia has been attracting the electrical and electronics companies such as Intel, Dell and Panasonic. However, the share of the high-skilled labour only consists of less than 30% of total employment.[60] This is attributed to its lack of educational and training facilities to equip its workforce with science and engineering skills.[61] Therefore, Malaysia should improve its training program and provide quality education institutions so that it can move towards technology-intensive and knowledge-intensive industries.

The economy of *Thailand* is driven by the manufacturing and tourism sectors. Thailand has established garment and automobile manufacturing production unit.[62] Its employment in manufacturing and service is at 15% and 45%, respectively.[63] On the other hand, 40% of its workforce still works in the rural agricultural sector, and the contribution of the sector to economic growth has been reducing in the past few years.[64] Thailand should introduce a program to bring its agriculture workforce to the booming industry in the manufacturing and services sectors to achieve greater growth. This can be achieved through the Thailand 4.0 economic model that transforms low-skilled labour into high-skilled labour to complement the growing manufacturing and services industries.[65]

The inflow of FDI has changed the labour landscape of *Indonesia*. Labour shifts from the agricultural sector to the manufacturing and services sectors currently makes up 47% of total employment in Indonesia.[66] Indonesia is also experiencing the wave of technological advancement with the rise of e-commerce and sharing economy that is shaping the change in the labour landscape.[67] Hence, Indonesia should equip its workforce with technological knowledge to increase its capacity so that it can absorb the technology-driven industry from trade diversification from China.

In the *Philippines*, agricultural sector remains the biggest contributor to employment, though this is changing as the Business Process Outsourcing (BPO) industry is growing.[68] Companies outsource part of their operations to the Philippines to reduce operating cost.[69] BPO includes

---

[59] Middle-skilled occupation is defined by employment as clerical, service and sales, skilled agricultural, machinists and assemblers. See International Labour Organization (2017).

[60] See International Labour Organization (2017).

[61] See Tan and Tang (2016).

[62] See Thailand Board of Investment (2015) and Watchravesringkan (2010) for more information on the automobile and garment industries in Thailand.

[63] See International Labour Organization (2019c).

[64] *Ibid.*

[65] See Thailand Board of Investment (2017) for more information on Thailand 4.0 initiative.

[66] The share of agricultural employment decreases from 55% in 1996 to about 32% in 2016. See International Labour Organization (2019a).

[67] *Ibid.*

[68] See International Labour Organization (2018, 2019d).

[69] See Tolentino (2017).

human resource management, telemarketing and accounting services. Its young and abundant labour force is driving the BPO industry.[70] The Philippines needs to enhance the skill set of its labour force in the IT industry so that they can handle the technical tasks required by the BPO.

Brunei should take the event of trade relocation as an opportunity to diversify its economy to be less reliant on the oil and gas industry. As of 2018, it is still far from having an innovative workforce that is skilful in Research and Development. Hence, Brunei should invest in its human capital development to remain competitive on the global market.

For *CLMV* countries, the workforce is largely unskilled. Investment in technical and vocational education and training (TVET) is needed to prepare these workers with the necessary industrial skill set for potential FDI inflow.

While low labour cost attracts labour-intensive and low-skilled industry to move its production plant to ASEAN, highly educated labour force can attract firms with knowledge-based and high value chain production. CLMV countries have a comparative advantage in the labour-intensive industry and had attracted garment factories to relocate to ASEAN. Singapore, Thailand, Malaysia and Brunei have middle-to high-skilled labour work forces with the ability to attract higher value chain production and knowledge-intensive firms. However, shortages in high-skilled labour are still prevalent in these countries. Skills development program is pivotal in these countries to develop a labour force that is high skilled and competitive.

4.2.3 Rising Middle-Class Consumers

Economic development in ASEAN in the past decades has contributed to the growth of a consumer class with higher purchasing power. The rise in middle-class consumers can be a driver of growth for ASEAN in terms of economic growth and as an attractive investment destination. Middle-class consumer in Asia is expected to increase from 500 million in 2010 people to over 3 billion people by 2030.[71] Another study by The Economist Intelligence Unit projects that the number of middle-class households in ASEAN will more than quadruple in the next 15 years, or a rise from 38 million to 161 million households.[72]

High economic growth in the last decades has resulted in an increase in the purchasing power of the people in ASEAN. The number of households with the household income above US$5000 is on the rise in ASEAN, and this see many people in the region from being able to afford only necessity goods such as food can now purchase other discretionary goods such as clothing and entertainment.[73] As more people moved from low income to middle income, they also purchase more consumption items, household appliances and luxury products. The increase in retail sales and household expenditure in ASEAN during the past years reflects the growing consumption pattern.[74]

[70] See Tolentino (2017).

[71] See United Nations Development Programme (2016).

[72] See The Economist Intelligence Unit (2016).

[73] See The Economist Intelligence Unit (2014).

[74] See PriceWaterhouseCoopers (2015) and United Nations Statistics Division (2018).

The growth in consumption applies across different categories of goods. A consumer report by the PWC shows growing consumption of Indonesia, Malaysia, Philippines, Thailand and Vietnam in food, beverages and tobacco, fashion and clothing, e-commerce, fast-moving consumer goods such as detergents and personal care items, and electronics goods such as laptop and smartphone.[75] The growth in consumption drives economic growth by creating demands for the goods and services.

When determining a location to set up production base or headquarters, firms consider many factors that form a conducive business and economic environment. One of the factors is the proximity to consumer base.[76] The growth in consumer demand in the region prompts global firms to expand to ASEAN to penetrate the new market. Moving production base to ASEAN would allow firms to move closer to the ASEAN consumers. A business outlook survey conducted by Amchan Singapore in 2018 finds that MNC and SME firms are considering expansion in ASEAN, partly due to the growth in domestic market as well as the rise in the middle-class consumer in the region.[77]

Other than the accessibility to both the US and the Chinese markets, businesses that are based in ASEAN could also access other markets and economies within the region. The low tariff rate for intra-ASEAN trade that hovers around the rate of 0–5% as well as the ease of the flow of goods across border are also incentives for businesses that wish to move their production base to the region.[78] This allows businesses to export their final product to the rest of ASEAN consumers at a lower cost as compared to exporting it from outside the ASEAN region.

With a vibrant developing economy, it is expected that the number of middle-class consumers in ASEAN will continue to increase in the future. These consumers are expected to be one of the drivers of growth for ASEAN through greater demand for goods and services as well as attracting businesses to set up a production base in the region to capture the growing consumer market.

4.2.4 Development of Hard and Soft Infrastructure

Infrastructure remains an important factor in attracting firms that are diversifying outside China. This section discusses the role of both hard and soft infrastructure in capturing the global supply chain that is relocating away from China. There are existing studies which suggest that better developed and higher quality infrastructure have proven to be more attractive to foreign investors.[79]

Here, hard infrastructure refers to physical infrastructures such as roads, railways, ports, power supply and telecommunications. Roads and railways facilitate the movement of goods and labour which reduce transportation cost and lead-time for goods as well as reducing commuting time for people. The availability of ports eases the flow of goods. Power supply such as electricity is essential for productions and other office functions. Telecommunications and digital devices made worldwide information transfer faster and more efficient. Soft infrastructure

[75] See PriceWaterhouseCoopers (2015).

[76] See Chen (2003).

[77] See The American Chamber of Commerce in Singapore and U.S. Chamber of Commerce (2017).

[78] See ASEAN Secretariat (2008).

[79] See Shah (2014) and Shah and Samdani (2015).

Figure 4.3: Infrastructure Index (0–100), by Countries and Regions

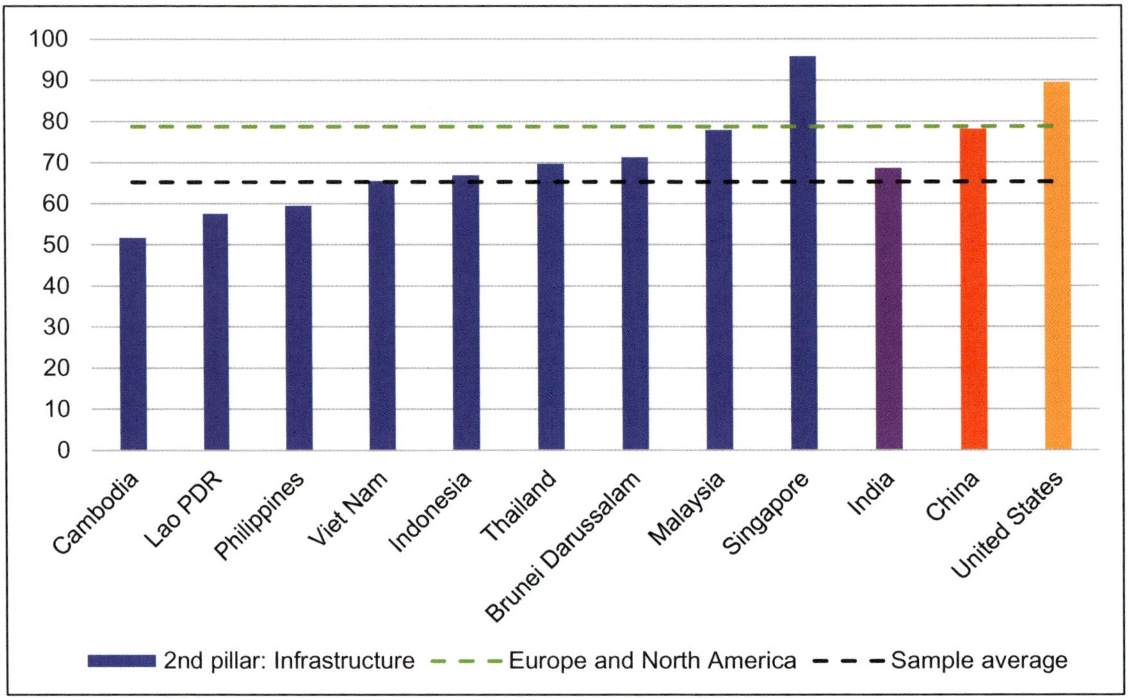

Source: Asia Competitiveness Institute based on The Global Competitiveness Report 2018.

concerns intangibles which support the functionality of the hard infrastructure and is measured by the quality of institutions and regulations.[80]

Figure 4.3 illustrates the quality and extension of the infrastructure in selected countries and regions.[81] Such comparison allows us to assess the attractiveness of ASEAN as an alternative investment destination to China. The infrastructure index shows that other than Cambodia, Lao PDR, Philippines and Vietnam, the rest of the ASEAN countries score above the world average in the infrastructure index. However, the quality and extension of the infrastructure in these countries, bar Singapore, still fall below China, United States and Europe and North America region. For instance, only 59.7% of the population have access to electricity in Cambodia, compared to 100% in United States, Singapore and Thailand.[82]

The infrastructure in ASEAN has improved rapidly in recent years but remains inadequate. Poor quality and neglect are prevalent.[83] A special report on infrastructure published by the Asian Development Bank suggests that the infrastructure investment gap in Southeast Asia remains wide.[84] Current investment in Southeast Asia is estimated to be at around US$55 billion, a shortfall of US$92 billion to meet the annual investment need from 2016 to 2020.[85]

---

[80] See Bhattacharyay (2009) and United Nations (2014).

[81] The infrastructure index measures the quality, coverage and efficiency of physical infrastructure.

[82] See The World Bank (2019).

[83] See Tongzon and Cheong (2013).

[84] See Asian Development Bank (2017a).

[85] *Ibid*.

Lack of adequate infrastructure is a factor of consideration for foreign firms during the relocation process. Current trends in production shift to ASEAN has seen companies taking infrastructure and market environment into account. Vietnam and Malaysia will reap the most benefit from the Information and Communications Technology (ICT) sector, particularly in low-end manufacturing production such as intermediate electronic components and consumer goods.[86] These countries attract ICT firms because they have better-developed transportation network and existing production network in manufacturing electronic products. Besides hard infrastructure, the existence of soft infrastructure also increases the attractiveness for foreign investors. For instance, Malaysia has a clear and stable corporate law system, and Vietnam adopts pro-growth policies that promote foreign investment.[87]

Therefore, it is important for ASEAN to invest in infrastructure development to benefit from trade relocation. For this reason, ASEAN countries are pursuing infrastructure investment through a multitude of policy initiatives as outlined in Sections 1.2 and 1.3. These policy initiatives and rise in infrastructure spending are crucial but may not have an immediate impact during this period of trade disruption as there is a time-lag between the planning and the completion of big infrastructure projects, and this applies for transportation networks such as roads and railways as well as power grids and telecommunication facilities. Construction of these hard infrastructure is not only costly, but often takes years to decades to manifest depending on the magnitude and complexity of the project and the efficiency of contracted firms.

ASEAN should continue to invest in quality roads, railways, energy grids and telecommunication networks for long-run economic development. For short-term gains from trade diversion, the development of these infrastructure must be accelerated to bridge the infrastructure gap. One of the ways to accelerate the process is to ensure that the supporting soft infrastructure is in place to prevent delays and ensure timely completion of projects. The Singapore Infrastructure and Urban Hub could serve this purpose by providing support in infrastructure projects such as legal advice, project development, financing and risk management.[88]

The development of soft infrastructure can be carried out rather quickly with enough political will and bureaucratic capability. Soft infrastructure complements hard infrastructure through several means including easing custom procedure, improving the ease of doing business and implementing business-friendly policies and incentives. This requires strong governance in the areas of regulations and law enforcement. As an example, Singapore has developed rapidly in the past few decades as a result of a strong and efficient government, making it a highly attractive investment location and easing the funding bottleneck choking infrastructure development. Therefore, the rest of ASEAN can emulate this success by adopting the same strategy in bureaucratic reform to develop its soft infrastructure.

Besides expediting the processes, a well-developed soft infrastructure could also complement the operation and maintenance of the hard infrastructure. Often, the economic value of the hard infrastructure is not only derived from the physical construction of these infrastructure, but also third-party services such as an integrated logistics network, regulations and customs clearance.[89]

---

[86] See The Economist Intelligence Unit (2018).

[87] *Ibid.*

[88] See Infrastructure Asia (2018).

[89] See Portugal-Perez and Wilson (2012).

For instance, improving the efficiency of custom procedures reduces the time taken to move goods in and out of the country. A recent initiative by ASEAN to improve third-party services include the ASEAN Single Window (ASW) that increases the efficiency of customs clearance by speeding up cargo clearance and reducing paperwork. Other benefits of a developed soft infrastructure include proper care and maintenance of the infrastructure. For instance, proper maintenance of energy grid ensures that the electricity supply in the country can be provided without disruption, tripping or blackout.

While inadequate hard infrastructure remains a weakness for ASEAN to be considered as an alternative for firms that are diversifying away from China, this can be remedied through improvements in soft infrastructure. The improvements in soft infrastructure such as having a strong regulatory process could accelerate the construction of hard infrastructure. Besides steering the construction process, a developed soft infrastructure could also improve the efficiency brought about by the hard infrastructure. Section 4.2.5 will discuss the necessary conditions for achieving quality soft infrastructure through the lens of governance and rule of law.

Having recognised that ASEAN is underfunding infrastructure projects, we now discuss some potential sources of much needed funding, including domestic funding, intra-ASEAN financing as well as extra-ASEAN financing.[90] Domestic funding for infrastructure project is raised through bonds or securities market from a single country. The financing is usually raised through domestic capital markets through medium- or long-term corporate bonds or commercial bank financing through loan issuance. Domestic capital markets encourage local firm participation by providing them with the access to funding.[91] However, domestic capital markets in the individual countries in ASEAN are often insufficient to fund big infrastructure projects.[92]

One recent initiative for intra-ASEAN financing is the establishment of the ASEAN Infrastructure Fund (AIF) in 2012 to address the region's infrastructure needs.[93] The fund is created to provide financing to sovereign or sovereign-guaranteed infrastructure projects in the region.[94] In December 2013, AIF provided US$25 million loan for the Java–Bali 500-Kilovolt Power Transmission Crossing project. The project is an expansion of the transmission networks from Java to Bali and will resolve power outages and blackouts that had occurred in Bali.[95]

In recent years, many countries in ASEAN have engaged with countries outside of the ASEAN region for infrastructure development. This includes the Belt and Road Initiative (BRI) from China as well as investment from Japan. China is looking to ASEAN due to slowing growth at home and Japan's presence in ASEAN is long established.[96] According to Figure 4.4, the investment from Japan has been consistent since 2010. Both countries look at ASEAN as a profitable investment destination due to its comparative advantage and growing economy. This is an opportunity that ASEAN can tap into to reduce its infrastructure gap within a short period of time, making it an even more attractive location for FDI.

---

[90] See Zen and Regan (2014).

[91] *Ibid.*

[92] *Ibid.*

[93] See Asian Development Bank (2019).

[94] *Ibid.*

[95] See Asian Development Bank (2016).

[96] See Sunaga (2017).

Figure 4.4: FDI Inflow to ASEAN by Source Country (in million US$), 2010–2017

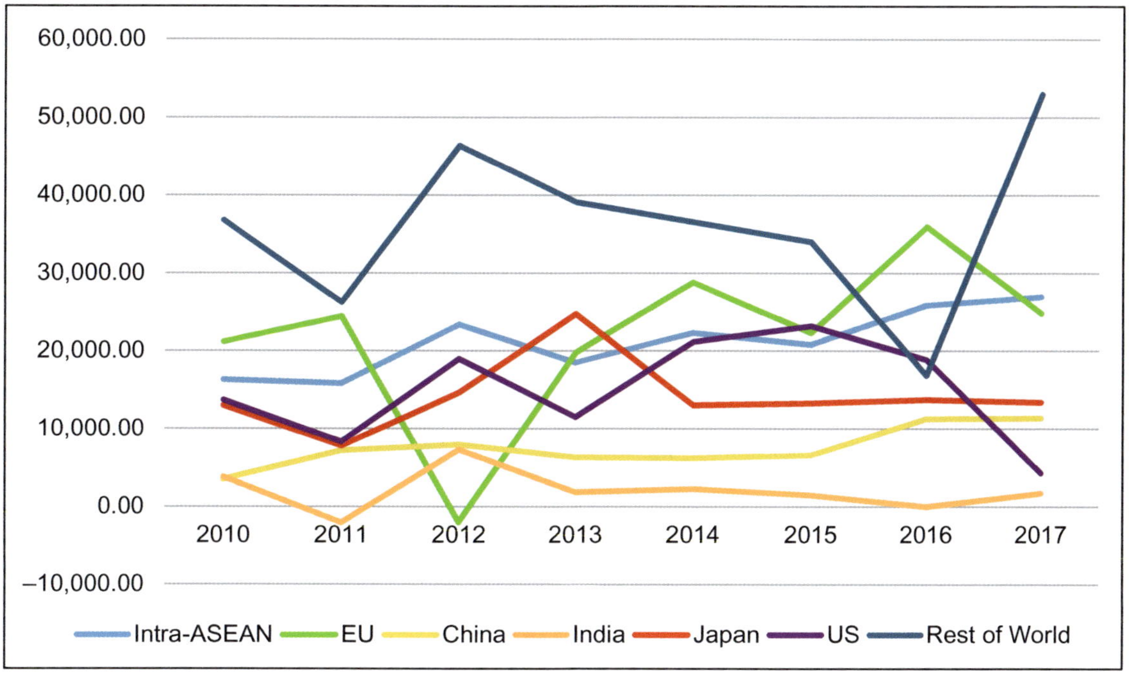

Source: Asia Competitiveness Institute based on ASEAN Secretariat.

Other than China and Japan, other international organizations also provide funding to infrastructure projects in ASEAN. Asian Development Bank provides financing for several ongoing projects with ASEAN that include Bangkok Mass Rapid Transit South Purple Line Project in Thailand and the Metro Manila Transport Project in Philippines.[97] Asian Development Bank has also co-funded Myanmar's Myingyan Power Plant along with Asian Infrastructure Investment Bank and International Finance Corporation.[98]

4.2.5 Corruption, Rule of Law and Quality of Governance

While increased costs from US tariffs on products exported from China have been cited as a significant reason for potential relocation,[99] it is necessary to also examine the structural reasons that were claimed to have triggered the initial wave of tariffs. The hostility demonstrated by the US administration against the Chinese government in the currently ongoing trade dispute has been grounded, among other reasons, in the alleged economic espionage, intellectual property theft, and general lawlessness and corruption exhibited by Chinese actors.[100] For instance, ever since 2017, at least three individuals have been charged with "attempting" or "conspiring" to "[spy] for China", alongside the (then) ongoing prosecution of five others for the "theft" or

[97] See Asian Development Bank (2017b, 2017c).

[98] See Asian Infrastructure Investment Bank (2016).

[99] See The American Chamber of Commerce in the People's Republic of China (2019).

[100] See The U.S. Department of Justice (2014).

"attempted theft" towards the "benefit of the Chinese government."[101] Specific areas of the alleged theft include the "high-volume manufacture and export of counterfeit goods", "trade secret theft", and "online piracy and counterfeiting."[102]

The other main allegation of corruption lies in the accusation that the Chinese government hinders the operation of the free market, in that it "uses foreign ownership restrictions...to require or pressure technology transfer from U.S. companies", "forces U.S. companies seeking to license technologies to Chinese entities to do so on non-market-based terms that favor Chinese recipients", and "directs and unfairly facilitates the systematic investment in, and acquisition of, U.S. companies and assets by Chinese companies to obtain cutting-edge technologies and intellectual property and generate the transfer of technology to Chinese companies."[103] These alleged infringements on the legal sanctity of the trade relations between the US and China therefore constitute the bulk of the justifications used by the Trump Administration in executing a host of trade and economic penalties against China.

Notably and as alluded to in Mr. Kausikan's article, ASEAN countries have not been exempted from similar scrutiny. In the 2018 Special 301 Report released by the USTR, several ASEAN member states[104] were raised as countries on the USTR's Priority Watch List and Watch List, which "call out foreign countries and expose the laws, policies, and practices that fail to provide adequate and effective IP protection and enforcement for U.S. inventors, creators, brands, manufacturers, and service providers."[105] Examples raised include Indonesia, which has been accused of enacting state-imposed "requirements for domestic manufacturing and technology transfer", or Thailand, for its lack of transparency in its dealings with relevant stakeholders in IP-related manners, for allowing the continued existence of "unauthorized collective management organizations" and "extensive cable and satellite signal theft", or in Vietnam, where "[c]apacity constraints related to enforcement continue, in part due to a lack of resources and IP expertise."[106] This section will systematically examine how these legal aspects manifest in ASEAN.

The legal climate in business contexts comprise multiple facets. Prominent indices qualifying these facets include those from the World Justice Project (WJP) Rule of Law Index, the United Nations (UN) Business for the Rule of Law Framework and the World Bank Worldwide Governance Indicators (WGI). The state of the legal climate in ASEAN tends to vary widely across member states, as demonstrated for instance in the annual survey conducted by The World Bank in 2017 (see Tables 4.1 and 4.2). With regard to the Rule of Law[107] indicator, member states like Singapore rank among the highest, while Myanmar and Cambodia lag far behind in the last places. A similar pattern can be observed with the

---

[101] See The U.S. Justice of Department (2014).

[102] See Office of the United States Trade Representative (2018a).

[103] *Ibid.*

[104] For instance, Indonesia is on the Priority Watch List, while Thailand and Vietnam are on the Watch List. ASEAN member states like Singapore, Malaysia and the Philippines are identified as countries being monitored by the USTR.

[105] See Office of the United States Trade Representative (2018a).

[106] *Ibid.*

[107] The Rule of Law index as defined by The World Bank WGI measures perceptions of the extent to which agents have confidence in and abide by the rules of society, and in particular the quality of contract enforcement, property rights, the police and the courts, as well as the likelihood of crime and violence. See The World Bank (2018).

Table 4.1: Worldwide Governance Indicators 2017 — Rule of Law in ASEAN Member States[108]

Country	Percentile Rank (Global)	Governance Score
Singapore	96.63	1.82
Brunei	74.52	0.65
Malaysia	64.9	0.41
Vietnam	55.77	0.07
Thailand	54.81	0.04
Indonesia	40.87	–0.35
Philippines	37.02	–0.41
Lao PDR	18.27	–0.88
Myanmar	16.83	–0.95
Cambodia	13.46	–1.06

Source: The World Bank.

Table 4.2: Worldwide Governance Indicators 2017 — Control of Corruption in ASEAN Member States

Country	Percentile Rank (Global)	Governance Score
Singapore	97.6	2.13
Brunei	75	0.71
Malaysia	58.17	0.03
Indonesia	48.08	–0.25
Thailand	42.79	–0.39
Philippines	39.9	–0.48
Myanmar	32.21	–0.56
Vietnam	31.73	–0.58
Lao PDR	15.87	–0.94
Cambodia	8.65	–1.29

Source: The World Bank.

indicator Control of Corruption[109]: member states like Singapore once again emerge as the highest, while Cambodia and Lao PDR fall far behind.

It is worth highlighting here that surveys of AmCham members and executives conducted in 2017 reflect a general dissatisfaction with and the desire for improvements in the legal climate

[108] Note: Governance Score: –2.5 to + 2.5. (Estimate of governance measured on a scale from approximately –2.5 to +2.5. Higher values correspond to better governance). Percentile Rank: 0–100. (0 corresponds to lowest rank and 100 to highest rank).

[109] The Control of Corruption index as defined by The World Bank WGI measures perceptions of the extent to which public power is exercised for private gain, including both petty and grand forms of corruption, as well as "capture" of the state by elites and private interests. See The World Bank (2018).

in business contexts across the majority of ASEAN economies, with anti-corruption measures and transparency identified among the top concerns.[110] Parallel to the rankings observed from the Worldwide Governance Indicators by The World Bank, executives' satisfaction with the legal climate[111] recorded the lowest scores in Lao PDR, Cambodia and Myanmar, while Singapore scored the highest.

Among the legal issues identified in the survey conducted by AmCham in 2018 as being the most problematic to business operations in ASEAN economies, the lack of clarity on regulations and enforcement, corruption at ports of entry, and legal systems that lack impartiality/provide limited protection for foreign parties rank the highest.[112] Other missing legal characteristics identified as crucial for attracting FDI in ASEAN by prominent institutional leaders include a higher degree of transparency in the development and enforcement of regulations, "strong dispute resolution mechanisms,"[113] "regulatory harmonization" in areas such as product safety, content requirements, and labelling, and "stable and transparent political systems that promote good governance."[114]

Many of these issues will indeed require a gargantuan amount of political willpower and effort to overcome, the effects of which can only be observed in the medium to long term. It is however for a multitude of reasons paramount that ASEAN member state governments work on these issues, both domestically and on an ASEAN-wide level.

In the long run, corruption has been found to hinder sustainable social, political and economic development.[115] In a report in 2016 on the costs of corruption by the IMF, the economic and social costs of corruptions from just bribes paid globally annually were estimated to be about US$1.5–2 trillion, or approximately 2% of global GDP[116]; the costs from various other types of corruption collectively are estimated to be even higher.[117] These costs are due in part to the raised transaction costs and inefficient utilisation of public resources.[118]

Empirical research by the Bingham Centre for the Rule of Law and British Institute of International and Comparative Law Investment Treaty Forum demonstrates a clear positive relationship between FDI and strong rule of law, most significantly involving the issues of lack of transparency of regulatory and legal rule-making processes; arbitrary or discriminatory treatment by host country government; and lack of recognition of intellectual property and contract rights[119] — aspects which feature prominently as the major concerns foreign investors and businesses have in their dealings with many ASEAN economies. These legal aspects are especially

---

[110] See The American Chamber of Commerce in Singapore and U.S. Chamber of Commerce (2017).

[111] As defined by the indicators on lack of corruption, laws and regulation, and legal system/contract sanctity. See The American Chamber of Commerce in Singapore, and U.S. Chamber of Commerce (2017).

[112] See The American Chamber of Commerce in Singapore and U.S. Chamber of Commerce (2017).

[113] ASEAN Studies Centre (2019).

[114] See The American Chamber of Commerce in Singapore and U.S. Chamber of Commerce (2017).

[115] See Aidt (2010) as cited in Loh *et al.* (2018). See also International Monetary Fund (2016) and Organisation for Economic Cooperation and Development (2014).

[116] See International Monetary Fund (2016).

[117] *Ibid.*

[118] See Organisation for Economic Cooperation and Development (2014), as cited in Loh *et al.* (2018).

[119] As cited in United Nations Global Compact (2015).

pertinent when one considers the current economic and political landscape, both in ASEAN and globally.

The technological developments that comprise the fourth industrial revolution are triggering fundamental changes across industries, not just in manufacturing, but also in management and even governance.[120] Developments in areas such as artificial intelligence (AI), energy storage, 3D printing, nanotechnology, robotics and quantum computing are triggering breakthroughs in the "scale, scope and complexity" of operations across the aforementioned industries.[121] The key results of these developments include the ability to remotely conduct various operations and transactions, the restructuring of logistics and global supply chains, and ultimately increased levels in efficiency and productivity.[122]

These indubitably limit the cost advantage of geographically dispersed supply chains, meaning that the competitive advantage that low-cost member economies like Vietnam and Lao PDR currently enjoy has a very limited lifespan. Essential for the continued business attractiveness and growth of these member states is economic restructuring towards higher value-added activities in production and services, accompanied with corresponding upgrades in infrastructure and its workforce.[123]

Many of these economies are however still heavily reliant on FDI from developed countries for the capital and the technological know-how required for such a shift.[124] The US for example is the largest single foreign direct investor in the ASEAN region, with American businesses indicating relatively high levels of interest in areas such as software/IT/telecommunications, healthcare and banking and finance.[125] Other heavyweights in the technological arena include Germany, the UK, Japan and South Korea,[126] and these, along with the US, have repeatedly emphasized the need for a fair, rules-based trade and business landscape.[127] This is underscored by the increasing pervasiveness of information technology in many aspects of communication and interaction between diverse parties — the potential for security breaches that arise from the inherent complexities within these systems is known to be high. Furthermore, in light of the relocation of the operations of Chinese companies to ASEAN countries, ASEAN economies will also be scrutinised to prevent their being used to circumvent US trade barriers.[128]

The current dependence of many ASEAN economies on FDI from countries such as the US for the necessary capital and technological know-how required for sustainable and competitive

[120] See Schwab (2016).

[121] *Ibid.*

[122] *Ibid.*

[123] See Khuong (2017).

[124] See Organisation for Economic Cooperation and Development (2018b).

[125] Respondents across ASEAN identified five sectors as offering the greatest promise for U.S. businesses in their response location: software/IT/telecommunications (38%), healthcare (36%), consulting (32%) banking and finance (32%) and education (30%). See The American Chamber of Commerce in Singapore and U.S. Chamber of Commerce (2017).

[126] See ASEAN Secretariat (2018a).

[127] See U.S. Department of Justice (2018).

[128] See ASEAN Studies Centre (2019).

economic performance means that ASEAN countries will have to demonstrate that they are trustworthy and reliable actors that play by established rules, regarding what constitutes a fair, rules-based trade and business landscape.

The move towards combating corruption in its diverse manifestations and concurrently strengthening the rule of law will be beneficial in a multitude of ways for ASEAN member states. In the context of the economic uncertainties triggered by the trade dispute between the US and China, the demonstration of determination by ASEAN member states to tackle these problem areas would increase their attractiveness as a destination for FDI and other business operations, and thereby both directly and indirectly positively influence general economic growth,[129] as elaborated upon in the following paragraph.

In a report on combating corruption by the OECD in 2014, the reduction of corruption is posited to contribute towards the decreased costs in business operations through removing the costs which arise directly through bribes and indirectly through the time, effort, uncertainty and opportunity costs which arise from extended negotiations.[130] Furthermore, in an age where corporate accountability is increasingly and publicly demanded for, both by global institutions and vocal interest groups on social media, ASEAN member states have a lot to gain in the case that they do implement strong(er) anti-corruption and rule of law measures. Many companies, especially those with a more customer-facing orientation, increasingly[131] seek to cement their reputation in the public sphere as ethical actors — the costs of being identified as unethical/corrupt actors include not just "reputational damage", but also the possibilities of "prosecution", "penalties" and "blacklisting".[132] Based on these factors, ASEAN countries with robust anti-corruption measures and rule of law conditions, especially those that subscribe to internationally recognised standards,[133] are thus more likely to attract companies to conduct business operations with them than those that do not.[134]

A legal climate that upholds the rule of law will also contribute in the long term to the socio-economic well-being of the countries involved. Increasing transparency and excising the forms of corruption that enable allocation of public resources towards industries that are not the most "value-for-money" or the most strategically necessary will enable the more efficient and expedient usage of these public resources. Studies have shown that there is a strong inverse correlation between corruption levels and the quality of government investments, services and regulations.[135] For instance, according to research gathered by the report from OECD, the lower the level of corruption, the likelier it is that infant mortality rates, school dropout rates and income inequality

---

[129] As cited in International Monetary Fund (2016): For instance, empirical research from Ugur and Desputa (2011) found that a "one-unit improvement in the perceived corruption index can lead to an increase of 0.59 to 0.86 percentage point in the growth rate of per capita GDP, depending on the sample of countries analyzed."

[130] See Organisation for Economic Cooperation and Development (2014).

[131] See Camilleri (2017).

[132] See Organisation for Economic Cooperation and Development (2014).

[133] For instance, all ASEAN member states have indicated commitment to WTO rules and the associated dispute settlement process for the enforcement of these rules. See World Trade Organization (2014).

[134] See Saminar *et al.* (2019).

[135] See Organisation for Economic Cooperation and Development (2014).

Table 4.3: Comparison of HDI Rankings, WGI CC Rankings and WGI RL Rankings across ASEAN for 2017[141]

Country	HDI Ranking (Global)	Percentile Rank WGI RL (Global)	Percentile Rank WGI CC (Global)
Singapore	9	96.63	97.6
Brunei	39	74.52	75
Malaysia	57	64.9	58.17
Thailand	83	54.81	42.79
Philippines	113	37.02	39.9
Indonesia	116	40.87	48.8
Vietnam	116	55.77	31.73
Lao PDR	139	18.27	15.87
Cambodia	146	13.46	8.65
Myanmar	148	16.83	32.21

Source: Asia Competitiveness Institute, based on The World Bank and United Nations.

levels are lower.[136] This trend can similarly be observed across ASEAN countries when one compares country rankings between the control of corruption,[137] rule of law[138] and on the UN Human Development Index (HDI)[139] (see Table 4.3).

The order of the countries ranked highest in their control of corruption tends to correspond to the rankings observed in the HDI.[140] Singapore, Brunei and Malaysia, which score among the top in control of corruption and rule of law indices are the top three countries in ASEAN for their HDI rankings, while countries like Cambodia and Lao PDR which score the worst in their control of corruption also receive the lowest scores for their HDI values. Especially then, for ASEAN member states which currently rank lowest on the control of corruption and rule of law indices, enacting measures to combat corruption and to improve the state of the rule of law would also contribute to the holistic development of their populace.

The legal uncertainty brought about by the wide range of legal systems and the prevalence of corruption throughout ASEAN has been argued to bring about "significant transactional costs" which hinder investment, consumption and growth in the region.[142] Institutional and business leaders have

[136] See Gupta (2002) as cited in Organisation for Economic Cooperation and Development (2014).

[137] See Table 4.2.

[138] See Table 4.1.

[139] HDI is a commonly used index for measuring socio-economic development across countries globally. It measures the indicators life expectancy at birth, expected years of schooling mean years of schooling and gross national income. See United Nations Development Programme (2016).

[140] See United Nations Development Programme (2016).

[141] Note: CC: Control of Corruption; RL: Rule of Law. For HDI rankings, Indonesia and Vietnam are both tied at the 116th position, with HDI Value of 0.694.

[142] As extracted from a speech by the Finance Minister of Singapore, Heng Swee Keat, during the ASEAN Law Conference held in Singapore in 2018. See Aw (2018).

contributed multiple perspectives on possible ways forward, for ASEAN to enhance trust in business transactions and technical and knowledge exchanges, both between member states and with external partners, and to be recognised as an even more legitimate and trusted actor on the international stage.

The *legal uncertainty engendered by the diversity of the legal landscape* across ASEAN has been mentioned as a key concern for foreign businesses and investors. Institutional developments targeted towards deepening ASEAN-wide integration include the connection and integration of the national single windows of the ASEAN Member States to accelerate the electronic exchange of trade and customs-related documents,[143] the ASEAN-wide Self-Certification Scheme, the ASEAN Good Regulatory Practices (GRP) Core Principles, the ASEAN Trade in Services Agreement (ATISA), the ASEAN Framework Agreement on the Facilitation of Inter-State Transport (AFAFIST), and the ASEAN Agreement on Electronic Commerce. Many of these however are still in their early stages, and leave considerable room for member states to interpret them however they deem most appropriate for their needs and abilities. Furthermore, several of these agreements like the ASEAN Good Regulatory Practices (GRP) Core Principles are non-binding, meaning members are technically not obliged to conform to them. These factors heighten the uncertainty about the actual effectiveness of these policies.

Strong dispute resolution mechanisms have also been raised as a legal element that stands on the wish list of businesses and investors. ASEAN could play on the strengths of some of its members in areas of international commercial arbitration, an area identified as increasingly meaningful in an age of international undertakings and transactions governed by contracts.[144] Singapore, for instance, was recognised in 2018 as the "most preferred arbitral institution in Asia", and the third-most preferred worldwide.[145]

One area that demands particular attention is the legal ecosystem in the digital realm. Digital transactions are increasingly forming the backbone of business relations, be it in the areas of e-payment, e-commerce or telecommunications. As mentioned previously, contemporary technological advancements have rendered interactions and transactions between parties internationally more complicated than ever. This engenders therefore the need for a *common cybersecurity framework* that assures the integrity and safety of the transactions between parties, a factor that will continue being regarded as crucial for corporate FDI allocations.[146] The move towards intra-ASEAN cooperation on ICT had its early roots in the 1990s, with the adoption of the e-ASEAN Framework agreement in 2000.[147] Subsequent initiatives included the adoption of the ASEAN Framework on Personal Data Protection, the ASEAN Framework on Digital Data Governance, a "series of five-year ASEAN ICT Master Plans", and a Work Programme on Electronic Commerce 2017–2025.[148]

The extent, however, to which these initiatives have been successfully implemented has varied widely, depending on the strategies various countries have undertaken. ASEAN member states

---

143 ASEAN Secretariat (2018d).

144 From speech by Heng Swee Keat during Asean Law Conference in 2018. See Aw (2018).

145 As extracted from a speech by the Finance Minister of Singapore, Heng Swee Keat, during the ASEAN Law Conference held in Singapore in 2018. See Aw (2018).

146 See The American Chamber of Commerce in Singapore and U.S. Chamber of Commerce (2017).

147 See ASEAN Secretariat (2018a).

148 *Ibid.*

exhibit widely varying levels of development in economic, infrastructural and institutional aspects, as reflected in the data shown in the Median Competitiveness Web Analysis in Chapter 2. These contribute significantly in turn to the differentiated abilities of the respective member states to implement the programmes required by the above-mentioned initiatives — member states have been found to enact the relevant laws, policies and regulations in markedly different ways.[149] This is consequently problematic, as regional integration in matters of cybersecurity fundamentally requires coordinated digital frameworks, which is presently not the case across ASEAN member states. For instance, findings from a joint study published in 2018 by the ASEAN Secretariat show for instance that a higher level of dispersion in responsibility assigned for executing the necessary steps tends to result in lower levels of success. Suggestions for improvement in this area include the concentration of responsibility in a single committee, so as to enhance leadership and accountability.[150] Member states with more developed levels of digital infrastructure could also share best practices and even conduct skills trainings with the other less-developed member states.[151]

The study also found that shortages in skilled manpower, low trust levels in online transactions and logistical hiccups in the areas of payment and delivery systems contributed negatively to the overall development of e-commerce in many ASEAN countries.[152] These aspects retard to varying extents the development of a stable cybersecurity ecosystem within ASEAN. Proposals to remedy these problems encompass both hard (infrastructural) and soft (skills training, informational and awareness campaigns) measures. The joint study by the ASEAN Secretariat and the UNCTAD recommends crafting policy measures to increase FDI in specifically the logistical and digital sectors.[153] In practical terms, the study also highlights how the effectiveness of these various policies would be greatly aided by the laying out of goals in clear and uncomplicated progressive steps.

As mentioned previously, anti-corruption measures were recorded from business executives as an area that should be given higher priority in many ASEAN member states. The measures mentioned in previous sections have to be implemented in tandem with the tackling of corruption, both in the public and private sectors. A study conducted in 2018 by the ASEAN CSR Network (ACN) and the Centre for Governance, Institutions and Organisations (CGIO) in five ASEAN member states[154] found, for instance, that due in part to the insufficient enforcement of anti-corruption measures towards companies, overall disclosure rates[155] of the largest companies still demonstrated much room for improvement, averaging at 56%.

---

[149] See ASEAN Secretariat (2018a).

[150] *Ibid.*

[151] Many institutional frameworks are already in place — for instance, all ASEAN member states have indicated commitment to the United Nations Convention against Corruption (UNCAC), a multilateral treaty negotiated by member states of the United Nations, where states parties are required to help each other prevent and fight against corruption through technical assistance. See Loh *et al.* (2018).

[152] See ASEAN Secretariat (2018a).

[153] *Ibid.*

[154] Namely Malaysia, Singapore, Thailand, the Philippines and Indonesia.

[155] Defined across 13 categories, namely: Publicly stated commitment to anti-corruption; Commitment to comply with laws; Leadership support; Code applied to all employees and directors; Training programme for all employees and directors; Code applied to agents; Code applied to suppliers; Gifts, hospitality, travel policies; Prohibition of facilitation payments; Disclosure of political contributions; Prohibition of retaliation for reporting; Confidential reporting channel and Regular programme monitoring. See Loh *et al.* (2018).

In member states like Thailand, where it is legally required for companies to disclose compliance and transparency, disclosure rates were higher.[156] The report identified the implementation of strict guidelines such as "The 15 Principles of Good Corporate Governance" by the Stock Exchange of Thailand towards public companies as a significant contributor towards the high disclosure rates.[157] Improvements in disclosure rates over the past few years in countries like Indonesia and Malaysia, two of the lowest ranking countries in this report, were also attributed to the introduction of corporate governance guidelines and legislation.[158]

However, the establishment of committees, guidelines and institutions does not automatically translate into reduced corruption. An OECD report in 2018 found, for instance, that the establishment of anti-corruption measures such as the Public Financial Management Reform Program, the Anti-Corruption Law and the Asset Declaration Law, alongside the election of an Anti-Corruption Unit in Cambodia was met with scepticism by European firms, against a backdrop of bribery.[159] This is supposedly due to its alleged lack of *de jure* and *de facto* independence.[160] Efforts should be undertaken to ensure a more stringent division in the allocation of power.

Surveys of the business community in Cambodia also found great dissatisfaction with the lack of transparency regarding rules and regulations in business activities. A study by the WTO in 2017 found that common complaints included "missing information relating to regulatory requirements", "inconsistent application and interpretation of regulations across agencies", "frequent changes of administrative practices" and "alleged discretionary applications of rules constitute limitations to an otherwise open regime".[161] Recent initiatives to include unofficial translations of regulations into English, as well as to shift registration processes for businesses to an online platform are in part being enacted in order to reduce the possibilities for corruption and thereby to increase investor confidence.

Corruption can also be tackled proactively from the corporate side. The study by the ACN and the CGIO found that a two-pronged approach worked best in combating corruption in business transactions, namely through the inclusion of not just internal staff but also external stakeholders in companies' anti-corruption policy.

4.3 Concluding Remarks

The escalation of tensions between the US and China will no doubt have negative consequences on global macroeconomic performance and by extension on heavily export-dependent regions like ASEAN.[162] As the possibility for a quick resolution seems unlikely, firms and investors will look towards alternative markets in an attempt to diversify. This likely forms the premise on

---

[156] See Loh *et al.* (2018).

[157] *Ibid.*

[158] Namely the Corporate Governance Guideline for Public Companies that were introduced by the Financial Services Authority (OJK) in Indonesia and the Malaysian Anti-Corruption Commission (MACC) Amendment Bill in Malaysia.

[159] See Organisation for Economic Cooperation and Development (2018a).

[160] *Ibid.*

[161] As cited in Organisation for Economic Cooperation and Development (2018a).

[162] See United Nations (2019b).

which the "short-sighted" analysts alluded to in Mr. Kausikan's article draw the conclusion of ASEAN benefiting.

However, in the course of this chapter, it has been demonstrated that ASEAN, regardless of the US–China trade war, has already been gaining traction as an alternative investment location. This trend is being driven by a confluence of various factors; these include the desire of foreign firms to diversify, the macroeconomic landscape in and out of ASEAN and even the policies of China. The greatest potential of ASEAN as a collective stems from its diversity and ability to integrate despite these differences. As demonstrated in Sections 4.2.1 and 4.2.2 firms are able to tap into the various advantages of individual ASEAN member states to fulfil requirements for different segments of production chain while maintaining the properties of an integrated supply chain.

While recognising the many positive strengths and initiatives that have been taken by ASEAN member states, we note that there are indeed many issues that urgently require attention within ASEAN in order for the very much valid concern that these potential benefits would only be in the short-term to be avoided. As rightly observed by Mr. Kausikan, the concept of credibility will play a key factor in ASEAN being able to compete and attract investments. This can only be established through sound governance and rule of law which forms the basis through which ASEAN can address its other weaknesses, from lacking infrastructure to regional disputes.

Through the US–China trade war, ASEAN is now being presented with a clear opportunity to advance and accelerate its development agenda and propel itself towards the goal of being the fourth largest economy by 2030. Regardless of and in fact especially in the event of eventual slowed global growth due to increased conflicts, ASEAN member states must take urgent steps to remedy the weaknesses highlighted and leverage on its strengths to mitigate the potential negative impacts.

References

Aidt, Toke S. 2010. "Corruption and Sustainable Development." Faculty of Economics, University of Cambridge. https://doi.org/10.17863/CAM.5249.

ASEAN Economic Community. 2017. "ASEAN Economic Community 2025 Consolidated Strategic Action Plan."

ASEAN Secretariat. 2008. "ASEAN Economic Community Blueprint." Jakarta.

ASEAN Secretariat. 2013. "ASEAN Investment Report 2012." Jakarta.

ASEAN Secretariat. 2018a. "ASEAN Investment Report 2018 — Foreign Direct Investment and the Digital Economy in ASEAN." Jakarta.

ASEAN Secretariat. 2018b. "ASEAN Key Figures 2018." Jakarta.

ASEAN Secretariat. 2018c. "ASEAN Statistical Highlights 2018." Jakarta.

ASEAN Secretariat. 2018d. "ASEAN Economic Integration Brief." https://asean.org/storage/2018/02/AEIB_3rd-Issue_v3-Ready-Print-Single-Page.pdf.

ASEAN Studies Centre. 2019. "ASEAN Focus: State of Southeast Asia: 2019 Survey." ASEAN Studies Centre, ISEAS-Yusof Ishak Institute.

Asian Development Bank. 2016. "ASEAN Infrastructure Fund." Philippines.

Asian Development Bank. 2017a. "Meeting Asia Infrastructure Needs." Philippines.

Asian Development Bank. 2017b. "Thailand: Bangkok Mass Rapid Transit South Purple Line Project." Transaction Technical Assistance.

Asian Development Bank. 2017c. "The Republic of the Philippines: Preparing the Metro Manila Transport Project, Phase 1." Transaction Technical Assistance.

Asian Development Bank. 2019. "ASEAN Infrastructure Fund (AIF)." https://www.adb.org/site/funds/funds/asean-infrastructure-fund.

Asian Infrastructure Investment Bank. 2016. "Connecting Asia for the Future: Annual Report and Accounts 2016."

Aw, Cheng Wei. 2018. "Legal Community Can Help Asean Move Towards Greater Economic Integration: CJ Menon." *The Straits Times*, 26 July. https://www.straitstimes.com/singapore/legal-community-can-help-asean-move-towards-greater-economic-integration-cj-menon.

Azevedo, Roberto. 2018. "Trade Policy Review Body: Overview of Developments in the International Trading Environment." World Trade Organization, 11 December. https://www.wto.org/english/news_e/spra_e/spra249_e.htm.

Bhattacharyay, Biswa Nath. 2009. "Infrastructure Development for ASEAN Economic Integration." Working Paper. ADBI Working Paper Series. Asian Development Bank Institute.

Biswas, Rajiv. 2018. *Emerging Markets Megatrends*. Palgrave Macmillan.

Business, Julia Horowitz, CNN. 2018. "Huawei CFO Meng Wanzhou Arrested in Canada." *CNN*, 6 December. https://www.cnn.com/2018/12/05/tech/huawei-cfo-arrested-canada/index.html.

Buzan, Barry. 2004. *The United States and the Great Powers: World Politics in the Twenty-First Century*.

Camilleri, Mark Anthony. 2017. "The Corporate Social Responsibility Notion." In *Corporate Sustainability, Social Responsibility and Environmental Management*. Springer International Publishing AG.

Chen, Tain-Jy. 2003. "Network Resources for Internationalization: The Case of Taiwan's Electronics Firms." *Journal of Management Studies* 40 (5): 1107–1130.

Congressional Research Service. 2001. "China–U.S. Aircraft Collision Incident of April 2001: Assessments and Policy Implications." U.S. Congress. https://fas.org/sgp/crs/row/RL30946.pdf.

European Commission. 2019a. "EU–China — A Strategic Outlook." European Comission. https://ec.europa.eu/commission/sites/beta-political/files/communication-eu-china-a-strategic-outlook.pdf.

European Commission. 2019b. "EU–Japan Trade Agreement Enters into Force." 24 March. http://europa.eu/rapid/press-release_IP-19-785_en.htm.

Gupta, Sanjeev. 2002. "Does Corruption Affect Income Inequality and Poverty?" *Economics of Governance* 3 (1): 23–45.

Horowitz, Julia. 2018. "Meng Wanzhou: Huawei CFO Arrested in Canada, Faces Extradition to United States." *CNN*, 6 December. https://edition.cnn.com/2018/12/05/tech/huawei-cfo-arrested-canada/index.html.

Huang, Eustance. 2018. "Malaysia Finance Minister Lim Guan Eng on US–China Trade War." *CNBC*, 13 September. https://www.cnbc.com/2018/09/13/malaysia-finance-minister-lim-guan-eng-on-us-china-trade-war.html.

Infrastructure Asia. 2018. "Our Network." Infrastructure Asia. https://www.infrastructureasia.org/Our-Network.

International Labour Organization. 2017. "Malaysia: Employment and Environmental Sustainability Fact Sheets 2017."

International Labour Organization. 2018. "Skills and the Future of Work: Strategies for Inclusive Growth in Asia and the Pacific."
International Labour Organization. 2019a. "The ILO in Indonesia." Jakarta.
International Labour Organization. 2019b. "The ILO in Malaysia." Bangkok.
International Labour Organization. 2019c. "The ILO in Thailand." Bangkok.
International Labour Organization. 2019d. "The ILO in the Philippines."
International Labour Organization. 2019e. "The ILO in Viet Nam." Hanoi.
International Monetary Fund. 2016. "Corruption: Costs and Mitigating Strategies." International Monetary Fund. https://www.imf.org/external/pubs/ft/sdn/2016/sdn1605.pdf.
International Monetary Fund. 2018. "Myanmar Selected Issues." IMF Country Report 18/91. Washington, D.C.: International Monetary Fund.
International Monetary Fund. 2019. "World Economic Outlook Update, January 2019: A Weakening Global Expansion." https://www.imf.org/en/Publications/WEO/Issues/2019/01/11/weo-update-january-2019.
Jendrzejczyk, Mike. 2000. "China's Accession to the WTO and Human Rights." 16 February. https://www.hrw.org/legacy/campaigns/china-99/china-testimony0216.htm.
Khuong, M.Vu. 2017. "ICT Diffusion and Production in ASEAN Countries: Patterns, Performance, and Policy Directions." *Telecommunications Policy* 41 (10): 962–977.
Kim, Tae. 2018. "China Says New Tariffs on US Goods Worth $60 Billion Effective on September 24." *CNBC*, 18 September. https://www.cnbc.com/2018/09/18/china-says-new-tariffs-on-us-goods-worth-60-billion-effective-sept-24.html.
Loh Lawrence, Thi Phuong Thao Nguyen, Ping Lee Shiau, and Thomas Thomas. 2018. "Corporate Disclosure on Business Integrity in ASEAN." ASEAN CSR Network and Centre for Governance, Institutions and Organisations, NUS Business School.
Maurer, Maria Rueda. 2017. "Supply Chain Trade and Technological Transfer in the ASEAN + 3 Region." *China Economic Review* 46: 277–289.
Ministry of Commerce, People's Republic of China. 2018. "Regular Press Conference of Ministry of Commerce." 21 June. http://english.mofcom.gov.cn/article/newsrelease/press/201807/20180702761813.shtml.
Ministry of Trade and Industry, Singapore. 2018. "European Union and Singapore Sign Free Trade and Investment Protection Agreements." Singapore: Ministry of Trade and Industry. https://www.mti.gov.sg/-/media/MTI/Microsites/EUSFTA/Press-Release-on-Signing-of-EUSFTA--EUSIPA-on-19-Oct-18--v2.pdf.
Nissan. 2019. "Nissan Announces New Mid-Term Business Plan for the ASEAN Region." 24 March. https://nissannews.com/es/nissan/lac/releases/1f5fa5b2-c0d2-461b-a7b2-682db9569f91?mode=print.
Office of the United States Trade Representative. 2017. "Initiation of the Section 301 Investigation; Hearing; and Request for Public Comments: China's Acts, Policies, and Practices Related to Technological Transfer, Intellectual Property and Innovation." https://ustr.gov/sites/default/files/enforcement/301Investigations/FRN%20China301.pdf.
Office of the United States Trade Representative. 2018a. "2018 Special 301 Report." USTR. https://ustr.gov/sites/default/files/files/Press/Reports/2018%20Special%20301.pdf.
Office of the United States Trade Representative. 2018b. "USTR Finalizes Tariffs on $200 Billion of Chinese Imports in Response to China's Unfair Trade Practices." Press Release. https://ustr.gov/about-us/policy-offices/press-office/press-releases/2018/september/ustr-finalizes-tariffs-200.
Office of the United States Trade Representative. 2019. "The People's Republic of China-US–China Trade Facts." 24 March. /countries-regions/china-mongolia-taiwan/peoples-republic-china.

Organisation for Economic Cooperation and Development. 2014. "Integrity in Practice." OECD. https://www.oecd.org/cleangovbiz/49693613.pdf.

Organisation for Economic Cooperation and Development. 2018a. "Chapter 4. Improving Business Regulation in Cambodia." *OECD Investment Policy Reviews.*

Organisation for Economic Cooperation and Development. 2018b. "Economic Outlook for Southeast Asia, China and India 2018: Fostering Growth Through Digitalisation." OECD. https://www.oecd.org/dev/SAEO2018_Preliminary_version.pdf.

Portugal-Perez, Alberto, and John S. Wilson. 2012. "Export Performance and Trade Facilitation Reform: Hard and Soft Infrastructure." *World Development* 40 (7): 1295–1307.

PriceWaterhouseCoopers. 2015. "2015–2016 Outlook for the Retail and Consumer Products Sector in Asia."

Saleh, Ali Salman, Thi Lan Anh Nguyen, Denis Vinen, and Arsalan Safari. 2017. "A New Theoretical Framework to Assess Multinational Corporations' Motivation for Foreign Direct Investment: A Case Study on Vietnamese Service Industries." *Research in International Business and Finance* 42: 630–644.

Saminar, Sabir, Rafique Anum, and Abbas Kamran. 2019. "Institutions and FDI: Evidence from Developed and Developing Countries." *Financial Innovation*, February. https://doi.org/10.1186/s40854-019-0123-7.

Schwab, Klaus. 2016. "The Fourth Industrial Revolution: What It Means, How to Respond." World Economic Forum: Global Agenda. 14 January. https://www.weforum.org/agenda/2016/01/the-fourth-industrial-revolution-what-it-means-and-how-to-respond/.

Seow, Bei Yi. 2019. "British Manufacturer Dyson to Relocate Corporate Headquarters to Singapore." *The Straits Times*, 23 January. https://www.straitstimes.com/business/companies-markets/british-manufacturer-dyson-to-relocate-corporate-headquarters-to.

Shah, Mumtaz Hussain. 2014. "The Significance of Infrastructure for FDI Inflow in Developing Countries." *Journal of Life Economics* 1 (2): 1–16.

Shah, Mumtaz Hussain, and Saima Samdani. 2015. "Impact of Trade Liberalization on FDI Inflows to D-8 Countries." *Global Management Journal for Academic & Corporate Studies* 5 (1): 31–38.

Sharma, Shalendra D. 2010. "China as the World's Creditor and the United States as the World's Debtor. Implications for Sino-American Relations." *China Perspectives* 2010 (2010/4). http://journals.openedition.org/chinaperspectives/5346.

Sunaga, Kazuo. 2017. "Japan–ASEAN Partnership." https://www.asean.emb-japan.go.jp/files/000243811.pdf.

Tan, Kim Song, and James T. H. Tang. 2016. "New Skills at Work: Managing Skills Challenges in ASEAN-5." Research Collection School of Economics.

Tan, Kong Yam, Tilak Abeysinghe, and Khee Giap Tan. 2015. "Shifting Drivers of Growth: Policy Implications for ASEAN-5." *Asian Economic Papers* 14 (1): 157–173. https://doi.org/10.1162/ASEP_a_00331.

Thailand Board of Investment. 2015. "Thailand's Automotive Industry The Next Generation."

Thailand Board of Investment. 2017. "Thailand 4.0 Means Opportunity for Thailand."

The American Chamber of Commerce in Singapore and U.S. Chamber of Commerce. 2017. "ASEAN Business Outlook Survey 2018." The American Chamber of Commerce in Singapore and the U.S. Chamber of Commerce.

The American Chamber of Commerce in the People's Republic of China. 2019. "2019 China Business Climate Survey Report 2019 中国商务环境调查报告." The American Chamber of Commerce in the People's Republic of China (AmCham China).

The Economist Intelligence Unit. 2014. "What Does the Average ASEAN Consumer Look Like?"

The Economist Intelligence Unit. 2016. "ASEAN Cities: Stirring the Melting Pot."

The Economist Intelligence Unit. 2018. "Creative Disruption: Asia's Winners in the US–China Trade War."

The Straits Times. 2019. "Law Proposed to Ban US Chip Sales to Huawei, ZTE." *The Straits Times*, 18, January. https://www.straitstimes.com/world/united-states/law-proposed-to-ban-us-chip-sales-to-huawei-zte.

The World Bank. 2018. "Worldwide Governance Indicators." The World Bank.

The World Bank. 2019. "World Development Indicators." World Bank.

Tolentino, Maria Catalina M. 2017. "Philippine Report on Employment Trends and Policies: Can the Duterte Administration End Contractualization?"

Tongzon, Jose, and Inkyo Cheong. 2013. "The Challenges of Developing a Competitive Logistics Industry in ASEAN Countries." *International Journal of Logistics Research and Applications* 17 (4): 323–338.

Ugur, Mehmet, and Nandini Dasgupta. 2011. "Evidence on the Economic Growth Impacts of Corruption in Low-Income Countries and Beyond." *EPPI-Centre Report 1914*.

Ujikane, Keiko. 2016. "Japan Shifts Investment From China to Southeast Asia." *Bloomberg*, 31 May, sec. Business. https://www.bloomberg.com/news/articles/2016-05-30/southeast-asia-is-winning-more-japanese-investment-than-china.

United Nations. 2014. "Report of the Multi-Year Expert Meeting on Transport, Trade Logistics and Trade Facilitation on Its Second Session." Geneva: United Nations.

United Nations. 2019a. "2017 International Trade Statistics Yearbook." New York.

United Nations. 2019b. "Key Statistics and Trends in Trade Policy 2018." Geneva: United Nations Conference on Trade and Development.

United Nations Development Programme. 2016. "Human Development Report 2016."

United Nations Global Compact. 2015. "Business for the Rule of Law Framework." UN Global Compact, United Nations.

United Nations Statistics Division. 2018. "Table 3.2 Individual Consumption Expenditure of Households, NPISHs, and General Government at Current Prices." UNdata. 2018. http://data.un.org/Data.aspx?d=SNA&f=group_code%3A302.

U.S. Census Bureau Foreign Trade Division. 2019a. "Top Trading Partners — December 2017." 24 March. https://www.census.gov/foreign-trade/statistics/highlights/top/top1712yr.html.

U.S. Census Bureau Foreign Trade Division. 2019b. "US Trade in Goods with China." 24 March. https://www.census.gov/foreign-trade/balance/c5700.html.

U.S. Chamber of Commerce. 2017. "Made in China 2025: Global Ambitions Built on Local Protection." U.S Chamber of Commerce. https://www.uschamber.com/sites/default/files/final_made_in_china_2025_report_full.pdf.

U.S. Congress. 2018. "H.R. 4747 Bill." https://www.congress.gov/115/bills/hr4747/BILLS-115hr4747ih.pdf.

U.S. Department of Commerce. 2019a. "Commerce Initiates Antidumping Duty and Countervailing Duty Investigations of Imports of Fabricated Structural Steel from Canada, China, and Mexico." https://

enforcement.trade.gov/download/factsheets/factsheet-multiple-fabricated-structural-steel-ad-cvd-initiation-022619.pdf.

U.S. Department of Commerce. 2019b. "Section 232 Investigations: The Effect of Steel Imports on National Security." 24 March. https://www.commerce.gov/page/section-232-investigation-effect-imports-steel-us-national-security.

U.S. Department of Justice. 2014. "U.S. Charges Five Chinese Military Hackers for Cyber Espionage Against U.S. Corporations and a Labor Organization for Commercial Advantage." 19 May. https://www.justice.gov/opa/pr/us-charges-five-chinese-military-hackers-cyber-espionage-against-us-corporations-and-labor.

U.S. Department of Justice. 2018. "Attorney General Jeff Sessions Announces New Initiative to Combat Chinese Economic Espionage." The United States Department of Justice. https://www.justice.gov/opa/speech/attorney-general-jeff-sessions-announces-new-initiative-combat-chinese-economic-espionage.

Watchravesringkan, Kittichai (Tu). 2010. "The Competitive Position of Thailand's Apparel Industry: Challenges and Opportunities for Globalization." *Journal of Fashion Marketing and Management: An International Journal* 14 (4): 576–597.

Wei, Yingqi, Xiaming Liu, David Parker, and Kirit Vaidya. 1999. "The Regional Distribution of Foreign Direct Investment in China." *Regional Studies* 33 (9): 857–867.

World Trade Organization. 2010. "WTO DS362: China — Measures Affecting the Protection and Enforcement of Intellectual Property Rights." 19 March. https://www.wto.org/english/tratop_e/dispu_e/cases_e/ds362_e.htm.

World Trade Organization. 2014. "Connecting to Global Markets: Challenges and Opportunities: Case Studies Presented by WTO Chair-Holders." WTO. https://www.wto.org/english/res_e/booksp_e/cmark_full_e.pdf.

World Trade Organization. 2015. "WTO DS431: China — Measures Related to the Exportation of Rare Earths, Tungsten and Molybdenum." 20 May. https://www.wto.org/english/tratop_e/dispu_e/cases_e/ds431_e.htm.

World Trade Organization. 2019. "Trade Policy Review Body — Annual Report by the Director-General on the Overview of Developments in the International Trading Environment, October 2017–October 2018." World Trade Organization. https://docs.wto.org/dol2fe/Pages/FE_Search/FE_S_S006.aspx?Query=@Symbol=%20(wt/tpr/ov/21*)&Language=ENGLISH&Context=FomerScriptedSearch&languageUIChanged=true#.

Zen, Fauziah, and Michael Regan. 2014. "Financing ASEAN Connectivity." ERIA Research Project Report 2013. Economic Research Institute for ASEAN and East Asia.

Chapter 5
Concluding Remarks and Future Research Agenda

5.1 Summary of Key Findings

Through this year's publication of the *Annual Competitiveness Analysis and Impact Estimation of Exchange Rates on Trade in Value-Added of ASEAN Economies,* the Asia Competitiveness Institute (ACI) at the Lee Kuan Yew School of Public Policy (LKYSPP), National University of Singapore (NUS) contributes to the existing literature on the ASEAN-10 by providing an insight into the development and competitiveness of each individual member in the ASEAN bloc. By using innovative data analyses to back up and shape our recommendations, ACI's value-add comes in the merging of quantitative and qualitative measures to contribute towards advancing policy formulation.

The scope and depth of the factors covered through the whole course of this publication ensures that an entire host of actors — be it governments, regional institutions or businesses — will find something of value in seeking to further understand ASEAN through this book.

The book starts with Chapter 1 presenting an introduction to the region's development since its founding in 1967, with special attention paid to recounting the events that happened in the past year of 2018. In particular, 2018 marks the 51st year of the ASEAN bloc's inauguration, as well as the three-year anniversary of the establishment of the ASEAN Economic Community (AEC).[1] The rapid growth of the region underlines the efforts and commitment made by the ASEAN leaders towards developing the bloc to its fullest potential. Besides putting into place many domestic measures to facilitate growth within the region — for example, through the promotion of intra-ASEAN trade — the ASEAN-10 have also consistently worked towards a deepening of economic relations with the rest of the world. This has taken the form of various influential and significant initiatives such as the Regional Comprehensive Economic Partnership (RCEP) and the Comprehensive and Progressive Trans-Pacific Partnership (CPTPP). The ASEAN bloc has come a long way and still has much more potential for growth as outlined in Section 1.2. However, as assessed in Section 1.3, the ASEAN-10 must also keep a close eye on both the existing and upcoming challenges that they have to face. In this regard, the insightful speech by Mr. Lawrence Wong, Minister for National Development and Second Minister for Finance on "Infrastructure Development For Economic Competitiveness" proves timely and apt, as Mr. Wong outlines the need for quality infrastructure in the region. In addition to infrastructure bottlenecks, the three other main areas of focus we have identified for the region are global and domestic geopolitical instabilities, the Fourth Industrial Revolution and issues surrounding environmental sustainability.

This is thus followed by Chapter 2 that produces an in-depth assessment of annual competitiveness rankings, shedding light on which areas the individual ASEAN member states can

[1] Established in 2015.

improve in. The competitiveness index is constructed using a holistic set of 121 indicators spanning four different dimensions, namely (i) Macroeconomic Stability, (ii) Government and Institutional Setting, (iii) Financial, Businesses and Manpower Conditions, and (iv) Quality of Life and Infrastructure Development. This allows us to measure the multilayered aspects of competitiveness that goes beyond just looking at the economy alone. In this year's edition, we also continue with the previous years' value-addition of the Shapley Weights methodology that furthers the objectivity and robustness of our data computations.

Generally, in terms of overall competitiveness, results in this book remain roughly similar to the ones obtained last year. Singapore and Malaysia still remain the top two economies, as they have been for the past 15 years. Brunei comes in third, followed by Thailand. Indonesia remains at fifth place for 15 years running, while the Philippines and Vietnam stay at sixth and seventh places, respectively, as they have been stuck at for the past five years. Lastly, Cambodia, Laos and Myanmar still come in as the bottom three economies — a pattern they have not deviated from since 2000. These results hold robust under the Shapley Weights methodology.

Further, we identify the 20% top and bottom indicators for each of the member countries and conduct a policy simulation exercise for all. This also forms the basis on which grounded, country-specific policy recommendations are made by the ACI. In the *What-if* simulation, the weakest 20% of indicators are raised to the regional average, while all else is held constant. The results of the study poignantly show that if more resources were directed to Vietnam and Myanmar's weakest areas in particular, they would both experience a rank increase of two spots, thus lessening the development divide that exists in ASEAN. Moreover, all economies in ASEAN experience an increase in standardised scores, indicating the need to look into these areas to enable growth.

Chapter 3 shifts its focus from domestically centred issues and looks at the impact of Real Effective Exchange Rates (REER) on ASEAN members' trade in value-added goods and services. Given the ASEAN region's reliance on exports as an engine of growth, its integration into the global value chain (GVC) and prevailing macroeconomic conditions is essential for its success. The empirical study conducted found that first, a positive relationship exists between Gross Exports and Foreign Direct Investment (FDI). This underlines the necessity for ASEAN to sustain a sanguine investment environment that is receptive to investors. This is followed also by a positive relationship between Gross Exports and Foreign Real Gross Domestic Product (GDP), once again delineating ASEAN's high reliance on trade. The bloc must hence be careful of risk factors stemming from external macroeconomic shocks. Lastly, results from the study emphasised that a competitive devaluation of exchange rates will not necessarily lead to a boost in exports due to the significant share of FVA in ASEAN's goods and services. On the other hand, while there still exists evidence of a negative relationship between exchange rate appreciation and gross exports for the ASEAN region, this is offset by an integration into GVCs. However, this is not to say that exchange rate volatility is insignificant, as increased volatility still has a dampening effect on exports performance which is not fully offset by neither FVA nor GVCs. It thus highlights the management of exchange rate volatility as an important priority for the bloc. These results then allow us to consider a variety of policy recommendations in the three areas of investment environment, exposure to external shocks and exchange rate management.

Once again, considering the ASEAN region's outwards-orientation and export-led growth, Chapter 4 carries on by looking at global macroeconomic trends and its impact on the bloc. Specifically, the chapter discusses the implications of the increasing trade disruptions and the global uncertainty it has engineered. In this regard, we have benefited greatly from the shrewd discernment of Mr. Bilahari Kausikan, Chairman of the Middle East Institute at the National University of Singapore, and former Permanent Secretary at the Ministry of Foreign Affairs of Singapore, who has kindly shared his thoughts on the effects that the US–China trade war will have on the ASEAN region. We further his article by providing a backdrop to the US–China trade disruptions, and carefully analyse ASEAN's standing in the situation. This is especially significant given that a global trend of diversification and production dislocation is already underway, with many looking at ASEAN as an attractive destination.

5.2 Policy Implications for ASEAN

5.2.1 East Asian Development Model as Applied to ASEAN

Given the turbulent international, regional and domestic conditions highlighted throughout this book, it is imperative to now turn to setting the future agenda and growth path for the ASEAN nations. This section thus first explores the applicability of the East Asian Development Model in the context of the ASEAN bloc.

The term "East Asian Miracle" was first coined by the World Bank (1993) in their report that analysed the rise of several High Performing Asian Economies (HPAEs), namely Japan, the Four Asian Tigers[2] (Hong Kong, Singapore, Taiwan, South Korea), and the newly industrialised economies (NIEs) of Thailand, Malaysia and Indonesia. These countries stood out for their exceptional and sustained growth rates which were coupled with declining income inequality and a rapid rise in standards of living.[3]

While there has been much debate on first, whether there is truly a single and unified model of development that exists between these eight economies, and second, what exactly constitutes this model of development, there are still some generalities that have given rise to the existence of what is termed the East Asian Development Model (EADM). The EADM is most prominently characterised by a highly interventionist government that actively participates in the developmental process via the promotion of economic growth. This is in combination with (i) the pursuance of export-driven strategies, especially that of industrial policies,[4] (ii) high amounts of savings and investments, and (iii) large funding channelled into the accruement of human capital and infrastructure. Essentially, it is "state-directed capitalism [that combines] the dynamic aspects of a market-oriented economy with the advantages of centralized government planning and direction" (Park, 2002); a state-led developmental model that takes on an active role in the market precisely by determining market forces. In this way, the EADM comes in nicely as a

[2] Also known as the Four Asian Dragons or Four Little Dragons. See Birdsall *et al.* (1993).

[3] See Berger and Hsiao (1989) and Tan *et al.* (2017c).

[4] Protection of infant industries and promotion of exports.

middle ground between Adam Smith's laissez-faire, solely market-based economics and the proponents of state-led development.

5.2.1.1 *The Flying Geese Pattern*

The export-led strategy of industrialisation that characterises the EADM can be further expressed through the Flying Geese Pattern (Akamatsu, 1962). To sum up briefly, the Flying Geese model posits that production processes, along with capital investment and development, are devolved from a developed economy, the lead goose, to the developing economies, which take on the roles of the follower geese. In this manner, the developing economies can employ a "catching up process" of industrialisation that follows the sequence of M–P–X. The developing economies first start off exporting primary goods while importing (M) consumer goods from the lead goose. Over time, however, the developing economies start to be capable of import-substitution and begin to produce (P) these consumer goods domestically. As the lead goose starts to lose its cost competitiveness, it shifts its production bases — particularly the manufacturing sector — to the developing economies. This leads to an inflow of capital investment and development from the lead goose to the developing economies. Finally, as the developing economies manage to successfully diversify and rationalise their own industries, they are able to now export (X) their own domestically produced goods to other developed economies. The "catching up" process is now complete as the developing economies have now, themselves, become developed through export-led industrialisation. These newly developed economies then take on the role of playing the "lead goose" to other developing economies, thereby repeating the cycle. There is hence a constant switching of roles as different economies play the different roles of "lead goose" and "follower geese".[5]

There are thus three main pillars that make up the Flying Geese model. The first two were briefly mentioned earlier as they are the vehicles of the "catching up" process/export-led policies of the EADM. They are, first, the diversification and rationalisation of industries, and second, pro-trade-oriented (PROT) foreign direct investment (FDI). As developing economies grow with PROT-FDI from the developed economy, they are able to switch towards more capital-intensive industries (diversification) as well as take on more efficient modes of production (rationalisation) through technological transfer, economies of scale, and so on. This leads to even greater PROT-FDI, thus growing the economies even further.

However, there is also one last pillar to the Flying Geese model: the concept of agreed specialisation. As the cycle of developing economies transitioning to developed economies continues on, there will be an eventual convergence in exports and industries due to homogeneity. Hence, in order to avoid international conflicts, countries should agree on an equilibrium amount and type of goods to specialise in producing — in essence, an equally agreed upon division of labour. As Kojima (2000) further expands, "there are a number of ways in which such agreed specialization can emerge, either explicitly or de facto within a regionally integrated group, because the integration assures mutual liberalization of trade and investment".

[5] See Akamatsu (1962) and Tan *et al.* (2017c).

Figure 5.1: GDP Per Capita (constant 2010 US$), 1985–2017

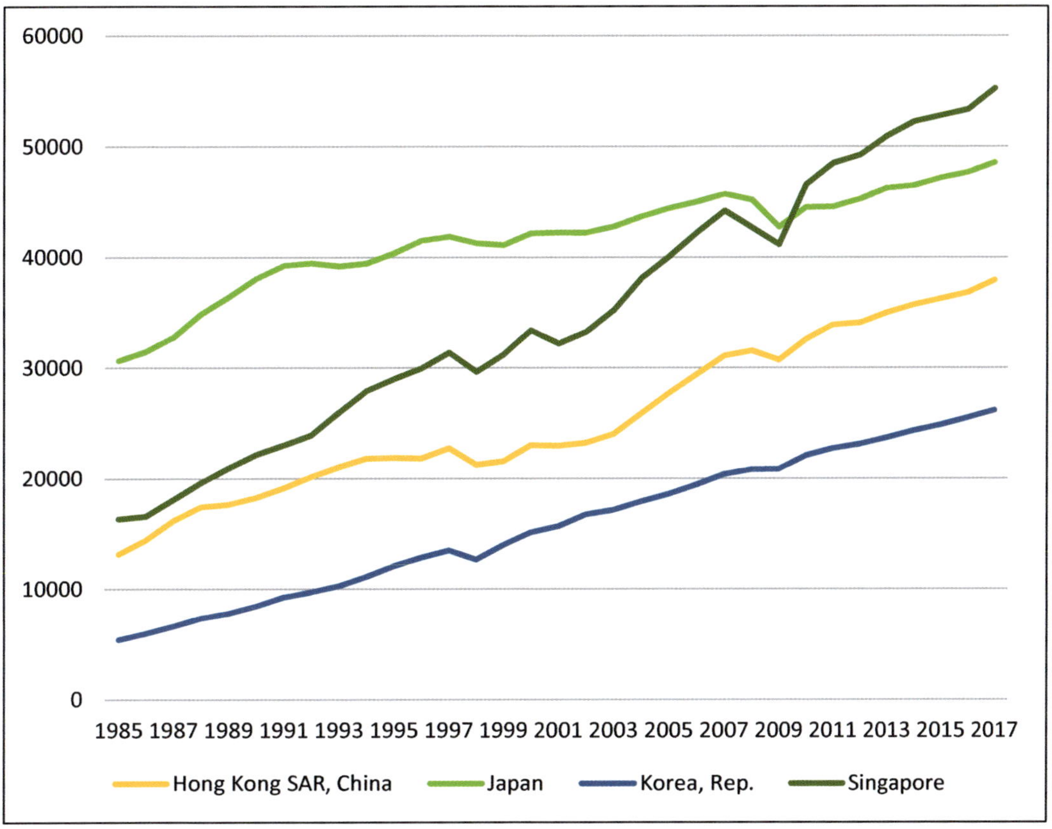

Source: Asia Competitiveness Institute based on data from World Bank, World Development Indicators.

In Akamatsu's theorisations, Japan took on the role of the lead goose with the Four Asian Tigers as the follower geese, who then had a cascading effect on the other NIEs, explaining the East Asian Miracle and solidifying the successes of the EADM. For example, as illustrated in Figure 5.1, South Korea, Hong Kong and Singapore all experienced a rising real GDP per capita in tandem with Japan's throughout the entire period of 1985–2017. This is in conjunction with Singapore even overtaking Japan in 2010 with a GDP per capita of US$46,569.68 versus Japan's US$44,507.68.

5.2.1.2 *Applicability of the EADM*

However, it still remains to be seen whether the EADM can successfully be put into place across all countries. While the aforementioned countries have experienced a strong growth trajectory, majority of the other ASEAN countries still rank comparatively low in terms of GDP per capita. Much has also changed since the development of these models — on the world stage, aforementioned mega-trends such as the rise of trade restrictive measures[6] and the dawning of the Fourth

[6] See Chapter 4.

Industrial Revolution[7] have significantly altered the possibilities of growth pathways. In light of all these factors, it is hence timely to take a step back and reflect upon the true applicability of the EADM to the ASEAN region.

5.2.1.3 *Structural Transformation of the Economy Through Export-Oriented Industrialisation*

As traced out in Chapter 3, the ASEAN region is highly dependent on exports as a crucial engine of growth.

In addition, this has been accompanied by a structural transformation of the region's economy: the structure of its outputs have by and large shifted from the low-cost, labour-intensive sectors of agriculture and industry to the more capital goods-intensive sector of services. For example, even though Cambodia comes in as the country where services have contributed the least to GDP at 39.8%, it is significant to note that the services sector still remains the main engine of growth, with agriculture and industry accounting for 23.4% and 30.9% of GDP, respectively (Figures 5.2–5.4). More importantly, there has also been decrease in the amount that agriculture contributes towards GDP in the majority of ASEAN countries, with a concurrent increase in the industry and services sectors towards making up greater portions of GDP.

Despite this, zooming into the individual countries, a stark development divide becomes apparent among the ASEAN members. For instance, in 2017, the agricultural sectors in Cambodia and Myanmar contributed to over 20% of GDP. This is in comparison to economies like Singapore, where agriculture made up only 0.03% of GDP, with the bulk of its GDP coming from the services sector at 70.44%. Furthermore, as seen in Table 5.1 which reflects country income classifications

Figure 5.2: Agriculture, Forestry, and Fishing, Value-Added as a Percentage of GDP in 2000 and 2017

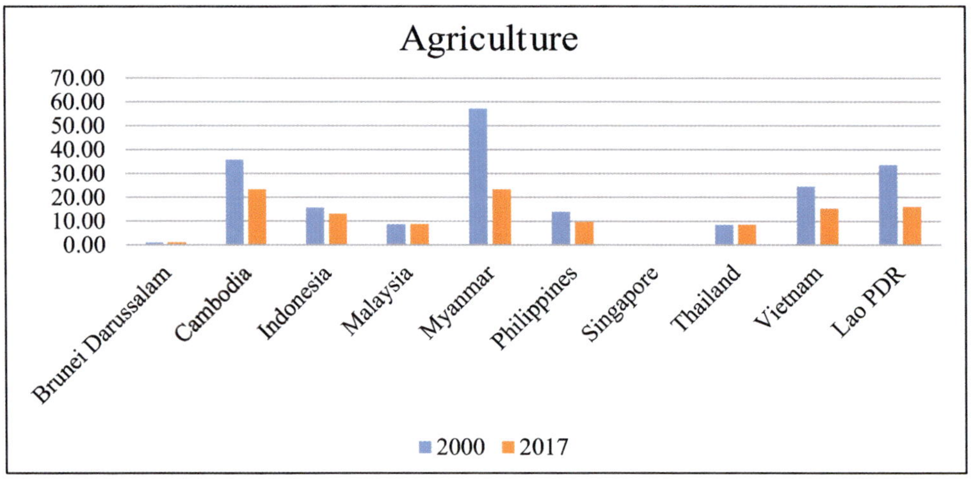

Source: Asia Competitiveness Institute based on data from World Bank, World Development Indicators.

[7] See Chapter 1.

Figure 5.3: Industry (including construction), Value-Added as a Percentage of GDP in 2000 and 2017

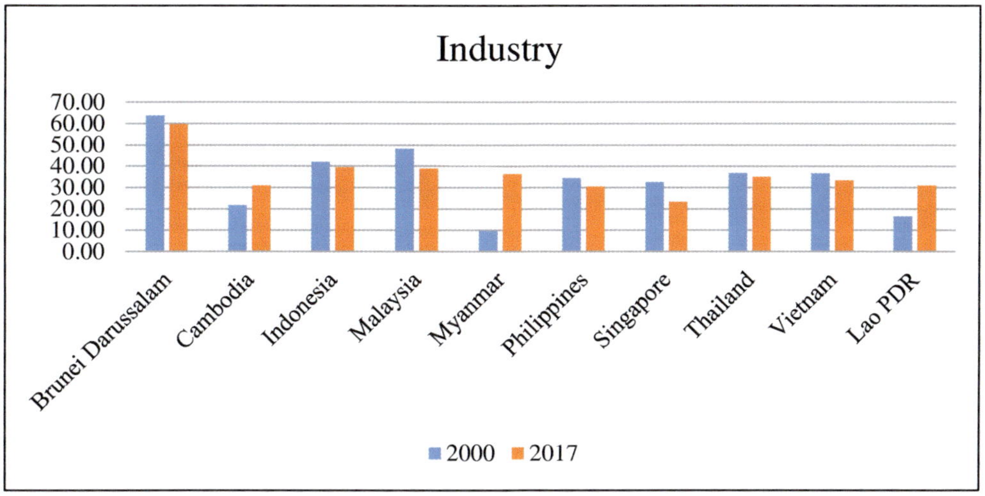

Source: Asia Competitiveness Institute based on data from World Bank, World Development Indicators.

Figure 5.4: Services, Value-Added as a Percentage of GDP in 2000 and 2017

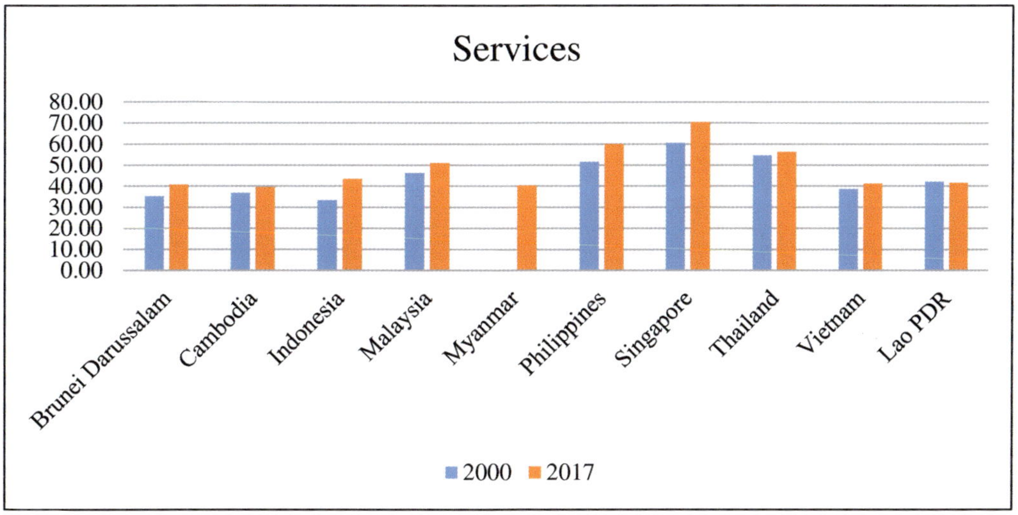

Note: No data for Myanmar in 2000.
Source: Asia Competitiveness Institute based on data from World Bank, World Development Indicators.

carried out by the World Bank,[8] only Singapore and Brunei were considered high-income economies in 2017, followed by Thailand and Malaysia who were considered upper-middle economies. On the other hand, the rest of the ASEAN members come in as lower-middle-income economies.

[8]According to the World Bank, "low-income economies are defined as those with a GNI per capita, calculated using the World Bank Atlas method, of $995 or less in 2017; lower middle-income economies are those with a GNI per capita between $996 and $3,895; upper middle-income economies are those with a GNI per capita between $3,896 and $12,055; high-income economies are those with a GNI per capita of $12,056 or more".

Table 5.1: World Bank Income Classification

	1990	1995	2000	2005	2010	2015	2017
Brunei Darussalam	H	H	H	H	H	H	H
Cambodia	L	L	L	L	L	LM	LM
Indonesia	L	LM	L	LM	LM	LM	LM
Lao PDR	L	L	L	L	LM	LM	LM
Malaysia	LM	UM	UM	UM	UM	UM	UM
Myanmar	L	L	L	L	L	LM	LM
Philippines	LM	LM	LM	LM	LM	LM	LM
Singapore	H	H	H	H	H	H	H
Thailand	LM	LM	LM	LM	UM	UM	UM
Vietnam	L	L	L	L	LM	LM	LM

Note: H — High Income, L — Low Income, LM — Lower Middle, UM — Upper Middle.
Source: Asia Competitiveness Institute based on the World Bank.

For example, Singapore's real GDP per capita stood at US$55,235.51 compared to Cambodia and Myanmar's at US$1137.22 and US$1489.51, respectively.

As evidenced by the previous segments, Singapore is part of the "East Asian Miracle" and is often called upon as "the most successful" of the four Asian Dragons[9] — the small city–state has arguably already made its transition into the ranks of the "developed economies" in the Flying Goose Pattern. Already, it comes in as the second most competitive country in the world according to the 2018 World Economic Forum's Global Competitiveness Index 4.0.

Singapore hence has the potential to serve as a "lead goose" to the rest of the ASEAN member states. Singapore's status as a key services, finance and technological hub presents a chance for the region to benefit intangibly from its skills and technological transfers. Given the efforts made towards an integrated ASEAN,[10] inflows into Singapore might also have spillover benefits for the whole region.

The strength of Singapore's economy stands to be beneficial to the rest of the ASEAN nations. As elaborated in Chapter 3, trade and production in ASEAN is increasingly tied to wider GVCs. Singapore's reputation as a key hub will attract higher-level investments and headquartering of transnational corporations. This pushes Singapore forward while also increasing the attractiveness of other ASEAN economies as preferred locations for manufacturing and industrial activities by supplementing the low-skilled low cost labour that form their comparative advantage.

Hence, while the export-led industrialisation strategies propounded by the EADM might have been transitional periods that allowed the Four Asian Tigers to successfully advance their economies, there exists a real threat of the less-developed members of the ASEAN region becoming stuck in the middle income trap.[11] As detailed in Table 5.1 and as mentioned above, many of the

[9] See Huff (1995).
[10] See Chapter 1.
[11] See Tan *et al.* (2015).

economies in the ASEAN region are classed as middle-income. Although there have been significant movements, such as the graduation of Cambodia and Myanmar from lower-income economies to lower-middle-income economies, the rest of the ASEAN bloc has remained stuck at their current income level since 1990.

The risk of the middle-income trap further increases with the rise of the Fourth Industrial Revolution[12] that both the EADM and Flying Geese model do not take into account. For instance, the usage of machinery erodes the cost-competitiveness of low-skilled industries, causing a country to be stuck in a continual process of having to further reduce its production costs in order to compete. As a result, it first becomes more and more reliant on cheap labour and second, is unable to move up the value chain. Applied to the Flying Geese Model, the Fourth Industrial Revolution also reduces the opportunities for developing economies to hinge on the outflow of developed economies' production processes, as the latter could choose to retain some of their production bases in their own countries instead.

Both the EADM and the Flying Geese Pattern have therefore been criticised for failing to capture larger global trends. Aside from the rise of digitalisation, the global geopolitical climate also needs to be further accounted for. Considering the increasing amount of trade restrictions and trade disruptions happening around the world,[13] export-led growth and open-market policies might not be the best strategies to pursue. This is especially relevant for the less-developed economies in the ASEAN region, as a simulation exercise carried out by Cline (1982) showed that given the flood of manufacturing exports following a widespread adoption of the EADM, 80% of industrial country markets for developing economies' manufacturing exports would be subject to potential protective action. This hence highlights that blindly following the EADM might result in a fallacy of composition — where what is good for one individual country might not be beneficial if adopted by all.

While Akamatsu's (1962) solution to export overproduction is the aforementioned agreed specialisation, whether or not this concept can be applied realistically is still debatable. Countries might be unwilling to come to an agreement, as evidenced by the various trade disputes happening globally. Issues of competition and cooperation among countries are more complex in reality and cannot be easily captured in a singular model. As expressed in Chapter 4, trade tensions may also extend beyond economics and into the geopolitical realm by reducing the involved countries' soft power and macroeconomic stability.

As part and parcel of the industrialisation strategy, it is therefore essential for ASEAN members to leverage their export-led growth with domestic demand. This is so that its economy will be more self-sustaining and less dependent on external factors, such as global value chains as laid out in Chapter 3 that are prone to shocks such as trade disruptions. The ASEAN region hence needs to increase the value of its economy by diversifying its economies and supporting MSMEs.

While there have been some attempts at doing so, ASEAN members also have to be careful about the kinds of industries they choose to nurture. For example, Malaysia's measures aimed at the protection of its domestic automobile sectors have been laudable; however, it is not in sync

[12] See Chapter 1.

[13] See Chapter 4.

with the larger global movement towards the rationalisation of the automobile industry.[14] Thus, while the issue earlier was of producing too much in a phase of protectionism, the problem here is paradoxically protecting too much in a globalised world. The ASEAN region therefore must make sure to strike a careful balance between the two.

The economic growth gained from export-led industrialisation strategies leads us to the next factor of the EADM. As mentioned earlier, countries that were part of the East Asian Miracle by and large all had high rates of savings and investments.

5.2.1.4 *Savings and Investments*

As evidenced by Figures 5.5 and 5.6, savings and investments in the ASEAN region are prone to fluctuations.

In terms of savings, Cambodia and Laos experienced the greatest overall increases in their savings rates from the period of 2000–2017. Cambodia's savings increased from 6.57% to 21.4% of GDP, while Laos' grew from 5.9% to 21.9%. While Brunei and Singapore have maintained their high savings rates at 53.0% and 53.5% of GDP, respectively, in 2017, Brunei's savings seem to be on a downwards trend. Malaysia experienced the greatest decrease in savings from 46.1% in 2000 to 32.5% of GDP in 2017. However, given that the world average of gross domestic savings rate was 28.1% in 2017, the ASEAN region seems to be doing well in terms of savings — Singapore and Brunei come in fourth and sixth place for the highest savings rate in the world, with Macao being the first at 65.9% of GDP.

Figure 5.5: Gross Domestic Savings as a Percentage of GDP

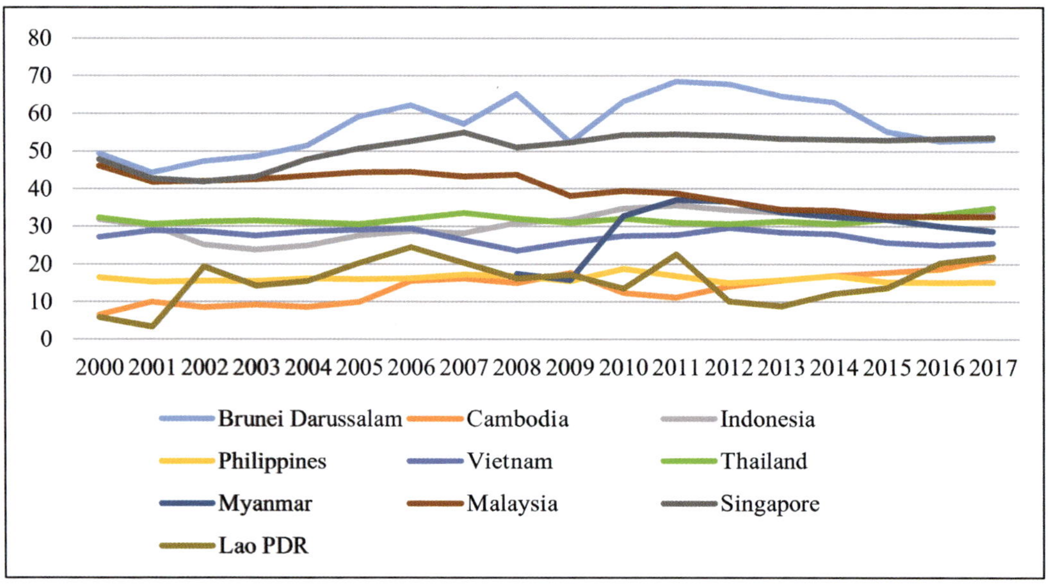

Note: Data for Myanmar only start in 2008.
Source: Asia Competitiveness Institute based on data from World Bank, World Development Indicators.

[14] See Freeman and Hew (2002).

Figure 5.6: Gross Capital Formation as a Percentage of GDP

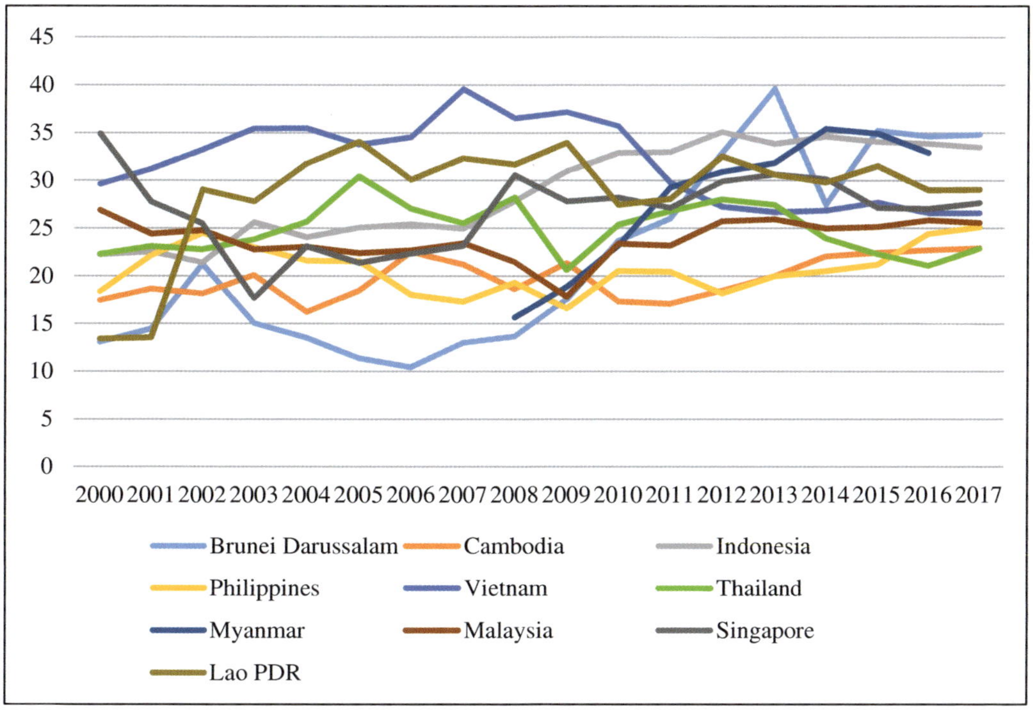

Note: Data for Myanmar are only from 2008–2016.
Source: Asia Competitiveness Institute based on data from World Bank, World Development Indicators.

Investment-wise, Brunei and Laos have experienced the highest surges in gross capital formation rates as a percentage of GDP. Brunei's investments grew from 13.1% to 34.8% from 2000 to 2017, while Laos' increased from 13.4% to 29.4%. Indonesia and Philippines also experienced notable increases from 22.2% to 22.4% and 18.4% to 25.1%, respectively. However, investment rates for Singapore have dropped from 34.9% in 2000 to 27.6% in 2017, while Vietnam's investment rates seem to be on a downward trend to a plateau. Given that China and India had gross capital formation rates of 44% of 31% of GDP in 2017, the ASEAN region still has room for improvement in this aspect.

One way to do so is to increase FDI inflows with the aim of financing capital formation.[15] Although FDI inflows into ASEAN are higher than that of the world average, it is essential to note that Singapore received 45.7% of FDI inflows into the ASEAN region. In contrast, other economies like Philippines, Malaysia, Myanmar and Lao PDR attract less than 10% of the region's inflows.[16] It is hence crucial to increase FDI inflows for the rest of the ASEAN economies as it allows for greater opportunities of infrastructure development and skills transfer.

However, one significant point to note here is the shifting patterns of FDI inflows and roles played by transnational corporations. As international production chains become more common,

[15] Notably, FDI does not always have to go into creating capital formation — for example, if FDI is used to cover a company's loan, it will be not be considered part of gross capital formation.

[16] See Chapter 1.

firms are less likely to look towards producing even more goods. Instead, they are likely to look towards adopting existing overseas competitors through mergers and acquisitions (M&A).[17] Given the lack of soft infrastructure, geopolitical instability and lower levels of innovation, the lower-income ASEAN economies are not as well-equipped in this aspect.[18] This also further supports the aforementioned point that more resources need to be directed towards building up a robust, diversified economy.

Countries can also look to increase their investment rates by spending more on human capital and infrastructure, thus leading us to the third leg of the EADM.

5.2.1.5 *Social Funding into Human Capital and Infrastructure*

As mentioned earlier, countries that were identified as part of the East Asian Miracle placed large importance on financing the areas of human capital and infrastructure.[19] The ASEAN region has experienced an extensive upsurge in its standard of living. Poverty reduction has taken place with a significant decrease in the percentage of population below the $1.25 (PPP) line from 47% in 1990 to 14% in 2015. Literacy rates have almost reached a full 100%, with the literacy rates of 15–24 year olds standing at 97% in 2015 (ASEAN Secretariat 2017). There have also been corresponding decreases in infant mortality rates, increases in access to electricity, as well as increases in mobile phone, as expressed in Figures 5.7–5.9. The overall increase in quality of life

Figure 5.7: Mortality Rate, Infant (per 1,000 live births), 1990–2017

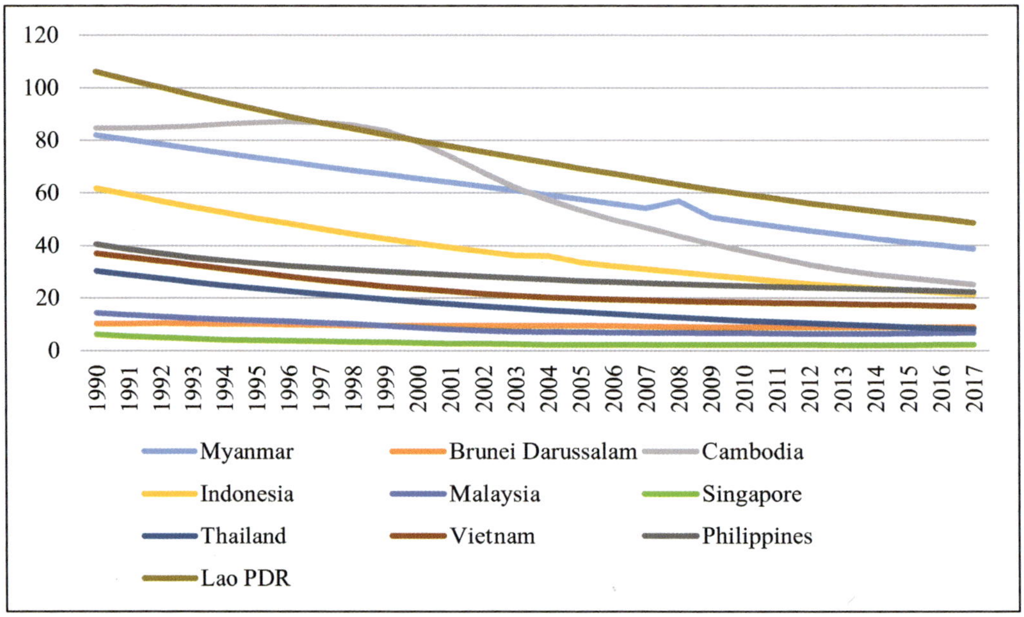

Source: Asia Competitiveness Institute based on data from World Bank, World Development Indicators.

[17] See Freeman and Hew (2002).

[18] See Chapter 1.

[19] See Tan *et al.* (2017b) for more on the importance of human capital to ASEAN development.

Figure 5.8: Access to Electricity by Percentage of Population, 1990–2016

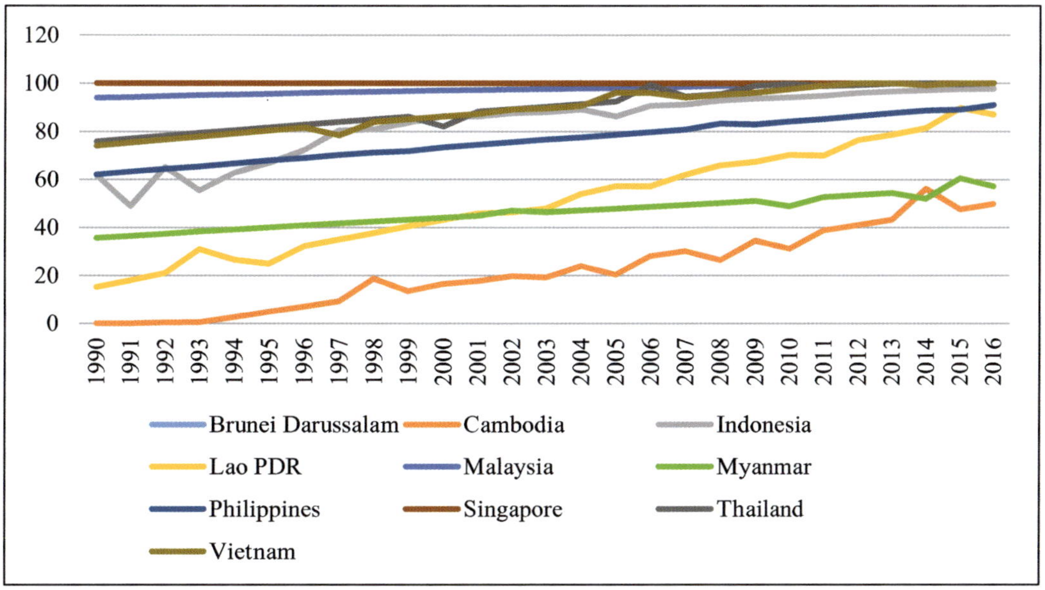

Source: Asia Competitiveness Institute based on data from World Bank, World Development Indicators.

Figure 5.9: Mobile Cellular Subscriptions (per 100 people), 1990–2017

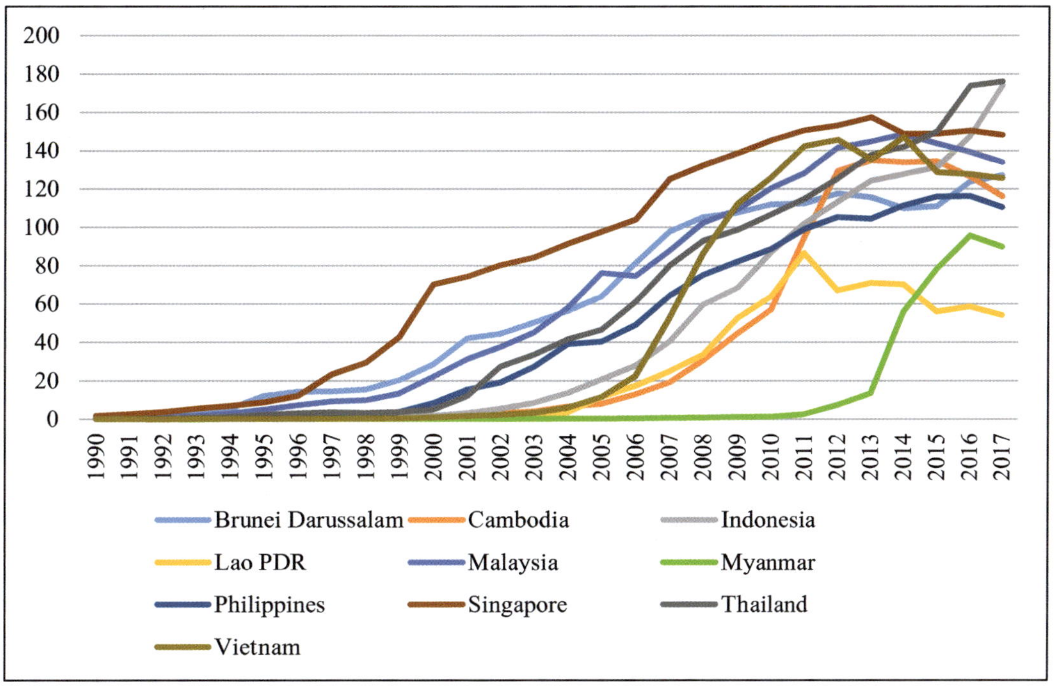

Source: Asia Competitiveness Institute based on data from World Bank, World Development Indicators.

Table 5.2: Human Development Index (HDI), 1990–2017

HDI Rank	Country	1990	1995	2000	2005	2010	2015	2017
9	Singapore	0.718	0.883	0.898	0.908	0.923	0.936	0.939
39	Brunei Darussalam	0.782	0.507	0.49	0.5	0.557	0.613	0.606
57	Malaysia	0.643	0.52	0.471	0.48	0.538	0.584	0.588
83	Thailand	0.574	0.8	0.83	0.857	0.87	0.876	0.88
113	Philippines	0.586	0.598	0.552	0.582	0.608	0.627	0.627
116	Indonesia	0.528	0.564	0.606	0.753	0.793	0.809	0.814
116	Viet Nam	0.475	0.489	0.53	0.58	0.616	0.655	0.667
139	Lao PDR	0.4	0.784	0.81	0.831	0.825	0.854	0.856
146	Cambodia	0.364	0.618	0.647	0.673	0.693	0.706	0.713
148	Myanmar	0.359	0.722	0.743	0.77	0.808	0.854	0.853

Source: Asia Competitiveness Institute based on Human Development Index, United Nations Development Programme.

is further reflected by the jumps made by ASEAN members in the Human Development Index (HDI) seen in Table 5.2.

However, while the basic standard of living of the ASEAN bloc might have improved, the region is still very much lacking in both hard and soft infrastructure as well as various other socio-demographic dimensions. The rankings of the ASEAN countries' in the HDI are testament to the amount of development that the region still has to undergo. For instance, six out of the 10 ASEAN members — Philippines, Indonesia, Vietnam, Lao PDR, Cambodia and Myanmar — still appear in the bottom 100 countries out of a total of 189.

As outlined above, ASEAN countries can increase their investment rates through social financing. This would result in the growth of domestic demand, and provide injections into the economy that would reap rounds of benefits due to the multiplier effect. Investments made into the research and development sectors, in particular, would also strengthen the possibility of escaping the middle-income trap and movement up the global value chain. This is because it boosts innovation and productivity, thus allowing for structural change and diversification of the economy into one that is more high value. At the same time, it can also help mitigate the issue of insufficient intellectual property creation in ASEAN, which entails an unhealthy reliance on costly technological imports.[20]

5.2.2 Developmental Bottlenecks

Throughout the book thus far we have visited, through different contexts, a few key issues preventing ASEAN from achieving its desired growth outcomes and higher standards of living. These issues can be condensed into three key developmental bottlenecks — (i) financing, (ii) infrastructure and (iii) production. These three bottlenecks have long been recognised and

[20] See Wattanapruttipaisan (2004).

we will see that they do not stand independently and are deeply intertwined.[21] As has been previously expressed, ASEAN has been severely underinvesting in infrastructure; within this singular issue one can see the interlinkages between the financing and infrastructure bottlenecks. The lack of financing is in this case a constraint preventing the resolution of infrastructure bottlenecks. This lack of infrastructure then forms a vicious cycle as quality infrastructure is an important factor in attracting FDI and firm's decision to invest in and shift production to ASEAN. This then exacerbates the third bottleneck as countries are unable to achieve the economic growth needed to reach higher standards of living.

The potential pathways to relieving these bottlenecks have been discussed as well and it is worth reiterating that ASEAN is now at a key moment in its development where the necessary inputs to relieve the three bottlenecks are all within reach if the various member states act with urgency to capitalise on various macroeconomic events such as shifting global value chains, growing FDI, the multitude of regional integration initiatives and the demographic dividends of the various member states.

This section will depart from the production and economy-focused analysis of earlier chapters and provide a discussion on the more direct impacts of relieving the first two bottlenecks on the region's people, businesses and sustainability.

5.2.2.1 *Financing Bottleneck*

We begin with the first bottleneck, financing. In Section 5.2.1, we have demonstrated the mismatch between ASEAN's high saving rates and its investments. Throughout the book we have also emphasised that ASEAN as a whole is attracting increasing amounts of FDI; this is not a new phenomenon to the region. Prior to the Asian Financial Crisis in 1997/98, we can observe that FDI played an increasingly larger proportion of Gross Fixed Capital Formation in the region. It is thus evident that ASEAN has the resources needed to relieve this bottleneck (Figures 5.10 and 5.11).

We can thus realistically discuss the potential impacts of rising FDI on standards of living and sustainable development in ASEAN.[22] The theory behind how FDI contributes to development is an extensively studied phenomenon.[23] In general, the benefits of FDI are thought to accrue from increased economic growth and technological development.[24] The direct effect of FDI on poverty is theorised to be realised through the direct channels of employment provision and human capital development. The outcome of poverty reduction from increased FDI has already been empirically observed in various ASEAN economies.[25] However, the actual direction of causality is nothing quite as straightforward. Empirical analysis on the nexus of FDI and economic growth find evidence through bidirectional causality between FDI and GDP, that is to say,

[21] See Yamazawa (1994).

[22] See Tan *et al.* (2017a) for empirical study on financing and economic growth.

[23] See Rajan and Gopalan (2012) for detailed discussion on the impact of FDI on Asia.

[24] *Ibid.*

[25] See Jalilian and Weiss (2002) and Mirza and Giroud (2004).

Figure 5.10: ASEAN FDI Inflows (millions current US$)

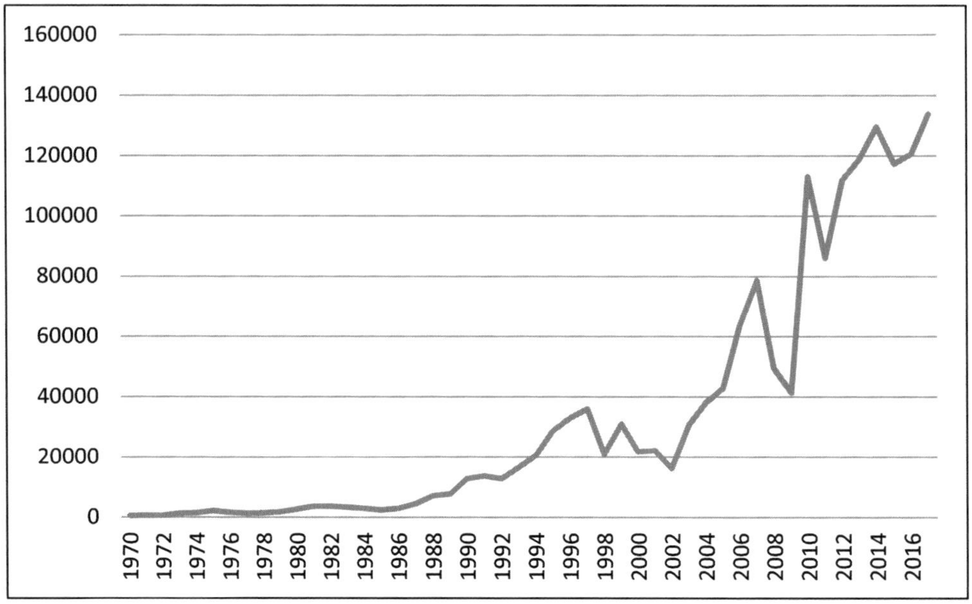

Source: Asia Competitiveness Institute based on UNCTAD.

Figure 5.11: ASEAN FDI Inflows (% Gross Fixed Capital Formation)

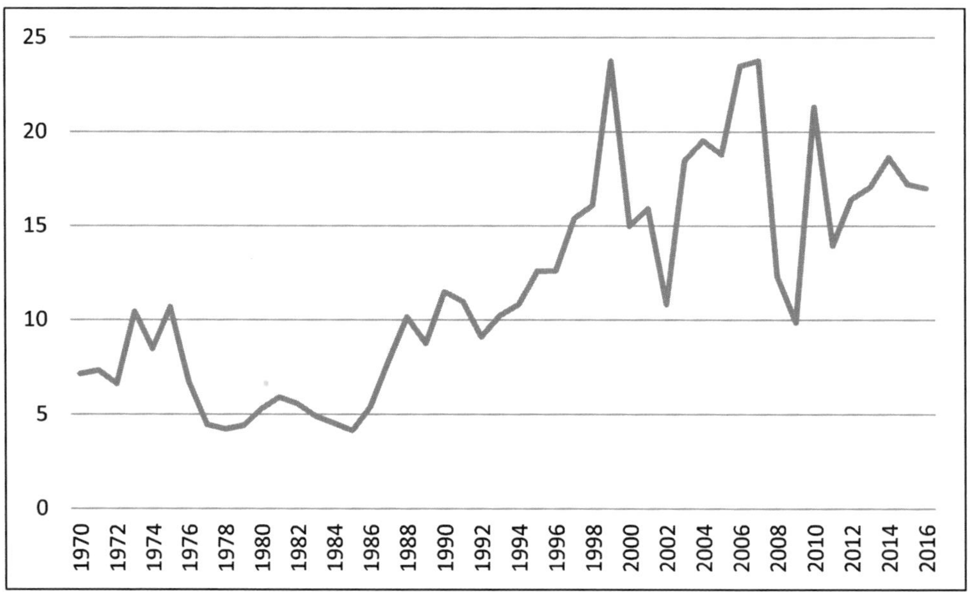

Source: Asia Competitiveness Institute based on UNCTAD.

higher FDI and GDP may form a feedback loop.[26] This then poses a risk to ASEAN as the already developed economies are likely to attract greater shares of FDI, which the less-developed economies greatly need to accelerate growth. Evidence to this effect may be found in Figure 5.12.

[26] See Chowdhury and Mavrotas (2006), Li and Liu (2005) and Omri *et al*. (2014).

Figure 5.12: Percentage of FDI Inflow to ASEAN by Host Country, 2010–2017

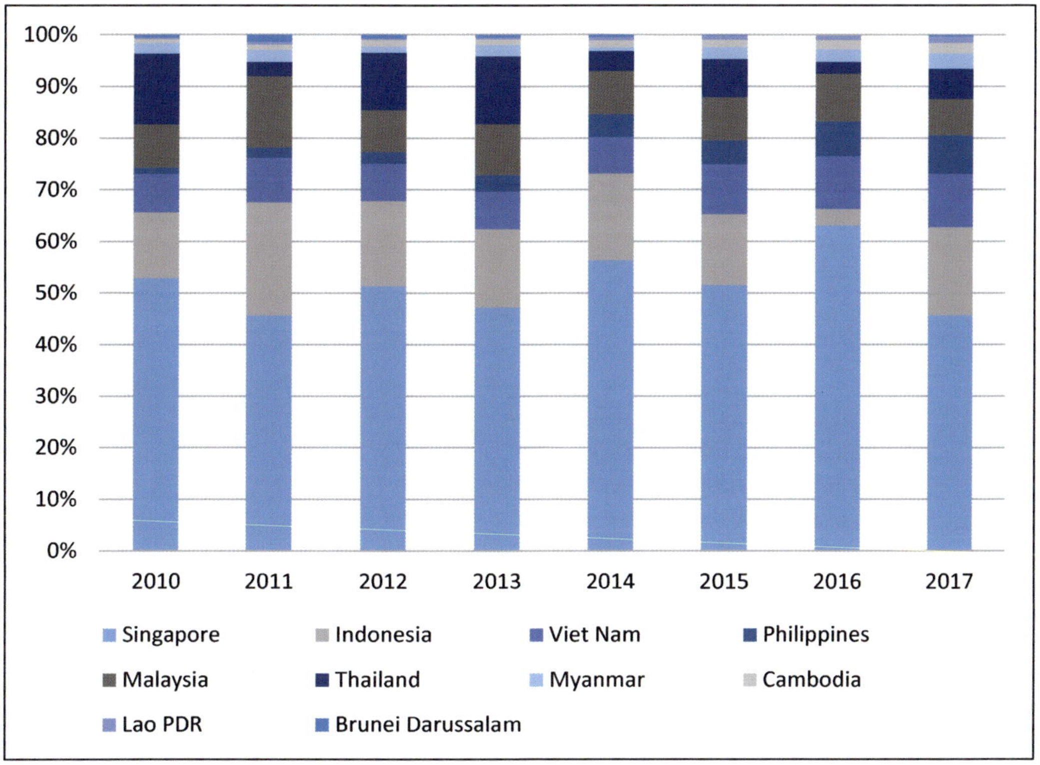

Source: Asia Competitiveness Institute based on ASEAN Secretariat.

Fortunately, not only is the total amount of FDI rising, it can be observed that the share accruing to less-developed ASEAN economies is rising. In this case, it is very much a case of both a larger pie and more equitable distribution.

Given the evidence of bidirectional relationships between FDI and GDP, properly managed FDI inflows can provide an avenue for sustained growth in ASEAN. The caveats to this have also been well studied. In order to sustain this trend, ASEAN member states need to improve human capital, technological capacity, integrate into the global economy and maintain stability.[27] The inflow of FDI also has the potential to alleviate the infrastructure bottleneck as described in Section 5.2.1.

A second development in terms of relieving the financing bottleneck has to do with access to finance. Access to finance for the purposes of responding to macroeconomic challenges such as infrastructure and environmental sustainability has been previously addressed, these were largely addressed through the context of major participants such as governments and MNCs. Going forward we will examine what access to financing can do for the Micro, Small and Medium Enterprises (MSMEs) of the region.[28] This is a key issue to examine as MSMEs form a major component of the ASEAN economy, providing between 51.7% and 97.2% share of total employment in ASEAN economies. The ASEAN Strategic Action Plan for SME Development

[27] See Zhang (2001), Borensztein *et al.* (1998) and Thangavelu and Narjoko (2014).

[28] See Tan and Tan (2014a).

2016–2025 has made increased access to finance and enhanced market access and internationalisation which are key strategic goals to be achieved.[29]

As observed in Figure 5.5, ASEAN has a high savings rate. This large pool of potential financing is now being made available to MSMEs and this has major impacts on the continued development of the region. Given that MSMEs contribute the share of employment in the region, the continued success of these enterprises is thus key to reducing unemployment and reduce poverty in the region. The increased access to financing and internationalisation will also enable the MSMEs to avoid being displaced by the inflow of MNCs as MSMEs also gain the ability access to wider international markets both for financing and consumers.[30] This addresses the constraints of the relatively small domestic markets of individual ASEAN economies.

This is especially key to maintaining sustainable long-term growth as a healthy MSME environment allows for the development of an industrial base, innovation and entrepreneurship that is essential for transition to knowledge-based economies.[31] The need for this transition has already been highlighted in Chapter 4. It worth noting that even Singapore, the ASEAN member state that is considered the most competitive in the region is facing challenges in fostering innovation in response to the fourth industrial revolution.

5.2.2.2 *Infrastructure Bottleneck*

While earlier discussions of infrastructure largely focused on the provision of infrastructure for the purpose of achieving economic growth, in this discussion focused on sustainable growth and standards of living, the concept of sustainable infrastructure must be examined.

Before furthering the discussion, it is important to introduce the concepts of sustainable development. As famously laid out in the 1984 World Commission on Environment and Development report "Our Common Future", "Sustainable development is development that meets the needs of the present without compromising the ability of future generations to meet their own needs" which encompasses two key concepts "the concept of 'needs', in particular the essential needs of the world's poor, to which overriding priority should be given" and "the idea of limitations imposed by the state of technology and social organization on the environment's ability to meet present and future needs."[32]

The effect of infrastructure on standards of living is well understood. The provision of basic infrastructure addresses fundamental necessities such as water, healthcare and energy. The benefits of infrastructure development on economic growth have been previously discussed and this growth is ultimately beneficial to standards of living.[33]

However, there are additional dimensions to the benefits of infrastructure beyond "a rising tide raising all boats" approach. A 2013 IMF study finds that infrastructure development reduces income inequality. The study concludes that ASEAN-5 economies stand to not only enhance productivity and growth through infrastructure development but also achieve it in an inclusive manner,

---

[29] See ASEAN Secretariat (2015).

[30] See Tan and Tan (2014b).

[31] See Yamazawa (1994) and Chia (2014).

[32] See World Commission on Environment and Development (1987).

[33] See Barro (1990).

effectively reducing poverty.[34] The sustainability dimension also has to do with intergenerational equity, the development of hard infrastructure, as this book has repeatedly stressed, requires extensive investments and long build-up time.[35] The discussion of sustainable development of infrastructure is thus one of both intra and intergenerational equity.[36]

It is thus telling that sustainable infrastructure formed the first key point of Minister Wong's speech in Chapter 1. A 2018 UN environment report paints a stark and urgent picture of the state of sustainable urban infrastructure in ASEAN. ASEAN is facing rising urbanisation, urban population in ASEAN is projected to increase by 205 million residents by 2050. In order to maintain reasonable standards of living, provisions of basic infrastructure necessities such as water, energy and transport must be met. For a more concrete example of the importance of sustainable infrastructure, in March of 2019, the Philippines in the midst of a severe water shortage in Metro Manila turned to Singapore for help.[37] For context, Singapore is a small island nation with a lack of natural fresh water sources and has kept water at the core of government policies turning it into a global leader in water policy. To quote Singapore's founding Prime Minister Lee Kuan Yew, "Every other policy has to bend at the knees for our water survival. Water is a precious resource; without it you die. You can live without energy ... But without water you dehydrate and die."[38] This singular event casts in sharp relief the real human consequences of long-term sustainability of infrastructure in both extremes, the failure to account for it and a persistent emphasis on it.

Fortunately, as we have previously discussed, not only are the relevant policies in place, the macroeconomic conditions ASEAN currently finds itself in are ideal for implementing much needed sustainable infrastructure development.

This concept of sustainability over time is key as infrastructure projects require both a high initial capital investment as well as recurrent expenditures to maximise welfare benefits. This implies that for the benefits of infrastructure development to be maximised over time, governments must be able to fund the upkeep cost.[39] This concept of sustainable government expenditures will be further examined in ACI's future research.

5.3 Future Research Agenda: Welfare Spending and Budget Sustainability in ASEAN

The European sovereign debt crises which occurred in the aftermath of the Global Financial Crisis (GFC), most notably the Greek insolvency of 2011–2012, has brought fiscal sustainability issues into the spotlight. However, fiscal sustainability does not only matter "when there is a fiscal house on fire".[40] Sufficient public funding is critical to finance investments and development programmes which help an economy overcome the impediments to growth and achieve sustainable and inclusive development. Moreover, ample fiscal resources provide governments

[34] See Seneviratne and Sun (2013).

[35] See Padilla (2002).

[36] See Pearce (1988).

[37] See Hermesauto (2019).

[38] See https://www.gov.sg/microsites/everydropcounts for more information on Singapore's water policy.

[39] See Ghosh and Rajan (2007) and Tsoukis and Miller (2003).

[40] See Buiter (2014).

with the necessary war chests to pursue counter-cyclical policies to shorten economic downturns and cushion the effects of recessions on employment. In contrast, concerns over the fiscal health of an economy may trigger adverse reactions in financial markets while also harming business confidence, thus planting the seeds for a financial and/or an economic crisis.

Like their counterparts in East Asia, policy-makers in the member economies of the Association of Southeast Asian Nations (ASEAN) have decisively unleashed various fiscal stimulus packages in response to the pronounced impacts of the GFC on trade and overall economic growth, particularly during the climax of the crisis over the second half of 2008 and the first half of 2009. While it is often believed that these fiscal interventions have contributed to the region's recovery, the stimulus packages might have raised public debt levels and the debt servicing costs for these economies.[41] Furthermore, Adams *et al.* (2010) have raised the concerns that the GFC might have marked a watershed in the region's fiscal outlook whereby the remarkable fiscal consolidation which has been happening since the Asian Financial Crisis (AFC) will be replaced with a less conservative philosophy. Indeed, as Rajan *et al.* (2015) have argued, while developing ASEAN economies might still have considerable fiscal space in the aftermath of the GFC, policy-makers must be mindful of potential dangers of contingent liabilities which are building up in these economies.

Fiscal sustainability becomes even more important when set in the broader context of ASEAN's development trajectory. As has been emphasised in this book, a key priority for the regional economies in the next phase of their development will be to resolve the many infrastructure bottlenecks which have hampered their growth. This will require large investment outlays, hence considerable fiscal resources. Moreover, as noted in Tan *et al.* (2018), ageing population is a long-term challenge for ASEAN economies. Countries with a rapidly growing elderly population may face increasing pressure to boost social spending, particularly on pension and healthcare. Further, an ageing population may also create impediments for economic growth, which will impede the governments' ability to generate revenue to meet their rising spending needs. Given the importance of the topic, the Asia Competitiveness Institute (ACI) has undertaken to study fiscal situations among ASEAN's economies and their future prospects.

References

Adams, Charles, Benno Ferrarini, and Donghyun Park. 2010. "Fiscal Sustainability in Developing Asia." *ADB Economics Working Paper Series No.* 25. Asian Development Bank (ADB), Manila.

Akamatsu, Kaname. 1962. "A Historical Pattern of Economic Growth in Developing Countries." *The Developing Economies* 1 (s1): 3–25. https://doi.org/10.1111/j.1746-1049.1962.tb01020.x.

ASEAN Secretariat. 2015. "ASEAN Strategic Action Plan for SME Development 2016–2025." https://asean.org/wp-content/uploads/2012/05/3-SAP-SMED-Final.pdf.

ASEAN Secretariat. 2017. "ASEAN Statistical Report on Millennium Development Goals 2017." Jarkata: ASEAN Secretariat. https://asean.org/storage/2012/05/ASEAN_MDG_2017.pdf.

Barro, Robert J. 1990. "Government Spending in a Simple Model of Endogeneous Growth." *Journal of Political Economy* 98 (5, Part 2): S103–S125. https://doi.org/10.1086/261726.

[41] See Adams *et al.* (2010).

Berger, Peter L., and Hsin-huang Michael Hsiao. 1989. "In Search of an East Asian Development Model." *Economic Development and Cultural Change* 38 (1): 201–206. https://doi.org/10.1086/451785.

Birdsall, Nancy M., Jose Edgardo, L., Campos, Chang-Shik Kim, W., Max Corden, Lawrence (editor MacDonald, Howard Pack, John Page, Richard Sabor, and Joseph E. Stiglitz). 1993. "The East Asian Miracle: Economic Growth and Public Policy: Main Report (English)." 12351. The World Bank. http://documents.worldbank.org/curated/en/975081468244550798/Main-report.

Borensztein, E., J. De Gregorio, and J.-W. Lee. 1998. "How Does Foreign Direct Investment Affect Economic Growth?" *Journal of International Economics* 45 (1): 115–135. https://doi.org/10.1016/S0022-1996(97)00033-0.

Chia, Siow Yue. 2014. *The ASEAN Economic Community: Progress, Challenges, and Prospects*. Edward Elgar Publishing. http://www.elgaronline.com/view/9781783479276.00017.xml.

Chowdhury, Abdur, and George Mavrotas. 2006. "FDI and Growth: What Causes What?" *The World Economy* 29 (1): 9–19. https://doi.org/10.1111/j.1467-9701.2006.00755.x.

Cline, William R. 1982. "Can the East Asian Model of Development Be Generalized?" *World Development* 10 (2): 81–90. https://doi.org/10.1016/0305-750X(82)90039-0.

Freeman, Nick J., and Denis Hew. 2002. "Rethinking the East Asian Development Model." *ASEAN Economic Bulletin Singapore* 19 (1): 1.

Ghosh, Amit, and Ramkishen S. Rajan. 2007. "A Survey of Exchange Rate Pass-Through in Asia." *Asian-Pacific Economic Literature* 21 (2): 13–28. https://doi.org/10.1111/j.1467-8411.2007.00199.x-i1.

Hermesauto. 2019. "Philippines Turns to Singapore to Ease Water Crisis in Metro Manila." Text. *The Straits Times*. 20 March. https://www.straitstimes.com/asia/se-asia/philippines-turns-to-spore-to-ease-water-crisis-in-metro-manila.

Huff, W. G. 1995. "What is the Singapore Model of Economic Development?" *Cambridge Journal of Economics* 19 (6): 735–759.

Jalilian, Hossein, and John Weiss. 2002. "Foreign Direct Investment and Poverty in the ASEAN Region." *ASEAN Economic Bulletin* 19 (3): 231–253.

Kojima, Kiyoshi. 2000. "The 'Flying Geese' Model of Asian Economic Development: Origin, Theoretical Extensions, and Regional Policy Implications." *Journal of Asian Economics*, 375–401.

Li, Xiaoying, and Xiaming Liu. 2005. "Foreign Direct Investment and Economic Growth: An Increasingly Endogenous Relationship." *World Development* 33 (3): 393–407. https://doi.org/10.1016/j.worlddev.2004.11.001.

Mirza, Hafiz, and Axèle Giroud. 2004. "Regionalization, Foreign Direct Investment and Poverty Reduction: Lessons from Vietnam in ASEAN." *Journal of the Asia Pacific Economy* 9 (2): 223–248. https://doi.org/10.1080/1354786042000207353.

Omri, Anis, Duc Khuong Nguyen, and Christophe Rault. 2014. "Causal Interactions between CO2 Emissions, FDI, and Economic Growth: Evidence from Dynamic Simultaneous-Equation Models." *Economic Modelling* 42 (October): 382–389. https://doi.org/10.1016/j.econmod.2014.07.026.

Padilla, Emilio. 2002. "Intergenerational Equity and Sustainability." *Ecological Economics* 41 (1): 69–83. https://doi.org/10.1016/S0921-8009(02)00026-5.

Park, Jong H. 2002. "The East Asian Model of Economic Development and Developing Countries." *Journal of Developing Societies* 18 (4): 330–353. https://doi.org/10.1177/0169796X0201800403.

Pearce, David. 1988. "Economics, Equity and Sustainable Development." *Futures*, Special Issue Sustainable Development, 20 (6): 598–605. https://doi.org/10.1016/0016-3287(88)90002-X.

Ramkishen S. Rajan and Sasidaran Gopalan. 2012. "What Is the Impact of Foreign Direct Investment on Asian Growth and Development?" In *Exchange Rates and Foreign Direct Investment in Emerging Asia: Selected Issues and Policy Options*, 95–118. Routledge. http://www.taylorfrancis.com/.

Seneviratne, Miss Dulani, and Mr Yan Sun. 2013. *Infrastructure and Income Distribution in ASEAN-5: What Are the Links?* International Monetary Fund.

Tan, Khee Giap, Sasidaran Gopalan, and Phuong Anh Nguyen Le. 2017a. "Financial Deepening and Economic Growth in Transition Economies of Southeast Asia: A Geweke Causality Analysis." *Review of Pacific Basin Financial Markets and Policies* 20 (03): 1750016. https://doi.org/10.1142/S0219091517500163.

Tan, Khee Giap, Luu Nguyen Trieu Duong, and Lian Xiao. 2017b. "Empirical Analysis of Growth Slowdown in Asean." *The Journal of Developing Areas* 51 (3): 363–376. https://doi.org/10.1353/jda.2017.0078.

Tan, Khee Giap, Le Phuong Anh Nguyen, and Trieu Duong Luu Nguyen. 2017c. *2016 Annual Competitiveness Analysis and Growth Slowdown Analysis for ASEAN-10.* Singapore: World Scientific.

Tan, Khee Giap, Nguyen Le Phuong Anh, and Ye Ye Denise. 2015. "Development Growth Models for Singapore and Malaysia: A Geweke Causality Analysis." *Journal of Centrum Cathedra: The Business and Economics Research Journal* 8 (2): 165–186. https://doi.org/10.1108/JCC-08-02-2015-B005.

Tan, Khee Giap, Trieu Duong Luu Nguyen, Hui Yin Chuah, and Duy Nguyen. 2018. *2017 Annual Competitiveness Analysis and Impact of Exchange Rates on Foreign Direct Investment Inflows to ASEAN Economies.* Asia Competitiveness Institute — World Scientific Series. Singapore: World Scientific. https://doi.org/10.1142/11065.

Tan, Khee Giap, and Kong Yam Tan. 2014a. "Foreign Direct Investment (FDI), Productivity Spillovers and the Role of Small and Medium Enterprises (SMEs) Financing: An Overview." *Journal of International Commerce, Economics and Policy* 05 (03): 1403002. https://doi.org/10.1142/S1793993314030021.

Tan, Khee Giap, and Yan Yi Tan. 2014b. "Promoting SMEs and Enhancing Labor Productivity in Singapore: A Policy Analysis." *Journal of International Commerce, Economics and Policy* 05 (03): 1440012. https://doi.org/10.1142/S1793993314400122.

Thangavelu, Shandre M., and Dionisius Narjoko. 2014. "Human Capital, FTAs and Foreign Direct Investment Flows into ASEAN." *Journal of Asian Economics*, Special Issue on the ASEAN Economic Community, 35 (December): 65–76. https://doi.org/10.1016/j.asieco.2014.11.002.

Tsoukis, Chris, and Nigel J Miller. 2003. "Public Services and Endogenous Growth." *Journal of Policy Modeling* 25 (3): 297–307. https://doi.org/10.1016/S0161-8938(03)00026-7.

Wattanapruttipaisan, Thitapha. 2004. "Innovation Is ASEAN's Achilles Heel." *The Straits Times*, 30 November. https://asean.org/?static_post=innovation-is-asean-s-achilles-heel-by-thitapha-wattanapruttipaisan-for-the-straits-times.

World Commission on Environment and Development. 1987. *Our Common Future*. Oxford, New York: Oxford University Press.

Yamazawa, Ippei. 1994. "Promotion of SMEs for Industrial Upgrading in ASEAN: A Japanese Proposal for Industrial Co-Operation." *ASEAN Economic Bulletin* 11 (1): 16–24.

Zhang, K. H. 2001. "Does Foreign Direct Investment Promote Economic Growth? Evidence from East Asia and Latin America." *Contemporary Economic Policy* 19 (2): 175–185. https://doi.org/10.1111/j.1465-7287.2001.tb00059.x.

Appendix 1

Competitiveness Analysis of ASEAN-10 Economies, 2000–2015 — List of Indicators

No.	Indicator	Unit	Reversed Indicator*
1	**Macroeconomic Stability**		
1.1	**Economic Vibrancy**		
1.1.01	Gross Domestic Product	US Dollars, Constant 2000 Prices	
1.1.02	Real GDP Growth	Percentage Change Per Annum	
1.1.03	GDP Per Capita	US Dollars, Constant 2000 Prices	
1.1.04	Output Agriculture (Value Added)	US Dollars, Constant 2010 Prices	
1.1.05	Output Industry (Value Added)	US Dollars, Constant 2010 Prices	
1.1.06	Output Services (Value Added)	US Dollars, Constant 2010 Prices	
1.1.07	Gross Domestic Savings	Percentage of GDP	
1.1.08	Gross Fixed Capital Formation	Percentage of GDP	
1.1.09	Inflation	Percentage Change Per Annum	R
1.1.10	Money Supply Growth (M2)	Percentage Change Per Annum	R
1.2	**Openness to Trade and Services**		
1.2.01	Current Account Balance	Percentage of GDP	
1.2.02	Exports of Goods and Services	US Dollars, Current Market Prices	
1.2.03	Imports of Goods and Services	US Dollars, Current Market Prices	
1.2.04	Openness to Trade	Ratio	
1.2.05	International Tourism Receipts	US Dollars, Current Market Prices	
1.3	**Attractiveness to Foreign Investors**		
1.3.01	Foreign Direct Investment Inflows	US Dollars, Current Market Prices	
1.3.02	Foreign-Owned Companies	Survey Data	
1.3.03	Corporate Income Tax	Percentage of Profit	R
1.3.04	Lack of Discrimination Against Investors	Survey Data	
1.3.05	Levelness of Playing Field	Survey Data	
1.3.06	Transparency of Processes for Investors	Survey Data	
1.3.07	Business Impact of Rules on FDI	Survey Data	
2	**Government and Institutional Setting**		
2.1	**Government Policies and Fiscal Sustainability**		
2.1.01	Government Revenue (Including Grants)	US Dollars, 2000 Constant Prices	
2.1.02	Tax Revenue	US Dollars, 2000 Constant Prices	

(Continued)

(Continued)

No.	Indicator	Unit	Reversed Indicator*
2.1.03	Tax Revenue/Government Revenue	Percentage	
2.1.04	Government Consumption Expenditure	Percentage of GDP	
2.1.05	External Debt	US Dollars, Current Market Prices	R
2.1.06	International Reserves	US Dollars, Current Market Prices	
2.1.07	Net Foreign Assets	US Dollars, Current Market Prices	
2.1.08	International Monetary Fund Credit	US Dollars, Current Market Prices	R
2.1.09	Budget Balance	Percentage of GDP	
2.1.10	Tax Burden	Percentage of GDP	R
2.1.11	Money Supply (M2)	Percentage of GDP	
2.1.12	Deposit Interest Rate	Percentage	
2.1.13	Lending Rate	Percentage	R
2.1.14	Interest Rate Spread	Percentage	R
2.1.15	Exchange Rate Appreciation	Annual Average Percentage Change (Local Currency Unit per US Dollar)	R
2.2	**Institutions, Governance and Leadership**		
2.2.01	Quality of Government Policies	Survey Data	
2.2.02	Government Effectiveness	Survey Data	
2.2.03	Government Environmental Protection Policies	Percentage of Total Territorial Area	
2.2.04	Quality of Central Bank/Monetary Authority	Survey Data	
2.2.05	Government Stability	Survey Data	
2.2.06	Government Responsiveness	Survey Data	
2.2.07	Quality of Political Leadership	Survey Data	R
2.2.08	Political System Risk	Survey Data	R
2.2.09	Legislature/Parliament (Functioning of Government System)	Survey Data	
2.2.10	Strength of Auditing and Reporting Standards	Survey Data	
2.2.11	Institutional Sophistication	Survey Data	
2.2.12	Bureaucracy/Red Tape	Survey Data	
2.2.13	Lack of Corruption	Survey Data	
2.2.14	Lack of Cronyism	Survey Data	
2.2.15	Lack of Market Distortion due to State Ownership	Survey Data	
2.3	**Competition, Regulatory Standards and Rule of Law**		
2.3.01	Corporate Governance	Survey Data	
2.3.02	Quality of Regulatory Environment	Survey Data	
2.3.03	Transparency of Government	Survey Data	
2.3.04	Monopolies and Cartel	Survey Data	

(Continued)

(*Continued*)

No.	Indicator	Unit	Reversed Indicator*
2.3.05	Policy Towards Private Enterprise Rating	Survey Data	
2.3.06	Ease of Starting Business	Index Value	R
2.3.07	Barriers to Trade	Survey Data	
2.3.08	Intellectual Property Rights Protection	Survey Data	
2.3.09	Regional Competitiveness	Survey Data	
2.3.10	Quality of Judiciary	Survey Data	
2.3.11	Effectiveness of Legal System	Survey Data	
2.3.12	Integrity of Legal System	Survey Data	
2.3.13	Quality of Police	Survey Data	
2.3.14	Political Change	Survey Data	
3	**Financial, Businesses and Manpower Conditions**		
3.1	**Financial Deepening and Business Efficiency**		
3.1.01	Claims on Private Sector	Annual Growth as Percentage of Broad Money	
3.1.02	Domestic Credit to Private Sector	Percentage of GDP	
3.1.03	Quality of Banking and Financial System	Survey Data	
3.1.04	Domestic Credit Provided by the Financial Sector	Percentage of GDP	
3.1.05	Listed Domestic Companies	Number	
3.1.06	Market Capitalisation	US Dollars, Current Market Prices	
3.1.07	Total Value of Stocks Traded	Percentage of GDP	
3.1.08	Sovereign Debt Risk	Number	R
3.1.09	Quality of Stock Market Regulatory Authority	Survey Data	
3.2	**Labour Market Flexibility**		
3.2.01	Labour Force	Number	
3.2.02	Unemployment Rate	Percentage	R
3.2.03	Cost of Production Labour	US Dollars, Current Market Prices	R
3.2.04	Availability of Scientists and Engineers	Survey Data	
3.2.05	Cost of Management Staff	US Dollars, Current Market Prices	R
3.2.06	High-Quality Management Staff	Survey Data	
3.2.07	Extent of Staff Training	Survey Data	
3.2.08	Labour Market Rating	Survey Data	
3.3	**Productivity Performance**		
3.3.01	Agriculture, Value Added Per Worker	US Dollars, 2010 Constant Prices	
3.3.02	Industry, Value Added Per Worker	US Dollars, 2010 Constant Prices	
3.3.03	Services, Value Added Per Worker	US Dollars, 2010 Constant Prices	

(*Continued*)

(*Continued*)

No.	Indicator	Unit	Reversed Indicator*
4	**Quality of Life and Infrastructure Development**		
4.1	**Physical Infrastructure**		
4.1.01	Population	Number	
4.1.02	Local Road System	Survey Data	
4.1.03	Rail Facilities	Survey Data	
4.1.04	Airport Facilities	Survey Data	
4.1.05	Port Facilities	Survey Data	
4.1.06	Electric Power	Survey Data	
4.1.07	Access to Water	Percentage of Population	
4.1.08	Access to Sanitation	Percentage of Population	
4.2	**Technological Infrastructure**		
4.2.01	Telecommunications System	Percentage of GDP	
4.2.02	Telephone Main Lines	Number Per 100 Persons	
4.2.03	Internet Subscribers	Number Per 100 Persons	
4.2.04	Cellular Mobile Telephone Subscribers	Number Per 100 Persons	
4.2.05	Networked Readiness Index	Survey Data	
4.2.06	Personal Computers	Number Per 100 Persons	
4.2.07	Information and Communication Technology (ICT) Expenditure	Percentage of GDP	
4.3	**Standard of Living, Education and Social Stability**		
4.3.01	Literacy Rate	Percentage	
4.3.02	Primary Schooling	Percentage	
4.3.03	Secondary Schooling	Percentage	
4.3.04	University and Post-Graduate Education	Percentage	
4.3.05	Human Development Index	Composite Statistic	
4.3.06	Health Expenditure	Percentage of GDP	
4.3.07	Urban Population	Percentage of Total Population	
4.3.08	Urban Population Growth	Percentage Per Annum	
4.3.09	Public Security and Safety	Survey Data	
4.3.10	Freedom of Press	Survey Data	R
4.3.11	Freedom of Speech	Survey Data	R
4.3.12	Access to Print Media	Index Value	
4.3.13	Freedom of Religion	Survey Data	R
4.3.14	Religious Unrest	Survey Data	
4.3.15	Labour Unrest	Survey Data	

(*Continued*)

(*Continued*)

No.	Indicator	Unit	Reversed Indicator*
4.3.16	Social Unrest	Survey Data	
4.3.17	Labour Activism	Survey Data	R
4.3.18	Daily Organic Water Pollutant Emissions	Kilogram Per 100 Persons	R
4.3.19	Air Quality	Micrograms Per Cubic Metre	R
4.3.20	Traffic Congestion	Number of Vehicles Per Kilometre of Road	R

Note: * R indicates that the indicator is a reversed indicator.
Source: Asia Competitiveness Institute.

Appendix 2
Competitiveness Analysis — The Algorithm

A step-by-step description of the ranking process is described below for N economies, M practical indicators and C environments, with each environment comprising S sub-environments.

(1) Compute the mean value of practical indicator j ($j = 1, \ldots, M$),

$$\bar{X}_j = \frac{1}{N}\sum_{i=1}^{N} X_{ij}$$

where X_{ij} represents the value that economy i ($i = 1, \ldots, N$) takes for practical indicator j.

(2) For each practical indicator j ($j = 1, \ldots, M$), calculate its standard deviation (SD),

$$\text{SD}_j = \sqrt{\frac{1}{N}\sum_{i=1}^{N}\left(X_{ij} - \bar{X}_j\right)^2}$$

(3) Compute the standardised value of indicator (SVI) that each economy i ($i = 1, \ldots, N$) takes under each of the practical indicators j ($j = 1, \ldots, M$),

$$\text{SVI}_{ij} = \frac{X_{ij} - \bar{X}_j}{\text{SD}_j}$$

(4) Compute the "ranked" standardised value of indicator (RSVI) that each economy i ($i = 1, \ldots, N$) takes under each of the practical indicators j ($j = 1, \ldots, M$):

$$\text{RSVI}_{ij} = \begin{cases} \text{SVI}_{ij}, & \text{if a higher value is better} \\ -\text{SVI}_{ij}, & \text{if a lower value is better} \end{cases}$$

(5) For each of the practical indicators j ($j = 1, \ldots, M$), a ranking can be obtained for cities: cities with a higher value of RSVI for indicator j are ranked ahead of those with a lower value.

(6) For each economy i ($i = 1, \ldots, N$), calculate the RSVI for each sub-environment k ($k = 1, \ldots, S$) belonging to environment l ($l = 1, \ldots, C$),

$$\text{Raw\_RSVI}_{i,lk} = \frac{1}{y_{lk}}\sum_{p=1}^{y_{lk}} \text{RSVI}_{i,j_{lk,p}}$$

$$\text{Mean\_RSVI}_{lk} = \frac{1}{N}\sum_{i=1}^{N} \text{Raw\_RSVI}_{i,lk}$$

$$\mathrm{SD\_RSVI}_{lk} = \sqrt{\frac{1}{N}\sum_{i=1}^{N}\left(\mathrm{Raw\_RSVI}_{i,lk} - \mathrm{Mean\_RSVI}_{lk}\right)^2}$$

$$\mathrm{RSVI}_{i,lk} = \frac{\mathrm{Raw\_RSVI}_{i,lk} - \mathrm{Mean\_RSVI}_{lk}}{\mathrm{SD\_RSVI}_{lk}}$$

where y_{lk} is the total number of practical indicators under sub-environment k of environment l and $(\mathrm{RSVI}_{i,j_{lk,1}}, \ldots, \mathrm{RSVI}_{i,j_{lk,y_{lk}}})$ are the RSVIs for economy i that make up sub-environment k of environment l.

(7) For each economy i ($i = 1, \ldots, N$), calculate the RSVI for each environment l ($l = 1, \ldots, C$),

$$\mathrm{Raw\_RSVI}_{i,l} = \frac{1}{S_l}\sum_{k=1}^{S_l}\mathrm{RSVI}_{i,lk}$$

$$\mathrm{Mean\_RSVI}_{l} = \frac{1}{N}\sum_{i=1}^{N}\mathrm{Raw\_RSVI}_{i,l}$$

$$\mathrm{SD\_RSVI}_{l} = \sqrt{\frac{1}{N}\sum_{i=1}^{N}\left(\mathrm{Raw\_RSVI}_{i,l} - \mathrm{Mean\_RSVI}_{l}\right)^2}$$

$$\mathrm{RSVI}_{i,l} = \frac{\mathrm{Raw\_RSVI}_{i,l} - \mathrm{Mean\_RSVI}_{l}}{\mathrm{SD\_RSVI}_{l}}$$

where $(\mathrm{RSVI}_{i,l1}, \ldots, \mathrm{RSVI}_{i,ls})$ are the RSVIs for the S sub-environments under each environment l.

(8) Overall rank score of economy i ($i = 1, \ldots, N$),

$$\mathrm{Raw\_R}_{i} = \frac{1}{C}\sum_{l=1}^{C}\mathrm{RSVI}_{i,l}$$

$$\mathrm{Mean\_R} = \frac{1}{N}\sum_{i=1}^{N}\mathrm{Raw\_R}_{i}$$

$$\mathrm{SD\_R} = \sqrt{\frac{1}{N}\sum_{i=1}^{N}\left(\mathrm{Raw\_R}_{i} - \mathrm{Mean\_R}\right)^2}$$

$$\mathrm{R}_{i} = \frac{\mathrm{Raw\_R}_{i} - \mathrm{Mean\_R}}{\mathrm{SD\_R}}$$

Economies with a higher R_i are ranked ahead of those with lower value of R_i, and the economy with the highest R_i is the most competitive economy.

Step (5) provides the ranking of each economy for each individual practical indicator. To achieve this ranking, Step (4) adjusts the value of the SVIs so that a higher value will lead to a better ranking in terms of "competitiveness". Depending on the nature of the indicator in question, a higher or lower value may reflect a more "competitive" economy. Take, for instance, the practical sub-indicators "Gross Domestic Product (GDP)" and "Unemployment Rate". A higher GDP but a lower "unemployment rate" suggest better economic performance which makes an economy more "competitive". In most cases where a higher value is better (e.g., GDP), the SVIs of regions are considered, and those with a higher SVI value will have a better ranking. However, for indicators where the inverse is true (e.g., Unemployment Rate), the "negative SVI" values are compared between economies and a lower SVI value will lead to a better ranking. Step (4) thus seeks to make all standardised values of all practical indicators consistent for ranking purposes.

Step (6) determines the sub-environment rankings of each economy. The average RSVI of all the indicators in the sub-environment are calculated, restandardised across all the economies and compared to other economies. Economies with a higher average RSVI rank better in the sub-environment.

To arrive at the ranking for each environment, the RSVIs of the sub-environments are averaged and restandardised across all economies as detailed in Step (7). Finally, Step (8) requires the RSVI values of each environment to be averaged and restandardised across all economies to determine the overall ranking of the economy. Economies with a higher RSVI are ranked ahead of those with a lower RSVI.

Although the number of sub-environments and indicators may vary for each environment, the aggregate score for each environment is given an equal weight which is 25% of the ASEAN-10 Overall Competitiveness Index. This method is repeated and applied consistently across all economies to ensure precision of the ranking. Mathematically, this can be illustrated as follows:

ASEAN-10 Overall Competitiveness Index
= 25% × (Macroeconomic Stability)
+ 25% × (Government and Institutional Setting)
+ 25% × (Financial, Businesses and Manpower Conditions)
+ 25% × (Quality of Life and Infrastructure Development)

Appendix 3
The Shapley Value Methodology

We will present the "Bottom-up" approach in this appendix. We start with indicator-level computation, then sub-environment- and environment-level computation, and finally the index construction.

Indicator Level

For each indicator $i \in I$ and each economy $e \in E$, the standardised value (or z-score) is

$$\mathrm{SV}_{ei} = \frac{X_{ei} - \overline{X}_i}{\mathrm{SD}_i}, \tag{1}$$

where X_{ei} is the data input for economy e in indicator i, $\overline{X}_i = \frac{1}{E}\Sigma_{e=1}^{E} X_{ei}$ is the mean value of the indicator i, and $\mathrm{SD}_i = \sqrt{\frac{1}{E}\Sigma_{e=1}^{E}(X_{ei} - \overline{X}_i)^2}$ is the standard deviation of the indicator i.

Now, let v^I be the characteristic function of the indicators, where v^I: $2^I \rightarrow \mathbb{R}$. Then for each indicator $i \in I$, $v^I(i)$: $\mathbb{R}^E \rightarrow \mathbb{R}$, which reflects that the value of indicator i is derived from X_{ei} for all $e \in E$. As we involve large number of indicators in our case studies, for the ease of numerical computation, we simply define that

$$v^I(i) = \sum_{e=1}^{E} |\mathrm{SV}_{ei}|. \tag{2}$$

The absolute value is used, as (1) it guarantees the positiveness of $v(i)$ which is required by the definition of Shapley value; and (2) the simple sum of the z-scores is zero, i.e. $\Sigma_{e=1}^{E}\mathrm{SV}_{ei} = 0$.

We further assume the Additivity of the characteristic function v^I, i.e.

$$v^I(i \cup j) = v^I(i) + v^I(j) \quad \text{for any indicator i}, j \in I. \tag{3}$$

With all these defined, we are able to proceed with the computation of the Shapley value Φ_i^I of indicator $i \in I$.

$$\Phi_i^I = \sum_{\mathbb{I} \subseteq I \setminus \{i\}} \frac{|\mathbb{I}|!(I - |\mathbb{I}| - 1)!}{I!}(v^I(\mathbb{I} \cup i) - v^I(\mathbb{I})) \quad \text{for all } i \in I \tag{4}$$

With the assumption of Additivity, Equation (4) can be simplified as

$$\Phi_i^I = \sum_{\mathbb{I} \subseteq I \setminus \{i\}} \frac{|\mathbb{I}|!(I - |\mathbb{I}| - 1)!}{I!} (v^I(\mathbb{I} \cup i) - v^I(\mathbb{I}))$$

$$= \sum_{\mathbb{I} \subseteq I \setminus \{i\}} \frac{|\mathbb{I}|!(I - |\mathbb{I}| - 1)!}{I!} v^I(i) = v^I(i). \quad (4^*)$$

Then the indicator weight w_i^I based on Shapley value is simply

$$w_i^I = \frac{\Phi_i^I}{\sum_{j=1}^I \Phi_j^I} = \frac{v^I(i)}{\sum_{j=1}^I v^I(j)}. \quad (5)$$

Economically, the Shapley value of each indicator i, Φ_i^I, measures the inequality among all the economies. The higher the Φ_i^I of an indicator i, the more divergent the performance across different economies. More weight, w_i^I, will thus be assigned to i. If a government has the aim of reducing inequality, it should implement policies to improve the indicators with more weight.

Sub-Environment Level and Environment Level

For each economy $e \in E$, the computed data of any sub-environment $s \in S$ is determined by the indicators comprised, i.e. I_s. Equation (5) has determined the weight of each indicator, and let $w_i^{I_s}$ be the weight of indicator $i \in I_s$. Thus, formally, the computed data of any sub-environment $s \in S$ for any economy $e \in E$ is

$$X_{es} = \sum_{i=1}^{I_s} w_i^{I_s} SV_{ei}. \quad (6)$$

Similar to the indicator-level analysis, we have the standardised score for sub-environment $s \in S$ is SV_{es}.

Let $v^S : 2^S \to \mathbb{R}$ be the characteristic function for the sub-environments. Then for each sub-environment $s \in S$, $v^S(s) : \mathbb{R}^S \to \mathbb{R}$ represents that the value of sub-environment s is derived from X_{es} for all $e \in E$. We have

$$v^S(s) = \sum_{e=1}^{E} |\mathrm{SV}_{es}|. \quad (7)$$

By the Additivity assumption, the Shapley value of each sub-environment $s \in S$ is

$$\Phi_s^S = v^S(s), \quad (8)$$

and the weight of each sub-environment is

$$w_s^S = \frac{\Phi_s^S}{\sum_{j=1}^S \Phi_j^S} = \frac{v^S(s)}{\sum_{j=1}^S v^S(j)}. \quad (9)$$

The construction of Shapley value and the weight associated with each environment is similar to the analysis above, and thus is omitted. Let $v^N : 2^N \to \mathbb{R}$ be the characteristic function for the environments. The Shapley value of each environment $n \in N$ is

$$\Phi_n^N = v^N(n), \tag{10}$$

and the weight of each environment is

$$w_n^N = \frac{\Phi_n^N}{\sum_{j=1}^N \Phi_j^N} = \frac{v^N(n)}{\sum_{j=1}^N v^N(j)}. \tag{11}$$

The economic interpretation of Φ_s^S and Φ_n^N are the same as the indicators'. They capture the inequality across all the economies at the sub-environment level and environment level, respectively. The higher the weights w_s^S and w_n^N, the more divergent the performance across different economies. Thus, government attention should be drawn to such sub-environment and environment.

Index Construction

In order for us to construct the final index to rank all the economies. First, we find the final computed score for each economy $e \in E$, i.e.

$$F_e = \sum_{n=1}^N w_n^N \mathrm{SV}_{en}, \tag{12}$$

where SV_{en} is the standardised value for economy e under environment n.

Then, we standardised the final computed score,

$$R_e = \frac{F_e - \bar{F}}{\mathrm{SD}_F}, \tag{13}$$

where $\bar{F} = \frac{1}{E}\Sigma_{e=1}^E F_e$ and $\mathrm{SD}_F = \sqrt{\frac{1}{E}\Sigma_{e=1}^E (F_e - \bar{F})^2}$.

All the economies, $e \in E$, will be ranked according to the value R_e, which is also the index score for each economy.

Asia Competitiveness Institute - World Scientific Series

(Continued from page vi)

2017 Impact Estimation of Exchange Rate on Foreign Direct Investment Inflows and Annual Update of Competitiveness Analysis for 34 Greater China Economies
by Tan Khee Giap, Zhang Xuyao, Leong Puey Ei & Tan Yang En Isaac (Lee Kuan Yew School of Public Policy, NUS, Singapore)

2017 Annual Competitiveness Analysis and Impact of Exchange Rates on Foreign Direct Investment Inflows to Sub-National Economies of India
by Tan Khee Giap, Sasidaran Gopalan, Jigyasa Sharma & Leong Puey Ei (Lee Kuan Yew School of Public Policy, NUS, Singapore)

2017 Annual Competitiveness Analysis and Impact of Exchange Rates on Foreign Direct Investment Inflows to Sub-National Economies of Indonesia
by Tan Khee Giap, Mulya Amri, Nursyahida Ahmad & Diamanta Vania Lavi (Lee Kuan Yew School of Public Policy, NUS, Singapore)

2016

2016 Annual Competitiveness Analysis and Growth Slowdown Analysis for ASEAN-10
by Tan Khee Giap, Nguyen Le Phuong Anh & Luu Nguyen Trieu Duong (Lee Kuan Yew School of Public Policy, NUS, Singapore)

2016 Growth Slowdown Analysis by Income Thresholds and Annual Update of Competitiveness Analysis for 34 Greater China Economies
by Tan Khee Giap, Wang Peng & Xie Teleixi (Lee Kuan Yew School of Public Policy, NUS, Singapore)

Inaugural 2016 Ease of Doing Business Index on Attractiveness to Investors, Business Friendliness and Competitive Policies (EDB Index ABC) for 21 Sub-National Economies of India
by Tan Khee Giap, Sasidaran Gopalan, Jigyasa Sharma & Tan Kong Yam (Lee Kuan Yew School of Public Policy, NUS, Singapore)

2016 Annual Competitiveness and Growth Slowdown Analysis for Sub-National Economies of India
by Tan Khee Giap, Sasidaran Gopalan, Anuja Tandon & Tan Kong Yam (Lee Kuan Yew School of Public Policy, NUS, Singapore)

2016 Growth Slowdown Analysis, Ease of Doing Business Index, and Annual Competitiveness Studies of Indonesia's Sub-National Economies
by Tan Khee Giap, Mulya Amri, Nursyahida Ahmad & Tan Kong Yam (Lee Kuan Yew School of Public Policy, NUS, Singapore)

2016 Annual Competitiveness Analysis and Development Strategies for Indonesian Provinces
by Tan Khee Giap, Mulya Amri & Nursyahida Ahmad (Lee Kuan Yew School of Public Policy, NUS, Singapore)

2015

2015 Annual Competitiveness Analysis, Agricultural Productivity and Development Vision for ASEAN-10
by Tan Khee Giap, Nguyen Le Phuong Anh, Sasidaran Gopalan & Luu Nguyen Trieu Duong (Lee Kuan Yew School of Public Policy, NUS, Singapore)

2015 Estimation of Agricultural Productivity and Annual Update of Competitiveness Analysis for Greater China: Optimising Agricultural Productivity and Promoting Innovation Driven Growth
by Tan Khee Giap, Yuan Randong & Xie Teleixi (Lee Kuan Yew School of Public Policy, NUS, Singapore)

2015 Agricultural Total Factor Productivity and Competitiveness Analysis for States and Federal Territories and Five Regions of India: Annual Competitiveness Update and Evidence on the Agricultural Development Models for Selected Indian States
by Tan Khee Giap, Sasidaran Gopalan & Anuja Tandon (Lee Kuan Yew School of Public Policy, NUS, Singapore)

2015 Agricultural Productivity, Decentralisation, and Competitiveness Analysis for Provinces and Regions of Indonesia
by Tan Khee Giap, Nurina Merdikawati, Mulya Amri & Tan Kong Yam (Lee Kuan Yew School of Public Policy, NUS, Singapore)

2015 Annual Competitiveness Analysis and Development Strategies for Indonesian Provinces
by Tan Khee Giap, Mulya Amri, Nurina Merdikawati & Nursyahida Ahmad (Lee Kuan Yew School of Public Policy, NUS, Singapore)

2014

2014 Annual Competitiveness Ranking and Simulation Study for ASEAN-10 and Development Strategies to Enhance Asia Economic Connectivity
by Tan Khee Giap, Sangiita Yoong Wei Cher, Sasidaran Gopalan & Nguyen Le Phuong Anh (Lee Kuan Yew School of Public Policy, NUS, Singapore)

2014 Annual Provincial and Regional Competitiveness Analysis for Greater China Economies: Development Strategies under the New Normal
by Tan Khee Giap, Yuan Randong & Sangiita Yoong Wei Cher (Lee Kuan Yew School of Public Policy, NUS, Singapore)

2014 Regional Competitiveness Analysis and a Master Plan on Regional Development Strategies for India: Annual Competitiveness Update and Evidence on Economic Development Model for Selected States of India
by Tan Khee Giap, Linda Low, Kartik Rao & Tan Kong Yam (Lee Kuan Yew School of Public Policy, NUS, Singapore)

2014 Provincial and Inaugural Regional Competitiveness Analysis: Safeguarding Indonesia's Growth Momentum
by Tan Khee Giap, Nurina Merdikawati, Mulya Amri & Tan Kong Yam (Lee Kuan Yew School of Public Policy, NUS, Singapore)

2014 Annual Competitiveness Analysis and Development Strategies for Indonesian Provinces
by Tan Khee Giap, Nurina Merdikawati, Mulya Amri & Blake Harley Berger (Lee Kuan Yew School of Public Policy, NUS, Singapore)

2013

Annual Analysis of Competitiveness, Simulation Studies and Development Perspective for 34 Greater China Economies: 2000–2010
by Tan Khee Giap, Yuan Randong, Sangiita Yoong Wei Cher & Yang Mu (Lee Kuan Yew School of Public Policy, NUS, Singapore)

Annual Analysis of Competitiveness, Simulation Studies and Development Perspective for 35 States and Federal Territories of India: 2000–2010
by Tan Khee Giap, Linda Low, Tan Kong Yam & Kartik Rao (Lee Kuan Yew School of Public Policy, NUS, Singapore)

Competitiveness Analysis and Development Strategies for 33 Indonesian Provinces
by Tan Khee Giap, Mulya Amri, Linda Low & Tan Kong Yam (Lee Kuan Yew School of Public Policy, NUS, Singapore)